The Basic Guide to SuperVision and Instructional Leadership

Second Edition

Carl D. Glickman

University of Georgia

Stephen P. Gordon

Texas State University

Jovita M. Ross-Gordon

Texas State University

PEARSON

Boston · New York · San Francisco
Mexico City · Montreal · Toronto · London · Madrid · Munich · Paris
Hong Kong · Singapore · Tokyo · Cape Town · Sydney

Executive Editor and Publisher: *Stephen D. Dragin*
Series Editorial Assistant: *Anne Whittaker*
Marketing Manager: *Darcy Betts*
Editorial Production Service: *Omegatype Typography, Inc.*
Composition Buyer: *Linda Cox*
Manufacturing Manager: *Megan Cochran*
Electronic Composition: *Omegatype Typography, Inc.*
Cover Administrator: *Linda Knowles*

For related titles and support materials, visit our online catalog at www.pearsonhighered.com.

Between the time website information is gathered and then published, it is not unusual for some sites to have closed. Also, the transcription of URLs can result in typographical errors. The publisher would appreciate notification where these errors occur so that they may be corrected in subsequent editions.

Library of Congress Cataloging-in-Publication Data

Glickman, Carl D.
   The basic guide to supervision and instructional leadership / Carl D.
Glickman, Stephen P. Gordon.—2nd ed.
          p.   cm.
   Includes bibliographical references and index.
   ISBN-13: 978-0-205-57859-7 (pbk.)
   ISBN-10: 0-205-57859-4 (pbk.)
   1. School supervision.   I. Gordon, Stephen P.   II. Ross-Gordon,
Jovita M.   III. Title.
   LB2806.4.G557   2009
   371.2'03—dc22

                                                        2008009493

Printed in the United States of America

10 9 8 7 6 5 4 3 2   12 11 10 09 08

Allyn & Bacon
is an imprint of

www.pearsonhighered.com

ISBN-10:   0-205-57859-4
ISBN-13:   978-0-205-57859-7

To our faculty, student, and staff colleagues
at Texas State University
and the University of Georgia

Contents

4   Adult and Teacher Development within the Context of the School: Clues for Supervisory Practice   41

5   Reflections on Schools, Teaching, and SuperVision   72

part THREE   Interpersonal Skills   91

6   Supervisory Behavior Continuum: Know Thyself   93

7   Developmental Supervision: An Introduction   103

8   Directive Control Behaviors   114

part SIX   Function of SuperVision   321

Preface

Our aim for this brief edition of *SuperVision and Instructional Leadership* is to provide the reader with a shorter version of the traditional book (now in its seventh edition) while maintaining the critical concepts and proposals found in the long version. We worked on this edition with a great sense of concern. This sense of concern was based on two realities. First, educators are increasingly losing their authority to make decisions about education—including decisions about what the curriculum should consist of, how students should be taught, and how student learning should be assessed. Second, as the economic gap between the "haves" and "have-nots" in our society increases, there is a corresponding widening of the educational gap. Low-income students, minority students, and other students placed at risk are failing and dropping out of school at an alarming rate. The field of supervision has a moral obligation to address both of these realities. Regarding the loss of decision making, our colleague John Smyth (2005) argues that supervision needs to become a "firewall" between harmful policies and authentic instructional improvement at the district, school, and classroom level. In other words, supervisors can assist teachers to meet external mandates while using the best practices to meet the learning needs of students, but they also must work with teachers and others to change policies that are harmful to students. Regarding the second reality, supervision can assist teachers to work for social justice at the school and classroom level, and through that work influence their communities and the larger society.

In view of the concerns described, this second edition places considerable emphasis on school and teacher empowerment as well as diversity and social justice. This edition also emphasizes supervisor reflection and self-critique as a means of improving the supervisory process.

Readers familiar with earlier editions of this or the full text will note updating of the following topics:

- A proposal for a new paradigm for supervision, one in which supervision is collegial rather than hierarchical, the province of teachers as well as supervisors, focused on teacher growth rather than compliance, based on teacher collaboration, and characterized by continuous reflective inquiry (Chapter 1)
- Effective schools research and the transition to school improvement research (Chapter 3)
- Connections between school and community development (Chapter 3)
- The integration of adult learning and adult development theories with instructional supervision (Chapter 4)

- Developmental supervision, the supervisory behavior continuum, and four interpersonal approaches to supervision (directive control, directive informational, collaborative, and nondirective) (Chapters 7–12)
- Technical skills of supervision: assessing, planning, observing, research, program evaluation, and teacher evaluation (Chapters 13–15)
- The tasks of supervision: direct assistance, group development, professional development, curriculum development, and action research (Chapters 16–20)
- Examples of model professional development (Chapter 18) and action research programs (Chapter 20)
- Shared governance for instructional improvement: premises, principles, and models (Chapter 20)
- Change, including discussions of change from the leader's view, change from the teacher's view, chaos theory applied to school and classroom change, and creating a culture for change (Chapter 21)

This edition also includes new material that:

- Addresses issues of equity in school and classroom practice (Chapters 2, 3, 5, 12, 16, 19, 20, 22)
- Discusses the need to improve classroom and school culture (Chapters 1, 2, 3, 5, 16, 19, 20, 21, 22)
- Describes how supervisors can critique their own performance (Chapters 5, 6, 8, 9, 10, 11, 12)
- Cautions against reductionist approaches to instructional improvement (Chapter 5), conferencing (Chapter 7), planning (Chapter 13), observing (Chapter 14), the change process (Chapter 21), and educational reform (Chapter 22)
- Critically examines No Child Left Behind and legislated learning (Chapters 13, 19, 21, 22)
- Presents new forms of action research (Chapter 20)
- Argues for radically changing the conditions of teaching (Chapter 21)

We hope that this second edition continues to signal the need for all of us—writers and readers—to think, challenge, and practice the promise of schools, education, and democracy.

Acknowledgments

It is impossible to acknowledge all those who have contributed to the development of this book. A host of colleagues—school practitioners, graduate students, and university faculty members—have provided us with settings, collaborations, and discussion for field-testing developmental and democratic propositions about supervision. We are grateful to Miguel G. Guajardo and Sarah Nelson of Texas State University for reviewing new material for this edition. Many thanks to doctoral student and graduate assistant Erin Ronder for her outstanding research and editing. We would also like to thank reviewers Carol L. Higy, University of North Carolina, Pembroke; Stacey Rutledge, Florida State University; Vernon G. Smith, Indiana University Northwest; and Marilyn Tallerico, Binghamton University.

Reference

Smyth, J. 2005. *New direction for supervision: When teachers give students power over their learning.* Paper presented at the annual meeting of the Council of Professors of Instructional Supervision, Athens, GA, October.

PART I

Introduction

SuperVision for Successful Schools

Take a walk with us. First, let's step into Finnie Tyler High School, with a student body of 1,200 in a lower- to middle-class urban neighborhood. A sign by the entrance tells all visitors to report to the office. In the halls, we see students milling around, boys and girls talking in groups, couples holding hands, one couple intertwined romantically in a corner. The bell rings and students scurry to class. We find the school office and introduce ourselves to the secretary and school principal, who are expecting our visit. They welcome us and assure us that we may move around the school and talk to students, teachers, and other staff. The school population has been notified of our visit and understands that we have come to see how Tyler High School operates. The principal tells us we will find Tyler a pleasant place. Equipped with a floor plan of classrooms and other facilities, we continue on our way.

The principal's description is accurate: Students seem happy and uninhibited, socializing easily with each other even during instruction time. Teachers joke with students. In the faculty lounge, we hear laughter that rises, falls, and then rises again. Several teachers have told us about the traditional Friday after-school gatherings at the local pizza parlor, where teachers and administrators socialize over a drink.

Classrooms vary considerably from each other; teachers tell us they can teach however they wish. Most teachers stand at the front of the room, lecturing, asking questions, and assigning seatwork. Some, however, take a less structured approach, allowing students to work alone or in small groups. There is an unhurried atmosphere. Students move at a leisurely pace, and classes seldom start on time. Teachers of the same subjects use the same textbooks but otherwise seem to have discretion to function as they please. As one seven-year veteran teacher at this school sums it up: "We have an ideal situation. We like each other, and the administration leaves us alone. I am observed once a year. I have one faculty meeting a month to attend. I love the other teachers and we have a great time together. The kids are fine, not as academic as they should be, but this school is a nice place for them. I wouldn't want to teach anyplace else."

Now let's drive across town to Germando Elementary School, with 600 students, located in a wealthy, suburban part of the city. Again, we follow the sign to the office. A few students are standing with their noses against the wall by their classroom doors. Otherwise, the halls are vacant and still; all classroom doors are shut. In the principal's office sit two students with tears in their eyes, obviously fearful of their impending conference with the principal. The principal welcomes us and hands us a preplanned schedule of times to visit particular teachers. She tells us not to visit any classroom during instructional time. "I think you will find that I run a tight ship," she says. "Teachers and students know exactly what is expected of them and what the consequences are for ignoring those expectations. Teachers are here to teach, and I see to it that it happens."

Moving down the halls, we are struck by the similarity of the classrooms. The desks are in rows; the teacher is in front; the school rules are posted on the right of the chalkboard. At the first recess time, the students seem to erupt onto the playground. Expecting to find a group of teachers in the faculty lounge, we are surprised to find only two people. One is knitting and the other is preparing a cup of coffee. All the other teachers have remained in the classrooms, either alone or with one other teacher.

Continuing our observation after recess, we find that teachers at each grade level not only work with the same textbooks but are on the same pages as well. When we ask about this, one teacher tells us that the principal has standardized the entire curriculum and knows what is being taught in every classroom at each moment of the day. At the first faculty meeting in August, the principal lays out materials, schedules, and time lines developed by the central office. We ask how the principal can enforce such procedures, and the teacher replies, "She asks for weekly lesson plans, visits my room at least once every two weeks, and has other central office personnel visit and report back to her."

In the classrooms we visit, students are generally quiet but restless. They appear attentive; those who are not are disciplined. Teachers are mostly businesslike; some show warmth toward their students, others do not. We conclude our visit with three separate interviews of teachers. It seems that teaching in Germando is perceived as a job to do. Whether one likes them or not, the principal's rules and regulations are to be followed. Teachers mention that when they have attempted to make modest changes in their instruction, they have been told to drop the changes and return to the school plan. All three mention the teacher who last year refused to follow the reading textbook and was subsequently forced to resign.

Finnie Tyler High School and Germando Elementary School are examples of real schools. Which is the successful school? Which has better attendance, attitudes, and achievement? *Neither does!* Both are ineffective, mediocre schools. The successful schools in the same system are quite different from either. Our first conclusion might be that these schools are very different. Tyler High School appears to have little supervision of instruction, whereas Germando has too much. According to the definition of instructional supervision presented in this book, however, *neither* school has effective instructional supervision. It also might appear that Tyler meets teachers' individual needs, whereas Germando meets organizational goals set by the principal. In successful schools, however, individual needs are fulfilled through organizational goals. In these two schools, *neither* need is being met. Finally, the working environments in these two schools only appear to be dissimilar; soon we will see how similar they really are.

The last school on our tour is Progress Middle School. Our first stop at Progress is the school office, where we are informed by the school secretary that the principal will meet with us at the end of the period. The principal is teaching Mr. Simmons's class while Simmons observes another teacher as part of a peer coaching program involving a number of teachers. The secretary invites us to wait for the principal in the teachers' lounge, where several teachers are spending their preparation period. As we relax with a soda, we listen to an animated discussion among the teachers concerning an interdisciplinary unit of instruction they are planning. The teachers are brainstorming alternative teaching and assessment strategies for the unit and discussing how these strategies could be connected to the unit's theme.

Soon the principal joins us and invites us on a tour of the school. During the tour, we note that classroom environments are work oriented, as well as warm and supportive. In some classrooms, students are involved in hands-on inquiry. In other classrooms, cooperative learning is taking place. In still others, teachers are challenging students to reflect on lesson content by using higher-level questioning and inviting student opinions on the lesson topic. A commonality across all classrooms is students engaged in active learning. Teachers give students feedback on their performance and provide alternative learning opportunities and special attention to those experiencing difficulties.

After school, we attend a meeting of the school leadership council, made up primarily of teachers. The council is considering action research proposals submitted by faculty liaison groups. Each proposal is focused on improvement of curriculum and instruction. Much of the debate among council members is concerned with whether or not the proposed research will assist in meeting the school's vision, mission, and goals agreed on two years earlier by the entire faculty. At times the debate becomes heated. Clearly the council is taking its decision making seriously. The principal is a voting member of the council, but does not have veto power over council decisions, which are made by majority rule.

Germando Elementary is an example of a *conventional school*—characterized by dependency, hierarchy, and professional isolation. Finnie Tyler is an example of a *congenial school*—characterized by friendly social interactions and professional isolation. A successful school like Progress Middle School is a *collegial school*—characterized by purposeful adult interactions about improving schoolwide teaching and learning. Professional respect is a by-product of discussing issues with candor, accepting disagreements as integral to change, and respecting the wisdom and care of all for arriving at educational decisions for students.

Collegial schools establish learning goals for all students consistent with the responsibility of education in a democratic society. These schools are always studying teaching and learning, setting common priorities, making decisions about internal changes and resource allocations, and assessing effects on student learning. These schools are driven by (1) a covenant of learning—mission, vision, and goals; (2) a charter for schoolwide, democratic decision making; and (3) a critical study process for informing decisions and conducting action research (Glickman, 1993, 2003). In effect, successful schools create a "SuperVision" of instruction, democratically derived and studied, that gives purpose and direction to the common world of adults.

SuperVision: A New Name for a New Paradigm

Like schools, supervision can be conventional, congenial, or collegial. Throughout most of its history supervision has operated from within a conventional paradigm (world view), attempting to control teachers' instructional behaviors. As we've stated previously, based on what we know about successful schools, the time has come to move from conventional schools (still dominant in the United States) and congenial schools (less prevalent but still present throughout the nation) toward collegial schools (growing in number and success). *A "paradigm shift" toward the collegial model, if it is to succeed, must include a shift away from conventional or congenial supervision toward collegial supervision.* This view of supervision includes all of the following:

1. A collegial rather than a hierarchical relationship between teachers and formally designated supervisors
2. Supervision as the province of teachers as well as formally designated supervisors
3. A focus on teacher growth rather than teacher compliance
4. Facilitation of teachers collaborating with each other in instructional improvement efforts
5. Teacher involvement in ongoing reflective inquiry (Gordon, 1997, p. 116)

Jo Blase captures the spirit of this new collegial approach to supervision in the following description:

Leadership is shared with teachers, and it is cast in coaching, reflection, collegial investigation, study teams, explorations into the uncertain, and problem solving. It is position-free supervision wherein the underlying spirit is one of expansion, not traditional supervision. Alternatives, not directives or criticism, are the focus, and the community of learners perform professional—indeed, moral—service to students. (cited in Gordon, 1995)

Collegial supervision, then, stands in sharp contrast to traditional approaches to supervision (Keedy and Simpson, 2002).

Given the fact that the historic role of supervision has been inspection and control, it is not surprising that most teachers do not equate supervision with collegiality. When teachers have been asked to make word associations with the term *instructional supervision,* most of the associations have been negative, as indicated by the following list (Gordon, 1997, p. 118):

Control	Directive
Step-by-step	Irrelevant
Lack of creativity	Waste of time
Lack of free choice	Restricting
Evaluation	Rules
Negative	Dog and pony show
Nonexistent	Big brother
Jumping through hoops	Intimidating
Boring	Constantly under watch
Paperwork	Anxiety
Bureaucrat	Boss
Monitoring instruction	Stress
Guidelines for testing	Need for detailed lesson plans
Authority	Administrative micro management
Unrealistic	Yuck!

The dictionary definition of supervision is to "watch over," "direct," "oversee," "superintend." The history of instructional supervision is viewed most often as an instrument for controlling teachers. In a series of recent studies, Richard Ingersoll (2003) concludes that the flight from education of both new and experienced educators is due to the external control of teachers' work lives. It seems that a new term for describing the collegial model of instructional leadership espoused in this book is in order. Therefore the first word in the title of this new edition is *SuperVision,* a term that denotes a common vision of what teaching and learning can and should be, developed collaboratively by formally designated supervisors, teachers, and other members of the school community. The word also implies that these same persons will work together to make their vision a reality—to build a democratic community of learning based on moral principles calling for all students to be educated in a manner enabling them to lead fulfilling lives and be contributing members of a democratic society.

Supervisory Glue as a Metaphor for Success

We can think of supervision as the *glue* of a successful school. Supervision is the function in schools that draws together the discrete elements of instructional effectiveness into whole-school action. Research shows that those schools that link their instruction and classroom management with professional development, direct assistance to teachers, curriculum development, group development, and action research under a common purpose *achieve their objectives* (Bernauer, 2002; Calhoun, 2002; MacKenzie, 1983). In other words, when teachers accept common goals for students and therefore complement each other's teaching, and when supervisors work with teachers in a manner consistent with the way teachers are expected to work with students, then—and only then—does the school reach its goals. Regardless of a school's grade span, socioeconomic setting, or physical characteristics, successful schools have a common glue that keeps a faculty together and creates consistency among a school's various elements. The glue is the process by which some person or group of people is responsible for providing a link between individual teacher needs and organizational goals so that individuals within the school can work in harmony toward their vision of what the school *should* be (Bernstein, 2004).

Effective supervision requires knowledge, interpersonal skills, and technical skills. These are applied through the supervisory tasks of direct assistance to teachers, curriculum development, professional development, group development, and action research. This adhesive pulls together organizational goals and teacher needs and provides for improved learning.

Who Is Responsible for SuperVision?

Mark Zelchack, an experienced teacher, has been appointed as a mentor for Julie, a beginning teacher in his elementary school. At the beginning of the school year, Mark orients Julie to the school, the curriculum, and her responsibilities. Mark visits Julie's classroom on a regular basis, has conferences with her, and is helping her to carry out an instructional improvement plan that they designed collaboratively.

Jane Simmons is a school principal. She has recently initiated a clinical supervision program with a group of volunteer teachers. In a typical clinical cycle, Jane holds a preconference with a teacher in which they discuss the teacher's plan for a future lesson. They also discuss nonjudgmental data that the teacher wishes Jane to collect while observing the lesson. After observing the class and collecting the desired data, Jane shares the data with the teacher during a postconference. The postconference is nonevaluative, aimed at interpreting the data and helping the teacher to plan improvement goals and strategies for reaching those goals.

Michele Carver is a lead teacher. She is released from teaching for three periods a day to help other teachers improve their instruction. This year Michele has conducted professional development programs on cooperative learning and teaching thinking skills, and has provided expert coaching to teachers who are attempting to transfer their new instructional skills to their classrooms. Recently, Michele has been elected chairperson of her school's instructional improvement committee.

Briget Myers is a first-grade teacher. She is a member of a collegial peer-coaching triad. This week she is scheduled to observe two other first-grade teachers who are attempting to use some of the same balanced literacy strategies that Briget is trying out with her own first-graders. She hopes not only to provide her colleagues with useful observation data, but also to pick up ideas on how she can better implement balanced literacy in her own classroom.

The educators discussed here carry out a variety of roles within their schools. However, they all participate in supervision during at least part of their working day. Our definition of supervision is identical to leadership for the improvement of instruction. This definition allows for instructional leadership to be viewed as a function and process rather than a role or position. Educators throughout the school system—from the top to the bottom of its organizational chart—can engage in the function and process of supervision.*

Organization of This Book

Figure 1.1 demonstrates the scope and organization of this book. For those in supervisory roles, the challenge to improving student learning is to apply certain knowledge, interpersonal skills, and technical skills to the tasks of direct assistance, group development, curriculum development, professional development, and action research that will enable teachers to teach in a collective, purposeful manner uniting organizational goals and teacher needs. As the supervisor allows teachers to take greater control over their own professional lives, a school becomes a dynamic setting for learning.

To facilitate such collective instructional improvement, those responsible for supervision must have certain prerequisites. The first is a *knowledge* base. Supervisors need to understand the exception—what teachers and schools can be—in contrast to the norm—what teachers and schools typically are. They need to understand how knowledge of adult and teacher development and alternative supervisory practices can help break the norm of mediocrity found in typical schools. Second, there is an *interpersonal skills* base. Supervisors must know how their own interpersonal behaviors affect individuals as well as groups of teachers and then study ranges of interpersonal behaviors that might be used to promote more positive and change-oriented relationships. Third, the supervisor must have *technical skills* in observing, planning, assessing, and evaluating instructional improvement. Knowledge, interpersonal skills, and technical competence are three complementary aspects of supervision as a developmental function.

*To avoid awkwardness of writing, from here on we will use the spelling of SuperVision only in particular headings. The point is that SuperVision and instructional leadership are integrated and interchangeable concepts.

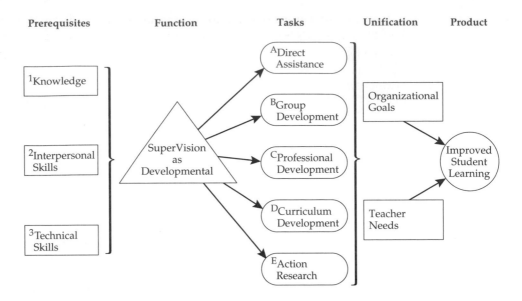

FIGURE 1.1 *SuperVision for Successful Schools*

Supervisors have certain educational tasks at their disposal that enable teachers to evaluate and modify their instruction. In planning each task, the supervisor needs to plan specific ways of giving teachers a greater sense of professional power to teach students successfully. Those supervisory tasks that have such potential to affect teacher development are direct assistance, group development, professional development, curriculum development, and action research. Direct assistance *(A)* is the provision of personal, ongoing contact with the individual teacher to observe and assist in classroom instruction. Group development *(B)* is the gathering together of teachers to make decisions on mutual instructional concerns. Professional development *(C)* includes the learning opportunities for faculty provided or supported by the school and school system. Curriculum development *(D)* is the revision and modification of the content, plans, and materials of classroom instruction. Action research *(E)* is the systematic study by a faculty of what is happening in the classroom and school with the aim of improving learning.

By understanding how teachers grow optimally in a supportive and challenging environment, the supervisor can plan the tasks of supervision to bring together organizational goals and teacher needs into a single fluid entity. The unification of individual teacher needs with organizational goals in "a cause beyond oneself" has been demonstrated to promote powerful instruction and improved student learning.

Figure 1.1, therefore, presents the organization of this textbook in a nutshell. Part II will be devoted to essential knowledge. Part III will deal with interpersonal skills. Part IV will explain technical skills the supervisor needs, and Part V will discuss the application of such knowledge and skills to the tasks of supervision.

Finally, Part VI will suggest ways of applying knowledge, skills, and tasks to integrate individual needs with organizational goals to achieve needed change and instructional success.

Supervision and Moral Purpose

Supervision based on moral purpose begins with the school community asking two broad questions:

1. What type of society do we desire?
2. What type of educational environment should supervision promote in order to move toward the society we desire?

If even part of the answer to the first question involves a democratic society in which all members are considered equal, then the answer to the second question must involve creating an educational environment that prepares students to be members of that democratic society. We can take this one step further and say that the answer involves creating a school that mirrors the democratic society we desire.

We ground this book in a SuperVision of the good school; one that delivers on the promise of education that promotes a better democracy for all (see Glickman, 2003; Gordon, 2001). To do so, we cannot think of ourselves as first-grade teachers, high school mathematics teachers, middle school counselors, central office specialists, high school principals, or superintendents. These positions are reflections of where we locate our bodies to go to work, but the names don't reflect where we need to locate our minds and our hearts. Educators are the primary stewards of the democratic spirit. The total of our efforts is far greater than the particulars of our job (Glickman, 1998b).

The democratic impulse for renewing education continues to resonate in the thoughts of many local teachers, parents, administrators, and citizens in schools throughout this country—perhaps among more people than ever before. However, schools blessed with such far-sighted people are still in the margin. The challenge to bring an inclusive definition of democracy as the guiding principle into public education is enormous (Glickman, 1998a, 1999; Scheurich, 1998). We have been here before and we might fall short once again. But, whether we succeed or simply keep the spirit alive, we will have let other generations of educators and citizens know that this is the most important fight in which to engage—the democratic education of our students for a just and democratic society.

REFERENCES AND RECOMMENDED READINGS

Bernauer, J. 2002. Five keys to unlock continuous school improvement. *Kappa Delta Phi Record,* 38(2), 89–92.

Bernstein, E. 2004. What teacher evaluation should know and be able to do: A commentary. *NAASP Bulletin, 88,* 80–88.

Calhoun, E. F. 2002. Action research for school improvement. *Educational Leadership, 59*(6), 18–24.

Glickman, C. D. 1993. *Renewing America's schools: A guide for school-based action.* San Francisco: Jossey-Bass.

Glickman, C. D. 1998a. Educational leadership for democratic purpose: What do we mean? *The International Journal of Leadership in Education, 1*(1), 45–53.

Glickman, C. D. 1998b. *Revolutionizing America's schools.* San Francisco: Jossey-Bass.

Glickman, C. D. 1999. A response to the discourse on democracy: The dangerous retreat. *The International Journal of Leadership in Education, 2*(1), 43–46.

Glickman, C. D. 2002. The courage to lead. *Educational Leadership, 59*(8), 41–44.

Glickman, C. D. 2003. *Holding sacred ground: Courageous leadership for democratic schools.* San Francisco: Jossey-Bass.

Gordon, S. P. 1992. Paradigms, transitions, and the new supervision. *Journal of Curriculum and Supervision, 8*(1), 62–76.

Gordon, S. P. (Ed.). 1995, April. *Newsletter of the Instructional Supervision Special Interest Group of the American Educational Research Association.*

Gordon, S. P. 1997. Has the field of supervision evolved to a point that it should be called something else? *Yes.* In J. Glanz and R. F. Neville (Eds.), *Educational Supervision: Perspectives, issues, and controversies* (pp. 114–123). Norwood, MA: Christopher-Gordon Publishers.

Gordon, S. P. 2001. The good school. *Florida Journal of Educational Leadership, 1*(2), 13–15.

Ingersoll, R. 2003. *Who controls teachers' work: Power and accountability in America's schools.* Cambridge, MA: Harvard University Press.

Keedy, J. L., and Simpson, D. S. 2002. Principal priorities, school norms, and teacher influence: A study of sociocultural leadership in the high school. *Journal of Educational Administration and Foundations, 16*(1), 10–41.

MacKenzie, D. E. 1983. Research for school improvement: An appraisal of some recent trends. *Educational Researcher, 12*(4), 8.

Scheurich, J. J. 1998. The grave dangers in the discourse on democracy. *The International Journal of Leadership in Education, 1*(1), 55–60.

Waite, D. 2000. Identity, authority, and the heart of supervision. *International Journal of Educational Reform, 9*(4), 282–291.

PART II

Knowledge

Part II examines the prerequisite knowledge for supervision. Chapter 2 will consider the pessimistic news—why schools are typically ineffective. The causes of ineffectiveness will be traced to the teaching career and the school environment. Chapter 3 will explain the optimistic news found in school research on characteristics of successful schools, with particular attention to those work environment factors within the province of supervision. Chapter 4 will explain how optimal adult development contrasts with the teaching career. Chapter 5 will look at how supervisory practices might respond to helping teachers develop and eliminate the causes of ineffectiveness. While moving from pessimism to optimism to realism, we will be riding through highly explosive grounds. Reactions of delight, anger, chagrin, hope, and disagreement are to be expected as current research challenges us to rethink typical supervisory practices.

The Norm
Why Schools Are as They Are

Dan Lortie (1986) wrote about the concept of structural strain, describing teachers of today who still work under school conditions of long ago (see Kottkamp, Provenzo, and Cohn, 1986). He and others have studied the work environment of schools and how work conditions promote or inhibit teacher development and instructional improvement. Our eyes must be wide open as we examine historical aspects of schools, teachers, and leadership. We must acknowledge that schools cannot be left alone to do business as usual if we are serious about lasting instructional improvement.

The Work Environment or Culture of Schools

The study of values, beliefs, myths, rituals, symbols, heroes, shamans, and storytellers in organizations is well documented in the literature (Bolman and Deal, 2002; Deal, 1985). It may seem technically incorrect to apply the term *culture* to professional settings; the term is appropriated from the anthropological studies of largely intact and isolated communities of people. However, the concept of culture helps us reexamine schools as places of human community with peculiar histories and stories. When we grasp the underlying values of our particular school as a work environment, we can consciously act to reshape the organization into a purposeful collection of individuals who believe that schools are for students, for learning, and for improvement rather than for insularity, self-protection, and complacency.

How does it happen that in the same school district, teachers in two schools view their work so differently from each other? In Meadow Valley Middle School, teachers come to school within 15 minutes of the required arrival time and leave school 15 minutes after the last bell. If a teacher arrives earlier or stays later, other teachers' questions and glances make that teacher feel as if he or she shouldn't be working more than the required time. To do so is to violate an unspoken norm that teachers have come to accept about the proper amount of time to spend in school. Yet, one and a half miles across town, at the other middle school in the same district, the norms about proper time are different. At Mountain View Middle School, teachers are in their classrooms 45 minutes ahead of time, sharing coffee with each other, organizing materials, and conferring with individual students. One hour after school each day, the majority of staff are still there, working industriously in their own rooms, conducting tutorials, calling parents, and checking on tomorrow's plans. If a teacher arrives later or leaves earlier, the questions and glances of other teachers make him or her feel that a taboo is being violated.

Teachers in both schools work under the same district regulations, yet their expectations about work in their particular school are quite different. Why is this so? How does this come about? What have been the enduring norms of schools and how have they been established? The answers to these questions are quite important if we are to know how to intervene in our own schools to minimize resistance and capitalize on school beliefs that give impetus to student learning.

The Legacy of the One-Room Schoolhouse

Discussing the present work environment of schools without discussing the one-room schoolhouse would be comparable to talking about issues in Western democracies without acknowledging the Magna Carta. Most existing beliefs and expectations about schools can be traced to the idyllic-looking, clapboard one-room schoolhouses of pioneer times. The teacher was responsible for the total instruction of all students, the maintenance of the building, keeping the stove filled with wood, and cleaning the floors. Our first schoolteachers were seen as working in an honorable but menial profession, poorly paid, but second only to the preacher in prestige (Lortie, 1975).

In the one-room schoolhouse, the teacher was responsible for all that transpired within its four walls; therefore, collective action in a school was automatic. What the teacher wanted to do about curriculum and instruction was what the school did! This legacy of independence, isolation, and privatization of teaching remains alive and well in many schools today. Instead of having physically separated one-room schoolhouses, we often see the one-room schoolhouses repeated every few yards down a school corridor. Each teacher sees his or her students, within the four walls, as his or her own school. Although the old one-room school is physically gone, it still holds a pervasive grip on the minds and actions of many teachers and schools.

The sense of classrooms as being private places is in direct contrast to the research on norms of improving schools.

> Research suggests that the schools with the greatest student learning going on are those which do not isolate teachers, but instead encourage professional dialogue and collaboration. Teaching in effective schools is a collective, rather than individual enterprise. (Freiberg and Knight, 1987, p. 3)

The one-room schoolhouse of pioneer times has spawned a deep-seated institutional belief among educators that is characterized by isolation, psychological dilemmas, routine, inadequate induction of beginning teachers, inequity, lack of career stages, lack of professional dialogue, lack of involvement in school decisions, lack of a shared technical culture, and conservatism. Many educators accept that these characteristics are simply part of school culture, and there is little doubt that they pervade the minds and beliefs of most teachers and administrators. However, instructional leaders are questioning whether beliefs and practices acceptable in the past are appropriate for the present, or whether we need to initiate a new culture based on purposeful and collective beliefs about school, students, and teaching. Let's look at the characteristics of today's education that are derived from the one-room schoolhouse of bygone days.

Isolation

The isolation and individualism of teachers has been observed in all major studies of their work environment. As an example of this isolation, Dreeben (1973) noted:

> Perhaps the most important single property of classrooms, viewed from a school-wide perspective, is their spatial scattering and isolation throughout school buildings; and because teachers work in different places at the same time, they do not observe each other working . . . the implications of this spatial isolation are far reaching. (p. 468)

Dreeben further wrote:

> Unlike hospitals and law firms, for example, where new recruits to medicine and law learn their trade as apprentices by performing work tasks of gradually increasing difficulty under close supervision, schools provide a less adequate setting—the classroom—for work and training activities to occur simultaneously. (p. 470)

As Dreeben pointed out, classrooms are set up structurally in such a way that teachers are difficult to supervise, do not receive feedback from others, and cannot work collaboratively. During a typical workday, a teacher will talk to only a few other adults—on the way to the classroom in the morning, for 20 minutes or so at lunch and recess, and at the end of the day on the way out of the building.

While teaching, teachers in most schools are invisible to each other and lack any concrete knowledge of what other teachers are doing in their classrooms.

Sarason (1996) points out that *physical* teacher isolation can lead to *psychological* isolation:

> What does it mean to go through a work day with no sustained personal contact with another adult? Being and talking with children is not psychologically the same as being and talking with peers. . . . When one is almost exclusively with children—responsible for them, being vigilant in regard to them, "giving" to them—it must have important consequences. *One of the consequences is that teachers are psychologically alone even though they are in a densely populated setting.* It is not only that they are alone, but they adapt to being alone. (p. 133; emphasis in original)

Teachers who have experienced long-term psychological isolation tend to view their work environment as limited to *their* classroom, *their* students, and *their* teaching. Although their isolation was initially involuntary, over time they have adapted to and accepted the tradition of isolation (Sarason, 1996); they now resist opportunities for professional dialogue and collaboration with other teachers that might arise.

Psychological Dilemma and Frustration

The teacher's work environment is marked by incessant psychological encounters. In just a few minutes of observation, one might see a teacher ask a question, reply with a smile to a student's answer, frown at an inattentive student, ask a student to be quiet, put a hand on a student's shoulder, and begin to lecture. Teachers have thousands of such psychological encounters in a normal school day (Jackson, 1968). A look, a shrug, and a word all have intended meanings between teacher and students.

Each day an elementary teacher meets with 25 to 35 students for six and one-half hours. A secondary teacher meets with 100 to 150 students for five to seven 50-minute periods. All this human interaction takes place in a 900 square-foot room, where a teacher must instruct, manage, discipline, reinforce, socialize, and attend to multiple occurrences. This crowded professional life makes teachers wish for smaller classes to reduce the psychological demand of constant decision making.

To maintain their own sanity in the face of an overload of psychological encounters and an inability to attend to the psychological needs of each student in a confined and regulated workplace, teachers often cope by routinizing classroom activity. The classroom routine for students becomes similar to the outside routine for teachers. For example, a science teacher might have students listen to a 20-minute presentation, followed by a 10-minute question-and-answer period and then by 20 minutes of seatwork. An elementary teacher might have three reading groups who rotate to him or her for 15 minutes each; each group reads aloud, responds to teacher questions, and then does worksheets. By routinizing what happens within the classroom, a teacher avoids making hundreds of decisions. The routinization of teaching allows the teacher to avoid the inherent conflict between being overwhelmed psychologically by the responsibility for teaching a large number of students, and being aware of neglecting the personal needs of individual students. In interpersonal terms, teaching closely resembles clinical psychology, but it takes place in an environment more like that of factory production.

Routine of the Teaching Day

The routine of the teaching day is imposed by administrative fiat, school board policy, and state guidelines. Every classroom teacher is required to be at school before students enter and to remain until they have departed. In primary or elementary schools, a teacher has specific times for recess and lunch, as well as approximate time allocations for teaching a given subject (for example, 45 minutes for reading, 30 minutes for mathematics, 30 minutes twice a week for social studies). The teacher is assigned a certain number of students and has responsibility for them for the entire day and school year. He or she is expected to remain physically in the assigned classroom for the entire school day, with the exception of recess, lunch, or special classes. Outside the classroom, teachers also have scheduled responsibilities for lunch, recess, and dismissal. In middle schools, junior high schools, and senior high schools, the school day is different from that of elementary schools but still has a set routine. A secondary teacher will have four to seven different classes of students meeting at specific times each day for an extended period (11, 18, or 36 weeks). Again, the teacher begins and dismisses each class at a prescribed time and has regular duties outside the classroom (for example, monitoring the lunchroom, halls, or bathrooms).

Regardless of grade level, teachers do not schedule their own time or determine the number or type of students. Unlike more autonomous professionals, teachers do not put up a shingle on the door, ask clients to arrange for appointments, or take Wednesday mornings off. Teachers do not have the right to make changes in their schedule. Imagine a teacher asking the school secretary to clear his or her schedule for several hours so he or she can attend to other business. School goes on, students keep coming, the bells keep ringing, and teachers cannot make individual readjustments of their professional time.

Of course, elementary and secondary teachers often do make readjustments within the assigned time, within their four walls, with their assigned students, and with instruction. School time, however, is imposed. Starting and ending times, numbers of students, physical locations for teaching, and extra duties are set for the duration, and a teacher has little control. The routines the school as a workplace imposes are more like those of the factory than those of high-status professions. The punch-in, punch-out clock may not be visible in the entering hallway of the school, but nonetheless it exists.

Sarason (1996) raises a critical question concerning the effects of routine on teachers and students:

> *If teaching becomes neither terribly interesting nor exciting to many teachers, can one expect them to make learning interesting or exciting to children? If teaching*

becomes a routine, predictable experience, does this not have inevitable consequences for life in the classroom? The model classroom does not allow me other than to conclude that children and teachers show most of the effects of routinized thinking and living. (p. 200; emphasis in original)

Inadequate Induction of Beginning Teachers*

Teaching has been a career in which the greatest challenge and most difficult responsibilities are faced by those with the least experience—a strange state of affairs indeed! Beginning teachers in many schools are faced with a number of environmental difficulties: inadequate resources, difficult work assignments, unclear expectations, a sink-or-swim mentality, and reality shock (Colley, 2002; Gordon, 1991; Gordon and Maxey, 2000; Johnson and Kardos, 2002). As we describe these difficulties, we invite you to reflect on your own first year of teaching and to recall if they were part of your entrance to the profession.

Inadequate Resources.   If a teacher makes known that he or she will not be returning in the fall, then after the last day of school other teachers will often descend on the vacant classroom and remove materials that will be useful to them. Not only are instructional materials removed but also desks, tables, and chairs! In their place are put those discarded items and furniture that no one else wants. Additionally, teachers may jockey around for the more spacious, better lighted classrooms. Thus, for the incoming year, the neophyte teacher with the least amount of experience often steps into the physically least desirable classroom in the school, with discards for furniture and equipment and few instructional materials.

Difficult Work Assignments.   Experienced staff and administration will often arrange for the "problem" children and/or lowest-achieving groups of students to be assigned to the newest teacher. In addition, the least interesting and most difficult courses usually are assigned to beginners (Johnson, 2001; Kurtz, 1983; Stansbury, 2001). New teachers are often given larger classes and more duties than experienced teachers (Birkeland and Johnson, 2002; Romatowski, Dorminey, and Van Voorhees, 1989).

Unclear Expectations.   A common complaint among first-year teachers is that they are never sure what is expected of them as professionals (Johnson and Kardos, 2002; Kurtz, 1983). Administrators, other teachers, parents, and students express conflicting expectations of the beginner, leaving the neophyte in a quandary about whose expectations he or she should try to meet. A failure to socialize novice teachers into a professional community leads to what Corcoran (1981) has called the "condition of not knowing" (p. 20).

*Adapted from *How to Help Beginning Teachers Succeed* by Stephen P. Gordon. Copyright 1991 by the Association for Supervision and Curriculum Development. Reprinted by permission.

Sink-or-Swim Mentality.   For a variety of reasons, beginning teachers are left on their own to "sink or swim." Administrators and experienced teachers tend to view the first year of teaching as a necessary "trial by fire" through which all neophytes must pass. Many experienced colleagues are reluctant to provide assistance to beginning teachers. Some veterans think it is only fair that new teachers should pass through the same trials and tribulations that they navigated when they were beginners. Some see it as a process that "weeds out" weak teachers, allowing only the strong to survive. Other experienced teachers are reluctant to assist beginners because of the norms of individualism and privacy that pervade the school culture.

Beginners often are reluctant to ask the principal or colleagues for help when they are experiencing management or instructional problems. This is due to the fact that teaching is the only profession in which a novice is expected to assume the same (or more) responsibilities at the same level of competence as experienced colleagues. Novice teachers often do not ask for help because they fear that a request for assistance will call into question their professional competence. In fact, neophytes often go to great lengths to conceal their classroom problems (Newberry, 1978).

Reality Shock.   Veenman defined *reality shock* as "the collapse of the missionary ideals formed during teacher training by the harsh and rude reality of classroom life" (1984, p. 143). Individuals tend to enter teaching with idealized visions of what it will be like. Classroom management problems, student learning difficulties, and the environmental difficulties already discussed tend to destroy those ideals rather quickly. Moreover, neophytes are faced with the numbing realization that they are unprepared to deal with the harsh realities of teaching. This realization can lead to disillusionment and professional paralysis (Corcoran, 1981).

Effects of Environmental Difficulties.   The environmental problems just discussed can cause tremendous stress and eventually lead to physical and emotional problems. Novice teachers tend to have more negative attitudes about themselves, their teaching, their profession, and students at the end than at the beginning of their first year of teaching (Gordon, 1991). Between one-third and one-half of teachers drop out of the profession within their first seven years of teaching (Metropolitan Life, 1985), with up to 15 percent leaving each of the first two years (Schlechty and Vance, 1981). Many of the most promising teachers are the ones who leave the profession early in their careers (Harris and Collay, 1990; Schlechty and Vance, 1981). Finally, as a result of their initial negative experiences, many teachers who stay in the profession develop a survival mentality, a narrow set of teaching methods, and resistance to experimentation and change that may last throughout their teaching careers (Huling-Austin, 1986; Romatowski, Dorminey, and Van Voorhees, 1989).

In recent years many school districts have initiated beginning teacher assistance programs (sometimes called teacher induction programs) in an effort to address these problems. These programs often include assigning experienced teachers to mentor novice teachers. Chapter 18 includes a description of a successful beginning teacher assistance program.

Inequity

The inequity between experienced and beginning teachers is not the only type of disparity often found in conventional districts and schools. Schools located in lower-income communities often are not provided the same resources as other schools in the same district. The physical facilities in low-income schools may be in ill repair and even present health and safety hazards. Class sizes in low-income schools often are larger than middle- or upper-class schools. Textbooks and instructional materials may be woefully out of date or nonexistent. Low-income schools may be shortchanged on human resources as well. Many teachers in low-income schools are teaching outside of their field (Ingersoll, 2002). New teachers often stay at low-income schools only until they are eligible to transfer to other schools, creating problems with faculty and school stability. The personnel problems in low-income schools often are blamed on the difficulty and frustration of teaching low-achieving students, but the major cause is that districts seldom provide either sufficient resources and incentives to attract the most qualified teachers or sufficient support to retain them.

Low-income, minority, and other marginalized students in conventional schools with diverse student bodies can also experience inequity. Many low-income students often are placed in remedial tracks where they miss out on the richer, higher-level curriculum taught to other students. In many conventional schools, there is little or no attempt to consider the culture or learning styles of minority students when designing curriculum, selecting instructional materials, or preparing lessons. Worse still, both unconscious and overt racism go unchallenged by supervisors and teachers in some schools. It may not be easy or comfortable for educators in conventional schools to critically examine inequity, but admitting its presence is the first step in removing it from our schools.

Unstaged Career

More prestigious professions avoid such an abrupt transition from student to full professional. Physicians, lawyers, engineers, and scientists all experience several transition years of apprenticeship, internship, and junior membership on the job before they qualify for full rights and responsibilities in the profession. However, teaching historically follows a different paradigm. The negative characteristic that perhaps most significantly differentiates the teaching profession from others is the absence of stages in a teacher's professional career.

More prestigious occupations have rigorous screening and requirements. Furthermore, they have a transitional or proving-ground stage; only when an aspirant has been judged competent by senior members does the junior member step into the next stage of the career, which provides high visibility, greater challenge, a substantial increase in salary, and responsibility for monitoring and judging the next wave of junior members. For example, a law school graduate must pass the bar exam and then serve as a clerk, as a legal aide, or as a junior member of a law firm. He or she works behind the scenes on writing and research that are credited to his or her superior. After proving competence over time, however, the lawyer then becomes a partner in a firm, a public prosecutor or defender, or an independent attorney. This movement brings visibility and stature in the profession and the right to have one's own apprentices to do the less challenging, less exciting work.

Teaching, on the other hand, has been unstaged from entry to exit. Education majors take courses, spend time in schools, perform as student teachers, and then graduate from college into their own classrooms as teachers. After that, no matter how many years they continue to teach, they do not move into another stage. The 20-year veteran teacher has the same classroom space, number of students, and requirements as the first-year teacher. Furthermore, for each year of experience, a teacher realizes a salary increase identical to that received by all others of comparable experience.

Lack of Dialogue about Instruction

Generally, people in schools do not talk about their work—teaching—with each other. DeSanctis and Blumberg (1979) found that the length of instruction-related discussion among teachers in a typical schoolday in a high school in New York was two minutes. Little's (1982) study of schools, Rosenholtz's (1985) review of effective schools, and Pajak and Glickman's (1987) study of 15 exemplary elementary and secondary schools in three improving districts pointed to one essential dimension of successful schools: Professionals constantly talk with each other, in a problem-solving, action-oriented way, about teaching. This talk is generated through faculty and committee meetings, in-service workshops, observations and conferences, faculty lounge contacts, and other informal occasions. This talk is of a specific nature: teaching and learning of students. Of course, teachers talk with each other in all schools, but the talk is of a more social nature—telling stories about students, parents, administrators, and community and school events.

For teachers to talk often and seriously with each other about the core of their job—instruction and curriculum—is a rarity in many schools. Time is not planned for it to occur. Faculty meetings are information giving, and when school concerns are raised, they are often deflected to noninstructional matters such as schedules, district policies, extracurricular responsibilities, and building maintenance.

The public school as a work institution is unique in that a collection of adults can be employed as professionals within the same physical setting, with a common responsibility for providing their particular services to the same group of clients (students), and not be frequently and intensively engaged with each other in discussions on how to improve their services. Again, the lack of such dialogue is related to the one-room schoolhouse legacy, which accepts isolation, privacy, and lack of career stages as the norms of teaching.

Lack of Involvement in Schoolwide Curriculum and Instructional Decisions

If teachers don't see each other at work, don't talk with each other about their work, and see teaching as what goes on within their own four walls, it is not surprising that they are not given the opportunity, time, or expectations to be involved in decisions about curriculum and instruction beyond their four walls. Goodlad's (1984) study of schooling found that teachers' involvement in decisions about curriculum and instruction was virtually nil. Blumberg (1987) has referred to one of the basic problems with public schools as "institutions premised on having mature, competent adults as employees, yet treating these same adults as children when it comes to deciding and operationalizing their work." Boyer (1983) has been even more adamant, referring to schools as impoverished intellectual climates for adults. The norm in most schools is that teachers are not expected to contribute experience, knowledge, and wisdom to decisions about the common good of educating students.

Lack of a Shared Technical Culture

Colleagues within a shared technical culture possess common purpose, expertise, and methods for analyzing and solving problems. They have developed sophisticated performance standards and communicate through a shared technical language. Imagine that a team of surgeons is about to perform a heart transplant operation. Each member of the team shares extensive knowledge of the cardiovascular system as well as state-of-the-art surgical procedures that will be used during the operation. The purpose of the surgery, as well as the technical means for achieving that purpose, are clear to each team member. Both in planning and performing the operation, the surgeons communicate in a complex technical language, much of which would be difficult for a layperson to understand. During the operation, the surgeons receive precise feedback from advanced technology and each other on the patient's condition. Should complications arise during the operation, the surgeons will rely on their expertise and each other to analyze the problem and take corrective action. The patient's survival is never assured, but the shared technical culture of the surgical team greatly enhances the patient's chances for recovery.

Unlike advanced professional communities, most schools are not characterized by shared technical cultures. Isolation, lack of dialogue, inadequate induction, and lack of involvement in schoolwide decisions all inhibit the development of such cultures among teachers. Based on his classic sociological study of schools and teachers, Lortie's (1975) description of school culture is in sharp contrast to the shared technical culture we have been discussing.

There is little "state of the art." . . . The image projected is more individualistic, teachers are portrayed as an aggregate of persons each assembling practices consistent with his experience and peculiar personality. It is not what "we the colleagues" know and share which is paramount, but rather what I have learned from experience. (p. 79)

Lortie concluded that the lack of a shared technical culture means that "the teacher's craft . . . is marked by the absence of concrete models for emulation, unclear lines of influence, multiple and controversial criteria, ambiguity about assessment timing, and instability in the product" (p. 136). Lortie's seminal research about nontechnical school cultures and their effects on teachers was carried out in the mid-1970s. Unfortunately, more recent studies have found that most schools still lack sophisticated technical cultures and are still characterized by unclear goals, uncertainty about what constitutes effective instruction, idiosyncratic teaching, and ambiguous assessment (Rosenholtz, 1989).

Conservatism

The lack of a shared technical culture and the resulting ambiguity and uncertainty foster teacher conservatism. One aspect of this conservatism is a set of restricted, teacher-centered instructional methods. After reviewing data from observations of more than 1,000 classrooms, John Goodlad (1984) concluded the following:

The domination of the teacher is obvious in the conduct of instruction. Most of the time the teacher is engaged in either frontal teaching, monitoring students' seat work, or conducting quizzes. Relatively rarely are students actively engaged in learning directly from one another or in initiating processes of interaction with teachers. When students work in smaller groups, they usually are doing the same thing side by side, and these things tend to be determined by the teacher. (pp. 123–124)

Beyond reliance on traditional teaching methods, less obvious aspects of conservatism can be observed in most schools, including the following:

- An emphasis on short-range rather than long-range instructional goals
- Satisfaction of successes with individual lessons, students, and projects rather than with the continuous growth of all students
- Reliance on personal experience rather than educational research
- Narrow limits on the types and degree of collegiality and collaboration in which teachers are willing to engage
- A reflexive resistance to curricular or instructional innovations

Such conservatism is not surprising considering the isolation and psychological dilemmas found in the traditional school environment. The irony is that the conservatism that results largely from the other environmental problems we have described tends to hinder efforts to solve those very same problems.

Blaming the Victim and Structural Strain

A Nation at Risk (National Commission on Education, 1983), a report highly critical of public education in America, intensified a tendency for politicians, policy makers, and the general public to blame educators for the low academic achievement of many K–12 students. This and similar national reports reinforced the perception that problems in public education were caused by incompetent, inconsiderate, and self-serving teachers and administrators. The general consensus among elected officials that public education was in deep trouble was not accompanied by a will to increase funding for teacher education, teacher pay, or school improvement. Rather, the solution of choice across the nation was legislation designed to control and monitor the work of educators and the curriculum taught to students. This "legislated learning" (Wise, 1988) includes state-mandated curriculum, statewide teacher evaluation systems, and high-stakes achievement tests.

Researchers on school reform and student learning are telling us loud and clear that we cannot improve education by simply legislating higher standards and higher stakes. To this point, policy makers do not appear to be listening. Moreover, none of the popular legislated reforms are aimed at improving the school as a culture or workplace. Thus, the problems described earlier in this chapter remain largely unaddressed. In fact these problems are aggravated by the external control brought about by legislated reform and the diminishing ability of teachers to engage in professional decision making.

Either the work environment of schools must be altered or we must accept that, regardless of extrinsic rewards, schools are not the place for our best teachers and thinkers. Supervision of instruction can play a strong role in reshaping the work environment to promote norms of collegiality and collective action, or supervision can remain another control apparatus "to keep teachers in their place." We can then continue to blame the victims for not shaking the institutional chains that shackle every attempt to work together in the instructional interest of all students.

Viewing School Culture in the Context of the Larger Culture

Our discussion of legislated learning opens the door to consideration of how other forces in the larger culture affect schools, and how educators should respond to these forces. In one sense, of course, we want our public schools to serve our culture, inculcating students with democratic values, preparing them to be contributing members of society, and so forth. We would be naïve, however, if we did not realize that there are factors in our culture that can have negative effects on teachers and their students. Donald Thomas and William Bainbridge (2002), for example, argue that there are a variety of public policies that harm children's education:

- Millions of children in the United States live in poverty and without proper health care, which prevents them from developing their full cognitive potential.
- Most of America's schools are underfunded. Schools in low wealth states and districts are especially hard hit, with inadequate instructional materials, little technology, unsafe buildings, and less-qualified teachers.
- Poorly regulated child-care centers across the nation damage children's creativity and development.
- The federal government, although requiring special accommodations for students with disabilities, provides inadequate funding for such assistance.

Beyond harmful public policies, we must not forget that many of the social evils that have long victimized so many of our citizens are still present and are still harming our nation's children. These include racism, classism, sexism, homophobia, and religious prejudice, to name a few. We would be foolish to ignore the fact that these evils exist, not only in the larger culture, but also inside our schools (Kao, 2004; Weiner, 2003).

How should schools address the societal problems that impinge on our children's growth and development? There are increasing calls for educators to become more politically active regarding policy issues that affect student learning. Political action can start with local educators forming partnerships with parents, the community, nearby universities, and the corporate sector (Fullan, 1999). Political action might take the form of working with the media to assure accurate reporting on policy issues, or communicating concerns to state and national legislators (Biddle and Berliner, 2002). Perhaps the most effective means of political action for educators, not surprisingly, is educating fellow citizens and policy makers on critical issues that relate to teaching and learning. Some harmful policies, of course, will stay in place despite the best efforts of educators and their allies to bring about change. In these cases, educators must use their creativity to meet ill-advised government mandates in ways that will not interfere with quality curriculum and instruction.

Regarding the deeper societal problems of prejudice and discrimination, in the short term it is possible for schools to become oases of equity and social justice. However, this can happen only as a result of the school community critiquing its structures, curriculum, instruction, and assessment practices; continuously reflecting on the relationships and interactions of administrators, teachers, students, and parents; and critically examining assumptions at the deepest levels of school culture. The school community must engage in continuous identification and analysis of aspects of the school culture that work against democratic learning and personal empowerment (Weiner, 2003).

In the long term, our schools can become society's primary vehicle for developing a more democratic and just society. Students can develop understanding and tolerance for others, and a commitment to democratic principles, the common good, and the well being of all men and women. This can be accomplished through developing schools as moral communities characterized by democratic learning, with opportunities for applying that learning locally and connecting it to communities across the nation and around the globe.

REFERENCES AND RECOMMENDED READINGS

Biddle, B. J., and Berliner, D. C. 2002. Unequal school funding in the United States. *Educational Leadership, 59*(8), 48–59.

Birkeland, S., and Johnson, S. M. 2002. What keeps new teachers in the swim? *Journal of Staff Development, 23*(4), 18–21.

Blumberg, A. 1987. *A discussion on the effects of local, state, and federal mandates on supervisory practices.* Annual conference of the Council of Professors of Instructional Supervision, Philadelphia, November.

Bolman, L. G., and Deal, T. E. 2002. Leading with soul and spirit. *School Administrator, 59*(2), 21–26.

Boyer, E. L. 1983. *High school: A report on secondary education in America.* New York: Harper & Row.

Colley, A. C. 2002. What can principals do about new teacher attrition? *Principal, 81*(4), 22–24.

Corcoran, E. 1981. Transition shock: The beginning teacher's paradox. *Journal of Teacher Education, 32*(3), 19–23.

Deal, T. E. 1985. The symbolism of effective schools. *Elementary School Journal, 85*(5), 601–620.

DeSanctis, M., and Blumberg, A. 1979. *An exploratory study into the nature of teacher interactions with other adults in the schools.* Paper presented at the annual meeting of the American Educational Research Association, San Francisco, April.

Dreeben, R. 1973. The school as a workplace. In R. M. Travers (Ed.), *Second handbook of research on teaching* (pp. 450–473). Chicago: Rand McNally.

Freiberg, H. J., and Knight, S. 1987. *External influences of school climate.* Paper presented at the annual meeting of the American Educational Research Association, Washington, DC, April.

Fullan, M. 1999. *Change forces: The sequel. Philadelphia.* Philadelphia: Falmer Press.

Goodlad, J. I. 1984. *A place called school.* New York: McGraw-Hill.

Gordon, S. P. 1991. *How to help beginning teachers succeed.* Alexandria, VA: Association for Supervision and Curriculum Development.

Gordon, S. P., and Maxey, S. 2000. *How to help beginning teachers succeed.* Alexandria, VA: Association for Supervision and Curriculum Development.

Harris, M. M., and Collay, M. P. 1990. Teacher induction in rural schools. *Journal of Staff Development, 11*(4), 44–48.

Huling-Austin, L. 1986. What can and cannot reasonably be expected from teacher induction programs. *Journal of Teacher Education, 37*(1), 2–5.

Ingersoll, R. M. 2002. Deprofessionalizing the teaching profession: The problem of out-of-field teaching. *Educational Horizons, 80*(1), 28–31.

Jackson, P. W. 1968. *Life in classrooms.* New York: Holt, Rinehart & Winston.

Johnson, H. R. 2001. Administrators and mentors: Keys in the success of beginning teachers. *Journal of Instructional Psychology, 28*(1), 44–49.

Johnson, S. M., and Kardos, S. M. 2002. Keeping new teachers in mind. *Educational Leadership, 59*(6), 12–16.

Kao, G. 2004. Social capital and its relevance to minority and immigrant populations. *Sociology of Education, 77*(2), 172–175.

King, D. 2002. The changing shape of leadership. *Educational Leadership, 59*(8), 61–63.

Kottkamp, R. B., Provenzo, E. F., Jr., and Cohn, M. M. 1986. Stability and change in a profession: Two decades of teacher attitudes. 1964–1984. *Kappan, 67*(8), 559–567.

Kurtz, W. H. 1983. Identifying their needs: How the principal can help beginning teachers. *NASSP Bulletin, 67*(459), 42–45.

Little, J. W. 1982. Norms of collegiality and experimentation: Workplace conditions of school success. *American Educational Research Journal, 19*(3), 325–340.

Lortie, D. C. 1975. *School teacher: A sociological study.* Chicago: University of Chicago Press.

Lortie, D. C. 1986. Teacher status in Dade County: A case of structural strain. *Kappan, 67*(8), 568–575.

Metropolitan Life. 1985. *Former teachers in America.* New York: Author.

National Commission on Education. 1983. An open letter to the American people. A nation at risk: The imperative for educational reform. *Education Week, 2*(31), 12.

Newberry, J. 1978. The barrier between beginning and experienced teachers. *The Journal of Educational Administration, 16*(1), 46–56.

Pajak, E., and Glickman, C. 1987. *Dimensions of improving school districts.* Presentation to the annual conference of the Association for Supervision and Curriculum Development, New Orleans, March.

Romatowski, J. A., Dorminey, J. J., and Van Voorhees, B. 1989. *Teacher induction programs: A report.* (ERIC ED 316 525)

Rosenholtz, S. J. 1985. Effective schools: Interpreting the evidence. *American Journal of Education, 93*(3), 352–388.

Rosenholtz, S. J. 1989. *Teachers' workplace: The social organization of schools.* New York: Longman.

Sarason, S. B. 1996. *Revisiting the culture of the school and the problem of change.* New York: Teachers College Press.

Schlechty, P. C., and Vance, V. S. 1981. Do academically able teachers leave education? The North Carolina case. *Kappan, 63*(2), 106–112.

Shulman, L. S. 1987. *Teaching alone, learning together: Needed agendas for the new reforms.* Paper presented at Conference on Restructuring Schooling for Quality Education, San Antonio, August.

Stansbury, K. 2001. What new teachers need. *Leadership, 30*(3), 18–21.

Thomas, M. D., and Bainbridge, W. L. 2002. No child left behind: Facts and fallacies. *Phi Delta Kappan, 83,* 781–782.

Veenman, S. 1984. Perceived problems of beginning teachers. *Review of Educational Research, 54*(2), 143–178.

Weiner, L. 2003. Why is classroom management so vexing to urban teachers? *Theory into Practice, 42*(4), 305–312.

Wise, A. E. 1988. The two conflicting trends in school reform: Legislated learning revisited. *Kappan, 69*(5), 328–333.

The Exception
What Schools Can Be

When we analyze the definitions of school success, we find great divergence in goals and practices. What do we mean by school success, and how do we measure it? Is the measure of school success short term—higher achievement scores on standardized basic skills tests? Is school success measured by improved student attitudes toward learning, social behavior, displays of creative work, critical writing or thinking, attendance, grades, promotion, retention, or community or extracurricular participation? The instructional goals that a school sets and how these goals are measured reflect how the staff members collectively understand and prioritize their beliefs about education. A successful school is foremost an organization that defines good education for itself, through its goals and desired practices, and then engages in achieving that vision (Glickman, 1987b).

Early Effective Schools Research

Beginning in the mid-1970s, research began to focus on individual schools that are exceptional, that consistently achieve results far superior to those of schools in general. In composition of student body, location, socioeconomic setting, and per-pupil expenditure, these schools do not differ from schools in general. Yet whether they are in poor urban areas or in wealthy suburbs, they succeed while others fail.

Ronald Edmonds, after discovering that the results of his own research were consistent with those of other independent investigations, was confident enough to predict that *all schools could be effective.*

> It seems to me, therefore, that what is left of this discussion are three declarative statements: (a) We can, whenever and wherever we choose, successfully teach all children whose schooling is of interest to us; (b) We already know more than we need to do that; and (c) Whether or not we do it must finally depend on how we feel about the fact that we haven't so far. (1979, p. 22)

How can one make such bold statements? Edmonds (1979) conducted three different studies. His first study was of 2 inner-city schools in Detroit; the second was of 55 effective schools in the Northeast (discovered by reanalyzing the Coleman study); and the third included 20 schools in inner-city New York. Edmonds's findings were consistent with those of other early effective schools studies. He found that effective schools were distinguished by the presence of

- Strong leadership
- A climate of expectation
- An orderly but not rigid atmosphere
- Communication to students of the school's priority on learning the basics
- Diversion of school energy and resources when necessary to maintain priorities
- Means of monitoring student (and teacher) achievement

The Second Wave of Effective Schools Research

Beginning in the latter half of the 1980s a new wave of effective schools research was carried out. These new studies, relying on more sophisticated research designs and new statistical analysis techniques (Creemers, 1996), tended to result in longer lists of correlates than the early effects research (Levine and Lezotte, 1990; Mortimore et al., 1988; Teddlie and Stringfield, 1993). After reviewing "second wave" effective schools research generated in a number of countries, Austin and Reynolds (1990, pp. 168–174) reported the following characteristics of effective schools:

- Site management
- Leadership
- Staff stability
- Curriculum and instructional articulation and organization
- Staff development
- Maximized learning time
- Widespread recognition of academic success
- Parental involvement and support

- Collaborative planning and collegial relationships
- Sense of community
- Clear goals and expectations commonly shared
- Order and discipline

In addition to supporting the early effective schools research on the need for such things as strong leadership, order, and agreed-on priorities, the second wave of research introduced new correlates such as site-based management, professional development, parental involvement, and teacher collaboration and collegiality.

Context Studies in Effective Schools Research

Traditional effective schools research has been criticized for reporting characteristics common to effective schools while ignoring differences between schools from various contexts (Hannaway and Talbert, 1993). Examples of context include location (urban, suburban, rural), socioeconomic status (SES), students' ethnicity and race, and school level (elementary, middle, or high school).

Makedon (1992) maintains that schools identified as effective have not closed the achievement gap between students of low and middle socioeconomic status. Cook, Semmel, and Gerber (1995) reported that in schools seeking to apply effectiveness research, general student achievement increased, but special education student achievement decreased. Pierce (1991) concluded that implementation of factors identified in effective schools research has failed to bring about significant achievement gains for language minority students. The fact that implementation of "traditional" effective schools has often failed to raise the achievement of low-income (Gustafson, 2002), minority, and special needs students has led to effectiveness research aimed specifically at these groups.

Context studies on schools with high-achieving low-income and minority students (Pierce, 1991; Reyes, Scribner, and Scribner, 1999; Stedman, 1987) have identified a number of school characteristics including

- Respect for racial pluralism
- A culture of caring
- Basic skills supplemented with rich academic programs
- Shared governance involving leaders, teachers, parents, and students
- Professional development to help teachers address cultural and special needs
- Teaching aimed at preventing academic problems

Has Effective Schools Research Outlived Its Usefulness?

Soon after publication of the first effective schools studies, school districts across the nation began to plan and implement programs designed to apply the research to their own schools. By the early 1990s over half of the school districts in America were implementing programs based on effective schools research (Reynolds and Stoll, 1996). Such efforts are still going on today. Yet many educators have raised concerns about using the effective schools research as the basis of school reform. One concern is that effective schools have usually been identified by student scores on standardized literacy and mathematics tests, despite the fact researchers have warned against using such tests to judge a school's performance (Cuban, 1998). Another concern is that effective schools research is *correlational;* there is a significant positive correlation between the identified characteristics and the chosen measure of school effectiveness, but the research has not shown that these characteristics *cause* the effectiveness they have been associated with. Yet another problem with the effectiveness research is discussed by Hill (1998):

> School effectiveness research has not found a satisfactory way of dealing with the fact that schools and school education are essentially about growth, progress, and change. Researchers have been reduced to taking snapshots of phenomena, to focusing on achievement rather than rates of progress of students, and on measuring current status rather than charting change over time. (p. 428)

For these reasons as well as continuing problems in research design and methodology, many experts believe that effective schools research has outlived its usefulness and that it is time to base school reform efforts on a new research paradigm (Cuban, 1998; Hill, 1998; Slavin, 2002).

The Legacy of Effective Schools Research

Despite criticism of effects research, it has left a positive legacy (Taylor, 2002). It has disproven the earlier conclusions by Coleman, Jencks, and others that socioeconomic status determines student achievement and that schools and teachers have little effect on student learning. Larry Cuban (1998) points out that basic values of effective schools reformers of the early 1970s—that all children can learn, the importance of academic achievement, the need for accountability—have now been adopted by those who make and influence public policy.

Joseph Murphy (1992) suggests that since effective schools correlates tend to change in different studies and contexts, educators need to move beyond a narrow interpretation of school effectiveness to a set of broad principles that underlie the various correlates. Murphy maintains that these principles constitute the real legacy of the effective schools research and include the following:

1. All students can learn.
2. Schools should focus on student outcomes and rigorously assess progress toward reaching those outcomes.
3. Schools should assume a fair share of the responsibility for student learning.

4. Schools should be structurally, symbolically, and culturally linked, providing for consistency and coordination throughout the school community (pp. 165–168).

Although the legacy of effective schools research is secure, the prevalent opinion of researchers is that this body of research, *by itself,* provides an insufficient basis for school reform. Additional research beyond the effects studies is necessary. This leads us to the topic of school improvement research.

From Effective Schools to School Improvement

Although effective schools research is still being carried out, over the last several years *school improvement research* has taken center stage. Before reviewing the research in this area, let's discuss differences between the two types of research. As noted by Bennett and Harris (1997), effects research asks the question "What do effective schools look like?" and school improvement research asks "How do schools improve over time?" Effects research examines inputs, throughputs, and outputs and emphasizes organizational structure, while school improvement research is focused on school culture and the change process (Bennett and Harris, 1997; Bernauer, 2002; Fullan, 2002; Harris, 2002; Rust and Friedus, 2001). Effects research takes statistical snapshots of performance measures and their correlates, while school improvement research is concerned with long-term growth, often examined through case studies (Bollen, 1996). In short, school improvement research is concerned with the *how* of successful schools. Although the specific characteristics of successful school improvement efforts vary somewhat across the research on school improvement (see Hopkins, Ainscow, and West, 1994; Joyce, Calhoun, and Hopkins, 1999; Levine, 1991; Little, 1982; Rosenholtz, 1989; Teddlie and Stringfield, 1993; Wasley, Hampel, and Clark, 1997), a consensus has emerged on the most important factors. Figure 3.1 provides a composite list of these characteristics.

After reviewing both the effective schools and the school improvement research, it becomes clear that these are not entirely separate types of research. Rather, effects research has informed and provided a foundation for school improvement research. Together, the two types of studies provide us with a knowledge base for developing successful schools.

Studies have pointed out that a successful school can vary considerably from other successful schools in the degree of community involvement, school leadership, and change initiation (Hallinger and Murphy, 1987; Purkey and Smith, 1983; Davies, 2002). There is ample research on school improvement to inform us of the different paths, factors, and actors of school success. However, we can say with confidence that participants in successful schools show a remarkable tendency to see themselves as being involved in "a cause beyond oneself."

- Varied sources of leadership, including teacher leadership
- Consideration of individual school context and culture
- Parental involvement
- Shared vision and continuous revisioning
- External and internal support, including time, moral, and technical support
- Focus on teaching and learning
- Ongoing professional development, including continuous analysis, reflection, and growth
- Instructional dialogue
- Teacher collaboration
- Democratic, collective inquiry, including action research
- Integration of improvement efforts into a coherent program
- Data-based feedback on improvement efforts using multiple measures

FIGURE 3.1   *Characteristics of Improving Schools*

A Cause beyond Oneself

Later chapters on observation, direct assistance, professional development, and curriculum development will explain how a supervisor can use the research on effective classroom practice with teachers. For now, however, the outside-the-classroom but within-the-school factors that correlate with or predict school success provide the more significant issue. *Every major research study on successful schools has noted the organizational phenomenon of collective action, agreed-on purpose, and belief in attainment* (Pratzner, 1984; Rosenholtz, 1985). On the other hand, every major research study on ineffective schools has noted an absence of such purpose. Successful schools do not happen by accident: Supervision is the force that shapes the organization into a productive unit.

Clearly, one characteristic of successful schools is that each teacher has "a cause beyond oneself." Teachers do not view their work as simply what they carry out within their own four walls. In successful schools, teachers see themselves as part of the larger enterprise of complementing and working with each other to educate students. For successful schools, education is a collective rather than an individual enterprise.

Connecting School Improvement to the Local Community and Larger Society

Successful school improvement efforts extend beyond school walls. School improvement needs to connect to the community in a number of ways. First, it is important that parents and other community members be involved in planning, implementing, and assessing school improvement efforts. The days of limiting parent and community involvement in schools to parent–teacher conferences, bake sales, and chaperoning field trips quickly is coming to an end. Parents and community members need to be involved in decision making about the school's mission and goals, as well as in helping educators and students to reach improvement goals. This shared decision making can be accomplished in a number of ways, including parent and community representatives on school councils, open forums with parent and community members, and parent surveys on school needs and improvement efforts (Doyle, 2004; Sanders and Lewis, 2005).

Successful schools do not treat parents and community members as outsiders. Rather parents are welcome in successful schools and invited to participate in a variety of school and classroom activities. Many successful schools now include parent councils, as well as parent centers coordinated and staffed by parents and serving as hubs for parent and community involvement in the school. In addition to sharing school turf and decision making with parents, educators need to interact with parents and families on a regular basis in community centers, neighborhoods, and homes. Many parents are unable to visit schools on a regular basis because of work schedules, transportation problems, or anxiety based on past negative experiences with schools. Educators need to reach out to parents in such circumstances, to collaborate not only in the education of individual children but also in decisions about school improvement.

It is important to connect school improvement and community development. Davies (2002) argues that "school success and community success are linked. Public schools are seldom able to be much better than neighborhoods and surrounding communities. Neighborhoods and communities are seldom able to stay healthy and attractive without good schools" (p. 392). Schools and community agencies can coordinate community services such as health care, social services, recreation programs, and community activities. Proponents of "full-service community schools" propose that schools become hubs of education *and* community services (Dryfoos, 2002).

Arrington and Moore (2001) assert "when we purposely involve students in learning experiences that stretch far beyond the school walls into the community and the world, we provide motivation and relevance that can make a difference in children achieving school success" (p. 56). A number of teaching and learning models that connect students to the community and larger society are being incorporated into school improvement efforts. Three such models are service learning, place-based learning, and democratic learning.

- *Service learning* integrates the curriculum with community service and occurs only when service is accompanied by academic learning. In service learning, students analyze community issues, choose a service project, plan activities, perform the service, and engage in individual and group reflection on the project (Arrington and Moore, 2001). Service learning can take place within any content area and often cuts across several content areas.

- *Place-based learning* uses social, cultural, and natural aspects of the students' local environment as the context for learning. Smith (2002) provides a snapshot of place-based learning:

> When Environment Middle School students go to Brookside Wetlands . . . their water samples and inventories of macro invertebrates, collected and compiled over the course of the year, become part of a report on the . . . Bureau of Environmental Studies. The project allows for a direct rather than mediated experience of the world. The water is cold—the mud, slippery. And when the class spots two geese threatening with outstretched necks a third who tries to cross the invisible boundary that marks their territory, everyone watches in silence. (p. 31)

In place-based learning, students produce rather than consume knowledge, teachers are co-learners and guides rather than instructors, and students solve real-world problems (Smith, 2002; Powers, 2004).

• *Democratic learning* asks students to integrate their self concerns with concerns about the larger world and the common good. Students decide on a common theme, often dealing with race, class, gender, or issues of diversity. Within the common theme, small groups and individuals can develop their own questions and projects. The questions that students ask in democratic learning tend to focus on serious social issues, such as war and peace, the environment, and the family. As students explore issues, they engage in rigorous academic work, display high-level cognitive skills, show mutual respect, and build community (Beane, 2002; Marri, 2005).

The connections between school and community development recently were illustrated to one of the authors serving on a blue ribbon panel asked to select the most outstanding school systems from a large number of nominated districts. The selection process included on-site visits to finalists' district offices as well as their elementary, middle, and high schools. In asking educators, parents, and community members in each district to discuss school–community relationships, the panel was surprised that interviewees in the most outstanding districts and schools initially had significant difficulty answering this question. The reason given for this difficulty was most interesting: The schools were such an integral part of the communities they served, and the communities were so closely associated with their schools, that it was difficult to consider school and community as separate entities and thus difficult to talk about their "relationship." Whether in urban, suburban, and rural settings, the schools were considered the centers of their communities in the outstanding districts. The schools felt a strong obligation to serve the communities in which they were located, and community members felt an equally strong obligation to serve their schools. In short, the educators, parents, and other community members the panel interviewed considered school and community development less as two separate processes to be linked and more as one and the same process.

The supervisor's role in connecting schools with their communities and the larger society should mirror the role of teachers in that same venture. The supervisor becomes a co-learner and facilitator as teachers, students, and communities explore ways to use partnership to improve student learning, develop communities, and, ultimately, improve society.

SUMMARY

Supervision must be viewed as developmental if schools are to become more successful. Supervision must not only respond to current teacher performance but also encourage greater involvement, autonomous thinking, and collective action by teachers. The first order of business for a supervisor is to build the staff into a team. In order to improve school instruction, a supervisor has to work with staff to create a professional togetherness. They must share a common purpose for their instruction and they must have confidence that their collective action will make a difference in their students' lives.

Gaining knowledge of successful schools and effective classrooms is only the first step in improving schools. Using such knowledge in one's own school demands skill and practice. Skill and practice flow from knowledge. We have seen that the research on school success converges on the concept of a cause beyond oneself or a belief in collective action. To use that knowledge, a supervisor needs further understanding about teaching and the teaching profession to understand why such a cause beyond oneself does not occur naturally in schools.

REFERENCES AND RECOMMENDED READINGS

Arrington, H. J., and Moore, S. D. 2001. Infusing service learning into instruction. *Middle School Journal, 32*(4), 55–60.

Austin, G., & Reynolds, D. 1990. Managing for improved school effectiveness: An international survey. *School Organization, 10*(2/3), 167–178.

Beane, J. A. 2002. Beyond self-interest: A democratic core curriculum. *Educational Leadership, 59*(7), 25–28.

Bennett, N., and Harris, A. 1997. *Hearing truth from power? Organization theory, school effectiveness, and school improvement.* Paper presented at the Annual Meeting of the American Educational Research Association, Chicago, March.

Bernauer, J. 2002. Five keys to unlock continuous school improvement. *Kappa Delta Pi Record, 38*(2), 89–92.

Bollen, R. 1996. School effectiveness and school improvement: The intellectual and policy context. In D. Reynolds, R. Bollen, B. Creemers, D. Hopkins, L. Stoll, and N. Lagerweij, *Making good schools: Linking school effectiveness and school improvement.* New York: Routledge.

Brookover, W., Beady, C., Flood, P., Schweiter, J., and Wisenbaker, J. 1979. *School social systems and students' achievement: Schools can make a difference.* New York: Praeger.

Chubb, J. E., and Moe, T. M. 1990. *Politics, markets, and America's schools.* Washington, DC: The Brookings Institute.

Cook, B. G., Semmel, M. I., and Gerber, M. M. 1995. *Are recent reforms effective for all students?* Paper presented at the annual meeting of the American Educational Research Association, San Francisco, April. (ERIC ED 385 012)

Creemers, B. 1996. The school effectiveness knowledge base. In D. Reynolds, R. Bollen, B. Creemers, D. Hopkins, L. Stoll, and N. Lagerweij, *Making good schools: Linking school effectiveness and school improvement* (pp. 36–58). New York: Routledge.

Cuban, L. 1998. How schools change reforms: Redefining reform success and failure. *Teachers College Record, 99*(3), 453–477.

Davies, D. 2002. The 10th school revisited: Are school/family/community partnerships on the reform agenda now? *Phi Delta Kappan, 83,* 388–392.

Doyle, L. H. 2004. Leadership for community building: Changing how we think and act. *The Clearing House, 77*(5), 196–199.

Dryfoos, J. 2002. Full-service community schools: Creating new institutions. *Phi Delta Kappan, 83,* 398–399.

Edmonds, R. 1979. Effective schools for the urban poor. *Educational Leadership, 37*(1), 15–24.

Fullan, M. 2002. The change leader. *Educational Leadership, 59*(8), 16–20.

Fullan, M. 2005. Turnaround leadership. *The Educational Forum, 69*(2), 174–181.

Glickman, C. D. 1987a. *Concepts of change in school systems improving criterion-referenced test scores.* Paper presented at the annual meeting of the American Educational Research Association, Washington, DC.

Glickman, C. D. 1987b. Good and/or effective schools: What do we want? *Phi Beta Kappan, 68*(8), 622–624.

Glickman, C. D., and Pajak, E. F. 1986. *A study of school systems in Georgia which have improved criterion-referenced test scores in reading and mathematics from 1982 to 1985.* (ERIC ED 282 317)

Goodlad, J. I. 1984. *A place called school: Prospects for the future.* New York: McGraw-Hill.

Gustafson, J. P. 2002. Missing the mark for low-SES students. *Kappa Delta Pi Record, 38*(2), 60–63.

Hallinger, P., and Murphy, J. 1987. *Social context on school effects.* Paper presented at the annual meeting of the American Educational Association, Washington, DC, April.

Hannaway, J., and Talbert, J. 1993. Bringing context into effective schools research: Urban-Suburban differences. *Educational Administration Quarterly, 29*(2), 164–186.

Harris, A. 2002. *School improvement: What's in it for schools?* New York: Routledge Falmer.

Hill, P. W. 1998. Shaking the foundations: Research driven school reform. *School Effectiveness and School Improvement, 9*(4), 419–436.

Hopkins, D., Ainscow, M., and West, M. 1994. *School improvement in an era of change.* New York: Teachers College Press.

James, William, as cited in Stone, R. 1986. A higher horror of the whiteness. *Harper's, 273*(1639), 54.

Joyce, B., Calhoun, E., and Hopkins, D. 1999. *The new structure of school improvement: Inquiring schools and achieving students.* Philadelphia: Open University Press.

Levine, D. V. 1991. Creating effective schools: Findings and implications from research and practice. *Phi Delta Kappan, 72*, 389–393.

Levine, D. V., and Lezotte, W. 1990. *Unusually effective schools: A review and analysis of research and practice.* Madison, WI: National Center for Effective Schools Research and Development.

Little, J. W. 1982. Norms of collegiality and experimentation: Workplace conditions of school success. *American Educational Research Journal, 19*(3), 325–340.

Makedon, A. 1992. *Is Alice's world too middle class? Recommendations for effective schools research.* (ERIC ED 346 612)

Marri, A. R. 2005. Building a framework for classroom-based multicultural democratic education: Learning from three skilled teachers. *Teachers College Record, 107*(5), 1036–1059.

Mortimore, P., Sammons, P., Stoll, L., Lewis, D., and Ecob, R. 1988. *School matters.* Berkeley, CA: University of California Press.

Murphy, J. 1992. Effective schools: Legacy and future directions. In D. Reynolds and P. Cuttance (Eds.), *School effectiveness: Research, policy, and practice* (pp. 164–170). London: Cassell.

National Commission on Education. 1983. An open letter to the American people. A nation at risk: The imperative for educational reform. *Education Week, 2*(31), 12.

Pierce, L. V. 1991. *Effective schools for national origin language minority students.* Washington, DC: The Mid-Atlantic Equity Center.

Powers, A. L. 2004. An evaluation of four place-based education programs. *The Journal of Environmental Education, 35*(4), 17–32.

Pratzner, F. C. 1984. Quality of school life: Foundations for improvement. *Educational Researcher, 13*(3), 20–25.

Purkey, S. C., and Smith, M. S. 1983. Effective schools: A review. *Elementary School Journal, 83*, 427–452.

Reyes, P., Scribner, J. D., and Scribner, A. P. (Eds.). 1999. *Lessons from high performing Hispanic schools: Creating learning communities.* New York: Teachers College Press.

Reynolds, D., and Stoll, L. 1996. Merging school effectiveness and school improvement: The knowledge bases. In D. Reynolds, R. Bollen, B. Creemers, D. Hopkins, L. Stoll, and N. Lagerweij, *Making good schools: Linking school effectiveness and school improvement* (pp. 94–112). London and New York: Routledge.

Rosenholtz, S. J. 1985. Effective schools: Interpreting the evidence. *American Journal of Education, 93*(3), 352–388.

Rosenholtz, S. J. 1989. *Teachers' workplace: The social organization of schools.* New York: Longman.

Rust, F. O., and Freidus, H. (Eds.). 2001. *Guiding school change: The role and work of change agents.* New York: Teachers College Press.

Rutter, M., Maughan, B., Mortimore, P., Ouston, J., and Smith, A. 1979. *Fifteen thousand hours:*

Secondary schools and their effects on children. Cambridge, MA: Harvard University Press.

Sanders, M. G., and Lewis, K. C. 2005. Building bridges toward excellence: Community involvement in high schools. *The High School Journal, 88*(3), 1–9.

Scribner, A. P. 1999. High performing Hispanic schools: An introduction. In P. Reyes, J. D. Scribner, and A. P. Scribner (Eds.), *Lessons from high performing Hispanic schools: Creating learning communities.* New York: Teachers College Press.

Slavin, R. E. 2002. Evidence-based education policies: Transforming educational practice and research. *Educational Researcher, 31*(7), 15–21.

Smith, G. A. 2002. Going local. *Educational Leadership, 60*(1), 30–33.

Stedman, L. C. 1987. It's time we change the effective schools formula. *Phi Delta Kappan, 69*(3), 215–224.

Stringfield, S., and Teddlie, C. 1987. *A time to summarize: Six years and three phases of the Louisiana School Effectiveness Study.* Paper presented at the annual meeting of the American Educational Research Association, Washington, DC, April.

Taylor, B. O. 2002. The effective schools process: Alive and well. *Phi Delta Kappan, 83*(5), 375–378.

Teddlie, C., and Stringfield, S. 1993. *Schools make a difference: Lessons learned from a 10-year study of school effects.* New York: Teachers College Press.

Wasley, P., Hampel, R., and Clark, R. 1997. The puzzle of whole-school change. *Phi Delta Kappan, 78,* 690–697.

Adult and Teacher Development within the Context of the School

Clues for Supervisory Practice

▶ **Adults as Learners**
▶ **Adult and Teacher Development**
▶ **Development: Ebb and Flow**

This chapter will serve as a core for thinking and practicing supervision in a developmental framework. So far, we have defined "a cause beyond oneself" as a demarcation between the collective, thoughtful, autonomous, and effective staffs of successful schools and the isolated, unreflective, and powerless staffs of unsuccessful schools. Knowledge of how teachers can grow as competent adults is the guiding principle for supervisors in finding ways to return wisdom, power, and control to both the individuals and the collective staff in order for them to become true professionals. With the understanding of how teachers change, the supervisor can plan direct assistance, professional development, curriculum development, group development, and action research at an appropriate level to stimulate teacher growth and instructional improvement.

The research on adult learning and development has been prolific. We have attempted to distill the knowledge of adult and teacher development that has direct applications for supervision and supervisors. Readers who desire more detail should refer to the references at the end of the chapter. The use of such readily available and potentially rich knowledge about human growth can be extremely valuable to those who work with adults. If schools are to be successful, supervision must respond to teachers as changing adults.

Adults as Learners

Instructional improvement takes place when teachers improve their decision making about students, learning content, and teaching. The process of improving teacher decision making is largely a process of adult learning. Thus, research and theory on adult learning is an important component of the knowledge base for instructional supervision.

Intelligence

Two basic questions drove much of the early research on adult learning ability: Does ability to learn diminish with age? Are there differences between the learning process of adults and children? Thorndike (1928) was among the first to suggest that adult learning did not peak in youth and diminish steadily thereafter (a common belief of his day). Horn and Cattell (1967) identified two categories of intelligence: *fluid* and *crystallized.* Fluid intelligence, which depends heavily on physiological and neurological capacities, peaks early and explains why youth excel on tasks requiring quick insight, short-term memorization, and complex interactions (Merriam, Caffarella, and Baumgartner, 2006). Crystallized intelligence, assessed by untimed measures calling for judgment, knowledge, and experience, is more heavily influenced by education and experience. Hence, older individuals show an advantage when it is measured.

Contemporary theories of intelligence have extended the notion that intelligence consists of multiple components or factors. Most readers of this text will be familiar with Howard Gardner's theory of multiple intelligences (1983, 1999). Gardner initially posited seven types of intelligence (linguistic, logical-mathematical, musical, spatial, bodily kinesthetic, intrapersonal, and interpersonal). He later added naturalistic intelligence and suggested there are likely other forms of intelligence. Gardner's ideas are relevant to supervision. Supervisors can identify and utilize the learning strengths of individual teachers when assisting them with instructional improvement efforts. Supervisors can also assist teachers to gradually expand their repertoire of learning strategies.

Sternberg (1985, 1990) likewise has proposed a theory of intelligence, called a *triarchic theory of intelligence* because it consists of three subtheories, that may be helpful in thinking about the cognition of teachers. The first subtheory, referred to as *componential,* deals with cognitive processing, the ability traditionally discussed in trying to understand intellectual competence. The second subtheory is *experiential,* which suggests that assessing intelligence must consider not only mental components but also the level of experience from which they are applied. Sternberg, intrigued by the differences between novices and experts, has suggested that experience promotes both the ability to respond automatically to routine situations and to deal effectively with novel situations. Thus, novice teachers can be expected to require different types of supervision than those who are more experienced.

Although the first two subtheories deal with universal processes, Sternberg's third *contextual* subtheory deals with *socially influenced abilities*. Individuals are said to cope with life's challenges by adapting to the environment, shaping the environment, or selecting a different environment—all the while being influenced by what is considered appropriate and intelligent behavior within one's cultural milieu. This last contextual subtheory becomes important when one looks at how teachers deal with challenging situations. Some obviously have greater capacities than others to adapt to or change the classroom and school environment. Through appropriate supervision, teachers can be assisted in broadening their array of adaptation and change strategies. It is this kind of practical intelligence that intrigues Sternberg and other theorists who propose that not enough attention has focused on the demonstration of adult intelligence through the identification and solution of real-world problems.

Theories of Adult Learning

As research increasingly put to rest the question of whether adults could continue to learn, attention turned to how their learning differed from that of children. The focus of the following overview of adult learning theories will be on those theories that have received particular attention over recent decades as adult educators sought to answer this question. A chronological review of the literature on adult learning would reveal in greater detail what this brief overview will suggest—a recent shift from a psychological orientation (Knowles, 1980; Tough, 1971) toward a sociocultural orientation (Amstutz, 1999; Hansman, 2001; Hayes and Flannery, 2000).

Andragogy.   The *theory of andragogy,* popularized in this country by Malcolm Knowles, has become one of the better-known theories of adult learning in recent years. Knowles (1980) proposed four basic assumptions of adult learning:

1. Adults have a psychological need to be self-directing.
2. Adults bring an expansive reservoir of experience that can and should be tapped in the learning situation.
3. Adults' readiness to learn is influenced by a need to solve real-life problems often related to adult developmental tasks.
4. Adults are performance centered in their orientation to learning—wanting to make immediate application of knowledge.

Later, Knowles added a fifth assumption—that adult learning is primarily intrinsically motivated (Knowles, 1984). The theory of andragogy no longer receives the uncritical acceptance that it once did, with questions increasingly raised about the extent to which these assumptions are exclusively true of adults (Tennant, 1986), the extent to which self-direction is an actual versus a desirable preference of adult learners (Brookfield, 1986), and the conditions under which andragogy may or may not apply (Pratt, 1988; Rachal, 2002). Knowles himself, before his death in 1997, came to acknowledge that differences between adults and children as learners may be a matter of degree and situation rather than a rigid dichotomy. Nevertheless, the theory of andragogy is still accepted by many as a broad guide to thinking about adult learning (Merriam, 2001; Rose, Jeris, and Smith, 2005).

Self-Directed Learning.   Even as self-direction in learning was emerging as one of the most challenged assumptions within andragogy, a distinct body of theory and research on adults' self-directed learning (SDL) was evolving. Allen Tough (1971) is generally credited with providing the first comprehensive description of self-directed learning—learning which adults engage in systematically as part of everyday life and without benefit of an instructor. A long-standing body of research on this topic has documented the ubiquity of adults' self-directed learning and led to the development of numerous models of self-directed learning as well as several instruments intended to measure it (Merriam, 2001).

Self-direction has been alternatively conceptualized as a goal for adult learning, a process through which learning occurs, a characteristic of learners that may be enduring or situational, and an instructional model through which instructors in formal classrooms foster student control of learning. The implications of the concept of self-directed learning are numerous for those who seek to foster teachers' growth and development through developmental supervision. Supervision should foster rather than inhibit self-directed learning by matching supervisory behaviors with teachers' readiness for self-direction. It is important to recognize that not all adults appear to be equally ready for self-directed learning, nor is an individual equally prepared for self-directed learning in every situation. Variables like background knowledge and degree of confidence affect the level of support adults may need in their learning efforts (Pratt, 1988). Just as Grow (1991) recommends that instructors match their teaching style to the estimated stage of self-direction of adult learners, so too the effective supervisor will adapt his or her supervisory style in response the degree of self-directed readiness exhibited by the teacher in a given context.

Transformational Learning.   For some who question whether either andragogy or SDL theory represent a learning theory that is uniquely adult, transformative learning theory—proposed and revised most prominently by Jack Mezirow (2000)—offers an appealing alternative. This theory grew out of Mezirow's research with women reentering higher education. He offers the following definition of transformative learning:

> Transformative learning refers to the process by which we transform our taken-for-granted frames of reference (meaning perspectives, habits of mind, mind-sets) to make them more inclusive, discriminating, open, emotionally capable of change, and reflective so that they may generate beliefs and opinions that will prove more true or justified to guide action. (Mezirow, 2000, pp. 7–8)

Kegan (2000) contrasts transformative learning (changes in *how* we know) with informative learning (changes in *what* we know), adding that we all experience potentially important kinds of change that do not bring about a fundamental shift in our frames of reference.

Perspective transformation often is described as triggered by a significant life event, originally referred to by Mezirow as a disorienting dilemma. Perspective transformation also can occur in response to minor events that create an opportunity for reflection and redirection, or may occur when an accumulation of internal dilemmas create a growing sense of disillusionment (Taylor, 2000; English, 2005). A teacher's trigger for transformative learning may occur in a situation as obvious as experiencing failure for the first time when she accepts a new position in an urban setting, or as subtle as having a conversation with a gay student about the impact of other students' homophobic jokes on his learning.

Cranton (1994) recommends that the educator critically reflect on his or her own meaning perspective of being an educator. She also describes the processes by which the educator might accomplish this:

> The educator, in order to develop the meaning perspective of being an educator would: increase self awareness through consciousness-raising activities, make his or her assumptions about beliefs about practice explicit, engage in critical reflection on those assumptions and beliefs, engage in dialogue with others, and develop an informed theory of practice. (Cranton, 1994, p. 214)

The strategies Cranton suggests as useful in this process are varied, including writing journals, visiting the classrooms of colleagues, conducting criteria analysis of incidents that epitomize their notions of success or failure in practice, experimenting with practice, eliciting feedback from learners, and consulting or engaging in dialogue with colleagues.

Experience and Learning: Situated Cognition, Informal and Incidental Learning.   At the heart of numerous conceptions of adult learning and education dating back to Dewey (1938) and Lindeman (1926) is the centrality of experience to adult learning. This concern with experience is reflected in Knowles's (1980) inclusion of the importance of adult experience as one of his original four assumptions about adult learning (Gorard and Selwyn, 2005). It is also reflected in Kolb's inclusion of two phases focusing on experience (concrete experience and active experimentation) as part of his four-phase model of the adult learning cycle (1984).

The centrality of experience to learning takes on new dimensions when the emerging body of work on situated cognition is applied to adult learning. Many cite Brown, Collins, and Duguid (1989) as a seminal work in proposing a theory of situated cognition. Essentially, they propose that education is misconceived to the degree that it emphasizes the acquisition of decontextualized, abstract knowledge. They insist that lasting knowledge emerges as learners engage in authentic activity embedded in specific situations. Referring specifically to adult learning, Hansman (2001) states, "The nature of the interactions among learners, the tools they use within these interactions, the activity itself, and the social context in which the activity takes place shapes learning" (p. 45). Wilson (1993) suggests adults learn *in* experience as they act in situations and are acted upon by situations, rather than the traditional assumption that adults learn *from* experience. In line with situated cognition theory, teachers would most effectively acquire knowledge useful in a new situation by being directly immersed in real practice situations, with support from experienced colleagues whose methods might include modeling and coaching.

More recently, interest in the ties between adult learning and experience have been explored in examinations of learning in the workplace, which have found that much of the meaningful learning occurring in that context is of the informal and incidental variety (Kerka, 1998; Uys, Gwele, McInerney, Rhyn, and Tanga, 2004). Marsick and Watkins (1990, 2001) offer a theory of informal and incidental learning. Informal learning is usually intentional but less structured than formal learning. Examples include self-directed learning, networking, informal coaching, and mentoring. Incidental learning, on the other hand, is defined as a by-product of some other activity, and is most often tacit or unconscious at the time. The model they propose describes a progression of meaning making that they admit is neither as linear or sequential as their necessarily simplified model might suggest. They describe this progression as follows:

1. Learning typically begins with a trigger event that is framed in light of the person's worldview.
2. The experience itself is interpreted, assessing what is problematic or challenging about it. The context of the experience is interpreted simultaneously.
3. Alternative actions are considered and chosen.
4. Learning strategies are used to implement the desired solution, with context influencing the options.
5. A proposed solution is produced.
6. Outcomes are assessed.
7. Lessons are learned.
8. Concluding thoughts become a part of the framework for analyzing subsequent situations.

Marsick and Watkins suggest that supervisors wishing to help adults improve their informal learning might help them identify conditions in the sociocultural context that assist or conversely hinder more effective learning. Once such factors are identified, supervisors can help the learner deal with or change them.

Critical and Postmodern Theories of Adult Learning. Kilgore (2001) has offered a brief synopsis of the critical and postmodern perspectives of adult learning, analyzing both their similarities and differences. As she notes, each of these perspectives challenges pillars of adult learning theory such as andragogy and self-directed learning as exclusionary and overly focused on the individual. Both critical and postmodern perspectives share assumptions that knowledge is socially constructed, along with an interest in power as a factor in learning. They differ, however, in other significant ways. Critical theorists argue that hegemony (dominant influence or authority wielded by those in power) operates to preserve inequities linked to structures of privilege and oppression based on categories like race, ethnicity, gender, class, and age. In this view, learning involves reflecting on the hegemonic assumptions that often guide our practices and perhaps acting to change the practices as well as the assumptions (an example given by Kilgore is that of use and misuse of standardized tests). Social justice is viewed as a core value. Postmodern theorists, on the other hand, resist embracing *any* universal truth, emphasizing that knowledge is multifaceted and truths shift according to the experience and context of the knower.

Power is a consideration for each framework, but in different ways. For instance, critical theories are interested in how the status quo (e.g., an individualistic focus on learning that research suggests may be culturally biased toward certain groups) can be interrupted to create more emancipatory knowledge (e.g., a greater emphasis on group learning, which research suggests is more culturally relevant for some groups of learners). Power is seen as held by some over others; for instance, the traditional role of principals invests them with greater power than teachers. From the postmodern perspective, power is present in every relationship and can be exercised by anyone to one degree or another. We must analyze (or deconstruct) the situation to know how power is being used and by whom. In this view, teacher and parent participation in site-based management or participatory action research projects become tools both for producing knowledge collaboratively and for negotiating and rearranging power relationships.

Teachers as Adult Learners

Sternberg's (1985, 1990) work on the experiential component of adult intelligence indicates that novice teachers need to be supervised differently than experienced teachers. One example of this need for differentiation is that many beginning teachers have more difficulty assessing and responding to novel teaching situations and problems than their experienced colleagues, and thus are in need of more intensive support. Both Sternberg's (1985, 1990) and Gardner's (1983) research on multiple intelligences take us beyond differences between novice and experienced teachers and point to the need for identifying and utilizing different learning strengths of teachers at all levels of experience.

The need to individualize teacher learning, indicated by the literature on adult learning, stands in sharp contrast to the actual treatment of teachers. Many supervisors treat teachers as if they were all the same, rather than individuals in various stages of adult growth. In most schools, teachers receive the same in-service workshops, the same observations, and the same assessments. It is as if teachers were stamped out of teacher training institutes as identical and thereafter have no further need to be viewed as individual learners. The research on adults shows the lack of wisdom of such assumptions (Mathis, 1987; Zepeda, 2004).

Sternberg's (1985, 1990) discussion of socially influenced abilities points to the need for teachers to engage in learning aimed at developing a variety of strategies for adapting to or changing their classroom and school environment. Both Mezirow's (1981, 1990) and Brookfield's (1986) work on adult learning indicate that in order to learn and grow, teachers need to participate in a continuous cycle of collaborative activity and reflection on that activity, which requires the development of critical thinking abilities. Finally, the writings of Knowles (1980, 1984), Mezirow (1981, 1990, 2000), and Brookfield (1986) have all supported the notion of the supervisor facilitating teacher growth toward empowerment and self-direction.

Unfortunately, many schools do not foster collaborative action, reflection, critical thinking, or teacher empowerment. Rather, the hierarchical structure of many school systems—as well as the environmental problems of isolation, psychological dilemma, and lack of a shared technical culture discussed in Chapter 2—tends to work against the type of growth described in the adult learning literature.

Adult and Teacher Development

Literature on adult development can be seen as reflecting several distinct but related approaches. Just a few decades ago, the study of human development focused on children, and adulthood was either not a consideration or was thought to represent a period of stability. Theory and research on adult development for several decades emphasized development as an orderly progression. Because much of the work in this area was done by developmental psychologists, there was an emphasis on the change processes occurring in the individual with relatively little consideration to his or her interaction with the environment. Early approaches to adult development were rooted in such a tradition. Over time, alternative views of adult development evolved, with less concern for a universal progression and greater interest in the interaction between the individual and the social environment.

Subsequent sections of this chapter will discuss adult development according to these five subtopics: (1) stage development, (2) life cycle development, (3) transition events, (4) role development, and (5) sociocultural influences on adult development.

Stage Theories of Adult and Teacher Development

We will begin discussion of adult development by focusing on developmental stage theories. Levine (1989) delineated the characteristics of stages:

First and foremost is their structural nature. Each stage is a "structured whole," representing an underlying organization of thought or understanding. Stages are qualitatively different from one another. All emerge in sequence without variation; no stage can be skipped. Finally stages are "hierarchically integrated"; that is, progressive stages are increasingly complex and subsume earlier stages. Individuals always have access to the stages through which they have passed. Under ordinary circumstances or with proper supports, people will generally prefer to use the highest stages of which they are capable. (p. 86)

It may be helpful to look more closely at several specific stage theories.

Cognitive Development.   Piaget described four stages of cognitive development: sensorimotor, preoperational, concrete operations, and formal operations (Ginsburg and Opper, 1979). The person at the formal operations stage has already progressed beyond reasoning only for the "here and now" and can project into and relate time and space. A person at the formal operations stage uses hypothetical reasoning, understands complex symbols, and formulates abstract concepts.

Some researchers have found that formal thought is not demonstrated by all adults. Others question the extent to which cultural bias in the traditional Piagetian tasks plays a role in differential findings, particularly in non-Western cultures (Neimark, 1987). There has been considerable exploration of characteristic adult forms of thinking that go beyond Piaget's fourth stage to a postformal operations stage (Arlin, 1975; Kitchener, Lynch, Fischer, and Wood, 1993; Merriam, Caffarella, and Baumgartner, 2006; Riegel, 1973), with some positing alternative cognitive frameworks to describe adult thought (Perry, 1970, 1981). Terms like *dialectical thought* (Riegel, 1973; Kramer, 1983), *integrative thought* (Kramer, 1987), and *epistemic cognition* (Taranto, 1987) have been used to describe the highest stage of cognition observed in adults. A related strand of research has examined the meaning of wisdom (Clayton and Birren, 1980; Holliday and Chandler, 1986) often seen as the hallmark of advanced adult thinking. Taranto (1987) and Neimark (1987) pointed out that in real life, unlike in the typical Piagetian assessment tasks, adults must focus on ill-defined problems without definitive answers. Neimark contended that such thinking is best assessed by giving adults problems without clear-cut answers on which to make judgments. Figure 4.1 represents the adult cognitive developmental continuum.

Teachers' cognitive development was explored by Ammon and associates in a study of a two-year graduate teacher education program with an emphasis on Piagetian theory (Ammon, 1984). This emphasis was intended to teach the adult preservice and in-service teachers about child development as well as to promote

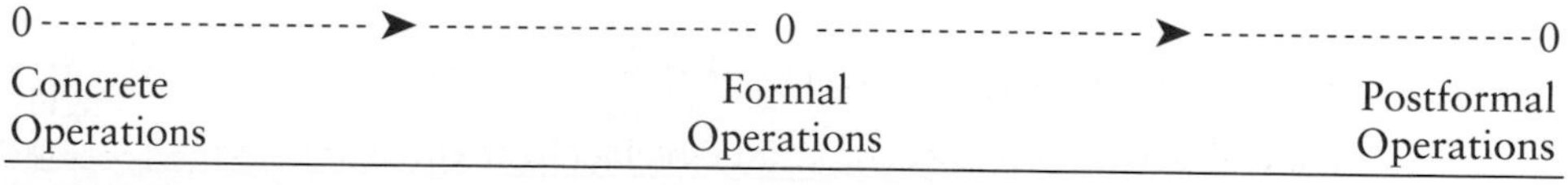

0 -------------------- ▶ -------------------- 0 -------------------- ▶ --------------------0
Concrete   Formal   Postformal
Operations   Operations   Operations

FIGURE 4.1   *Adult Cognitive Development Continuum*

the teachers' own development. As the teachers studied Piagetian and related developmental theory, their conceptions of students, learning, and teaching changed. They progressed from simplistic to more complex, interactive explanations of student behaviors, development, and learning. These teachers also moved from a conception of teaching as "showing and telling" to creating a learning environment designed to foster the students' learning and development. The teachers' views on learning shifted from passive reception to active construction. They also came to think of their roles differently, as facilitating learning rather than imparting knowledge.

Conceptual Development.   One developmental framework that is closely related to cognitive development and that has been studied significantly with teachers is that of conceptual development. Hunt and others defined *conceptual level (CL)* "in terms of (1) increasing conceptual complexity, as indicated by discrimination, differentiation, and integration and (2) increasing interpersonal maturity, as indicated by self-definition and self-other relations" (Hunt, Butler, Noy, and Rosser, 1978, p. 3). Hunt placed individuals on a continuum from most concrete (lowest CL) to most abstract (highest CL).

Persons of *low CL* evaluate things in a simple, concrete fashion. They tend to view issues in "black and white." Individuals of low CL have difficulty defining a problem they are experiencing and respond to the same problem in a habitual manner despite the fact that the repeated response is not solving the problem. They need to be shown how to solve the problem. Persons of *moderate CL* are becoming more abstract in their thinking. They can define the problem and generate a limited number of possible solutions but have difficulty formulating a comprehensive plan. They still need some assistance in solving a complex problem. Persons of *high CL* are abstract thinkers. They are independent, self-actualizing, resourceful, flexible, and possess a high capacity of integration. Figure 4.2 represents the conceptual development continuum.

High-concept teachers have been found to differ from low-concept teachers in terms of both teaching approach and teacher-generated classroom atmosphere. High-concept teachers rate higher on what are generally considered to be more positive characteristics (such as warmth, perceptiveness, empathy, flexibility, ingenuity, task effectiveness, smoothness, and consistency) and low-concept teachers rate higher on more educationally negative characteristics (such as innovativeness, rule orientation, punitiveness, and anxiety) (Harvey, White, Prather, Alter, and

| Low Conceptual Level (Concrete Thinking) | Moderate Conceptual Level (Moderately Abstract Thinking) | High Conceptual Level (Highly Abstract Thinking) |

FIGURE 4.2   *Conceptual Development Continuum*

Hoffmeister, 1966; Heck and Davis, 1973; Reiman and Thies-Sprinthall, 1998). Hunt and Joyce (1967) found correlations between teacher conceptual level and ability to use learners' needs as a basis for planning and evaluation. High-concept teachers used a greater range of learning environments and teaching methods. Similarly, Hopkins (1990) found that high stage teachers employed new methods of teaching at a rate four times greater than their counterparts at lower stages. A study of 52 teachers by Calhoun (1985) found that teachers with high conceptual thought provided more corrective feedback to students, gave more praise, and were less negative and punitive. These teachers were more varied in their instructional strategies and were able to elicit more higher-order conceptual responses from their students than teachers of moderate and lower levels of conceptual thought.

Moral Development.   Kohlberg and Armon (1984) identified three broad categories of morality: the preconventional level, the conventional level, and the postconventional level. They further delineated two stages of development within each of these levels, with the second stage more advanced and organized than the first. Across the three levels, reasoning shifts from a self-centered perspective to one that increasingly considers the perspectives and rights of others. The individual at Level I makes decisions from a self-centered orientation. At Level II, individuals "do the right thing" because that is what is expected according to social norms. Finally, at Level III, moral decisions serve to recognize the social contract and to uphold individual rights. Although conflicts between these principles and legal mandates are recognized as problematic in the lower stage of Level III, moral principles come to take precedence by the time an individual reaches the highest stage of moral development. Kohlberg sees the higher stages as superior, and he sees enhancing development as an appropriate aim for education. Figure 4.3 represents the moral development continuum.

It is important here to give mention to the work of Carol Gilligan (1979, 1982). Gilligan compared conclusions from Kohlberg's model of moral development with conclusions from her own research with women discussing personal decisions. People at the top of Kohlberg's stages worry about interfering with others' rights, whereas those at the top of Gilligan's stages worry about errors of omission, such as not helping others when you could. At Gilligan's highest stage, morality is conceived in terms of relationships, and goodness is equated with helping others. Gilligan proposed that a different conception of development emerges from the study of women's lives:

> This conception of morality as fundamentally concerned with the capacity for understanding and care also develops through a structural progression of increasing

0 - - - - - - - - - - - - - - - - - ➤ - - - - - - - - - - - - - - - 0 - - - - - - - - - - - - - - - - ➤ - - - - - - - - - - - - - - - 0

Preconventional   Conventional   Postconventional
Level   Level   Level

FIGURE 4.3 *Moral Development Continuum*

differentiation and integration. This progression witnesses the shift from an egocentric through a societal to the universal moral perspective that Kohlberg described in his research on men, but it does so in different terms. The shift in women's judgement from an egocentric to a principled ethical understanding is articulated through their use of a distinct moral language, in which the terms "selfishness" and "responsibility" define the moral problem as one of care. Moral development then consists of the progressive reconstruction of this understanding toward a more adequate conception of care. (1979, p. 442)

Several small-scale studies have investigated relationships between teachers' moral development and their understandings of teaching and learning. Johnston (1985) found that teachers scoring low on the same test of moral reasoning possessed a narrow conception of the on-task students (working quietly and individually on an assignment provided by the teacher). Teachers with the highest scores on moral reasoning considered students' perspectives and the complex, continuous nature of learning while resisting classifying students as on task or off task based solely on behavioral observation. Reiman and Parramore (1994) found first year teachers at higher moral reasoning levels to exhibit greater concern for the instructional needs of their students.

Ego Development.   Ego is both a process of striving for coherence and meaning in one's life and a structure with its own internal logic (Levine, 1989). This is one of the few developmental theories derived from the study of women, but it has been applied subsequently to numerous samples of women and men. Loevinger (1976) has identified 10 stages of ego development that individuals can pass through. Orientations toward symbiotic, impulsive, and self-protective behaviors are manifest in the early stages. In these lower stages, a person depends on others for solutions to problems. In the middle stages of ego development, the individual exhibits conventional behaviors. At the higher stages, the adult becomes individualistic, autonomous, and integrated. The person at the highest stage of ego development is able to synthesize what seem to be unrelated or opposing concepts to individuals at lower stages (Witherell and Erickson, 1978). Adults at the beginning point on the continuum might be classified as *fearful*. Those at the midpoint on the continuum can be called *conforming*. Adults at the end of the continuum (those with the most mature egos) are referred to as *autonomous*. Figure 4.4 represents the ego development continuum.

Cummings and Murray (1989) found that teachers at different levels described different roles of a teacher, with those at lower levels of ego development focusing on the role of the teacher as information disseminator and caregiver, and those at higher levels emphasizing the role of the teacher in helping students learn to learn. Based on their findings, they concluded that lower-level teachers may not

0 - - - - - - - - - - - - - - - - ➤ - - - - - - - - - - - - - - 0 - - - - - - - - - - - - - - - - ➤ - - - - - - - - - - - - - - 0
Fearful   Conforming   Autonomous

FIGURE 4.4   *Ego Development Continuum*

have the resources to cope with the intricacies of student–teacher relationships or with the complexity of the learning process.

Levels of Consciousness.   Robert Kegan (1994), a self-acknowledged neo-Piagetian, is a more recent entrant on the scene of adult developmental psychology with his theory of levels of consciousness.

As with the Piagetian shift from concrete to formal operations, the development of abstract thinking is a key characteristic of movement from the adolescent stage of *durable category* level to a more mature *cross-categorical* (or *third order*) *consciousness*. The person functioning at the cross-categorical level is capable of thinking abstractly, reflecting on his or her own emotions, and being guided by beliefs and values that insure loyalty to the larger community. At this stage the adult experiences a new construction of reality, with the needs, wants, and desires of others figuring as prominently as her own (Taylor and Marineau, 1995). Only with the transition from cross-categorical to *systems* (or *fourth order*) *consciousness,* however, does the individual move beyond defining himself or herself in terms of those duties, devotions, and values to become a truly independent and autonomous person. At this level we can look objectively at our own perspective, compare it with that of others, and work to reconcile differences. The systems level of consciousness is considered necessary to meet the various demands of modern adult life (parenting, partnering, working, continued learning), but Kegan (1994) contends many don't reach this stage until the their 30s or 40s, if at all. Finally, as is common with stage theories Kegan posits a level rarely achieved, *trans-systems* (or *fifth order*) *consciousness.* Dialectical thinking is associated with this level of consciousness, said to be rare before midlife.

Kegan's model suggests our expectations may be high, both for ourselves and others. In the preface to his book *In Over Our Heads: the Mental Demands of Modern Life,* he especially appeals to those who provide education, training, and supervision for other adults to be mindful of the mental demands we place on others. An example would be our expectation that teachers, even those recently graduated as traditional-age students, exhibit high levels of critical thinking and metacognitive skills, although he speculates these skills may not be fully evolved for many until their 30s and 40s. The emphasis Kegan places on continuing adult learning in the workplace as well as in other domains of adult life, along with his suggestion that teaching/coaching can stimulate developmental growth, makes this a promising model for future examination with practicing teachers. It also provides a framework that is consistent with the principles of developmental supervision. Figure 4.5 depicts the continuum of adult consciousness.

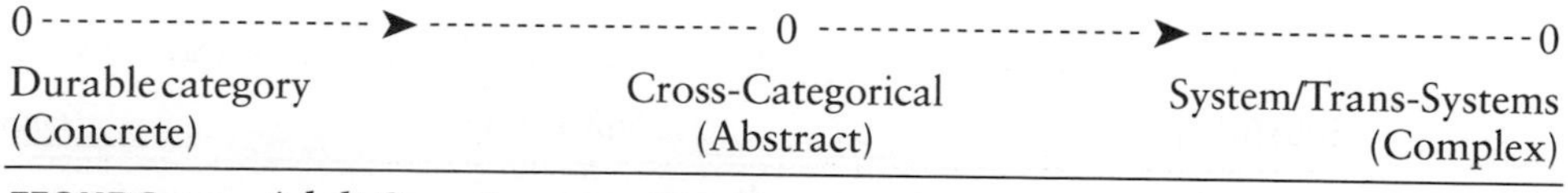

0 - - - - - - - - - - - - - - - - - ➤ - - - - - - - - - - - - - - - - - 0 - - - - - - - - - - - - - - - - - ➤ - - - - - - - - - - - - - - - -0

Durable category   Cross-Categorical   System/Trans-Systems
(Concrete)   (Abstract)   (Complex)

FIGURE 4.5 *Adult Consciousness Continuum*

Stages of Concern.   In the 1960s and early 1970s, Frances Fuller (1969) conducted pioneer studies of teacher concerns. In analyzing both her own studies and six others, she found that the responses by hundreds of teachers at various stages of experience showed different concerns.

Kimpston (1987), in a study examining both teacher and principal stages of concern, substantiated a steady increase in the stage of concern for most teachers. They also discovered that the nature of teachers' participation in staff development (sustained and active versus brief and episodic) had an impact of the emergence of higher stages of concern.

Teachers at the *self-adequacy* stage are focused on survival. They are concerned with doing well when a supervisor is present, getting favorable evaluations, and being accepted and respected by students and other teachers (Adams and Martray, 1981). Their primary concern is making it through the school day.

With survival and security assured, teachers think less of their own survival needs and begin to focus on *teaching tasks*. At this stage, teachers become more concerned with issues related to instructional and student discipline. They begin to think about altering or enriching the classroom schedule, the teaching materials, and their instructional methodology.

Superior teachers are at the highest stage of concern, referred to as the *teaching impact* stage. At this stage, teachers are most concerned with the impact on students' learning and well-being, even if it means departing from rules and norms. Academic concerns at this stage include diagnosing and meeting individual needs, sparking unmotivated students, and facilitating the intellectual and emotional development of students. The teacher with mature concerns also tends to be interested in the whole child, including interest in student health and nutrition, use of drugs by students, dropout prevention, and so on (Adams and Martray, 1981). The unfolding of teachers' concerns evolve on a continuum reflecting a shifting perspective, from "I" concerns to concerns for "my group" to concerns for "all students." Figure 4.6 represents the continuum of teacher concerns.

Integrating Stage Development Theories.   Investigators of adult and teacher development have postulated that the various developmental characteristics are related (Oja and Pine, 1984; Sullivan, McCullough, and Stager, 1970). Although somewhat speculative, these findings suggest that many teachers at a given level (low, moderate, or high) in one developmental characteristic may operate at the same general level in another developmental characteristic. Figure 4.7 reviews the six adult/teacher development continuums.

The majority of teachers appear to be in relatively moderate to low stages of cognitive, conceptual, moral, and ego development—probably no different from the adult population at large (Oja and Pine, 1981; Rest, 1986; Wilkins, 1980). So

FIGURE 4.6 *Teacher Concerns Continuum*

0 - - - - - - - - - - - - - ➤ - - - - - - - - - - - 0 - - - - - - - - - - - ➤ - - - - - - - - - - -0

| Low Developmental Stages | Moderate Developmental Stages | High Developmental Stages |

COGNITIVE

0 - - - - - - - - - - - ➤ - - - - - - - - - - - 0 - - - - - - - - - - ➤ - - - - - - - - - - -0

| Concrete | Formal | Postformal |

CONCEPTUAL

0 - - - - - - - - - - - ➤ - - - - - - - - - - - 0 - - - - - - - - - - ➤ - - - - - - - - - - -0

| Low (Concrete) | Moderate (Moderately Abstract) | High (Highly Abstract) |

MORAL

0 - - - - - - - - - - - ➤ - - - - - - - - - - - 0 - - - - - - - - - - ➤ - - - - - - - - - - -0

| Preconventional | Conventional | Postconventional |

EGO

0 - - - - - - - - - - - ➤ - - - - - - - - - - - 0 - - - - - - - - - - ➤ - - - - - - - - - - -0

| Fearful | Conforming | Autonomous |

LEVELS OF CONSCIOUSNESS

0 - - - - - - - - - - - ➤ - - - - - - - - - - - 0 - - - - - - - - - - ➤ - - - - - - - - - - -0

| Durable category (Concrete) | Cross-Categorical (Abstract) | System/Trans-Systems (Complex) |

TEACHER CONCERNS

0 - - - - - - - - - - - ➤ - - - - - - - - - - - 0 - - - - - - - - - - ➤ - - - - - - - - - - -0

| Self-Adequacy | Teaching Tasks | Teaching Impact |

FIGURE 4.7 *Teacher and Adult Stage Development*

Source: Figures 4.1 through 4.5 and 4.7 are adapted from Stephen P. Gordon, *Assisting the Entry Year Teacher: A Leadership Resource.* Published 1990 by the Ohio Department of Education, Columbus, Ohio.

what? What difference does it make that many teachers are not complex or autonomous? Perhaps one does not need higher-order thinking to teach. One could argue that if teaching is a simple enterprise with no need for decision making, then it would make little difference. In fact, if most teachers were autonomous and abstract, then trying to do a simple job would create great tension, resentment, and noncompliance. If teaching is a simple activity, schools need people who can reason simply. If teaching is complex and ever-changing, however, then higher levels of reasoning are necessary. A simple thinker in a dynamic and difficult enterprise would be subjected to overwhelming pressures.

Sociologists have documented the environmental demands posed by making thousands of decisions daily, by constant psychological pressure, and by expectations that the teacher must do the job alone—unwatched and unaided. A teacher daily faces up to 150 students of various backgrounds, abilities, and interests, some of whom succeed while others fail. Concrete, rigid thinking on the part of the teacher cannot possibly improve instruction. As Madeline Hunter (1986) has noted, "Teaching . . . is a relativistic situational profession where *there are no absolutes*" (italics in original).

Teacher improvement can only come from abstract, multiinformational thought that can generate new responses toward new situations. Glassberg's (1979) review of research on teachers' stage development as related to instructional improvement concluded:

> In summary these studies suggest that high stage teachers tend to be adaptive in teaching style, flexible, and tolerant, and able to employ a wide range of teaching models. . . . [E]ffective teaching in almost any view is a most complex form of human behavior. Teachers at higher, more complex stages of human development appear as more effective in classrooms than their peers at lower stages. (pp. 9–10)

The problem with the need for high-stage teachers is that, although the work by its nature demands autonomous and flexible thinking, teachers in most schools are not supported in ways to improve their thinking. The only alternative for a teacher in a complex environment who cannot adjust to multiple demands and is not being helped to acquire the abilities to think abstractly and autonomously is to *simplify and deaden the instructional environment.* Teachers make the environment less complex by disregarding differences among students and by establishing routines and instructional practices that remain the same day after day and year after year. Research on effective instruction (Berman and McLaughlin, 1978; Glatthorn, 2000; Hargreaves and Moore, 2000; O'Keefe and Johnston, 1989; Porter and Brophy, 1988; Rutter et al., 1979; Tieso, 2001) indicates that effective instruction is based on adaptation of curriculum and materials to local settings and particular learning goals. In other words, effective teachers think about what they are currently doing, assess the results of their practice, explore with each other new possibilities for teaching students, and are able to consider students' perspectives. Effective teaching has been misunderstood and misapplied as a set and sequence of certain teaching behaviors (review previous day's objectives, present objectives, explain, demonstrate, guided practice, check for understanding, etc.). This explanation of effectiveness is simply untrue, as can be seen in the prior reference to Hunter (1986) as well as in Berliner (quoted in Brandt, 1986). Rather, successful teachers are thoughtful teachers (Elliott and Schiff, 2001; Ferraro, 2000; Porter and Brophy, 1988).

Evidence of the relationship between high-stage attainment of teacher development and effective instructional practice can be found in several research studies. The works of Thies-Sprinthall and Sprinthall (1987), Phillips and Glickman (1991), Oja and Pine (1981), and Parker (1983) are particularly important because they suggest that teachers, when provided with a stimulating and supportive environment, can reach higher stages of development.

Life Cycle Development, Teachers' Life Cycles, and the Teaching Career

In discussing research on age-linked life cycle development, theorists have sought to define sequential and normative patterns of development. The pioneering theorists in this tradition tended to look at very broad age periods and the patterns or issues for resolution associated with them (Buhler, 1956; Erikson, 1950), whereas later theorists have tended to posit a greater number of specific age periods (Gould, 1978; Levinson et al., 1978).

The study by Daniel Levinson and his colleagues (1978) of 40 men in their mid-30s to mid-40s is among the most frequently cited studies of life cycle development. This research described how individuals alternate through periods of stability and transition in a life structure whose critical components typically revolve on work and family. An occupational dream is said to be formed during young adulthood and nurtured, frequently with the assistance of the spouse and a mentor. Levinson's work is a coherent treatment of changes in a person's life but has limitations in that the subjects were all middle-class males from a limited set of occupations. A number of subsequent studies of women have substantiated the model in part, but differences have been found in the timing and quality of transitions and the ages associated with transitional periods among women (Levinson and Levinson, 1996; Roberts and Newton, 1987). Some of the variability among women is related to whether they have followed a more traditionally female orientation to family versus a more typically masculine orientation to career during early adulthood (Lieblich, 1986; Roberts and Newton, 1987).

Occupational development of teachers appears to run counter to the needs of teachers as they progress through the adult life cycle. The work of Levinson and colleagues (1978) and Neugarten (1977) has pointed to early adulthood as a period of bravado, romance, and the pursuit of dreams. The young adult aged 20 to 35 is on an exciting search for status, comfort, and happiness in work, family, and friends. The middle years, ages 35 to 55, provide some disillusionment, reflection, and reordering of priorities according to a reassessment of one's capabilities and opportunities. In teaching, however, the young adulthood period, which should be one of romance, quickly becomes one of disillusionment. The young person of 24 or 25 who has entered teaching to pursue his or her dreams often finds after three years that work life is going nowhere. The job does not excite; the advancements do not exist; and the variety of work is nonexistent. The result can be intense boredom, leading to resignation—either *from* the job or *on* the job. What does it mean to education when a young teacher's natural inclination toward excitement and idealism is bound by a straitjacket of repetition?

Let's ask the next question. What happens when the natural inclination of the middle-aged teacher to reflect and reorder his or her teaching priorities confronts the same six periods of 30 students that he or she has faced for the past

20 years? One might expect a further despair of any impulse to change and to improve. Finally, what about the older teacher who is perceived by many as an anomaly, a relic who has remained in teaching because of inability to advance into administration or supervision. The acquisition of 30 years of experience coincides with the natural time for consolidating achievements and identifying one's remaining career objectives. Instead, there is only the same job—the same job as that of the new teacher down the hall, who might be the age of the older teacher's grandchild. Where is the sense of responsibility, generativity, and accomplishment in seniority? Old and new teachers are treated the same, accorded the same status, and expected to conform to the same routines.

Teaching appears to be a topsy-turvy occupation, running against the natural adult life cycle. Those who continue to make lasting improvement and enhance their students' educational lives should have our utmost respect. If not fortunate enough to be in a school that responds to and supports phases of the adult life cycle, the effective teacher truly transcends the system and educates in spite of, not because of, the school.

A small but growing body of literature focuses on the links between teacher development and issues related to the adult lifespan. Gehrke (1991) argued that we should more fully incorporate our understanding of adult development in developing programs for new teachers. This means both fostering the generative motivations of mature teachers and being sensitive to the fact that many young teachers are dealing with needs for intimacy. Levine (1987) argued that profitable activities that capitalize on young teachers' enthusiasm might include opportunities to work on new teaching methods, to develop curricula, and to initiate projects. The key is nurturing their need for innovation and adventure and helping them establish and cultivate close collegial relationships that meet their needs for intimacy.

Levine (1987) encouraged placing midlife teachers in situations permitting "a combination of teaching and administrative responsibilities that expands an adult's authority and mobility without sacrificing his or her expertise with children" (p. 16). Work on decision-making committees and mentorship of younger colleagues can provide such an outlet. Krupp (1987) argued that lack of career centrality and on-the-job retirement can be countered by bringing the older teachers' interests into the school. For instance, older teachers' interests in computers, photography, and gardening can be brought into the curriculum or extracurricular programs for students.

roles for beginning, mid, and older teachers

Transition Events

A third approach to adult development focuses more explicitly on the kinds of events associated with life transitions. Some theorists resist accepting the study of what are variably called *life events, critical events,* or *marker events* as part of the rubric of adult development because such a focus does not attempt to describe a universal, orderly sequence of development. However, Fiske and Chiriboga (1990) noted that just as the assumption of adult stability has given way to models of adult development "as a progression of orderly transformations over time," more recent models emphasize the role of transition events in our lives.

Life events have been typologized in a variety of ways. One typology, offered by Willis and Baltes (1980), seems to relate directly to the salience of the event for the individual. They talk about *normative age-graded events*—events that occur in many people's lives and that are anticipated around certain ages (such as marriage, birth of first child, and widowhood), *normative history-graded events*—those that affect large numbers of people in a given age cohort simultaneously (such as World War II and the Depression), and *nonnormative events*—those personal events that are not anticipated as part of the life course even though they may occur for many (such as divorce, unemployment, and unexpected illness). Events can be positive or negative, anticipated or unanticipated. Although events associated with expected transitions in adult lives are often the impetus for adult growth (Aslanian and Brickell, 1981), it appears to be the unanticipated event, even if negative, that may provide the greatest opportunity for change and growth (Fiske and Chiriboga, 1990; Krupp, 1982).

Neugarten (1977) and Neugarten and Neugarten (1987) studied the timing of events such as childbearing, occupational advancement and peaking, children leaving home, retirement, personal illness, and death of a spouse or close friend. Many of these events are common to all or most adults; the time of their occurrence, according to Neugarten, influences how the person responds and continues with life. For example, the Blum and Meyer (1981) study of the recovery of adult men from severe heart attacks highlighted the difference in timing of critical events. Young men were bitter and hostile toward their heart attack and couldn't wait to resume their previous lives. Middle-aged men were reflective about the heart attack and seriously weighed whether they wanted to continue to live as they had before. They contemplated changes in family relations, job, and living environments. Older men were accepting and grateful that the heart attack had left them alive with the opportunity to finish some of their desired retirement plans. As one can see, the same event—a heart attack—resulted in quite different reactions, depending on the time and age of the adult. Neugarten's interpretation of these differential responses relates to the experience of the events as "on time" versus "off time"—that is, occurring at an age considered socially appropriate or not.

Both personal transition events (marriage, birth of a child, divorce, death of a loved one) and professional transition events (entry into the profession, tenure, transferring schools, becoming a lead teacher or department chairperson) can have a significant impact on a teacher's career and teaching. Traditionally, personal and transitional events have been ignored and professional transitions have been given pro forma recognition by the school organization. Krupp (1987) has suggested that staff development programs providing an environment of trust and collegiality, as well as adult transition support networks within schools, can be an important means of assisting teachers as they prepare for anticipated change events, such as retirement, or cope with unanticipated changes, such as the sudden dependency of a parent. The support networks and professional development recommended by Krupp to assist teachers have been largely non-existent in schools.

One exception in recent years has been the emergence of beginning teacher assistance programs, including the assignment of support teams and mentors to novice teachers. Hopefully, beginners' assistance programs will become the foundation on which career-long support for personal and professional transitions becomes available. Beyond formal support programs, schools need to become the type of collegial, caring, growth-oriented communities that sustain teachers in time of transition.

Role Development

One of the most recent directions in work on adult development has emphasized adult social roles, generally examining how adult lives are characterized by interacting roles related to work or career, family life, and personal development. Juhasz (1989) has developed a model of adult roles that incorporates each of three major roles: family, work, and self. These roles are depicted as intertwining, sometimes in synchrony, sometimes with different momentum and force. This model emphasizes the active involvement of adults who take roles and choose which roles they will place emphasis on at given points in their lives, with self-esteem as the driving force "directing energies toward roles that will best enhance feelings of worth" (p. 307).

Merriam and Clark (1991, 1993) designed a questionnaire to study the relationship between life events in the domains of "work and love" (here broadly defined as in the instrumental and expressive components of life) and adult learning. In essence, people graphed their life patterns, using two separate lines to show the ups and downs in these two domains of life. Respondents were asked next to list major events occurring in the last 20 years of their adult life (age 18 or older) and to describe related learning experiences.

One of Merriam and Clark's most significant findings was the predominance of work-related learning for both men and women and the evidence that more learning occurs when things are going well in both arenas (work and family life). However, learning that led to a real perspective transformation most often was associated with coping with the difficult times in either work (e.g., being fired) or family life (e.g., losing a parent). Since much of the most significant adult learning appears to be from life experience, the role of the supervisor may be critical in helping teachers to experience growth as an outcome of unsettling life experiences in the professional, personal, or family domains. Although the supervisor need not and should not assume the role of therapist, one implication of the social roles models of adult development is that a teacher's personal, family, and professional roles interact with and affect each other, and need to be addressed holistically by supervision.

School systems and supervisors traditionally have been concerned only with teachers' professional roles, ignoring their personal and family roles. The few efforts intended to address the relationship of the three domains have been criticized as being beyond the scope of supervision, an inappropriate use of school resources, and superfluous to the improvement of teaching and learning. Yet, the literature on adult role development tells us that we cannot compartmentalize the personal, family, and professional aspects of a teacher's life. Put succinctly, teachers' other adult roles have direct effect on their instruction. Supervision, however, has largely failed to provide teachers with support to help them understand the interaction of their various adult roles, cope with role conflict and resulting stress, or develop the proper balance and synergy among alternative roles.

Beyond Universal Conceptions of Development: The Sociocultural Context of Adult Development

From the 1980s and through the present a significant body of research has emerged examining the impact of social structural variables (e.g., race, class, gender, disability, or sexual orientation) on adult development (Clark and Caffarella, 1999), with greatest emphasis on the effects of gender and race/ethnicity. The intent of some researchers has been to develop more robust and inclusive theories, describing a broader range of people than earlier theories. In other cases, especially for researchers informed by the postmodern resistance to "grand" theories, there has been no such attempt at "umbrella" theories of adult development (Kilgore, 2001). The latter researchers have been interested in offering previously unavailable pictures of adult development for individuals from groups previously marginalized in the construction of knowledge about adult development, as well as in illustrating how structural variables like gender, race, and class intersect in the construction of our identities (Sheared, 1999; Tisdell, 2000; Graue, 2005).

The Role of Gender in Adult Development.   Much of the literature examining the relationship of gender and adult development has looked specifically at women, in response to the initial claim that their lives and experiences were not accounted for in early development of adult development theory. Emerging theory and research have taken two forms, in some cases extending or adapting earlier work based primarily on men, and in other cases starting afresh with female or mixed gender samples. In the first strand is the work of Gilligan (1982), challenging Kohlberg's model of moral development (Kohlberg and Turiel, 1971). Her work suggested men and women base their moral decisions on different criteria, with women using an ethic of caring and men an ethic of justice. Similarly Joselson (1987) reexamined Erikson's stage theory of psychosocial development, postulating four potential outcomes of Erikson's identity stage for women. Primary among her findings was that maintaining a sense of connectedness and affiliation with others was crucial for women.

The second strand of research consists of studies based specifically on the lives of women. One of the most cited sources in this strand is that of *Women's Ways of Knowing* by Belenky, Clichy, Goldberger, and Tarule (1986). Resisting the notion of hierarchical stages, Belenky et al. point to the development of *voice* as central to women's development, and delineate five positions or categories in the development of women's knowledge: silence, received knowledge, subjective knowledge, procedural knowledge, and constructed knowledge. The developmental ideal is the integration of all five categories. Also representing this strand of research is the work of Peck (1986). She theorized women's lives as consisting of three contiguous layers, including an outermost core of sociohistorical context; a flexible, bidirectional "sphere of influence," consisting of the sum of multiple relationships; and, finally, a center core of self-definition. These spheres are presumed to be constantly interacting as women move through their lives. Caffarella and Olson (1993) summarized the research on women's development in terms of four themes: the centrality of relationships, the importance and interplay of social roles, the dominance of role discontinuities and change as the norm for women, and the diversity of experience across age cohorts. Given the predominance of women in the teaching workforce, it seems important that supervisors become familiar with those models of adult development that reveal the distinctive developmental concerns women may bring.

More recently, models of adult development whether based on men's or women's lives have been critiqued for their universalizing character, tending to ignore or discount diversity *among* men and women, and the degree to which individuals of each gender exhibit patterns described as typical of the opposite sex. For example, Anderson and Hayes (1996) found that both men and women value achievement as well as relationships, derive self-esteem from similar sources, and struggle with ongoing issues of holding on (connection) and letting go (separation). The tendency of these models to ignore diversity related to race, class, and culture has also been criticized. Harris (1995) examined how men from different subcultures viewed each of 24 cultural messages about masculinity, and described differences related to class, race, sexual orientation, and community of origin (city, urban, rural). This literature may help explain why some men are more willing to break mainstream cultural norms that discourage their entry into the elementary education teaching force.

● *The Role of Race and Ethnicity in Adult Development.*   Chavez and Guido-DiBrito (1999) provide an excellent overview of models of racial and ethnic identity, two prominent strands of work contributing to an understanding of the impact of race and ethnicity on adult learners. Cross (1971) and Cross, Jr. (1995) developed one of the earliest of these models, focusing on the development of racial identity among African Americans. According to this model, Blacks move from a stage of limited awareness of race (a stage Chavez and Guido-Dibrito question) to later stages of embracing first an Afrocentric identity and finally a multicultural identity. Similarly, Parham (1989) has focused on how experiences with negative differential treatment by others become the trigger for formation of racial identity among Blacks. Chavez and Guido-DiBrito (1999), on the other hand, posit that immersion in one's own racial group acts as the primary trigger for such identity development. Similarly they take issue with the focus on perceptions of other groups inherent in the most prominent model of White racial identity development, that of Helms (1993, 1995). Helms stresses interracial exposure as a powerful trigger for the development of a White racial identity that moves beyond a dominant group assumption of White superiority toward a nonracist frame. Chavez and Guidi-DiBrito argue that Helms's model places inordinate emphasis on the intersection of racial perceptions of others and racial perception of self. They are more intrigued by models of ethnic identity development.

For instance, a model of White ethnic identity by Katz (1989) identifies values and perspectives of White American cultural identity. These values include autonomy, competitiveness, and a linear sense of time, and can be contrasted with values such as harmony, balance, and respect for the wisdom of elders identified in Garrett and Walking Stick Garrett's (1994) model of Native American identity. Phinney (1990), on the other hand, developed a model describing an ethnic identity process that can be applied to all groups. She emphasizes two issues faced by members of nondominant groups: (1) dealing with stereotyping and prejudicial treatment by the dominant group, and (2) resolving the clash between the value systems of their own ethnic culture and that of the dominant culture by negotiating a bicultural value system.

Several implications for adult learning can be drawn from these models. The models generally suggest that while most individuals from White ethnic groups typically experience learning that is grounded in their own cultural norms, they may struggle with or resist learning in less familiar multicultural environments. This has implications for efforts in the area of diversity training. On the other hand, persons from nondominant cultural groups often have to learn to be at least bicultural in their learning if they are to succeed in "mainstream" learning environments. For instance, Alfred (2001) points to the development of bicultural competence as a factor in the career development of successful (tenured) African American women faculty. She also points to the assistive role that White male mentors played in some cases. Similarly teachers from nondominant groups are likely to find that they must learn to successfully navigate two or more cultures; their mentors need to remain sensitive to the challenges this presents.

Recent research on women's development and research on the place of race and ethnicity in identity development have challenged our thinking about the degree to which any single theory of adult development can adequately describe all adult lives. Yet these models can still provide a useful heuristic for thinking about the many ways in which adults continue to change throughout the course of their lives and the myriad forces which come to influence these changes. For those who seek to provide assistance to teachers, familiarity with this literature serves as a reminder of the tremendous differences among the adult learners who constitute the teaching force.

Review of Adult/Teacher Development Models

Table 4.1 presents a schematic review of the five conceptual frameworks for adult development. One thing all five approaches have in common is the supposition

TABLE 4.1 *Conceptual Models of Adult Development*

Universal, Orderly, Sequential		Interactive, Socially Contexted		
Hierarchical Stages	*Life Cycle Phases*	*Transition Events*	*Role Development*	*Sociocultural Variables*
Cognitive	*Goal Phases*	*Critical Events*	*Family, Work, and Self*	*Spheres of Influence*
Piaget, Perry	Buhler	Brim and Ryff	Juhasz	Peck
Moral	*Critical Issues*	*Stressful Events*	*Love, Work, and Learning*	*Women's Ways of Knowing*
Gilligan, Kohlberg	Erikson	Fiske et al.	Merriam and Clark	Belenky et al.
Conceptual	*Stability vs. Transition*	*On Time/Off Time*		*Ethnic Identity Development*
Hunt	Levinson	Neugarten		Phinney
Ego				
Loevinger				
Levels of Consciousness				
Kegan				
Concern				
Fuller				

that adult lives are characterized by change and adaptation. For teachers, as with all adult learners, the one thing we can be certain of is that things will not remain the same; thus, individuals will need to cope with changes as they arise. Supervision provides the opportunity for ascertaining the levels, stages, and issues of adult development in schools and assisting the teacher's professional development in the context of these realities.

Development: Ebb and Flow

Cognitive researchers have shown that stages of thinking vary according to the domain or topic (Case, 1986; Gardner, 1983; Sternberg, 1988). The same can be said for motivation. For example, Fred loves to teach art to his second-grade youngsters. He's constantly looking for ideas, finding materials, and expending energy to improve his art program. Yet when it comes to teaching mathematics, he puts in the required time, uses the worksheets, and muddles through the material. He never liked mathematics as a student and does not spend extra time on it. Suffice it to say that teachers, like all humans, are not static in their levels of thinking and commitment about all endeavors.

Furthermore, development can regress, recycle, or become blocked. Because one has reached a high level of development in one arena does not mean that level of development is consolidated eternally. *Experience* is a relative term; a teacher (or supervisor) with 30 years of teaching (or supervising) can still be inexperienced in many ways. Change the expectations of the jobs and/or change the clientele served, and suddenly there is an inexperienced person trying to figure out how to survive. Likewise, a first-year teacher may, after only a few months, be experienced and able to reason according to concerns beyond his or her own survival.

Alterations to a person's personal or professional situation can usher in regression in levels of thinking and levels of motivation. A highly committed and thoughtful faculty, who had made their school an exciting and successful place, was jolted when negotiations between the teachers' union and the school board resulted in a bitter strike. The immediate result on the school was that teachers retreated within their four walls, carrying out the letter of their contract and removing themselves from involvement in school curriculum and instruction issues. Most teachers retreated to a self-survival stage.

Teacher or adult development is not monolithic, linear, or eternal. The research on developmental stages provides lenses for viewing teachers individually and collectively as to their current levels of thinking and motivation about instructional improvement. Through such lenses, we can explore possible interventions to assist teachers individually and collectively to move into higher stages of development.

REFERENCES AND RECOMMENDED READINGS

Adams, R. D., and Martray, C. 1981. *Teacher development: A study of factors related to teacher concerns for pre, beginning, and experienced teachers.* Paper presented at the annual meeting of the American Educational Research Association, Los Angeles, April.

Alfred, M. V. 2001. Expanding theories of career development: Adding the voices of African American women in the White academy. *Adult Education Quarterly, 51,* 108–127.

Ammon, P. 1984. Human development, teaching and teacher education. *Teacher Education Quarterly, 11*(4), 95–108.

Amstutz, D. 1999. Adult learning: Moving toward more inclusive theories and practices. In T. C. Guy (Ed.), *Providing culturally relevant adult education: A challenge for the twenty-first century (New Directions for Adult and Continuing Education,* 82). San Francisco: Jossey-Bass.

Anderson, D. Y., and Hayes, C. L. 1996. *Gender, identity and self-esteem: A new look at adult development.* New York: Springer.

Arlin, P. K. 1975. Cognitive development in adulthood: A fifth stage. *Developmental Psychology, 11,* 602–606.

Aslanian, C. B., and Brickell, H. M. 1981. *Americans in transition.* New York: College Entrance Examination Board.

Baltes, P. B., and Baltes, M. 1980. Plasticity and variability in psychological aging: Methodological and theoretical issues. In C. Guerski (Ed.), *Aging and CNS.* Berlin: Schering.

Belenky, M. F., Clinchy, B. M., Goldberger, N. R., and Tarule, J. M. 1986. *Women's ways of knowing. The development of self, voice, and mind.* New York: Basic Books.

Berman, P., and McLaughlin, M. W. 1978. *Federal programs supporting educational change, Vol. 8. Implementing and sustaining innovations.* Santa Monica, CA: Rand Corporation. (ERIC ED 159 289)

Blum, L. S., and Meyer, R. 1981. *Developmental implications of myocardial infarction for mid-life adults.* Paper presented at the annual meeting of the American Educational Research Association, Los Angeles, April.

Brandt, R. S. 1986. On the expert teacher: A conversation with David Berliner. *Educational Leadership, 44*(2), 4–9.

Brim, O. J., and Ryff, C. D. 1980. On the properties of life events. In P. B. Baltes and O. G. Brim (Eds.), *Lifespan development and behavior, Vol. 3.* New York: Academic Press.

Brookfield, S. 1986. *Understanding and facilitating adult learning.* San Francisco: Jossey-Bass.

Brown, J. S., Collins, A., and Duguid, P. 1989. Situated cognition and the culture of learning. *Educational Researcher, 18*(1), 32–42.

Bruner, J. S. 1960. *The process of education.* Cambridge, MA: Harvard University Press.

Buhler, C. 1956. *From childhood to maturity.* London: Routledge and Kegan Paul.

Burden, P. R. 1982. *Developmental supervision: Reducing teacher stress at different career stages.* Paper presented at the annual conference of the Association of Teacher Educators, Phoenix, February.

Burke, P. J., Christensen, J. C., Fessler, R., McDonnell, J. H., and Price, J. R. 1987. *The teacher career cycle: Model development and research report.* Paper presented to the annual meeting of the American Educational Research Association, Washington, DC, April.

Caffarella, R. S., and Olson, S. K. 1993. Psychosocial development of women: A critical review of the literature. *Adult Education Quarterly, 43*(3), 125–151.

Calhoun, E. F. 1985. *Relationship of teachers' conceptual level to the utilization of supervisory services and to a description of the classroom instructional improvement.* Paper presented at the annual meeting of the American Educational Research Association, Chicago, April.

Case, R. 1986. The new stage theories in intellectual development. In M. Perlmutter (Ed.), *Perspectives on intellectual development,* Vol. 19. Hillsdale, NJ: Lawrence Erlbaum.

Chavez, A. F., and Guido-DiBrito, F. 1999. Racial and ethnic identity and development. In M. C. Clark and R. S. Caffarella (Eds.). *An update on adult development theory: New ways of thinking about the life course (New Directions for Adult and Continuing Education,* 84). San Francisco: Jossey-Bass.

Clark, M. C. and Caffarella, R. S. 1999. *An update on adult development theory: New ways of thinking about the life course (New Directions for Adult and Continuing Education,* 84). San Francisco: Jossey-Bass.

Clayton, V., and Birren, J. 1980. The development of wisdom across the lifespan: A reexamination of an ancient topic. *Lifespan Development and Behavior, 3,* 103–135.

Cranton, P. 1994. *Understanding and promoting transformative learning.* San Francisco: Jossey-Bass.

Cross, W. E. 1995. The psychology of Nigrescence: Revising the Cross model. In J. G. Ponterott, J. M Casa, L. A. Suzuki, and C. M. Alexander (Eds.), *Handbook of Multicultural Counseling.* Thousand Oaks, CA: Sage.

Cross, W. E. Jr. 1971. Toward a psychology of Black liberation: The Negro-to-Black convergence experience. *Black World, 20*(9), 13–27.

Cummings, A. L., and Murray, H. G. 1989. Ego development and its relation to teacher education. *Teaching and Teacher Education, 5*(1), 21–32.

Dewey, J. 1938. *Experience and education.* New York: Collier.

Elliott, V., and Schiff, S. 2001. A look within. *Journal of Staff Development, 22*(2), 39–42.

English, L. M. 2005. Historical and contemporary explorations of the social change and spiritual directions of adult education. *Teachers College Record, 107*(6), 1169–1192.

Erikson, E. H. 1950. *Childhood and society.* New York: Norton.

Erikson, E. H. 1963. *Childhood and society* (2nd ed.). New York: Norton.

Ferraro, J. M. 2000. *Reflective practice and professional development.* Washington, DC: ERIC Clearinghouse on Teaching and Teacher Education. (ERIC ED 449 120)

Fiske, M., and Chiriboga, D. A. 1990. *Change and continuity in adult life.* San Francisco: Jossey-Bass.

Freire, P. 1970. *Pedagogy of the oppressed.* New York: Herder and Herder.

Fuller, F. F. 1969. Concerns of teachers: A developmental conceptualization. *American Educational Research Journal, 6*(2), 207–266.

Gardner, H. 1983. *Frames of mind: The theory of multiple intelligences.* New York: Basic Books.

Gardner, H. 1999. *Intelligence reframed: Multiple intelligences for the 21st century.* New York: Basic Books.

Garrett, J. T., and Walking Stick Garrett, M. 1994. The path of good medicine: Understanding and counseling Native American Indians. *Journal of Multicultural Counseling and Development, 22,* 134–144.

Gehrke, N. J. 1979. Renewing teacher enthusiasm: A professional dilemma. *Theory into Practice, 18*(3), 188–193.

Gehrke, N. J. 1991. Seeing our way to better helping of beginning teachers. *Educational Forum, 55*(3), 233–242.

Gilligan, C. 1979. Woman's place in man's life cycle. *Harvard Educational Review, 49*(4), 431–446.

Gilligan, C. 1982. *In a different voice.* Cambridge, MA: Harvard University Press.

Gilligan, C. 1998. Remembering Larry. *Journal of Moral Education, 27*(2), 125–140.

Ginsburg, H., and Opper, S. 1979. *Piaget's theory of intellectual development* (2nd ed.). Englewood Cliffs, NJ: Prentice Hall.

Glassberg, S. 1979. *Developing models of teacher development.* (ERIC ED 171 658)

Glatthorn, A. A. 2000. *The principal as curriculum leader: Shaping what is taught and tested* (2nd ed.). Thousand Oaks, CA: Corwin Press.

Glickman, C. D. 1981. *Developmental supervision: Alternative approaches for helping teachers to improve instruction.* Alexandria, VA: Association for Supervision and Curriculum Development.

Glickman, C. D., and Tamashiro, R. T. 1982. A comparison of first year, fifth year, and former teachers on efficacy, ego development and problem solving. *Psychology in the Schools, 19*(4), 558–562.

Gonzalez Rodriguez, Y. E., and Sjostrom, Barbara R. 1998. Critical reflection for professional development: A comparative study of nontraditional adult and traditional student teachers. *Journal of Teacher Education, 49*(3), 177–186.

Gorard, S., and Selwyn, N. 2005. What makes a lifelong learner? *Teachers College Record, 107*(6), 1193–1216.

Gordon, S. P. 1990. *Assisting the entry-year teacher: A leadership resource.* Columbus: Ohio Department of Education.

Gould, R. L. 1978. *Transformations.* New York: Touchstone Books.

Graue, E. 2005. Theorizing and describing preservice teachers' images of families and schooling. *Teachers College Record, 107*(1), 157–185.

Grow, G. 1991. Teaching learners to be self-directed: A stage approach. *Adult Education Quarterly, 41*(3), 125–149.

Hansman, C. A. 2001. Context-based adult learning. In S. Merriam (Ed.), *The new update on adult learning theory* (*New Directions for Adult and Continuing Education,* 89). San Francisco: Jossey-Bass.

Hargreaves, A., and Moore, S. 2000. Curriculum integration and classroom relevance: A study of

teachers' practice. *Journal of Curriculum and Supervision, 15*(2), 89–112.

Harris, I. 1995. *Messages men hear: Constructing masculinities.* London: Taylor.

Harvey, O. J., Hunt, D. E., and Schroeder, H. M. 1961. *Conceptual systems and personality organization.* New York: Wiley.

Harvey, O. J., White, B. J., Prather, M., Alter, R., and Hoffmeister, J. 1966. Teachers' belief systems and preschool atmospheres. *Journal of Educational Psychology, 57,* 373–381.

Hayes, E., and Flannery, D. D. 2000. *Women as learners: The significance of gender in adult learning.* San Francisco: Jossey-Bass.

Heck, E. J., and Davis, C. S. 1973. Differential expression of empathy in a counseling analog. *Journal of Counseling Psychology, 20,* 101–104.

Helms, J. E. 1993. Introduction: Review of racial identity terminology. In J. E. Helms (Ed.), *Black and White racial identify: Theory, research and practice.* Westport, CT: Praeger.

Helms, J. E. 1995. An update of Helms' White and people of color racial identity models. In J. G. Ponterott, J. M. Casas, L. A. Suzuki, and C. M. Alexander (Eds.), *Handbook of Multicultural Counseling.* Thousand Oaks, CA: Sage.

Holliday, S. G., and Chandler, M. J. 1986. *Wisdom: Explorations in adult competence.* Basel, Switzerland: Karger.

Hopkins, D. 1990. Integrating staff development and school improvement: A study of personality and school climate. In B. Joyce (Ed.), *ASCD Yearbook: Changing school culture through staff development.* Alexandria, VA: Association for Supervision and Curriculum Development.

Horn, J. L., and Cattell, R. B. 1967. Age differences in fluid and crystallized intelligence. *Acta Psychologica, 26,* 107–129.

Hoy, W. K., and Miskel, C. G. 1982. *Educational administration theory, research and practice* (2nd ed.). New York: Random House.

Hunt, D. E. 1966. A conceptual systems change model and its application to education. In O. J. Harvey (Ed.), *Experience, structure, and adaptability* (pp. 277–302). New York: Springer-Verlag.

Hunt, D. E., Butler, L. F., Noy, J. E., and Rosser, M. E. 1978. *Assessing conceptual level by the paragraph completion method.* Toronto: Ontario Institute for Studies in Education.

Hunt, D. E., and Joyce, B. R. 1967. Teacher trainee personality and initial teaching style. *American Educational Research Journal, 4*(3), 253–255.

Hunter, M. 1986. To be or not to be—Hunterized. *Tennessee Educational Leadership Journal 12,* 70.

Jackson, P. 1968. *Life in classrooms.* New York: Holt, Rinehart and Winston.

Johnston, M. 1985. How elementary teachers understand the concept of "on-task": A developmental critique. *The Journal of Classroom Interaction, 21,* 15–24.

Johnston, M., and Lubomudrov, C. 1987. Teachers' level of moral reasoning and their understanding of classroom rules and roles. *Elementary School Journal, 88,* 65–78.

Josselson, R. 1987. *Finding herself: Pathways to identity development in women.* San Francisco: Jossey-Bass

Juhasz, A. M. 1989. A role-based approach to adult development: The triple helix model. *International Journal of Aging and Human Development, 29*(4), 301–315.

Katz, J. H. 1989. The challenge of diversity. In C. Woolbright (Ed.), *College unions at work.* Monograph, No. 11, 1–17. Bloomington, IN: Association of College Unions-International.

Kegan, R. 1994. *In over our heads: The mental demands of modern life.* Cambridge, MA: Harvard University Press.

Kegan, R. 2000. What "form" transforms?: A constructive-developmental perspective on transformational learning. In J. Mezirow et al. (Eds.), *Learning as transformation: Critical perspectives on a theory in progress.* San Francisco: Jossey-Bass.

Kerka, S. 1998. *New perspectives on mentoring.* ERIC Digest No. 194. (ERIC ED 418 249)

Kilgore, D. W. 2001. Critical and postmodern perspectives on adult learning. In S. B. Merriam (Ed.), *The new update on adult learning theory* (*New Directions for Adult and Continuing Education, 89*). San Francisco: Jossey-Bass.

Kimpston, R. D. 1987. Teacher and principal stage of concern regarding implementation of benchmark testing: A longitudinal study. *Teaching and Teacher Education, 3*(3), 205–217.

King, N. 1970. Clarification and evaluation of the two-factor theory of job satisfaction. *Psychological Bulletin, 74,* 18–31.

Kitchener, K. 1983. Cognition, metacognition and epistemic cognition. Three models of cognitive processing. *Human Development, 26,* 222–232.

Kitchener, K. S., Lynch, C. L., Fischer, K. W., and Wood, P. K. 1993. Developmental range of reflection judgement: The effect of contextual support and practice on developmental stage. *Developmental Psychology, 29*(5), 893–906.

Knowles, M. S. 1980. *The modern practice of adult education: From pedagogy to andragogy* (2nd ed.). Chicago: Association/Follett.

Knowles, M. S. 1984. *Andragogy in action: Applying modern principles of adult learning.* San Francisco: Jossey-Bass.

Kolb, D. A. 1984. *Experiential learning.* Englewood Cliffs, NJ: Prentice Hall.

Kohlberg, L., and Armon, C. 1984. Three types of stage models used in the study of adult development. In M. Commons, F. A. Richards, and C. A. Armon (Eds.), *Beyond formal operations: Late adolescent and adult cognitive development.* New York: Praeger.

Kohlberg, L., and Turiel, E. 1971. Moral development and moral education. In G. Lessor (Ed.), *Psychology and educational practice.* Chicago: Scott Foresman.

Kramer, D. A. 1983. Post-formal operations? A need for further conceptualization. *Human Development, 26*(2), 91–105.

Kramer, D. A. 1987. *Improved learning in aging: Implications for education.* Paper presented at Information and Aging: Coalitions for the Future, New Brunswick, NJ, April. (ERIC ED 283 098)

Krupp, J. 1982. *The adult learner: A unique entity.* Manchester, CT: Adult Development and Learning.

Krupp, J. 1987. Understanding and motivating personnel in the second half of life. *Journal of Education, 169*(1), 20–47.

Lave, J., and Wenger, E. 1991. *Situated learning: Legitimate peripheral participation.* New York: Cambridge University Press.

Levine, S. L. 1987. Understanding life cycle issues: A resource for school leaders. *Journal of Education, 169*(1), 7–19.

Levine, S. L. 1989. *Promoting adult growth in schools.* Boston: Allyn and Bacon.

Levinson, D. J. et al. 1978. *The seasons in a man's life.* New York: Knopf.

Levinson, D. J., and Levinson, J. D. 1996. *The seasons of a woman's life.* New York: Knopf.

Lieblich, A. 1986. Successful career women at midlife: Crises and transitions. *International Journal of Aging and Human Development, 23*(4), 301–312.

Lindeman, E. 1926. *The meaning of adult education.* New York: New Republic.

Loevinger, J. 1976. *Ego development.* San Francisco: Jossey-Bass.

Lortie, D. C. 1975. *Schoolteacher: A sociological study.* Chicago: University of Chicago Press.

Marsick, V. J., and Watkins, K. 1990. *Informal and incidental learning in the workplace.* London and New York: Routledge.

Marsick, V. J., and Watkins, K. E. 2001. Informal and incidental learning. In S. Merriam (Ed.), *The new update on adult learning theory (New Directions for Adult and Continuing Education,* 89). San Francisco: Jossey-Bass.

Mathis, C. 1987. Educational reform, the aging society and the teaching profession. *Journal of Education, 169*(1), 80–88.

McNeil, L. M. 1986. *Exit, voice and community: Magnet teachers' responses to standardization.* Presentation to the annual meeting of the American Educational Research Association, San Francisco, April.

McNergney, R. F., and Carrier, C. A. 1981. *Teacher development.* New York: Macmillan.

Merriam, S., and Caffarella, R. 1999. *Learning in adulthood* (2nd ed.). San Francisco: Jossey-Bass.

Merriam, S. B. 2001. Something old, something new: Adult learning theory for the twenty-first century. *New Directions for Adult and Continuing Education, 89*, 93–96.

Merriam, S. B., Caffarella, R. S., and Baumgartner, L. M. 2006. *Learning in adulthood: A comprehensive guide* (3rd ed.). San Francisco: Jossey-Bass.

Merriam, S. B., and Clark, M. C. 1991. *Lifelines: Patterns of work, love and learning in adulthood.* San Francisco: Jossey-Bass.

Merriam, S. B., and Clark, M. C. 1993. Learning from experience: What makes it significant? *International Journal of Lifelong Education, 12*(2), 129–138.

Mezirow, J. D. 1981. A critical theory of adult learning and education. *Adult Education, 32*(1), 3–24.

Mezirow, J. D., and associates. 1990. *Fostering critical reflection in adulthood. A guide to transformative and emancipatory learning.* San Francisco: Jossey-Bass.

Mezirow, J. M. 2000. Learning to think like an adult: Core concepts of transformation theory. In J. M. Mezirow & Associates (Eds.), *Learning as transformation: Critical perspectives on a theory in progress.* San Francisco: Jossey-Bass.

Neimark, E. D. 1987. *Toward a cross-cultural examination of adult thought.* Paper presented at the Satellite Conference of the International Society of the Study of Behavior Development, Beijing, May. (ERIC ED 291 869)

Neugarten, B. L. 1977. Personality and aging. In J. E. Birren and K. W. Schaie (Eds.), *Handbook of the psychology of aging.* New York: Van Nostrand Reinhold.

Neugarten, B., and Neugarten, D. 1987. The changing meaning of age. *Psychology Today, 21*(5), 29–33.

Oja, S. N. 1979. *A cognitive-structural approach to adult ego, moral, and conceptual development through in-service education.* Paper presented at the annual meeting of the American Educational Research Association, San Francisco, April.

Oja, S. N. 1988. *A collaborative approach to leadership in supervision: Program assessment report. Part B of the final report.* (ERIC ED 304 432)

Oja, S. N., and Pine, G. J. 1981. *Toward a theory of staff development.* Paper presented at the annual meeting of the American Educational Research Association, Los Angeles, April.

Oja, S. N., and Pine, G. J. 1984. *Collaborative action research: A two-year study of teachers' stages of development and school contexts.* Durham, NH: University of New Hampshire.

O'Keefe, P., and Johnston, M. 1989. Perspective taking and teacher effectiveness: A connected thread through three developmental literatures. *Journal of Teacher Education, 40*(3), 20–26.

Parham, T. 1989. Cycles of psychological Nigrescence. *The Counseling Psychologist, 17*(2), 187–226.

Parker, W. C. 1983. *The effect of guided reflection and role-taking on the interactive decision making of teachers.* Paper presented at the annual meeting of the American Educational Research Association, Montreal, April.

Peck, T. A. 1986. Women's self-definition in adulthood: From a different model? *Psychology of Women Quarterly, 10*(3), 274–284.

Perry, W. G. 1970. *Forms of intellectual and ethical development in the college years.* New York: Holt, Rinehart and Winston.

Perry, W. G. 1981. Cognitive and ethical growth: The making of meaning. In A. Chickering (Ed.), *The modern American college.* San Francisco: Jossey-Bass.

Phillips, M. D., and Glickman, C. D. 1991. Peer coaching: Developmental approach to enhance teacher thinking. *Journal of Staff Development, 12*(2), 20–25.

Phinney, J. S. 1990. Ethnic identify in adolescents and adults: Review of the research. *Psychological Bulletin, 108*, 499–514.

Piaget, J. 1955. *The language and thought of the child.* New York: World Publishing.

Porter, A. C., and Brophy, J. 1988. Synthesis of research on good teaching: Insights from the work of the Institute for Research on Teaching. *Educational Leadership, 45*(7), 78–85.

Pratt, D. D. 1988. Andragogy as a relational construct. *Adult Education Quarterly, 38,* 160–181.

Rachal, J. R. 2002. Andragogy's detectives: A critique of the present and a proposal for the future. *Adult Education Quarterly, 52*(3), 210–227.

Reiman, A. J., and Parramore, B. 1994. The first year of teaching: Assignment, expectations, and development. In S. Odell and M. O'Hair (Eds.), *Diversity and teaching.* Orlando, FL: Harcourt Brace Jovanovich.

Reiman, A. J., and Thies-Sprinthall, L. 1998. *Mentoring and supervision for teacher development.* New York: Longman

Rest, J. 1986. *Moral development: Advances in research and theory.* New York: Praeger.

Resta, V., Huling, L., and Rainwater, N. 2001. Preparing second-career teachers. *Educational Leadership, 58*(8), 60–63.

Riegel, K. 1973. Dialectical operations: The final period of cognitive development. *Human Development, 16,* 346–370.

Roberts, P., and Newton, P. M. 1987. Levinsonian studies of women's adult development. *Psychology and Aging, 2,* 154–163.

Rose, A. D., Jeris, L., and Smith, R. 2005. Is adult education a calling? Shaping identity and practice in steel mill learning centers. *Teachers College Record, 107*(6), 1305–1334.

Rutter, M., Maughan, B., Mortimore, P., Ouston, J., and Smith, A. 1979. *Fifteen thousand hours. Secondary schools and their effects on children.* Cambridge, MA: Harvard University Press.

Schlossberg, N. K. 1984. *Counseling adults in transition: Linking practice in theory.* New York: Springer.

Sheared, V. 1999. Giving voice: Inclusion of African American students' polyrhythmic realities in adult basic education. In T. C. Guy (Ed.), *Providing culturally relevant adult education: A challenge for the twenty-first century (New Directions for Adult and Continuing Education, 82).* San Francisco: Jossey-Bass.

Sprinthall, N. A., and Thies-Sprinthall, L. 1982. Career development of teachers: A cognitive developmental perspective. In H. Mitzel (Ed.), *Encyclopedia of educational research* (5th ed.). New York: Free Press.

Sternberg, R. J. 1985. *Beyond IQ: A triarchic theory of human intelligence.* New York: Cambridge.

Sternberg, R. J. 1988. *Triarchic mind: A new theory of human intelligence.* New York: Viking.

Sternberg, R. J. 1990. *Metaphors of mind: Conceptions of the nature of intelligence.* New York: Cambridge.

Sullivan, E. V., McCullough, G., and Stager, M. A. 1970. Developmental study of the relationship between conceptual, ego, and moral development. *Child Development, 41,* 399–411.

Taranto, M. 1987. *Wisdom and logic.* Paper presented at the annual symposium of the Jean Piaget Society, Philadelphia, May. (ERIC ED 282 099)

Taylor, K. 2000. Teaching with developmental intention. In J. Mezirow and Associates (Eds.), *Learning as transformation: Critical perspectives on a theory in progress.* San Francisco: Jossey-Bass.

Taylor, K., and Marienau, C. 1995. Bridging practice and theory for women's adult development. In *New Directions for Adult and Continuing Education, 65.* San Francisco: Jossey-Bass.

Tennant, M. 1986. An evaluation of Knowles' theory of adult learning. *International Journal of Lifelong Education, 5*(2), 113–122.

Terehoff, I. I. 2002. Elements of adult learning in teacher professional development. *NASSP Bulletin, 86*(632), 65–77.

Thies-Sprinthall, L., and Sprinthall, N. A. 1987. Experienced teachers: Agents for revitalization and renewal as mentors and teacher educators. *Journal of Education, 169*(1), 65–79.

Thorndike, E. L., and others. 1928. *Adult learning.* New York: Macmillan.

Tieso, C. 2001. Curriculum: Broad brushstrokes or paint-by-the-numbers? *The Teacher Educator, 36*(3), 199–213.

Tisdell, E. 2000. Feminist pedagogies. In E. Hayes and D. Flannery (Eds.), *Women as learners: The significance of gender in adult learning.* San Francisco: Jossey-Bass.

Tough, A. 1971. *The Adult's learning projects: A fresh approach to theory and practice in adult learning.* Toronto: Ontario Institute for Studies in Education.

Uys, L. R., Gwele, N. S., McInerney, P., Rhyn, L., and Tanga, T. 2004. The competence of nursing graduates from problem-based programs in South Africa. *Journal of Nursing Education, 43*(8), 352–361.

Whitbourne, S. K. 1986. *Adult development* (2nd ed.). New York: Praeger.

Wilkins, R. A. 1980. If the moral reasoning of teachers is deficient, what hope for pupils. *Kappan, 61*(8), 548–549.

Willis, S. L., and Baltes, P. B. 1980. Intelligence in adulthood and aging: Contemporary issues. In L. W. Poon (Ed.), *Aging in the 1980s: Psychological issues.* Washington DC: American Psychological Association.

Wilson, A. L. 1993. The promise of situated cognition. In S. Merriam (Ed.) *An update on adult learning theory* (*New directions for adult and continuing education,* 57). San Francisco: Jossey-Bass.

Witherell, C. S., and Erickson, V. L. 1978. Teacher education as adult development. *Theory and Practice, 17,* 229–238.

Zepeda, S. J. 2004. Leadership to build learning communities. *The Educational Forum, 68*(2), 144–151.

5

Reflections on Schools, Teaching, and SuperVision

As we seek ways to improve school and classroom instruction, we need to understand how present thinking, beliefs, and practices in the field of supervision interact with instruction and assumptions about students and teachers as learners. This chapter will show how issues of school and teaching effectiveness are not clearly answered by research, but instead must be resolved by human judgments about goals and purposes. We will also look at how supervisory beliefs are related to a particular educational philosophy or platform. Two instruments will then be provided to help clarify each person's personal supervisory belief, and we will examine how one's own supervisory belief fits along a control continuum. Finally, some propositions about supervisory belief and consequences for teacher development will be presented.

How do we reconcile the uncertainties of supervision, teaching, and instructional improvement? How do we know whether we are progressing in the desired direction? Unless we reflect on our own beliefs, there is little to steer us.

Sergiovanni and Starrat (1983) noted the importance of understanding one's personal supervisory beliefs:

> What is needed is some firm footing in principle. Some have called our often unexpressed constellation of principles a platform. Just as a political party is supposed

to base its decisions and actions on a party platform upon which it seeks election, so, too, supervisory personnel need a platform upon which, and in the light of which, they can carry on their work. With a clearly defined platform, they can begin to take a position relative to educational practices, looking beyond the surface behavior to probe for the real consequences of a variety of school practices. (pp. 226–227)

Knowing oneself as a supervisor is necessary before considering alternative practices and procedures. To move from a platform, we must first know where we are standing. Let's look at the human decisions that a supervisor must make about school improvement, teaching effectiveness, and one's purpose in working with teachers.

The Coast of Britain

Correct answers to questions about physical matters are human decisions. Answers about social and educative matters are even more clearly human judgments (see Glickman, 1987b). An example from geometry is illustrative. To the question, "How long is the coast of Britain?" the geometer Benoit Mandelbrot answered that the coast has no real length apart from human judgment (Hardison, 1986). If one uses a measurement scale of 100 miles to an inch to draw the British coastline, that coastline has large bays and capes. If one uses a scale of 10 miles to an inch, then new inlets and promontories appear. The coast becomes longer or shorter, depending on the scale used. Furthermore, what happens when measurement of the coast begins when the tide is coming in? Each incoming wave reduces the coast, and each outgoing wave lengthens the coast. Therefore, how does one find the length of the British coast? The question can be answered only by agreeing on the purpose of the measurement, the perspective and the unit of measurement to be used, and the particular time at which the measurement is to be made. The length of the coast is a mathematical fiction created so that humans can find a representation that will accomplish their purpose.

Effective and Good Schools: The Same?

In discussing questions about supervision, teaching, and school improvement, as in measuring the coast of Britain, there is no certainty about how to arrive at an answer. The issue of effective schools highlights the human values that drive school decisions and actions (Glickman, 1987a).

Many of the clarion calls for school reform cite the findings from research on effective teaching and effective schools as examples of how schools and classrooms should change. The reformers tell us that the goal of all schools should be effectiveness—as measured by such factors as students' scores on tests of basic skills, their attendance rates, and their performance on the Scholastic Aptitude Test (SAT). Furthermore, we ought to narrow the academic focus of the curriculum, test students more frequently, raise standards for promotion, and have teachers state specific, measurable objectives and follow a prescribed instructional approach that involves reviewing, explaining, demonstrating, guiding practice, checking for understanding, and summarizing. The findings of the recent research on effective teaching and effective schools are treated as scientific laws that apply to *all* teachers and *all* schools.

The findings of the research on effective teaching and effective schools are too often equated with what is desirable or good. By failing to distinguish between *effectiveness* and *goodness,* we avoid two central questions in education. The first question with which schools and school systems must deal is: What is good? Only after that question has been answered should we deal with the second question: How do we become effective? The current fascination with findings from the research on effectiveness has blinded schools and school systems to the more basic question of goodness.

Do higher SAT scores justify labeling a school "good" if the price for those higher scores has been an increase in the dropout rate? Are higher scores in reading and mathematics "good" if students gain them at the expense of time spent in studying science, social studies, art, or music? Is an average gain of eight points on reading test scores worth the increased allocation of time and resources to direct instruction in reading? Is that gain more desirable than maintaining current achievement levels in reading but devoting a greater proportion of class time to a whole-language approach that emphasizes creative writing or critical thinking? The research on effective schools and effective teaching does not answer these questions for us. The research is neutral: It does not choose our goals but simply tells us how to accomplish certain things (which may or may not be among our goals). Educators who care about the fate of all children must define *goodness* before they worry about *effectiveness;* as supervisors, we must first clarify our own definitions.

Changing Views: New Emphasis on Constructivist Teaching and Learning

In recent years the constructivist view has had increasing influence over teaching and learning in our nation's classrooms. Constructivism is an epistemology (a theory of the nature of knowledge) based on the work of a variety of philosophers, psychologists, and educators. Luminaries associated with constructivism include Immanuel Kant, Lev Vygotsky, John Dewey, Jean Piaget, Jerome Bruner, and Howard Gardner. Constructivism holds that people create new knowledge as a result of the interaction of their existing knowledge, beliefs, and values with new ideas, problems, or experiences. To the constructivist, knowledge is not universal, objective, or fixed, but is constructed or co-constructed by learners.

Although there are several different models of constructivism, these models can be classified into one of two broad categories. *Cognitive constructivism* is focused on the individual's intellectual development. It holds that learning is stimulated when the individual encounters an idea or experience that contradicts his or her present conception of reality. This discrepancy causes "cognitive conflict" and "disequilibrium" which stimulates the person to develop and assimilate new knowledge as a means of dealing with the discrepancy. The other broad category is *social constructivism,* which proposes that knowledge is not created by the individual but is constructed as a result of the individual's interaction with his or her social context. Furthermore, that interaction brings about changes to both the individual and the social context (Null, 2004).

What are the practical implications of constructivism for instruction? Airasian and Walsh (1997) discuss what a constructivist approach means for teachers and students:

> In a constructivist approach, teachers will have to learn to guide, not tell; to create environments in which students can make their own meanings, not be handed them by the teacher; to accept diversity in constructions, not search for the one "right" answer; to modify prior notions of "right" and "wrong," not stick to rigid standards and criteria; to create a safe, free, responsive environment that encourages disclosure of student constructions, not a closed, judgmental system. (p. 148)

> Students will also have to learn new ways to perform. They will have to learn to think for themselves, not wait for the teacher to tell them what to think; to proceed with less focus and direction from the teacher, not to wait for explicit teacher directions; to express their own ideas clearly in their own words, not to answer restricted-response questions; to revisit and revise constructions; not to move immediately on to the next concept or idea. (p. 448)

Table 5.1 further illuminates the constructivist approach to teaching and learning by comparing traditional to constructivist classrooms.

Instructional Improvement and Effective Teaching

Let's continue this reflection on practice by taking an innocuous statement about supervision that virtually no one would take issue with: The goal of supervision is to improve instruction. It sounds nice, until we ask for a definition of what type of instruction we wish to improve. Effective teaching, to a large extent, depends on what you are trying to teach. Consider the following examples:

- If the goal is for students to master basic skills, then effective teaching might involve explanation, demonstration, practice, feedback, and more practice.
- If the goal is for students to learn classical culture, then effective teaching might consist of reading the great works, lecture, and Socratic discussion.

TABLE 5.1 *Comparing Constructivist and Traditional Classrooms*

	Traditional Classroom	*Constructivist Classroom*
Educational Purpose	• Transmission of knowledge	• Construction of knowledge
Curriculum	• Content-centered • Rigid, sequential	• Problem-centered • Flexible, webbed
Instructional Focus	• Discrete pieces of information • Breadth	• Big ideas • Depth
Planning	• By teacher	• By teacher and students
Instructional Methods	• Lecture • Teacher questions with "correct" student responses • Student recitation • Student practice with teacher feedback • Independent student practice	• Open-ended discussion • Student-initiated questions • Problem solving • Inquiry, experimentation • Active learning • Cooperative learning • Self and group reflection on constructions
Assessment	• Distinct from learning • Intended to measure learning and grade students • Objective quizzes and tests • Designed externally or by teacher	• Integrated with learning • Co-planned by teacher and students • Seeks to understand student constructions • Authentic • Assessment of process and product equally important • Includes self, peer, and group assessment

- If the goal is for students to become problem solvers, then effective teaching might call for exposing students to real-world problems and encouraging active student involvement in testing possible solutions and reaching resolutions.
- If the goal is social development, then effective teaching might consist of structuring cooperative learning and community building activities.
- If the goal is personal development, then effective teaching might mean facilitation of students' self-directed learning and self-assessment.
- If the goal is critical inquiry, then effective teaching might require the teacher to challenge students' current values and assumptions, asking them to critique dominant belief systems, social structures, and power relationships.

A productive course of action is therefore to identify various instructional strategies that are effective in relation to identified instructional goals and individual students. If this proposition is accepted, the supervisor's role becomes one of assisting teachers to clarify school and classroom instructional goals, develop a variety of instructional strategies (direct instruction, constructivist teaching, cooperative learning, classroom dialogue, service learning, and so on), "mix and match" instructional strategies to learning goals and students, and assess the effects of instruction for the purpose of continuous improvement. With such a supervision emphasis, effective instruction is seen as the teacher's ability to use various ways of teaching according to a variety of learning goals and student learning styles.

To the mix of multiple learning goals and multiple instructional models, Ornstein (1990) adds the concept of *teaching style*:

> Teaching style is a truncated version of a personality and philosophical type. Everyone must develop his or her own style of teaching and feel comfortable in the classroom. In short, teachers must develop their own repertoire, relative to their own physical and mental characteristics and their students. Thus, there is no one ideal type but a multiple set of teacher types or styles. Teachers' style is a matter of choice and comfort, and what works for one teacher with one set of students may not work for another. (p. 84)

Teaching styles, of course, can change and broaden over time, allowing for the expansion of a teacher's repertoire of instructional strategies. However, attempting to force teachers to immediately adopt strategies that strongly conflict with their current teaching style is inconsistent with both the principles of adult learning and the concept of the teacher as a professional. It is better to initially invite teachers to learn and try out new strategies which are consistent with their current style, and then facilitate teachers' continued development of teaching style and repertoire over time.

Instructional improvement can be defined as helping teachers acquire teaching strategies consistent with their instructional goals and compatible with their general teaching styles that increase the capabilities of students to make wise decisions in varying contexts (with regard to peers, adults, academics, and life). Effective teaching consists therefore of those teaching decisions about actions, routines, and techniques that increase the decision-making capabilities of students.

Beliefs about Education

We've discussed how the definition of effective instruction depends on school and teacher instructional goals. Instructional goals, in turn, are ultimately based on beliefs concerning such things as the purpose of education, what should be taught, the nature of the learner, and the learning process. Whether or not they are conscious of it, teachers' and supervisors' educational philosophies have a significant impact on instruction and instructional improvement efforts. The following are summaries of educational platforms of three teachers with different beliefs about education.

> Joan Simpson believes that the purpose of education should be to transmit a prescribed body of basic knowledge, skills, and cultural values to students. To do this effectively, the teacher must exercise control over the classroom, lesson content, and students. Content should be broken first into discrete academic areas and then into small elements, and learning should take place in a series of small, sequential steps. All students should be expected to master the same content. Grades and other types of external motivation are necessary to assure student learning.

> Bill Washington believes that the purpose of education should be student growth, especially in inquiry and problem-solving skills. To promote such growth, the teacher conveys existing knowledge, but also encourages students to experiment in order to test old ideas and find solutions to new problems. Bill believes that since inquiry is most successful in a democratic environment, the teacher should share control of the learning environment with students. Because problem solving often takes place within a social context, students should learn social skills as well as academic content.

> Pat Rogers believes that each child is unique and that the primary purpose of education should be to meet students' individual needs. The teacher should foster the development of each student toward his or her fullest potential. This means addressing students as whole persons by fostering their physical, emotional, cognitive, moral, and social development. Such holistic education includes facilitating student self-inquiry. Pat believes that students should have as much control over their own learning environment as their maturity level permits. Teachers should base lessons on students' experience, concerns, and interests. Students should be allowed to participate in assessing their own learning.

The three educational platforms just described do indeed represent contrasting beliefs. Based on their educational beliefs, Joan Simpson, Bill Washington, and Pat Rogers, no doubt, have quite different definitions of instructional improvement and effective teaching. You may view one of these educational platforms as quite similar to your own, you may agree with parts of each, or you may have an entirely different set of beliefs. In any case, it is important for you to clarify your own educational beliefs. By reflecting on the following questions, you can begin to build your educational platform:

1. What should be the purpose of education?
2. What should be the content of the school curriculum?
3. Who should control the learning environment?
4. What should be the relationship of teacher and students?
5. Under what conditions is student learning most successful?
6. What motivates students to do their best in school?
7. What is your definition of effective teaching?
8. What personal characteristics are possessed by a successful teacher?

9. How should the teacher assess student learning?
10. What is your definition of a good school?

Supervision Beliefs

Most supervisors, of course, are former teachers. As a result, their views about learning, the nature of the learner, knowledge, and the role of the teacher in the classroom influence their view of supervision. After all, supervision is in many respects analogous to teaching. Teachers wish to improve students' behavior, achievement, and attitudes. Supervisors similarly wish to improve teachers' behavior, achievement, and attitudes. The supervisory platforms of three supervisors are described next. As you read these platforms, note the relationship between the beliefs they contain and the teacher beliefs present in the three educational platforms discussed earlier in this chapter.

Bob Reynolds believes that the purpose of supervision is to monitor teachers to determine if their instruction includes the elements of effective instruction. If those elements are observed, the supervisor should provide positive reinforcement to assure that they continue to be included in the teacher's lessons. Bob believes that if a teacher is not using, or is incorrectly using, the elements of effective instruction, the supervisor has a responsibility to provide remedial assistance by explaining and demonstrating correct instructional behaviors, setting standards of improvement, and monitoring and reinforcing the teacher's improvement efforts. In short, the supervisor should have primary responsibility for instructional improvement decisions.

Jan White believes that the purpose of supervision is to engage teachers in mutual inquiry aimed at the improvement of instruction. The supervisor and teacher should share perceptions of instructional problems, exchange suggestions for solving those problems, and negotiate an improvement plan. The improvement plan becomes a hypothesis to be tested by the teacher with the supervisor's assistance. Thus, Jan believes that supervisors and teachers should share the responsibility for instructional improvement.

Shawn Moore believes that the purpose of supervision should be to foster teacher reflection and autonomy and to facilitate teacher-driven instructional improvement. The supervisor should be concerned with the teacher's self-concept and personal development as well as the teacher's instructional performance. It is critical for the supervisor to establish a relationship with the teacher characterized by openness, trust, and acceptance. Shawn believes that the supervisor should allow the teacher to identify instructional problems, improvement plans, and criteria for success. The supervisor can assist the teacher's self-directed improvement through active listening, clarifying, encouraging, and reflecting. Thus, the teacher should have primary responsibility for instructional improvement decisions, with the supervisor serving as an active facilitator.

These descriptions show that supervisory platforms can be as varied as educational platforms. When we compare the educational platforms of Joan Simpson,

Bill Washington, and Pat Rogers with the supervisory platforms of Bob Reynolds, Jan White, and Shawn Moore, we can see that both types of platforms reveal basic beliefs about knowledge, human nature, and control. By answering the following questions, you can begin the process of clarifying your own beliefs about instructional supervision. We suggest that you write responses to the questions, save your responses, and reassess your supervisory platform after you have finished reading this text.

1. What is your definition of instructional supervision?
2. What should be the ultimate purpose of supervision?
3. Who should supervise? Who should be supervised?
4. What knowledge, skills, attitudes, and values are possessed by successful supervisors?
5. What are the most important needs of teachers?
6. What makes for positive relationships between supervisors and teachers?
7. What types of activities should be part of instructional supervision?
8. What should be changed about the current practice of instructional supervision?

Supervisory Platform as Related to Educational Philosophy

Many educators view discussions of educational philosophy as overly abstract and irrelevant to the real world of supervisors and teachers. Yet a supervisor's actions in working with teachers are based on supervisory beliefs, which in turn reflect a broader educational philosophy. Many different philosophies exist. Some, such as idealism and realism, date back to ancient times. Others, such as pragmatism and behaviorism, have been developed within the last century. Even more recent has been the emergence of progressivism, reconstructionism, and existentialism. Philosophies are numerous and overlapping, and many have historical roots in each other. To unravel the major philosophical trends in education, one must decipher how philosophies differ from each other and then build overriding conceptual categories. Each conceptual category or superphilosophy is created by grouping various philosophies that have central agreement on the nature and scope of education. In other words, there may be disagreement on the specific nature of knowledge, truth, and reality, yet they hang together as a general educational philosophy because they are in agreement on the purpose and treatment of education.*

With educational application in mind, divergent philosophies can be simplified and classified. Three major educational superphilosophies have direct relevance to supervision. These categories have been labeled, according to Johnson, Collins, Dupuis, and Johansen (1973), as essentialism, progressivism, and exis-

*The descriptions of philosophy in Chapter 5 are taken from C. D. Glickman and J. P. Esposito, *Leadership Guide for Elementary School Improvement: Procedures for Assessment and Change* (Boston: Allyn and Bacon, 1979), p. 20.

tentialism. We would like to substitute for progressivism the more general term *experimentalism,* as described by Van Cleve Morris (1961).

Essentialism

Essentialism as a philosophy is derived from idealism and realism. *Idealism,* which dates back to Plato, espouses a belief in absolutes: The world we live in is merely a reflection of reality. Reality, truth, and standards of morality exist beyond our common ways of knowing. Only by training the mind do we glimpse the ultimates. Yet training the mind is not sufficient in itself; it only brings the mind nearer to grasping reality. Divine revelation, insight, and faith are the necessary elements for ultimate knowledge of what exists. Therefore, idealism emphasizes truth and reality existing outside of people. It is absolute and unchanging. *Realism,* developed at the onset of the industrial age, places a similar emphasis on truth and reality being outside of people. Instead of humankind and the outer environment being separated from each other, realism maintains that humanity is part and parcel of that environment. The world is a preordained, mechanistic reality. All of existence operates according to scientific, cause-and-effect relations. It is as if existence is a clock that always runs according to mechanical principles governing levers, gauges, and gears. Humans have no existence apart from this clock; they are a part of the predetermined machine. Knowledge is learning how the machine works; truths are the scientific laws of regulation. Nothing exists outside the principles of nature. The purpose of education is to condition the mind to think in a natural, logical way. The mind should be trained to become consciously aware of the predetermined nature of the world.

Essentialism, created by William L. Bagley in 1938, encompassed the educational philosophies of idealism and realism. He took the ideas of knowledge being eternal and outside of humankind (idealism—absolutes; realism—natural laws) to form pedagogy. Essentialists emphasize that there is a body of timeless knowledge, both historical and contemporary, that is of value to the living.

Essentialism in terms of supervision emphasizes the supervisor as the person who teaches truths about teaching to teachers. Supervisors are those most knowledgeable about those absolute standards. Teachers are then handled mechanistically to systematize and feed content to students. As teachers digest these teaching truths, they move closer to being good teachers.

Experimentalism

As Western society became more industrialized, optimism and confidence in human ability to control nature emerged. The philosophy of *pragmatism* developed by Charles S. Pierce and William James emphasized what people can do to nature rather than what nature does to humankind. John Dewey, circa 1920, further expanded on the writings of James by putting the individual squarely in the context of society. Humans can both reform and be reformed by society. Dewey's philosophy is, of course, the well-known school of progressive thought.

Reconstructionism is a further offshoot of both pragmatism and progressivism. Richard Pratte (1971) cited the pamphlet *Dare the Schools Build a New Social Order,* written by George S. Counts in 1932, as a guiding document for the then radical notion that schools and students were the reformers of society.

Experimentalism emerges from the philosophies of pragmatism, progressivism, and reconstructionism. They hold in common a historical break from the more traditional philosophies of realism and idealism. The essentialist idea that knowledge, truth, and morality exist as absolutes outside of humans was rejected. The emerging faith in the scientific method, the ability of humans to create their own laws, principles, and machines, and the fact that such man-made inventions would work for them demanded an accompanying philosophy. Experimentalism provided that philosophy.

Reality was what worked. If a person could form a hypothesis, test it, and find it to work, then it was regarded as tentatively true. On repeated experimentation with the same results, it became real. Yet experimentalists would never claim an absolute truth. The human environment was believed to be constantly changing, so that what one can do and prove today may not be probable tomorrow. A new situation and a different approach may alter yesterday's reality. Experimentalists point to the historical evidence of Newton's law of gravity as a past truth that has given way to Einstein's theory of relativity; they believe that in time a new theory will replace Einstein's.

Morality is also viewed in relation to what works for humanity and human society. Morality is that behavior that promotes one's working with the group to achieve greater ends. To be wise is to understand how the environment (of things and people) affects oneself and how one might affect it. Whether action is moral or not is determined by the degree of progress that has been achieved by the group. The use of trial and error in a laboratory setting is the key to evaluating the outcome of action. Therefore, experimentalists do not view knowledge as absolute or external to human capabilities. Rather, knowledge is a result of the interaction between the scientific person and the environment.

The educational application of experimentalist thinking to supervision is well documented in the writing of Dewey. Teachers (as students) need to learn what are the truths of their time, but they should not rest content with that parcel of knowledge. Supervisors view schools as laboratories for working with teachers to test old hypotheses and to try new ones. Supervisors work democratically with teachers to achieve collective ends that will help everyone. Supervisors are not solely conveyors of age-old wisdom; they are both the conveyors of the rudimentary knowledge of the time and the guiders of trial-and-error, exploratory learning.

Existentialism

Existentialism as a school of thought is derived from the rejection of the other philosophies encompassed in essentialism and experimentalism. As such, it is a large category for many diverse philosophers. They have in common a scorn for rational, empirical, and systematic thinking as the way of knowing reality. As previously mentioned, the essentialists believe in rational thinking to help elevate the mind to uncover the absolutes of the universe. Experimentalists believe in rational, scientific thinking to explore and frame the relevant knowledge of the times. However, the existentialists believe that this same rational thinking restricts humans from discovering existence and therefore keeps them ignorant.

This philosophy has roots in the writings of Sören Kierkegaard in the mid-nineteenth century. It has been popularized in drama and literature by such exponents as Albert Camus and Jean-Paul Sartre. The current popular cults of transcendental thinking, meditation, and introspection (knowing oneself) have a kinship with existentialism. The basic tenet of the philosophy is that the individual is the source of all reality. All that exists in the world is the meaning the individual puts on his or her own experiences. There is no absolute knowledge, no mechanical working of the universe, and no preordained logic. To believe in such inventions is merely the narrow, incorrect way humans interpret their own experiences.

Beyond the individual exists only chaos. The only reality that exists is one's own existence. Only by looking within oneself can one discern the truth of the outside disorder. Humanity is paramount. Human dignity and worth are of greatest importance; they are the source and dispenser of all truth. With this realization, one acquires a profound respect for all human beings and their uniqueness. Human relations become very important, affirming individual worth and protecting the individual's right to discover his or her own truth. Morality is the process of knowing oneself and allowing others the freedom to do likewise. Faith, intuition, mysticism, imagery, and transcendental experiences are all acceptable ways of discovery. Humans are totally free, not shaped by others or restricted by the flux of the times. They hold within themselves the capacity to form their own destiny.

This philosophy of education, applied to supervision, means a full commitment to individual teacher choice. The supervisor provides an environment that enables the teacher to explore his or her own physical and mental capabilities. Teachers must learn for themselves. The supervisor does not dispense information and shies away from intrusively guiding a teacher. Supervisors help when needed, protect the rights of others to self-discovery, and encounter the teacher as a person of full importance.

Table 5.2 compares the three superphilosophies.

Checking Your Own Supervisory Beliefs

Let's step back and watch ourselves at work. First, we consider how we act with individual teachers and then with groups. Read the Supervisory Interpersonal Behavior Questionnaire for Working with Individuals, and select the approach you most often take.

Next, take a look at the interpersonal behaviors you typically use when meeting with groups of teachers. Please respond to the Supervisory Interpersonal Behavior Questionnaire for Working with Groups on page 86.

TABLE 5.2 *Comparing Three Superphilosophies*

	Essentialism	*Experimentalism*	*Existentialism*
View of Reality (knowledge, truth, morality)	Exists outside of humans, absolute, unchanging	Reality is what works; it is tentative, constantly changing	Individual is source of all reality; individual defines reality
How to Learn about Reality	Train the mind to think rationally	Interact with environment; experiment	Engage in self-discovery; create meaning
Application to Supervision	Supervisor is expert; mechanistically transmits instructional knowledge to teacher	Supervisor works democratically with teachers to test old hypotheses and try new ones	Supervisor facilitates teacher exploration and autonomous decision making

---

BOX 5.1   Supervisory Interpersonal Behaviors Questionnaire for Working with Individuals: A Scenario

The school day has just ended for students at Whichway School. Just as the teacher sits down at the desk, you (the supervisor) appear at the door and the teacher invites you in. "How is everything going?" you ask. Looking at the large stack of papers to correct, the teacher predicts a number of them will reflect that the students did not understand the work. "It's very frustrating working with this class. They have such a wide range of abilities!" Then the teacher mentions another source of frustration: "Some of the students are discipline problems and their behavior results in class disruption."

After further discussion, the teacher and you agree that you will come into the classroom to observe what is going on, followed by a conference to discuss the classroom visit.

A few days later, after you have observed in the classroom and carefully analyzed the collected information, you begin to plan for the conference. You consider a number of

approaches to use in the conference to help the teacher.

Approach A.   Present what you saw in the classroom and ask for the teacher's perceptions. Listen to each other's responses. After clarifying the problem, each of you can propose ideas. Finally, you will agree on what is to be done in the classroom. You will mutually identify an objective and agree to an action plan that both of you will work together to carry out. The plan is for both of you to make.

Approach B.   Listen to the teacher discuss what is going on in the classroom. If asked, you offer your perceptions regarding what you observed. Encourage the teacher to analyze the problem further, and ask questions to make sure the teacher is clear about his or her view of the problem. If the teacher requests your views on how to proceed, respond, but only if asked. Finally, ask the teacher to determine and detail the actions he or she will take and find out if you might be of further help. The plan is the teacher's to make.

Approach C. Share your observations with the teacher and tell the teacher what you believe to be the major focus for improvement. Ask the teacher for input into your observations and interpretations. Based on your own experience and knowledge, carefully delineate what you believe are alternative actions to improve the classroom and ask the teacher to consider and select from the options. The plan to follow is chosen by the teacher from the supervisor's suggestions.

Approach D. Present your beliefs about the situation and ask the teacher to confirm or revise the interpretation. After identifying the problem, offer directions to the teacher on what should be done and how to proceed. You can go into the classroom to demonstrate what you are telling the teacher to do, or tell the teacher to observe another teacher who does well in this particular area. Praise and reward the teacher for following

the given assignment. The plan is for you the supervisor to make.

Response.

Most often, I use Approach ___A___ .

Interpretation.

Approach A: A cluster of *collaborative behaviors* in which the supervisor and teacher share the decision making about future improvement.

Approach B: A cluster of *nondirective behaviors* in which the supervisor helps the teacher formulate his or her own decisions about future improvement.

Approach C: A cluster of *directive informational behaviors* in which the supervisor frames the teacher's choices about future improvement.

Approach D: A cluster of *directive control behaviors* in which the supervisor makes the decision for the teacher.

Source: Adapted from an instrument developed by Katherine C. Ginkel, 1983. "An Overview of a Study Which Examined the Relationship between Elementary School Teachers' Preference for Supervisory Conferencing Approach and Conceptual Level of Development," a paper presented at the annual meeting of the American Educational Research Association, Montreal, April. Used with permission of Katherine C. Ginkel.

The supervisory approaches in the Supervisory Interpersonal Behaviors Questionnaires correspond to the philosophies of essentialism, experimentalism, and existentialism, and are labeled *directive* supervision, *collaborative* supervision, and *nondirective* supervision. Glickman and Tamashiro (1980) wrote:

> Directive Supervision is an approach based on the belief that teaching consists of technical skills with known standards and competencies for all teachers to be effective. The supervisor's role is to inform, direct, model, and assess those competencies.
>
> Collaborative Supervision is based on the belief that teaching is primarily problem solving, whereby two or more persons jointly pose hypotheses to a problem, experiment, and implement those teaching strategies that appear to be most relevant in their own surroundings. The supervisor's role is to guide the problem-solving process, be an active member of the interaction, and keep the teachers focused on their common problems.

You (the supervisor) have just called on the science teachers to decide on a policy for allowing students to use laboratory equipment outside of regular class time. Many students have complained about not having enough class time for doing their experiments. The issue is how and when to free up more laboratory time for students (before school, at lunchtime, during study hall, after school) under the supervision of certified teachers. How would you work with the science teachers to make a decision?

Approach A. Meet with the staff and explain that they need to decide what to do about this issue. Present the information you have about the problem and ask for clarification. Paraphrase what they say and, once the teachers verify your summary, ask them to decide among themselves what they are going to do. Remain in the meeting, helping to move the discussion along by calling on people, asking questions, and paraphrasing, but do not become involved in making your own position known or influencing the outcome in any conscious way.

Approach B. Meet with the staff by first explaining that you have to make a decision that will meet the needs of students, teachers, and supervisor. Either by consensus or, if not, then by majority vote, make a decision. You should listen, encourage, clarify, and reflect on each staff member's perception. Afterwards, ask each member, including yourself, to suggest possible solutions. Discuss each solution; prioritize the list; and, if no consensus emerges, call for a vote. Argue for your own solution, but go along with the group's decision.

Approach C. Meet with the staff and explain to them that you have thought of several permissible actions that could remedy this situation. You would like them to discuss and agree on which of these actions or combinations of actions they would like to implement. Lay out the alternatives, explain the advantages and disadvantages of each, and then allow the group to discuss and decide among your alternatives.

Approach D. Meet with the staff and tell them you want their feedback before you make a decision about the issue. Make it clear that the staff's involvement is to be advisory. Ask for their suggestions, listen, encourage, clarify, and paraphrase their ideas. After everyone has had a chance to speak, decide what changes should be made. Tell them what you are going to do, when the changes will be made, and that you expect them to carry out the plan.

Response.

Most often, I would use Approach ___B___.

Interpretation.

Approach A: A cluster of *nondirective behaviors* in which the supervisor assists the group to make its own decision

Approach B: A cluster of *collaborative behaviors* in which the supervisor works as part of the group in making a group decision.

Approach C: A cluster of *directive informational behaviors* in which the supervisor works as the framer of choices among which the group is to decide.

Approach D: A cluster of *directive control behaviors* in which the supervisor makes the decision for the group.

Source: Adapted from an instrument developed by Katherine C. Ginkel, 1983. "An Overview of a Study Which Examined the Relationship between Elementary School Teachers' Preference for Supervisory Conferencing Approach and Conceptual Level of Development," a paper presented at the annual meeting of the American Educational Research Association, Montreal, April. Used with permission of Katherine C. Ginkel.

Non-Directive Supervision has as its premise that learning is primarily a private experience in which individuals must come up with their own solutions to improving the classroom experience for students. The supervisor's role is to listen, be nonjudgmental, and provide self-awareness and clarification experiences for teachers. (p. 76)

What Does Your Belief Mean in Terms of Supervisor and Teacher Responsibility?

Beliefs about supervision can be thought of in terms of decision-making responsibility (see Table 5.3). An essentialist philosophy is premised on the supervisor being the expert on instruction and therefore having major decision-making responsibility. A situation of high supervisor responsibility and low teacher responsibility is labeled *directive supervision.* An experimentalist philosophy is premised on the supervisor and teachers being equal partners in instructional improvement; equal supervisor and teacher responsibility is labeled *collaborative supervision.* Existentialist philosophy is premised on teachers discovering their own capacities for instructional improvement. Low supervisor responsibility and high teacher responsibility is labeled *nondirective supervision.*

As we clarify our own educational philosophy and supervisory beliefs, we rarely find a pure ideological position. Therefore, Sergiovanni's idea of a supervisory platform becomes helpful. What combination of various philosophies and beliefs do we consider important? Perhaps our beliefs are mainly essentialist and directive yet contain parts of experimentalism and collaboration; or perhaps we have another combination of beliefs. A particular platform is not right or wrong; rather, it is an assessment of the bits and pieces we use to create the floor we stand on.

Where You Stand Depends on Where You Sit: Effects of Culture on Beliefs

Our cultural background is an important aspect of what we believe about education. There is a natural tendency for members of the dominant culture to support curriculum and instruction that will transmit that culture to students. Students from minority cultures, however, may find it difficult to adapt to curriculum and instruction intended to convey the dominant culture, possibly resisting (sometimes

TABLE 5.3   *Relationship of Philosophy, Control, and Supervisory Belief*

Educational Philosophy	*Decision-Making Responsibility*	*Supervisory Belief*
Essentialism	Supervisor high, teacher low	Directive
Experimentalism	Supervisor equal, teacher equal	Collaborative
Existentialism	Supervisor low, teacher high	Nondirective

passively, sometimes actively) the transmission of that culture. This is not just a question of an unfortunate mismatch between dominant and minority cultures that eventually will be overcome as minority cultures are assimilated. Schools that marginalize the cultures of particular students marginalize those students as well. What is especially insidious about such marginalization is that educators may not realize their partial responsibility for its occurrence.

Educators' beliefs about education often are influenced by cultural assumptions they may not be aware of because the assumptions are so deeply ingrained and taken for granted. These assumptions can influence the curriculum that educators design, their relationships with students and parents, the lessons they plan, and so forth. Because of the influences of our cultural assumptions and beliefs on students, it is not sufficient for us to simply articulate our beliefs and then base educational goals and practices on those beliefs. Rather, we should attempt to identify and critically examine our cultural assumptions. Such critique, often done in dialogue with others, can cause us to change assumptions that have negative effects on colleagues and students.

Identifying and critiquing cultural assumptions is not easy for individuals and schools to do. It usually is necessary to begin by examining our actions, cultural artifacts, and espoused beliefs, and then begin to search below the surface of those actions, artifacts, and beliefs for underlying assumptions. At the individual level, this might mean reflecting on questions like the following:

- Do I have more difficulty working with some cultural groups than others? If so, why?
- How congruent are my espoused beliefs and actions when working with cultural groups different from my own?
- How does my cultural background influence my expectations of and interactions with parents?
- How does my cultural background contribute to my perceptions of effective teaching?
- How does my cultural background affect my expectations of students in general? My expectations of different student groups?

The questions above provide entry points for critical reflection that can expand our understanding of cultural assumptions. Questions like the following can assist groups to critically examine cultural effects on the school as an organization:

- How does the dominant culture inform our goals as a school? How do other cultures contribute to our goals?
- How is the dominant culture represented in our curriculum, including textbooks and curriculum materials? Are other cultures reflected positively in our curriculum?
- How do our cultural beliefs affect the way students are grouped and placed in various programs in our school?
- How do our cultural beliefs affect the school's disciplinary practices?
- How do our cultural beliefs affect the way we assess student learning?

- How do our cultural beliefs affect the way we interact with our students' families?

Another catalyst for changing beliefs is a better understanding of cultures different than our own, whether by reading literature about other cultures and about multicultural education, dialogue with students and colleagues from other cultures, interaction with parents and community members from different cultures in various community settings, or sharing of educational and leadership roles within the school with representatives of various cultures. Better understanding of cultures, especially when achieved through interaction with those cultures, can overcome personal bias, change educational beliefs, and ultimately inform a different and more diverse educational practice.

SUMMARY

We have examined the relationship of educational philosophy to supervisory belief and practice. You were asked to define what is meant by good and effective schools and teaching effectiveness and then to determine your own supervisory platform. We believe teachers will become collectively purposeful as they gain greater control over decisions for instructional improvement.

The following propositions about supervision that will enhance collective teacher actions are now possible:

- Proposition 1: *Supervisors should use a variety of practices that emanate from various philosophies and belief structures with developmental directionality in mind.* Directive, collaborative, and nondirective supervisory approaches are all valid as long as they aim to increase teacher self-control.
- Proposition 2: *As supervisors gradually increase teacher choice and control over instructional improvement, teachers will become more reflective and committed to improvement, and a sense of ethos or of a cause beyond oneself will emerge.*

Allowing for gradual choice will increase teacher abstraction and autonomy and lead to more altruistic, collective faculty action.

REFERENCES AND RECOMMENDED READINGS

Airasian, P. W., and Walsh, M. E. 1997. Constructivist cautions. *Phi Delta Kappan, 78*(6), 444–449.

Council of Professors of Instructional Supervision 1988. *Resolution on effective teaching.* Annual meeting, San Antonio, November.

Gardner, H. 1999. *Intelligence reframed: Multiple intelligences for the 21st century.* New York: Basic Books.

Ginkel, K. C. 1983. *An overview of a study which examined the relationship between elementary school teachers' preference for supervisory conferencing approach and conceptual level of development.* Paper presented at the American Educational Research Association, Montreal, Canada, April.

Glickman, C. D. 1987a. Good and/or effective schools: What do we want? *Phi Delta Kappan, 68*(8), 622–624.

Glickman, C. D. 1987b. Unlocking school reform: Uncertainty as a condition of professionalism. *Phi Delta Kappan, 69*(2), 120–122.

Glickman, C. D., and Tamashiro, R. T. 1980. Determining one's beliefs regarding teacher supervision. *Bulletin, 64*(440), 74–81.

Glickman, C. D., and Tamashiro, R. T. 1981. The supervisory beliefs inventory. In C. D. Glickman, *Developmental supervision: Alternative practices for helping teachers to improve instruction* (pp. 12–16). Alexandria, VA: Association for Supervision and Curriculum Development.

Hardison, O. B., Jr. 1986. A tree, a streamlined fish, and a self squared dragon: Science as a form of culture. *Georgia Review* (Summer), 394–403.

Humphries, J. D. 1981. Factors affecting the impact of curriculum innovation on classroom practice. Unpublished Ph.D. dissertation, University of Georgia.

Johnson, J. A., Collins, H. W., Dupuis, V. L., and Johansen, J. H. 1973. *Foundations of American education.* Boston: Allyn and Bacon.

Joyce, B., and Calhoun, E. 1994. Lessons in learning. *American School Board Journal, 81*(12), 37–40.

Joyce, B., Showers, B., and Rolheiser-Bennett, C. 1987. Staff development and student learning: A synthesis of research on models of teaching. *Educational Leadership, 45*(2), 11–23.

Joyce, B., and Weil, M. 1986. *Models of teaching.* Englewood Cliffs, NJ: Prentice Hall.

McLaughlin, M. W., and Marsh, D. D. 1978. Staff development and school change. *Teacher College Record, 80*(1), 69–74.

Morris, V. C. 1961. *Philosophy and the American school.* Boston: Houghton Mifflin.

Null, J. W. 2004. Is constructivism traditional? Historical and practical perspectives on a popular advocacy. *The Educational Forum, 68*(2), 180–188.

Ornstein, A. C. 1990. A look at teacher effectiveness research: Theory and practice. *NASSP Bulletin, 74*(528), 78–88.

Pratte, R. 1971. *Contemporary theories of education.* Scranton, PA: T. Y. Crowell.

Sergiovanni, T. J., and Starrat, R. J. 1983. *Supervision: Human perspectives* (3rd ed.) (pp. 226–227). New York: McGraw-Hill.

Showers, B. 1990. Aiming for superior classroom instruction for all children: A comprehensive staff development model. *Remedial and Special Education, 7*(3), 35–39.

Vanezky, R. L. 1982. *Effective schools for reading instructions.* Address to the California (Calfee) Reading Project, Stanford University, January.

PART III

Interpersonal Skills

The organization of this book was outlined in Figure 1.1 (Chapter 1). The prerequisites for supervision as a developmental function are knowledge, interpersonal skills, and technical skills. Part II examined the critical knowledge base. Part III will describe interpersonal skills, beginning in Chapter 6, which introduces the supervisory behavior continuum. Chapter 7 will introduce the theory of developmental supervision, and Chapter 8 will detail the use of directive control behaviors. Chapter 9 addresses directive informational behaviors, Chapter 10 discusses the use of collaborative behaviors, while Chapter 11 focuses on nondirective behaviors. Finally, Chapter 12 will discuss in detail the theory and practice of developmental supervision.

Knowledge of what needs to be done for teacher growth and school success is the base of a triangle for supervisory action (see Figure III.1). Knowledge needs to be accompanied by interpersonal skills for communicating with teachers and technical skills for planning, assessing, observing, and evaluating instructional improvement. We will now turn to understanding interpersonal skills in the context of educational supervision.

FIGURE III.1 *Prerequisite Dimensions for a Supervisor*

6

Supervisory Behavior Continuum

Know Thyself

This chapter looks at the range of interpersonal behaviors available to a supervisor who is working with individuals and groups of teachers. It will assess how supervisors typically behave with staff in school settings and then determine other behaviors that might be used skillfully and effectively. Later chapters will provide training in each of four clusters of interpersonal skills.

What are the categories of behaviors? After many years of collecting supervisors' observations in meetings with individuals and groups of teachers for purposes of making classroom or school decisions, broad categories of supervisory behaviors have been derived (Glickman, 1981, 2002; Wolfgang and Glickman, 1980). These categories encompass almost all observed supervisor behaviors that are deemed purposeful. A *purposeful* behavior is defined as one that contributes to the decision being made at the conference or meeting. The derived categories of supervisory behaviors are listening, clarifying, encouraging, reflecting, presenting, problem solving, negotiating, directing, standardizing, and reinforcing. Definitions of each category are as follows:

- *Listening:* The supervisor sits and looks at the speaker and nods his or her head to show understanding. Gutteral utterances ("uh-huh," "umm") also indicate listening.
- *Clarifying:* The supervisor asks questions and statements to clarify the speaker's point of view: "Do you mean that?" "Would you explain this further?" "I'm confused about this." "I lost you on. . . ."

- *Encouraging:* The supervisor provides acknowledging responses that help the speaker continue to explain his or her positions: "Yes, I'm following you." "Continue on." "Ah, I see what you're saying; tell me more."
- *Reflecting:* The supervisor summarizes and paraphrases the speaker's message for verification of accuracy: "I understand that you mean . . ." "So, the issue is . . ." "I hear you saying . . ."
- *Presenting:* The supervisor gives his or her own ideas about the issue being discussed: "This is how I see it." "What can be done is . . ." "I'd like us to consider . . ." "I believe that . . ."
- *Problem solving:* The supervisor takes the initiative, usually after a preliminary discussion of the issue or problem, in pressing all those involved to generate a list of possible solutions. This is usually done through statements such as: "Let's stop and each write down what can be done." "What ideas do we have to solve this problem?" "Let's think of all possible actions we can take."
- *Negotiating:* The supervisor moves the discussion from possible to probable solutions by discussing the consequences of each proposed action, exploring conflict or priorities, and narrowing down choices with questions such as: "Where do we agree?" "How can we change that action to be acceptable to all?" "Can we find a compromise that will give each of us part of what we want?"
- *Directing:* The supervisor tells the participant(s) what the choices are: "As I see it, these are the alternatives: You could do A . . . , B . . . , or C . . . Which of these make the most sense to you and which will you use?" *Or* the supervisor tells the participants what is to be done: "I've decided that we will do . . ." "I want you to do . . ." "The policy will be . . ." "This is how it is going to be." "We will then proceed as follows."
- *Standardizing:* The supervisor sets the expected criteria and time for the decision to be implemented. Target objectives are set. Expectations are conveyed with words, such as: "By next Monday, we want to see . . ." "Report back to me on this change by . . ." "Have the first two activities carried out by . . ." "I want an improvement of 25 percent involvement

1	2	3	4	5
Listening	Clarifying	Encouraging	Reflecting	Presenting

T _____

s

Clusters of behaviors: Nondirective

Key: T = Maximum teacher responsibility   S = Maximum supervisor responsibility
         t = Minimum teacher responsibility   s = Minimum supervisor responsibility

FIGURE 6.1 *The Supervisory Behavior Continuum*

by the next meeting." "We have agreed that all tasks will be done before the next observation."

- *Reinforcing:* The supervisor strengthens the directive and the criteria to be met by telling of possible consequences. Possible consequences can be positive, in the form of praise: "I know you can do it!" "I have confidence in your ability!" "I want to show others what you've done!" Consequences also can be negative: "If it's not done on time, we'll lose the support of . . ." "It must be understood that failure to get this done on time will result in . . ."

The foregoing categories of interpersonal supervisory behavior move participants toward a decision. Some supervisory behaviors place more responsibility on the teacher(s) to make the decision, others place more responsibility on the supervisor to make the decision, and still others indicate a shared responsibility for decision making. The categories of behaviors are listed in a sequence on the supervisory behavior continuum (Figure 6.1) to reflect the scale of control or power.

When a supervisor *listens* to the teacher, *clarifies* what the teacher says, *encourages* the teacher to speak more about the concern, and *reflects* by verifying the teacher's perceptions, then clearly it is the teacher who is in control. The supervisor's role is that of an active prober or sounding board for the teacher to make his or her own decision. The teacher has high control and the supervisor low control over the actual decision (big *T*, small *s*). This is seen as a *nondirective interpersonal approach.*

When a supervisor uses nondirective behaviors to understand the teacher's point of view but then participates in the discussion by *presenting* his or her own ideas, *problem solving* by asking all parties to propose possible actions, and then *negotiating* to find a common course of action satisfactory to teacher and supervisor, then the control over the decision is shared by all. This is viewed as a *collaborative interpersonal approach.*

When a supervisor *directs* the teacher in what the alternatives are from which the teacher might choose, and after the teacher selects, the supervisor *standardizes* the time and criteria of expected results, then the supervisor is the major

6 Problem Solving	7 Negotiating	8 Directing	9 Standardizing	10 Reinforcing

t

S

| Collaborative | | Directive Informational | Directive Control | |

FIGURE 6.1 *Continued*

source of information, providing the teacher with restricted choice (small *t*, big *S*). This is viewed as a *directive informational interpersonal approach.*

Finally, when a supervisor *directs* the teacher in what will be done, *standardizes* the time and criteria of expected results, and *reinforces* the consequences of action or inaction, then the supervisor has taken responsibility for the decision. (small *t*, big *S*). The supervisor is clearly determining the actions for the teacher to follow. These behaviors are called a *directive control interpersonal approach.*

Outcomes of Conference

Another way of clarifying the distinctions among supervisory approaches is by looking at the outcomes of the conference and determining who controls the final decision for instructional improvement.

Approach	*Outcome*
Nondirective	Teacher self-plan
Collaborative	Mutual plan
Directive informational	Supervisor-suggested plan
Directive control	Supervisor-assigned plan

In the nondirective approach, the supervisor facilitates the teacher's thinking in developing a self-plan. In the collaborative approach, both supervisor and teacher share information and possible practices as equals in arriving at a mutual plan. In the directive informational approach, the supervisor provides the focus and the parameters of possible actions, and the teacher is asked to choose within the supervisor's suggestions. In the directive control approach, the supervisor tells the teacher what is to be done. Nondirective provides maximum teacher choice; collaborative, mutual choice; directive informational, selected choice; and directive control, no choice in the outcome of the conference.

Valid Assessment of Self

As a school principal in New Hampshire, one of the authors regarded himself as operating a successful school and being accessible to teachers. He could document success by external evidence—state and national recognition the school had received and complimentary letters from numerous visitors. He documented his accessibility through casual discussions with teachers in the lounge and by having an open-office policy for every staff member who wished to speak with him. In his third year as a principal at this particular school, the superintendent asked all principals in the school system to allow teachers to evaluate principal performance. One item on the evaluation form was "Ability to Listen to Others," followed by a numerical scale of responses from 1 ("rarely listens") to 7 ("almost always listens"). Before giving the form to teachers, the author filled out the same evaluation form according to his own perception of his performance. He confidently circled the number 7 on "ability to listen." Once the teachers' responses were collected and results were received, he was amazed to find that the lowest teacher rating on the entire survey was on that very item on which he had rated himself highest. To the author's chagrin, there was an obvious discrepancy between his own perception of performance and staff perceptions.

Johari Window

The Johari Window (Luft, 1970; Janas, 2001) provides a graphic way to look at what we know and do not know about our behavior (see Figure 6.2). Visualize a window with four windowpanes. In this scheme, there are four windowpanes of the self in which behaviors are either known or not known by self (the supervisor) and others (the teachers). In windowpane 1, there are behaviors that both supervisor and teachers know the supervisor uses. This is the *public self*. For example, the supervisor knows that when he or she is anxious, speech will become halting and hesitant; teachers are also aware of what such speech indicates.

In windowpane 2 is the *blind self*—behaviors the supervisor practices that are unknown to the self but are known to teachers. For example, as a school principal, one of the authors was displaying behaviors toward teachers that he thought were listening behaviors, but teachers saw the same behaviors as a failure to listen. Of course, once one becomes aware of teachers' perceptions of those behaviors, the blind self becomes the public self.

In windowpane 3 is the *private self*—behaviors the supervisor has knowledge about but that teachers do not know. For instance, in new situations a supervisor might mask his or her unsureness by being extroverted in greeting others. Only the supervisor knows that this behavior is covering up insecurity; once the supervisor discloses this perception to others, the private self becomes public.

Finally, there is windowpane 4, the *unknown self*. There are actions a supervisor takes of which both supervisors and teachers are unaware. From time to time the supervisor might rapidly shift his legs while speaking behind a table.

	Known to Supervisor	Not Known to Supervisor
Known to Teachers	1. Public self	2. Blind self
Not Known to Teachers	3. Private self	4. Unknown self

FIGURE 6.2 *Adaptation of Johari Window*

Source: Adapted from Joseph Luft, *Group Processes: An Introduction to Group Dynamics* (New York: National Press Books, 1970).

Neither supervisor or teachers are aware of this leg movement. Perhaps a supervisor becomes irritated while a certain teacher is speaking. The supervisor may not know why she is irritated or even that she feels this way, and the teacher may not know either. The unknown self is unconscious to all; it becomes private, blind, or public only by circumstances that create a new awareness.

What does the Johari Window have to do with supervision? We cannot become more effective as supervisors unless we know what we are doing. We may, at our discretion, decide to keep parts of ourselves private. (For example, we may not want teachers to know all the details of our life and personality.) Yet we need to understand that by remaining largely private and not sharing the experiences that bind us as humans, we are creating a distance when we work with teachers. We may prefer formality and distance and may be able to document that such privateness accomplishes certain results. On the other hand, we must also accept that our privateness will be reciprocal, and that staff may not easily discuss personal situations that may affect teaching performance. First, we must be aware of how private or public we are with our staff and determine if we desire teachers to be the same way with us. Second, as supervisors, we cannot afford to be blind to our own behaviors and the effect of those behaviors on others. We can improve only what we know; to believe only our own self-perceptions is to court disaster.

The author's perception of his listening behavior as a principal is a case in point. As long as he saw himself as a wonderful, accessible listener, it did not seem probable that teachers were not coming to him with instructional problems. However, he discovered that on two different occasions teachers had gone to the superintendent about instructional problems of which he was unaware. After the superintendent had told him that teachers were going over his head, he angrily confronted the teachers with their "unprofessional" behavior. It did not occur to the author that he might have been the one at fault. After the staff evaluations, he could no longer delude himself. Many teachers were not telling him their concerns because they did not believe that he would really listen. The author had to face the fact that the staff did not see him as accessible. He might have avoided collecting such information, continued with his euphoric self-perception, and then been devastated as the school fell apart.

Cognitive Dissonance

Invalidity of perceptions creates *cognitive dissonance,* according to a model of motivation by psychologist Leon Festinger (1957). The model is based on the premise that a person cannot live with contradictory psychological evidence—that is, thinking of himself or herself in one way while other sources of information indicate that he or she is different. When the author's perception of his listening abilities were contradicted by teacher perceptions, mental turmoil or cognitive dissonance was created. For example, if you believe that you are a collaborative supervisor and then you receive feedback from teachers that you are a directive supervisor, this will cause cognitive dissonance. We must wrestle with disparate perceptions and reconcile them. If not, the two differing sources of information will continue to bother us. This mental anguish strives to resolve the question of what is it that we really do. The resolution can come about in three alternative ways (Hyman, 1975).

First, we can dismiss the source of contrary evidence as biased and untrue. For example, the principal might rationalize, "I really am a good listener; teachers marked me low because they didn't like the way I scheduled bus duties." Or the supervisor might think he or she really is collaborative: "Teachers simply don't understand what collaboration is." By dismissing the other source of information as erroneous, we can continue to believe that we are what we originally thought. No further change is necessary.

Second, we can change our own self-perception to conform to the other source of information and can then live with the new perception of ourselves. We accept that they are right and we are wrong; thus, our perception will now be theirs. For example, "I really was wrong about my listening abilities, and I now reconcile myself to being a poor listener," or "The supervisor is really not collaborative but instead is, as the teachers say, directive." Accepting the other source of information makes dissonance vanish so that no further change is necessary.

Third, we can accept our original self-perception as how we wish to be perceived, use the other source of information as an indicator of how we are currently perceived, and then change our behaviors to be more similar to our wish. In other words, our perception was not accurate, but it still represents what we want to be. In our example, the author thought he was a good listener, but others said that he was not; so he attempted to change his listening behaviors in order to become a good listener. The supervisor who claimed to be collaborative was made aware that others saw a directive style, and so changed behavior to become more collaborative.

The third alternative to resolving cognitive dissonance creates behavioral change. Whenever we have an idea of how we desire to be matched against the reality of how others see us, there exist conditions for individual change. The acknowledged gap between what is and what should be becomes a powerful stimulus to change. We change our behaviors and gather feedback from others to determine whether others are forming new perceptions of us and more positive results are forthcoming.

Comparing Self-Perceptions with Others' Perceptions

Box 6.1 provides an instrument that the supervisor uses to compare self-perceptions with teacher perceptions of supervisor performance. The *Supervisor Self-Assessment* is divided into four sections: "Professional Characteristics," "Skills," "Individual Assistance," and "Schoolwide Assistance," and yields a subscore for each section. The process of self-assessment begins with the supervisor completing and self-scoring the instrument. It is important to be totally open when completing the self-assessment, so as a general rule the supervisor should not be expected to share results with superiors or teachers. The supervisor next distributes the instrument to the teachers or a randomly selected sample of the teachers he or she supervises. It's important that the teachers complete and return the instruments anonymously.

BOX **6.1**   Supervisor Self-Assessment

Directions for Completing: Place next to each item a number (1, 2, 3, or 4) identifying the response that most nearly indicates your level of agreement with the item:

1. Strongly disagree
2. Disagree
3. Agree
4. Strongly agree

Section A: Professional Characteristics

___ 1. The supervisor is genuinely concerned with the growth and development of students.
___ 2. The supervisor is genuinely concerned with the growth and development of teachers.
___ 3. The supervisor is trustworthy.
___ 4. The supervisor treats teachers fairly.
___ 5. The supervisor is flexible.
___ 6. The supervisor is ethical.

Section B: Skills

___ 7. The supervisor displays communication skills.
___ 8. The supervisor displays needs assessment skills.
___ 9. The supervisor displays planning skills.
___ 10. The supervisor displays group facilitation skills.
___ 11. The supervisor displays problem-solving skills.
___ 12. The supervisor displays change agency skills.
___ 13. The supervisor displays observation skills.
___ 14. The supervisor displays conflict resolution skills.

Section C: Individual Assistance

___ 15. The supervisor effectively observes teaching and provides helpful feedback.
___ 16. The supervisor provides useful instructional resources.

___ 17. The supervisor fosters teacher reflection.
___ 18. The supervisor demonstrates effective teaching.
___ 19. The supervisor shares innovative instructional strategies.
___ 20. The supervisor effectively assists beginning teachers.
___ 21. The supervisor effectively assists teachers with instructional problems they are experiencing.
___ 22. The supervisor effectively assists teachers to plan for instruction.
___ 23. The supervisor effectively assists teachers to assess student learning.
___ 24. The supervisor effectively assists teachers to individualize instruction.

Section D: Schoolwide Assistance

___ 25. The supervisor effectively facilitates instructional dialogue among teachers.
___ 26. The supervisor fosters a positive school culture.
___ 27. The supervisor facilitates collective vision building.
___ 28. The supervisor fosters teacher collaboration for schoolwide instructional improvement.
___ 29. The supervisor fosters teacher empowerment.
___ 30. The supervisor effectively facilitates teachers' professional development.
___ 31. The supervisor effectively facilitates curriculum development.
___ 32. The supervisor effectively facilitates program evaluation.

Directions for Scoring: For the instrument completed by the supervisor, add the ratings for the items in each section to find subtotals. The range of possible subtotals for each section follows:

Section A: Professional Characteristics, from 6–24.

Section B: Skills, from 8–32.

Section C: Individual Assistance, from 10–40.

Section D: Schoolwide Assistance, from 8–32.

The overall rating (the sum of the four subtotals) ranges from 32 to 128.

For the instrument completed by teachers, calculate the mean scores for each item, section, and the overall rating. For example, if five teachers responded to the same item with ratings of 2, 3, 4, 4, and 5 respectively, the teachers mean rating for that item would be 3.6. For an example at the section level, if the subtotals on Section A from five teachers were 16, 18, 19, 21, and 22, the mean ratings for Section A would be 19.2. For the overall mean, if individual overall ratings by five teachers were 83, 92, 100, 112, and 118, the overall mean for teacher ratings would be 101.

After calculating item, section, and overall means of teacher responses, the supervisor can compare self-perceptions with teacher perceptions. When comparing self-ratings to teacher ratings on any particular item, the supervisor can reach a variety of conclusions.

1. Supervisor and teacher satisfaction with supervisor performance
2. Supervisor satisfaction and teacher dissatisfaction with supervisor performance
3. Supervisor dissatisfaction and teacher satisfaction with supervisor performance
4. Supervisor and teacher dissatisfaction with supervisor performance

Any of the last three conclusions can spur the supervisor to define improvement objectives and design action plans for enhancing instructional assistance.

Comparing Self-Perceptions with Recorded Behaviors

Another approach to cognitive dissonance as a catalyst for improving supervisory practice is comparing supervisor self-perceptions to data on actual behaviors. If a key supervisory process is to gather data on teacher classroom behaviors to assist instructional improvement, it makes sense for the supervisor to similarly analyze data on her or his own performance for the purpose of improved supervision. Data gathering while the supervisor is interacting with individual teachers or groups can be accomplished in a number of ways. Other supervisory personnel can observe a conference or meeting conducted by a supervisor and gather requested data. The supervisor or other personnel can tape a supervisory conference or meeting and review the recording for personal assessment or in collaboration with others. The supervisor can analyze documents that reflect supervisory behaviors, such as e-mails, memos, and observation reports that she or he has prepared to compare the supervisor's perceptions to recorded behaviors. Comparing perceptions to data can create cognitive dissonance as did the comparison of supervisor and teacher perceptions discussed previously. In fact, comparing supervisor perceptions to hard data may cause stronger cognitive dissonance than comparing supervisor perceptions to teacher perceptions, leading even more readily to changes in supervisory behaviors.

What types of data on supervisory performance should be gathered and analyzed? Data might be gathered on interpersonal behaviors in general. For example, in an attempted collaborative approach, are collaborative behaviors in evidence, or does the supervisor slip into directive or nondirective behaviors? Data also can be used to compare supervisory behaviors with different groups. Does the supervisor treat men and women differently? Hispanics and Whites? Younger and older teachers? If so, why is one group treated differently from the other? If equity is an educational goal, then equitable treatment of teachers by supervisors should be a model for teachers and students. By recording and analyzing supervisory behaviors through the lens of equity, the supervisor can recognize problems in this area and begin to improve her or his own performance.

SUMMARY

This chapter outlined the supervisory behavior continuum and the clustering of interpersonal behaviors into nondirective, collaborative, directive informational, and directive control approaches. Three assessment instruments were provided. A discourse on the Johari Window and cognitive dissonance was given so that we might check the perceptions of our beliefs and behaviors by those who are recipients of our behaviors. To compare our own supervisory beliefs and self-perceived interpersonal behavior with teacher perceptions of our behavior or with objective data is believed to be important in refining and changing behaviors.

We will next examine and practice the skills of each supervisory approach in terms of actual conferencing and meeting behaviors. Understanding how we behave as supervisors and then refining our present behaviors are the first steps toward acquiring new interpersonal skills.

REFERENCES AND RECOMMENDED READINGS

Festinger, L. 1957. *A theory of cognitive dissonance.* Stanford, CA: Stanford University Press.

Glickman, C. D. 1981. *Developmental supervision: Alternative practices for helping teachers improve instruction.* Alexandria, VA: Association for Supervision and Curriculum Development.

Glickman, C. D. 2002. *Leadership for learning: How to help teachers succeed.* Alexandria, VA: Association for Supervision and Curriculum Development.

Hyman, R. T. 1975. *School administrator's handbook of teacher supervision and evaluation methods* (pp. 46–47). Englewood Cliffs, NJ: Prentice Hall.

Janas, M. 2001. Getting a clear view. *Journal of Staff Development,* 22(2), 32–34.

Luft, J. 1970. *Group processes: An introduction to group dynamics.* New York: National Press Books.

Wolfgang, C. H., and Glickman, C. D. 1980. *Solving discipline problems: Alternative strategies for teachers.* Boston: Allyn and Bacon.

Developmental Supervision

An Introduction

This chapter provides an introduction to developmental supervision—a model that will be described in greater detail throughout the remainder of the text. We begin by sharing four case studies of developmental supervision in action. As you read the four case studies, compare them in relation to the following:

1. The teacher's levels of development, expertise, and commitment to solving the problem
2. The nature of the problem
3. The interpersonal behaviors of the supervisor, including any shifts in supervisory behavior that take place

Case Study One

After receiving complaints about Gerald Watson's teaching methods from students, parents, and other teachers, principal Martha Cozero observed Gerald's science class on several occasions. Regardless of lesson content or student population, all of the observed lessons followed the same pattern. First, seat by seat and row by row, students would take turns reading paragraphs from the science text. Next, Gerald would pass out a worksheet for students to complete independently. If students finished their worksheets before the end of class, they were told to begin their homework assignment, which always consisted of written exercises from the textbook. During independent seatwork, Gerald usually sat at his desk reading sports magazines, looking up only to give an "evil-eye" to students who were talking to each other or out of their seats.

Martha was not surprised by Gerald's "instructional" routine. She *was* surprised that he made no attempt at more active teaching even during her classroom observations. Martha used the first of several conferences with Gerald to try to find out more about his attitudes toward teaching science. He admitted that he rarely graded or returned the written assignments that he required students to complete. Gerald stated that he neither understood nor used the hands-on science program that the middle school science team had agreed to adopt the previous year. He had not attended the science team's after-school meetings that led to the decision to adopt the program. He had taken personal days rather than attend the all-day workshops during which science teachers developed skills necessary to implement the program. Gerald told Martha that he was six years away from retirement and saw no reason to learn new skills or use new teaching methods.

After reflecting on her classroom observations and conference with Gerald, Martha designed an improvement plan that she presented to him during their next conference. During that conference, she told Gerald that his current instructional strategies and failure to learn about or implement the school's science program were detrimental to student learning and that his approach to teaching science was unacceptable. She stated that Gerald's improvement goals would be to engage in more active teaching and make use of instructional strategies consistent with the science curriculum's goals. Martha mandated the following steps on Gerald's part:

1. End excessive reliance on students taking turns reading aloud from the science text
2. Reduce the use of worksheets as a primary instructional strategy
3. Review written assignments completed by students, providing students with feedback on their performance
4. Review the school district's written curriculum as well as teacher guides for the school's hands-on science program
5. Visit other science teachers' classrooms to observe the science program in action
6. Use more hands-on science activities consistent with the adopted science program

The principal made it clear that the goals and activities she presented were not optional. Martha listened to Gerald's concerns and answered questions about the action plan. She promised to provide him with resources and materials necessary to implement the new science program. Martha scheduled a series of classroom observations that would allow her to monitor Gerald's progress with the plan and provide him with assistance and feedback on the new instructional strategies he would be trying out.

Gerald reluctantly began to implement the mandated improvement plan. Although progress was slow, his teaching methods did begin to change. Some of Gerald's attempts at hands-on learning worked well, others did not. Students were enjoying the hands-on activities and demonstrating levels of interest and learning that Gerald had not thought possible. Eventually, he admitted to Martha that missing the workshops on the new curriculum had been a mistake. There were many gaps in his knowledge of the new curriculum that his readings and observations had not filled.

Martha decided that Gerald needed formal training in how to implement the science program if he was going to continue to improve his teaching. She also decided that the effort and progress he had made warranted allowing Gerald some choice in how that training should be acquired. Martha offered Gerald three options for learning more about the program: attendance at two days of in-service education on the program offered by the program's publisher at a nearby intermediate unit, after-school workshops to be presented by the science supervisor at the district's other middle school, or individualized training by Jim Adams, the science coordinator at Gerald's middle school. Gerald had always liked Jim so he told Martha that he preferred to receive training from a colleague just down the hall whom he could call on if he had problems implementing the curriculum. Jim agreed to work with Gerald, and Martha and Jim designed a plan to provide Gerald with several hours of individualized training and intensive classroom coaching.

Case Study Two

Veteran teacher Bill Levin was assigned as mentor to beginning teacher Janice Smith. Janice had joined the middle school teaching staff eager to try out a variety of innovative teaching strategies she had been introduced to during her teacher preparation program. Now, just two months into her teaching career, Janice was considering leaving the profession at the Thanksgiving break. After a few observations of Janice's teaching, Bill was convinced that Janice had considerable potential as a teacher, but that her classroom management problems might prevent her from reaching that potential. Although Janice had been exposed to brief discussions of student discipline problems in several of her teaching methods courses, she had never received systematic training in effective classroom management. Her lack of training and inexperience in dealing with middle school students was becoming increasingly apparent. On several visits to Janice's classroom, Bill observed considerable off-task behavior and numerous student disruptions. Rather than attempting to control the high noise level, Janice would first try to yell over the student conversations, then scream at disruptive students who had ignored her pleas to quiet down.

Janice knew she had classroom management problems but was not sure why the students behaved the way they did, or what she could do to improve the situation. Based on his observations and discussions with Janice, Bill made the following suggestions to the novice teacher:

1. Establish a set of rules and procedures for classroom behavior and determine natural consequences for students who fail to follow those rules and procedures
2. Share the rules and procedures with the students, explaining the rationale for each rule, procedure, and natural consequence
3. Give the students the opportunity to practice each rule and procedure under simulated conditions and provide them with feedback on their performance
4. Consistently enforce all rules and procedures, providing positive feedback for student compliance and carrying through on natural consequences for noncompliance

Bill offered to help Janice develop her rules and procedures, rehearse her presentation and explanation to students, and plan opportunities for students to practice new guidelines and receive feedback on their performance. Bill also suggested that Janice try out a number of nonverbal and verbal interventions to correct minor student misbehaviors before they reached a disruptive stage. He explained how in his own classroom he used nonverbal interventions such as eye contact, physical proximity, and touch control, as well as verbal interventions such as use of students' names, reminder of a rule or procedure, and explicit redirection. Bill invited Janice to visit his classroom and observe his classroom management techniques. He also offered to observe Janice's class as she implemented his suggested strategies and techniques, and to provide her with feedback based on the observations.

Janice agreed to try out Bill's recommendations. With considerable assistance from her mentor, she implemented the suggested strategies and techniques. After several weeks, most of the students in Janice's class had increased their amount of time on task considerably and student disruptions had decreased. Janice had made it through to Thanksgiving and was willing to give teaching another chance, at least until the end of the school year. She was still experiencing some problems with classroom management, particularly with three students who regularly ignored the rules and procedures she had set up, seemingly unaffected by the natural consequences intended to discourage disruptive behavior. Janice informed Bill that the classroom management system, although generally effective, had failed with these three students.

Bill was pleased with the progress Janice had made but concerned about the students who seemed to be immune to his protégée's new classroom management strategies and techniques. He knew that even a few students could disrupt Janice's entire class if she was unable to help them change their behavior. The mentor offered two possibilities for dealing with the three disruptive students. One was for Janice to work individually with each of the problem students to develop a behavior contract. In the contract, teacher and student would negotiate specific behavioral improvement goals, a time period for meeting the goals, teacher and student actions, assessment of student progress, and rewards and consequences.

The second possibility suggested by Bill was that Janice keep daily logs of disruptive behaviors by each of the three students. The initial record keeping would last for a period of two weeks, with the students required to sign log entries each day. At the end of the two-week period, Janice could assign the three students individual improvement plans aimed at reducing the types of behaviors recorded in the logs. Once the plan was initiated, Janice could record both positive and disruptive student behaviors in the logs in order to document student progress toward improvement goals.

When Bill asked Janice to select one of the two options, she asked if it would be agreeable to use parts of both strategies by first logging student behaviors for two weeks and then negotiating a behavioral contract with each of the three students. Bill agreed that this would be an appropriate synthesis of the two strategies. He offered to assist Janice in reviewing the log entries and writing the three behavioral contracts—an offer that Janice readily accepted.

Case Study Three

Social studies teacher Mike Phillips had requested a conference with George Cantinni, his department chairperson. Mike was not satisfied with the quality of discussions in his current events class. George asked Mike to describe the type of class discussions he wanted to take place. Mike replied that he wanted to foster students' "higher-level" thinking and open dialogue concerning important social and political issues. When George asked Mike what was preventing such discussion, he replied that he probably hindered class discussions himself by asking too many simple recall questions rather than questions that would spark student interest and discussion. Another problem Mike discussed was that typically only a few students participated in class discussions, and he had done little to encourage those who did not participate to join in.

Based on Mike's description of the problem, George suggested that changes in the way Mike structured class discussions might be in order. He proposed that Mike and he take a few minutes to write down ideas for improvement separately. After both had reflected on and listed potential actions, George asked Mike to share his ideas. Mike's possible actions included asking students more open-ended questions, giving the entire class more time to think about a question before calling on one of the students to respond, and randomly calling on students in order to increase student participation. George responded that he agreed with the first two suggestions. He added that while randomly calling on students to respond was appropriate in some situations, he did not believe that it was a viable way to foster the open, reflective dialogue that Mike was hoping for.

George introduced additional possible actions by building on ideas already suggested by Mike. He suggested that Mike refer to the upper five categories of

Bloom's taxonomy when planning discussion lessons, first to help determine the lesson's objectives and then to formulate relevant discussion questions. George reviewed Bloom's cognitive domain, which Mike vaguely recalled from his undergraduate years. To Mike's idea of giving the class time to think about questions before responding to them, George added the option of allowing students to discuss questions in small groups prior to whole-class discussion. Finally, George suggested that during whole-class discussions the class as well as individual students be provided adequate "wait time" to formulate their responses and that appropriate wait time also *follow* individual student responses.

Mike responded that he liked the idea of basing learning objectives and discussion questions on Bloom's taxonomy, but thought he might have trouble formulating the different types of questions. He asked George if he would be willing to help develop some questions for Mike's next few lessons. George agreed, and also offered to observe a few of Mike's lessons in order to record the number of questions asked within each category of Bloom's taxonomy. Mike replied that he would appreciate the feedback. Regarding George's suggestion of beginning discussions with small groups, Mike stated that for the time being he would prefer to lead whole-class discussions throughout his lessons. He said that he had a fairly good understanding of the different types of wait time, but would like to have some feedback on how many seconds he was allowing for each type of wait time. George agreed to collect data on Mike's wait time during the observations they had already agreed to. Mike and George also agreed that in addition to types of questions and wait time, George would track the number of students who participated in each class discussion.

After considerably more discussion, Mike and George had worked out an action plan for instructional improvement. The plan was written as follows:

Goal: to increase student participation in open discussion requiring student interpretation, application, analysis, synthesis, and evaluation.

Mike Phillips' Responsibilities:
1. Participate in the design of student learning objectives within each of Bloom's upper five categories of cognitive objectives (listed in goal statement)
2. Participate in the creation of open-ended discussion questions for each of the five types of learning objectives
3. Allow at least five seconds after asking an open-ended question for a student to respond, calling on volunteers only
4. Allow at least five seconds after calling on an individual student for the student to respond
5. Wait at least five seconds after a student has responded to an open-ended question before continuing the discussion

George Cantinni's Responsibilities:
1. Assist Mr. Phillips in designing student learning objectives based on the upper five categories of Bloom's taxonomy

2. Assist in creating open-ended discussion questions corresponding to stated objectives
3. Periodically observe Mr. Phillips' class discussions, collecting data on
   a. Frequency of teacher questions inviting student responses requiring interpretation, application, analysis, synthesis, and evaluation
   b. Duration of wait time after teacher questions, after calling on students to answer questions, and after student responses
   c. Frequency of each student's participation in open-ended discussions

Criteria for Success:
1. In selected classes, open-ended questions will be asked and related discussions held at each of the five upper levels of Bloom's taxonomy.
2. When appropriate, at least five seconds of wait time will be provided after asking open-ended discussion questions, after calling on students to respond to questions, and after student responses.
3. Each student will make at least one contribution to each open-ended class discussion.

Working closely with George over a period of several weeks, Mike made steady progress toward his instructional improvement goal. Eventually, George suggested that Mike had developed sufficient skill at writing open-ended discussion questions that he no longer needed George's assistance during his lesson planning. Mike agreed, but asked George if he would review Mike's discussion questions for a few weeks and give him feedback on their quality. George and Mike also decided that in lieu of additional classroom observations by George, Mike would record his next few class discussions on audiotape. He would review his own performance by analyzing the tapes. George agreed to review the tape of any class discussion for which Mike requested expert feedback.

Case Study Four

Stella Simpson was assistant principal for instruction at Kennedy Elementary School. She had organized a development option for teachers wishing to participate in an individualized professional development program. Maria Sanchez had some tentative ideas for a program that would provide development opportunities for herself and others and requested a meeting with Stella to discuss the plan.

During their meeting, Stella listened, reflected, clarified, and encouraged as Maria discussed a problem she saw emerging at the school. With the growing popularity of cooperative learning, a number of teachers had decided to try out cooperative strategies in their classrooms. Unfortunately, few of the teachers had received in-depth training in cooperative learning. Most had attended only a 60-minute awareness session provided at a recent districtwide in-service education day. Maria, who had received 30 hours of training in cooperative learning, was delighted that other teachers were taking an interest in the approach. However, based on her classroom observations as part of the school's peer-coaching program, she was concerned that many teachers did not have a clear grasp of the basic elements of a cooperative learning lesson and felt that without sufficient expertise, teachers' use of cooperative learning would be ineffective, and they would soon abandon it as an instructional strategy.

Stella paraphrased Maria's general concerns and then asked her to discuss specific problems teachers were having with cooperative learning. Maria replied that several teachers were attempting cooperative lessons without teaching students prerequisite social skills. She also stated that they were not building positive interdependence or individual accountability—two vital aspects of cooperative learning—into their lessons. Maria added that, based on her conversations with other teachers, these problems were not confined to teachers she had observed as a peer coach.

Stella agreed with Maria's observations. She had attended the same 30-hour training program as Maria, and her classroom observations verified Maria's concerns. Stella asked Maria for her perceptions of what could be done about the problem. As Maria presented her proposal, Stella continued to listen intently, sometimes paraphrasing Maria's statements, sometimes asking clarifying questions, other times encouraging Maria to elaborate. Maria proposed that she attend an advanced training program to develop additional expertise in cooperative learning as well as skills necessary to deliver a training program to other teachers. After completing the advanced program, Maria would deliver a series of evening workshops providing 30 hours of basic training on cooperative learning to interested teachers. Maria also suggested that she provide classroom coaching to the teachers attending her workshops in order to assist them to transfer skills learned in the workshops to their classrooms.

Stella asked Maria if she had considered the difficulties of attempting to provide instructional assistance to peers. Maria replied that she had considered the issue, but that since she would be working with volunteer teachers only, she did not see her peer status as a major problem. She reminded Stella that as a participant in the school's peer-coaching program she had successfully provided instructional assistance to many of the teachers who would attend the workshops. Also, she would not attempt to lead workshops for peers until she had received extensive leadership preparation.

Stella told Maria that if her plan was accepted, professional development funds could be used to pay for released time, the costs of Maria's leadership training, and the materials for the evening workshops that Maria would deliver. She said that no funds were available to pay Maria for the considerable amount of personal time and energy she would have to spend to make the program a success. Stella asked Maria if she was willing to make the extensive commitment that her new leadership role would require. After receiving an affirmative response, Stella asked Maria to put together a detailed proposal, including goals, activities, needed resources, criteria for success, a time line, and a tentative budget.

Developmental Supervision

The ultimate aim of the supervisor should be reflective, autonomous teachers facilitated by nondirective supervision. However, the fact that many teachers are functioning at developmental levels or in situations in which self-direction is not feasible means that the supervisor often must initially use collaborative, directive informational, or, in rare cases, directive control behavior. Each of the four case studies represents a different entry point for supervision. In each case, the supervisor based his or her initial supervisory approach on the teacher's levels of development, expertise, and commitment, as well as the nature of the situation.

The case studies provide examples of three phases of developmental supervision. In Phase 1, the supervisor diagnoses the teacher's developmental levels, expertise, commitment, and educational situation, and selects the interpersonal approach that creates the best supervisory match. In Phase 2, the supervisor uses the selected interpersonal approach to assist the teacher in instructional problem solving. In Phase 3 (illustrated in the first three case studies), the supervisor changes his or her interpersonal behavior in the direction of less supervisor control and more teacher control. Such a change in supervisory approach occurs only after the teacher has shown readiness to assume more decision-making responsibility.

In Case Study One, Martha Cozero determined that Gerald Watson was functioning at low levels of development, expertise, and commitment. She was convinced that Gerald's purposeless instructional routine was a serious impediment to student learning. Martha decided to use directive control behaviors in her initial supervisory approach. She identified the problem, presented Gerald with the instructional improvement goal, and directed him to carry out actions to reach the goal. Martha followed up by monitoring and providing feedback on Gerald's progress. Once Gerald had shown some improvement in teaching behaviors and motivation, Martha took a first step away from complete control, asking Gerald to choose one of three training formats.

In Case Study Two, novice Janice Smith's lack of classroom management and problem-solving skills created a different type of instructional problem. Janice initially had been highly motivated. She realized she had classroom management problems. What she needed was intensive assistance in identifying causes and solutions. After observing and conferencing with Janice, mentor Bill Levin decided to use directive informational behaviors during his initial assistance to Janice. Bill identified a goal for Janice of improved classroom management. He suggested a number of actions that she and he could take to move toward that goal. It was up to Janice to accept or reject Bill's suggestions. After Janice had made considerable progress under his mentorship, Bill encouraged her to choose from two alternative strategies for working with three students who displayed chronic discipline problems. Janice and Bill's negotiation and mutual agreement to integrate the two strategies represent movement toward a more collaborative relationship between novice and mentor.

In Case Study Three, Mike Phillips was able to define the problem he was experiencing and identify some causes, but he needed assistance in thinking through a plan to solve the problem. Chairperson George Cantinni decided to use a collaborative approach with Mike. After listening to Mike's perceptions, George shared his own point of view, then suggested that he and Mike both develop and exchange options for solving the problem. During the negotiation process, both Mike and George accepted, rejected, and proposed modifications to ideas presented by the other. Eventually, Mike and George reached mutual agreement on an action plan. George's suggestions several months later that Mike independently design his own discussion questions and tape and review his class discussions was an attempt to move away from collaborative and toward nondirective supervision. Their agreement that George would be available to review Mike's discussion questions and audiotapes indicated a transitional phase between collaborative and nondirective supervision.

In Case Study Four, teacher Maria Sanchez was clearly functioning at high levels of personal and professional development. Assistant principal Stella Simpson used nondirective interpersonal behaviors of listening, reflecting, clarifying, and encouraging as Maria discussed her concerns and proposal. Stella asked Maria to consider the consequences of her plan. Stella's request for a written proposal was made to encourage Maria to decide on details and standards and make a formal commitment to the plan.

Stella Simpson used noncontrolling interpersonal behaviors throughout Case Study Four, encouraging Maria Sanchez to assume full decision-making responsibility. Supervisors in the first three case studies used various levels of control, but *in each of the first three cases, the supervisor moved from more to less control and toward more decision-making responsiblity on the part of the teacher.* Developmental supervision thus is "developmental" in two ways. First, the entry-level supervisory approach is matched with the teacher's current developmental levels and the immediate situation. Second, supervisory behaviors are gradually modified to promote and accommodate long-range teacher development toward higher levels of reflection and problem-solving ability.

We purposefully provide case studies in this chapter demonstrating a clear match between the teacher's levels of development, expertise, and commitment with the supervisory approach. In the real world, other variables tend to enter the picture and interactions are more complex. The supervisory approach that the teacher is most comfortable with, although not necessarily the determining factor, should help decide which approach to use. The supervisor's level of comfort and expertise with various supervisory approaches must be considered. The specific problem that the supervisor and teacher are dealing with also should be a determining factor. The past relationship of the teacher and supervisor is yet another variable to be considered. Even if we had a totally valid and reliable way of measuring a teacher's levels of development, expertise, and commitment (which we don't), it is impossible to predict in advance all of the other variables that might need to be considered when selecting the best supervisory approach. This is why deciding on the best approach is a human decision, not the result of a predetermined formula. The decision should be based on observations and discussions with the teacher or group over time, combined with an assessment of the situation at hand.

SUMMARY AND A LOOK AHEAD

This chapter has provided a brief introduction to developmental supervision and case studies of supervisors using alternative supervisory approaches within a developmental frame.

Chapters 8 through 11 provide detailed discussions of the four supervisory approaches encompassed by developmental supervision. Chapter 12 includes in-depth discussions on the theory and application of developmental supervision.

Directive Control Behaviors

Supervisor: Have you been using the computers? I haven't seen any students at the desks.

Teacher: Well, I really don't think computers are such an important topic for seventh-grade mathematics. The students need training in basic geometry, not in how to play games with a computer.

Supervisor: As you know, part of the geometry curriculum is on a computer disk. It's not just fun and games. They could be learning geometry as they improve their technology skills.

Teacher: All this computer emphasis is ridiculous! It's another educational fad that's supposed to solve all our problems! I have enough trouble getting kids to learn what's in the book.

Supervisor: I understand your reservations about using the computer, but our school curriculum states that computers are to be used in seventh-grade mathematics. We're committed to doing so, particularly after spending so much money on the equipment and software.

Teacher: I think it's ridiculous.

Supervisor: That's beside the point. I want to see your kids using them.

Teacher: I'd rather not. Couldn't they teach computers in science class? After all, computers are science.

Supervisor: We're now using computers throughout the curriculum, including in science *and* in mathematics. I'd like to see at least one-third of your class begin the software program on plotting graphs by next Friday.

Teacher: Who's going to show them how to operate the program? I don't know how to.

Supervisor: Mrs. Techno, you were a participant in the computer class last summer. You know how to do it.

Teacher: I didn't understand the foggiest bit of it. Professor Wallenwood was a terrible teacher. He just paid attention to all those teachers who already had a computer background.

Supervisor: Well, I wasn't aware that you were unsure of how to use the software in class. I'll call Fred Tirtial, director of media, to come into your class next week to demonstrate how to use the program. I'll see to it that he gets the program started in your class, and then you continue with it.

Teacher: Any help would be appreciated.

Supervisor: You keep me posted, and we'll shoot for at least one group of your students working on the graphing program by a week from Friday.

Directive Control Continuum of Behaviors

It is evident in the previous scenario that the supervisor has taken over the teacher's problem. At first, the supervisor identified the problem by gathering information from his own observations and discussing this information with the teacher. Next, he told the teacher what to do and provided an explanation of why his suggestion would work. He concluded by reviewing the proposed action and reiterating his expectations for the teacher. The teacher was left with a concrete understanding of what she was expected to do. As we look at a typical sequence of behaviors along the supervisory behavior continuum (Figure 8.1), keep in mind that the sequence and frequency of behaviors will vary, especially in the beginning of the conference, but the directive control approach will end with the supervisor making the final decisions for the teacher. This chapter will accentuate directive behaviors that control teacher actions.

1. Presenting: *Identifying the problem.* The supervisor begins with a general idea of what the needs and difficulties are. Having used observations and gathered information from other sources, the supervisor tells the teacher what seems to be the problem: "I understand that there is a problem with . . ."

2. Clarifying: *Asking teacher for input into the problem.* The supervisor wants to gather direct information from the teacher about the problem prior to

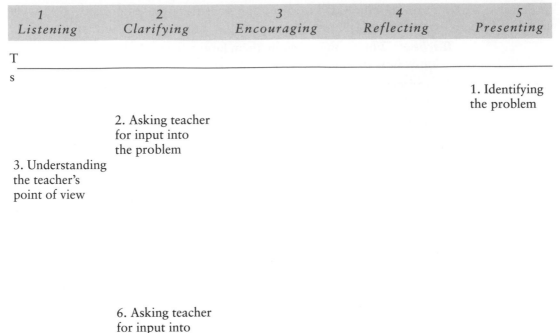

1 Listening	2 Clarifying	3 Encouraging	4 Reflecting	5 Presenting

T

s

1. Identifying the problem

2. Asking teacher for input into the problem

3. Understanding the teacher's point of view

6. Asking teacher for input into the expectations

Key: T = Maximum teacher responsibility   S = Maximum supervisor responsibility
        t = Minimum teacher responsibility   s = Minimum supervisor responsibility

FIGURE 8.1   *The Supervisory Behavior Continuum: Directive Control Behaviors*

the solution stage. This is done by using the teacher in an advisory capacity, asking the teacher such questions as: "How do you see the problem?" "Why do you think these conditions exist?"

3. Listening: *Understanding the teacher's point of view.* To gather maximum information in the shortest amount of time, the supervisor must attend carefully to what the teacher says. He or she listens both to the surface messages—"Computers are a waste of time"—and to underlying messages—"I don't know how to use them"—in formulating a complete problem.

4. Problem solving: *Mentally determining the best solution.* The supervisor processes the information and thinks, "What can be done?" After considering various possibilities, he or she selects the needed actions. The supervisor

6	7	8	9	10
Problem Solving	*Negotiating*	*Directing*	*Standardizing*	*Reinforcing*

t

S

4. Mentally
determining
best solution

5. Telling
expectations
for teacher

7. Detailing
and modifying
expectations

8. Repeating and
following up on
expectations

FIGURE 8.1   *Continued*

should be confident of indeed having a good, manageable solution to the
problem before conveying it to the teacher.

5. Directing: *Telling expectations to the teacher.* The supervisor tells the teacher
   in a matter-of-fact way what needs to be done: "I want to see you do the following . . ." The phrasing of the directive is important. Avoid timid, circular
   expectations: "Well, maybe you might consider doing . . ." "Don't you think
   it would be a good idea to . . . ?" The supervisor is not asking or pleading
   with the teacher, but *telling*. On the other hand, directing does not mean being
   vindictive, overbearing, condescending, or insulting. Avoid personal slights or
   paternalistic references: "I don't know why you can't figure out what needs to
   be done." "Why can't you get it right in the first place?" "Now listen, honey,
   I'm going to help you by . . ." A supervisor should state actions as *I* statements,

not as what others think. Tell the teacher what *I* want to happen, not what parents, other teachers, or the superintendent would want to see. A statement such as "If the superintendent saw this, he would tell you to do . . ." is hiding behind someone else's authority. The supervisor needs to make statements based on his or her own position, credibility, and authority.

6. Clarifying: *Asking the teacher for input into the expectations.* Possible difficulties with the supervisor's directive should be known before the teacher leaves the conference. For example, if circumstances exist that make teacher compliance with the directive impossible, it is better to adjust to those circumstances during the conference than to find out two weeks later why the plan failed. Therefore, after telling the teacher what is expected—"I want one-third of your students using the computers"—the supervisor needs to ask such questions as: "What do you need to carry out this plan?" "How can I help you carry out the plan?"

7. Standardizing: *Detailing and modifying expectations.* After considering the teacher's reactions to the directive, the supervisor solidifies the plan by building in the necessary assistance, resources, time lines, and criteria for expected success. The teacher is then told the revisions: "I can rearrange the visit time to . . . ," "I will find those materials for you," "I will arrange for you to attend . . . ," "I will change the time to three weeks."

8. Reinforcing: *Repeating and following up on expectations.* The supervisor reviews the entire plan and establishes times for checking on progress. The supervisor closes the meeting by making sure the teacher clearly understands the plan: "Do you understand what you're to do?" "Tell me what it is you're now going to do."

A History of Overreliance on Control

Historically, control has been used by supervisors as a first rather than last resort. The tradition has been to rely on controlling behaviors with all teachers in all situations (Gordon, 1992; Harpaz, 2005). At times, this has been done by tying supervision to summative evaluation systems requiring certain teaching behaviors. At other times, social pressure has been applied to force teacher conformity to generic "research-based" teaching methods (the research cited during such efforts often has been misinterpreted and oversimplified). Even worse, some supervisors wishing to reduce teacher resistance have combined control and manipulation, hoping to convince teachers that they have participated in a decision when in fact the supervisor knew all along what the decision would be.

We strongly disagree with supervisors using directive control behaviors with all teachers and in all situations. We also oppose using directive control behaviors indefinitely. Finally, in all cases, we oppose control through *manipulation*. Although we admit that directive control is necessary with some teachers and groups in some situations, we believe that it should be used only when no other supervisory approach is feasible. When using a directive control approach with a teacher or group, the supervisor should be ready to move away from directive control toward noncontrolling behaviors as soon as possible.

Issues in Directive Control

To many, directive control connotes an adversary relationship. It conjures up an image of the pushy, authoritarian boss at work. This is a stereotyped connotation, however. Being directive basically involves letting the other person know (1) what the supervisor is convinced will improve the teacher's instruction *and* (2) that the supervisor is willing to assume complete responsibility for that decision. A teacher might welcome knowing the depth and clarity of the supervisor's expectations. It is better to be up front about the directive than to pretend that teachers have decision-making power over issues that in reality they do not control. Some supervisors avoid being directive controlling by going through the directive informational, collaborative, or nondirective behaviors of involving staff when they've already made the decision. One might be able to succeed with such manipulation temporarily, but once staff members become aware that their involvement is of no significance, they will be resistant to further participation with the supervisor. With each issue, it is best to let teachers know the degree of their involvement, ranging from full involvement to none, rather than being nebulous. Anyone would prefer to work in a place where the game is *on,* not *under,* the table. Directive control should be viewed as being informative, decisive, and clear about what teachers have little control over. It also means listening and being willing to modify one's expectations according to reactions from teachers that point out errors in one's directives.

Another major issue raised by directive control behavior concerns power and authority. Unless a supervisor holds formal line authority over teachers, he or she cannot enforce directives. It is impossible to make the teacher do what he or she wants. Instead, a supervisor with a staff relationship can expect teachers to follow imposed plans only if they respect the supervisor and trust his or her judgment. The supervisor must demonstrate and convince the teachers of this superior expertise.

Directive control should be a measure of last resort when an immediate decision is needed. Other directive, nondirective, or collaborative approaches will normally ensure greater receptivity by teachers and greater likelihood of successful implementation of a decision, but decisions will take longer to make. Inevitably, when there are many people involved in a decision, discussion, conflict, and resolution will take more time than when only one person is deciding. However, not every instructional problem needs to be addressed at length; a supervisor using directiveness judiciously might actually save time for those decisions most important to staff. There are matters (such as scheduling or budgeting) in which teachers may not desire involvement. A supervisor who attempts to involve people in decisions they view as a waste of time is just as inept as one who does not involve people in decisions about which they care intensely.

At times, a supervisor with such authority does better by being directive and making the decision.

The issue of time includes the need for directive control in response to emergencies. When the flow of school life is interrupted by irate parents, student defiance, malfunctioning heaters, or media investigations, the supervisor may have to be unilaterally decisive. He or she will simply not have time to meet with teachers before responding. For example, a middle school principal was called at home by a newspaper reporter who sought her reaction to a fire marshal's report about unsafe cardboard partitions in a classroom of her school. The principal, totally unaware of the marshal's visit, refused comment and called the fire marshal to confirm the report. The marshal told her that all cardboard in classrooms was to be removed by the following morning. Deciding not to fight the fire marshal's orders and thus to avoid further newspaper attention, the principal told each teacher arriving at school the next morning of the fire marshal's report and told them to have their rooms cleared of all cardboard partitions before ten o'clock. She also informed them that they would meet later that afternoon to discuss the fire marshal's ruling and determine whether they wanted to appeal it. For the moment, she had used her own judgment. Later, when there was time to review the matter, she and the staff decided collaboratively to meet with the marshal about a proposal to reinstall cardboard partitions covered with fire-resistant plastic.

When to Use Directive Control Behaviors

Since directive behaviors raise issues of power, respect, expertise, and line and staff relationships, the following guidelines are given with caution. Directive control behaviors should be employed

1. When teachers are functioning at very low developmental levels
2. When teachers do not have awareness, knowledge, or inclination to act on an issue that a supervisor, who has organizational authority, thinks to be of critical importance to the students, the teachers, or the community
3. When teachers will have no involvement and the supervisor will be involved and totally accountable in carrying out the decision
4. When the supervisor is committed to resolving the issue and the teachers are not or when decisions do not concern teachers, and they prefer the supervisor to make the decision
5. When the supervisor does not have sufficient time to meet with teachers in an emergency

Moving from Directive Control toward Directive Informational Behaviors

In long-term supervisory situations and relationships, the supervisor should begin to shift from a directive control to a directive informational approach as soon as possible. Stabilizing an unstable situation or giving a teacher or group intensive support will tend to foster limited professional growth. Such growth is likely to continue only if the supervisor then begins to give the teacher or group limited opportunities to make decisions and assume some responsibility. One way to do this is to begin to allow the teacher or the group *"restricted choice."* For example, the supervisor might mandate an instructional improvement goal and then allow the teacher or group to choose from two or three clearly defined alternatives for meeting the goal. By doing this, the supervisor has begun movement toward directive informational supervision—an approach that is discussed in detail in the next chapter.

Critical Reflection on Directive Control Supervision

The supervisor should reflect critically on directive control behaviors both during and after their use. Questions that might assist critical reflection include the following:

- Are teacher developmental levels low enough or the situation critical enough to require my use of directive control behaviors?
- What effects will my use of directive control behaviors have on my long-term professional relationship with the teacher or group?
- Are the decisions made through the use of directive control behaviors likely to be implemented?
- What is my plan for moving away from directive control behaviors as soon as possible?

SUMMARY

Directive control supervision is used to transmit supervisor expectations to teachers clearly. Supervisors in a line position *over* teachers can use directive controlling language and enforce via hierarchical control. Supervisors in a staff position can only hope for compliance based on trust and credibility with teachers. Directive control supervision consists of behaviors of presenting, clarifying, listening, problem solving, directing, standardizing, and reinforcing (with line authority). The direction of presenting, problem solving, and directing is mostly from supervisor to teacher. Directive control behaviors are useful in limited circumstances when teachers possess little expertise, involvement, or interest with respect to an instructional problem and time is short. In these circumstances, directive control is not an adversarial or capricious set of behaviors, but an honest approach with teachers, such as to an emergency.

REFERENCES AND RECOMMENDED READINGS

Alberti, R. E., and Emmons, M. L. 1974. *Your perfect right: A guide to assertive behavior.* San Luis Obispo, CA: Impact.

Gordon, S. P. 1992. Paradigms, transitions, and the new supervision. *Journal of Curriculum and Supervision, 8*(1), 62–76.

Harpaz, Y. 2005. Teaching and learning in a community of thinking. *Journal of Curriculum and Supervision, 20*(2), 136–157.

Lucio, W. H., and McNeil, J. D. 1979. *Supervision: A synthesis of thought and action* (3rd ed.). New York: McGraw-Hill.

Mager, R. F., and Pipe, P. 1970. *Analyzing performance problems or "You really oughta wanna."* Belmont, CA: Fearon.

Smith, M. 1975. *When I say no, I feel guilty.* New York: Dial Press.

Directive Informational Behaviors

Supervisor: So, in conclusion, what I've observed is that 7 of your 26 students had little involvement in the discussion or question-and-answer period.

Teacher: Well, those seven who you are referring to show no interest in class. At least, if they are quiet, they don't interfere with the learning of others. However, I am surprised that they had such little involvement. I guess if they are quiet, I've just learned to tune them out.

Supervisor: I believe that a goal might be to involve those seven students actively in your future classes.

Teacher: I'd agree. None of my other classes are like this. If I only knew how to do that! When I call on them, they don't respond. When I give the class a controversial topic in U.S. history, most students jump right in, but Sheila, Aliendra, and the rest of them go blank, giggle, and seem not to care.

Supervisor: Well, based on my own experiences as a teacher and what I've seen others do with seemingly apathetic students, let me give you a list of possible actions. Think about them, and determine which of these are worth trying. First, you might establish individual contracts with each of those seven students, that they will be expected to participate at least twice in each class and can earn extra homework points for their participation. Second, you might move to the back and corners of the room during question-and-answer sessions. This is where most of these nonparticipating kids sit. In your lesson plans, make notes to call on each of these students at least once. Your physical presence close to them might help. Third, when you know that a topic to be introduced can be controversial, you might prep the students by using a cooperative learning format. Break the class into groups of three—put each of the nonparticipants with two active participants and ask each group to formulate a group position, with each member being responsible for reporting the position. Monitor the groups while they are working. At discussion times, occasionally call the nonparticipants to speak for the group. What do you think of these possibilities?

Teacher: Individual contracts for students aren't practical—other students would think I'm playing favorites. Moving around to the back and corners of the room is obvious, I could become more aware of doing that. The last idea of cooperative groups is one that I hadn't thought of with this class. I do that with my honors classes but never thought of using small groups here. I guess I assumed that it would be too confusing.

Supervisor: Which of these activities would you like to try?

Teacher: Moving to the back of the room, for sure! The cooperative learning, I'd like to try on a small scale to see how it would work. What do I need to do to prepare the groups to work together and how do I introduce the topic and task?

Directive Informational Continuum of Behaviors

The scenario, transcribed from a tape of an actual conference, shows a supervisor acting as the information source for the goal and activities of the improvement plan. The supervisor, through her observations, has determined a clear classroom goal for the teacher and directs the teacher to those activities she believes highly likely to achieve the goal. Notice that, through each step of the conference, the supervisor remains the information source but always asks and considers teacher feedback. Furthermore, the supervisor provides a range of alternatives from which the teacher is asked to choose. The scenario concludes with the teacher committing himself to using several activities. The supervisor then will detail with the teacher the what, when, and how of implementing the activities, set criteria for improvement, and reinforce the understanding of what is to be done. As we look at a sequence of directive informational behaviors (see Figure 9.1), keep in mind that the supervisor is constantly framing the direction and choices for the teacher.

1. Presenting: *Identifying the goal.* Based on the observation and previous experience she has with the teacher, the supervisor begins by reviewing her summarized observations and concluding with an interpretation that seven students being nonparticipants throughout a class period is problematic. Therefore, she sees an important goal as "involving all students."

2. Clarifying: *Asking the teacher for input into the goal.* The supervisor is careful not to move too quickly into a planning phase until she checks to see what the teacher thinks of her interpretation and goal. The teacher is surprised, agrees, and explains why these seven students have been neglected.

3. Listening: *Understanding the teacher's point of view.* The supervisor listens to determine if the teacher accepts the goal as an important one or if she needs to provide further explanation.

4. Problem solving: *Mentally determining possible actions.* The supervisor has given thought to some alternative actions that might be considered by the teacher. When the teacher explains the reasons for students being uninvolved and what has been done, the supervisor mentally prepares to lay out the alternative actions or suggestions.

5. Directing: *Telling alternatives for teachers to consider.* The supervisor carefully words the alternative actions as possibilities, based on her experience and knowledge, for the teacher to judge, consider, and respond to.

6. Listening: *Asking the teacher for input into alternatives.* The supervisor asks the teacher to react to her suggestions. The teacher has the opportunity now to give the supervisor information to modify, eliminate, and revise before finalizing the choices.

7. Directing: *Framing the final choices.* In a straightforward manner, the supervisor lays out what the teacher could do: "So, in the final analysis, these are the actions you could take . . ."

8. Clarifying: *Asking the teacher to choose.* The supervisor asks the teacher to decide and clarify which activities or combinations he will use.

9. Standardizing: *Detailing the actions to be taken.* At this juncture, the supervisor assists the teacher in developing the specifics of the activities (i.e., introduce cooperative learning, set up threesomes, identify one controversial topic, try for 15 minutes next Tuesday, etc.) and the criteria for success (i.e., "Let's see, when I come in next Thursday, whether four of these seven students can be called on and give prepared, on-target responses").

10. Reinforcing: *Repeating and following up on the plan.* The supervisor concludes the conference by restating the goal, the activities to be taken, the criteria for success, and the follow-up time for the next observation and/or conference.

Comparing Directive Control and Directive Informational Statements

Students in supervision courses using this text often have difficulty distinguishing between directive control and directive informational behaviors, especially when practicing the different behaviors during role plays. This is not surprising, since there is often a thin line between controlling and informational language. And yet that thin line is a critical one. The precise language of a supervisor using a directive

1 Listening	2 Clarifying	3 Encouraging	4 Reflecting	5 Presenting

T _____

s

1. Identifying
the goal

2. Asking teacher
for input into
the goal

3. Understanding
the teacher's
point of view

6. Asking teacher
for input into
the expectations

8. Asking teacher
to make a choice

Key: T= Maximum teacher responsibility   S = Maximum supervisor responsibility
        t = Minimum teacher responsibility   s = Minimum supervisor responsibility

FIGURE 9.1   *The Supervisory Behavior Continuum: Directive Informational Behaviors*

approach can be the difference between a successful and unsuccessful supervisory conference or group meeting. Figure 9.2 will help you distinguish directive control from directive informational statements by a supervisor.

The supervisor using directive control behaviors is analogous to a judge or policeman giving directives that must be followed (although the analogy eventually breaks down because we know of no district where teachers go directly to jail for failing to follow a supervisor's suggestions for instructional improvement!).

6	7	8	9	10
Problem Solving	*Negotiating*	*Directing*	*Standardizing*	*Reinforcing*

t

S

4. Mentally
determining
best solution

5. Telling
expectations
for teacher

7. Framing the
final choices

9. Determining
the actions to
be taken

10. Repeating
and following up
on plan

FIGURE 9.1 *Continued*

On the other hand, the supervisor using directive informational behaviors can be compared to a physician or attorney giving expert advice to a patient or client. The person receiving the advice does not have to follow it, but if they respect the expertise of the professional giving the advice they will probably conclude that it is in their best interest to act on the professional's suggestions. (If you begin to compare the salaries of physicians or attorneys with instructional supervisors, once again our analogy falls apart, but we've made our point!)

Directive Control (DC)	*Directive Informational (DI)*
It is essential that you improve your classroom management during your first-period math class.	I suggest the goal of improving your classroom management during your first-period math class.
One of my expectations is that you attend the classroom management workshop being offered by the district.	One alternative is for you to attend the classroom management workshop being offered by the district.
You need to have a written lesson plan prepared for each class. Each plan must include the following elements . . .	You could prepare more detailed lesson plans for this group. Each plan might include these additional elements . . .
You must include a wider range of instructional strategies in your lessons.	In my own teaching, I've found that using a wide range of instructional strategies improves student behavior and learning. You may wish to include a wider range of teaching strategies in your lessons.
Do you have any questions concerning these new expectations?	Do you have any questions concerning these possible actions?
You will be required to make the changes we've discussed in accordance with this written timeline.	Which of the alternatives that we have discussed do you wish to try out?
I will be observing your class again in four weeks, and I expect to see the following changes . . .	I would be willing to visit your class again in four weeks to observe your progress in implementing the changes you have selected.

FIGURE 9.2   *Directive Control versus Directive Informational Statements*

Issues in the Directive Informational Approach

Anyone who uses a directive informational approach needs to be aware of the degree of expertise that he or she has when delineating the choices available to others. Since the supervisor is placing himself or herself in the role of expert, the issues of confidence and credibility are crucial. The supervisor must be confident that he or she knows what practices will work in helping the teacher, because when the teacher chooses to use one or more of the supervisor's suggestions, the person ultimately responsible for the success or failure of the various practices will be the supervisor, not the teacher. After all, if I consider and select from your proposed actions, implement what you've suggested, and those actions don't work, I'm probably going to tell you the next time we meet, when we note that the goal is no closer to being achieved, "After all, I just did what you told me to do!"

The teacher is correct in holding the supervisor accountable for the results. Thus, the issue of credibility hovers above the directive informational approach.

Not only must the supervisor be confident that his or her own knowledge and experience are superior to and different from those of the teacher, but the teacher must also believe that the supervisor possesses a source of wisdom that he or she does not have. When confidence and credibility in the supervisor's knowledge are shared by both parties, and the teacher is either unaware, inexperienced, or stumped about what changes can be made, then the directive informational approach can be a most valuable set of behaviors to use.

When to Use Directive Informational Behaviors

Directive informational behaviors revolve on expertise, confidence, credibility, and limiting choice (Greiner, 1967). Therefore, they should be employed under the following circumstances:

1. When the teacher is functioning at fairly low developmental levels
2. When the teacher does not possess the knowledge about an issue that the supervisor clearly possesses
3. When the teacher feels confused, inexperienced, or is at a loss for what to do, and the supervisor knows of successful practices
4. When the supervisor is willing to take responsibility for what the teacher chooses to try
5. When the teacher believes that the supervisor is credible—a person who has the background and wisdom to know whereof he or she speaks
6. When the time is short, the constraints are clear, and quick, concrete actions need to be taken

Moving from Directive Informational toward Collaborative Behaviors

In directive informational supervision, the teacher or group is given some choice but the supervisor still assumes *primary* decision-making responsibility. In the collaborative approach, the teacher and supervisor share decision-making responsibility equally. Movement from directive informational to collaborative interaction is thus a matter of degree. The supervisor might begin that movement by suggesting an instructional improvement goal, asking the teacher or group to suggest one or two activities for moving toward the goal, and then suggesting a detailed action plan incorporating some of the teacher or group's proposed actions. Hopefully, the supervisor eventually will be able to enter a fully collaborative relationship with the teacher. This takes us to the topic of the next chapter—collaborative behaviors.

Critical Reflection on Directive Informational Supervision

Considering the questions below can assist the supervisor to reflect critically on the use of directive informational behaviors:

- Is my interaction with the teacher or group truly informational rather than controlling, both in terms of the technical language I use and the overall environment I create?
- Is the teacher or group provided alternative actions to consider that are clearly defined but also provide meaningful choice?
- Is the directive informational approach resulting in any unanticipated consequences?
- Is the directive informational approach working well with this teacher or group? Would another approach work better?

SUMMARY

Directive informational supervision is used to direct teacher(s) to consider and choose from clearly delineated alternative actions. The supervisor is the major source of information, goal articulation, and suggested practices. However, the supervisor is careful to solicit teacher input as he or she revises and refines the choices; ultimately, the teacher is asked to make a judgment as to which practices or combinations are feasible and realistic. Such an approach is useful when the expertise, confidence, and credibility of the supervisor clearly outweigh the teacher's own information, experience, and capabilities.

REFERENCES AND RECOMMENDED READINGS

Glickman, C. D. 2002. *Leadership for learning: How to help teachers succeed.* Alexandria, VA: Association for Supervision and Curriculum Development.

Grainer, L. E. 1967. Patterns of organizational change. *Harvard Business Review, 45*, 119–130. See the "decisions from alternatives approach."

Collaborative Behaviors

Teacher: I refuse to have Steve sent out of my class.

Supervisor: Don't you think being hit by him and being bruised is the last straw?

Teacher: No, I don't. It's my body and I don't think Steve meant it. He was angry and didn't know what he was doing.

Supervisor: Listen, he's been in fights with other students since the first day of school, and the latest episode of striking could have resulted in serious damage. We may have to remove him from your classroom.

Teacher: I know that you're thinking about my own welfare, but that kid is making progress. He's beginning to do some assignments and has been behaving better. The hitting incident was an accident. He's not bothering the other students too much.

Supervisor: Still, he may do better in a special classroom.

Teacher: I prefer he stay with me.

Supervisor: You know that whatever is done, we will both agree to do. You don't want him to leave and I think, for his own good, he should be given special attention. Steve is dangerous to you and the other students.

Teacher: I don't have anything against special attention. It's just that we've come so far and I hate to see him cut off from me and the class. He has a better chance to make it in our class than to begin all over in another class.

> *Supervisor:* Then you would be receptive to having him receive special attention as long as he stays in your class?
>
> *Teacher:* Yeah, I think so. I have no problem with a qualified person working with him in my classroom or even for a small part of the day outside of the classroom.
>
> *Supervisor:* That seems reasonable. I think that we are getting somewhere.

Collaborative Continuum of Behaviors

The foregoing script, based on a real conference, highlights collaborative supervisory behaviors. The supervisor wishes to resolve a problem that is shared equally with the teacher. The supervisor encourages the teacher to present his or her own perceptions and ideas. Yet the supervisor also honestly gives his or her own views. The result is a frank exchange of ideas. Both participants know they will have to agree on any course of action. In fact, when the disagreement becomes obvious, the supervisor restates the disagreement and reassures the teacher that they will have to find a mutual solution. Disagreement is encouraged, not suppressed. As the conversation continues, some openings for possible agreements become apparent, and the supervisor steers the conversation toward those ends. Finally, they will either agree to an action or wind up stalemated. A stalemate will mean further negotiating, rethinking, and even the possible use of a third-party mediator or arbitrator.

Figure 10.1 shows a prototype of collaborative behaviors according to the supervisory behavior continuum. A conference between supervisor and teacher begins with understanding each other's identification of the problem and concludes with mutual agreement on the final plan. The reader should think of the supervisory behaviors as a piano keyboard, with the musician beginning by hitting the keys on the left, then playing the keys back and forth, and culminating by hitting the middle key—negotiating.

1. Clarifying: *Identifying the problem as seen by the teacher.* First, ask the teacher about the immediate problem or concern: "Please tell me what is bothering you." "Explain to me what you see as the greatest concern."
2. Listening: *Understanding the teacher's perception.* You (the supervisor) want to have as much information about the problem as possible before thinking about action. Therefore, when the teacher narrates his or her perceptions, the full range of nondirective behaviors should be used (eye contact, paraphrasing, asking probing questions, and being willing to allow the teacher to continue talking): "Tell me more." "Uh huh, I'm following you." "Do you mean . . . ?"
3. Reflecting: *Verifying the teacher's perception.* When the teacher has completed his or her description of the problem, check for accuracy by summarizing the teacher's statements and asking if the summary is accurate: "I understand that you see the problem as . . . Is this accurate?"

4. Presenting: *Providing the supervisor's point of view.* Until this point, we have seen an abbreviated nondirective conference. Instead of asking the teacher to begin thinking of his or her own possible actions, however, you now move in and become part of the decision-making process. Give your own point of view about the current difficulty and fill in any information about the situation of which the teacher might be unaware: "I see the situation in this way." "The problem, as I see it, is . . ." (To minimize influencing the teacher's position, it is better for you to give your perceptions only after the teacher has given his or hers.)

5. Clarifying: *Seeking the teacher's understanding of the supervisor's perception of the problem.* In the same way that you paraphrased the teacher's statement of the problem and asked for verification, you now ask the teacher to do likewise: "Could you repeat what you think I'm trying to say?" Once you feel confident that the teacher understands your views, problem solving can begin.

6. Problem solving: *Exchanging suggestions of options.* If you and the teacher are familiar with each other and have worked collaboratively before, you can simply ask for a list of suggestions: "Let's both think about what might be done to improve this situation." Then listen to each other's ideas. If the teacher is not familiar with you or with the collaborative process, however, he or she may feel apprehensive about suggesting an idea that is different from the supervisor's. It might be better to stop the conference for a few minutes and have both supervisor and teacher write down possible actions before speaking: "So that we don't influence each other on possible solutions, let's take the next few minutes and write down what actions might be taken and then read each other's list." Obviously, once actions are in writing, they will not change according to what the other person has written. You the supervisor, therefore, have promoted a spectrum of personal ideas that are ready to be shared and discussed.

7. Encouraging: *Accepting conflict.* To keep the conference from turning into a competitive struggle, you need to reassure the teacher that disagreement is acceptable and that there will be no winners or losers: "It appears that we have some different ideas on how to handle this situation. By disagreeing we will find the best solution. Remember our agreement—we both have to agree with the solution before it will take place." You must genuinely believe that conflict between two caring professionals is productive for finding the best solution.

8. Negotiating: *Finding an acceptable solution.* After sharing and discussing, ask if there are suggestions common to both—"Where do we agree?"—and if there are suggestions markedly different—"Where do we differ?" If you find agreement, then the conference proceeds. But if there is a vast difference in suggestions, then you can take four sequential actions. First, check to see whether the differences are as vast as they appear by both you and the teacher explaining thoroughly what is meant by your respective suggestions. Second, if the disagreement is still real, then find out how convinced

1	2	3	4	5
Listening	*Clarifying*	*Encouraging*	*Reflecting*	*Presenting*

T

s

1. Identifying the
problem as seen
by the teacher

2. Understanding
the teacher's
perception

3. Verifying
teacher's
perception

4. Providing
supervisor's
point of view

5. Seeking teacher's
understanding of supervisor's
perception of problem

7. Accepting
conflict

10. Summarizing
final plan

Key: T = Maximum teacher responsibility   S = Maximum sup ervisor responsibility
        t = Minimum teacher responsibility   s = Minimum supervisor responsibility

FIGURE 10.1   *The Supervisory Behavior Continuum: Collaborative Behaviors*

each of you is that your suggestion be chosen: "How important is it to you that we do it your way?" If the importance of one person's suggestion is far greater than that of the other person's suggestion, then the question becomes whether one can give up his or her idea and live with the other's. Third, if grounds for agreement are not reached, you can consider a compromise: "How about if I give up this part of my suggestion and if you give up . . ." Or see if a totally new idea can be found: "Since we can't agree, let's drop our top choices for solutions and see if we can find another one."

6 Problem Solving	7 Negotiating	8 Directing	9 Standardizing	10 Reinforcing

t

S

6. Exchanging
suggestions
of options

8. Finding an
acceptable
action

9. Agreeing on
details of plan

FIGURE 10.1 *Continued*

9. Standardizing: *Agreeing on details of plan.* Once agreement on an acceptable action has been reached, the supervisor needs to attend to the details of time and place. When will the plan be implemented? Where will it take place? Who will help? What resources are needed? These details need to be discussed and agreed to so there will be a clarity and precision to the final plan.

10. Reflecting: *Summarizing the final plan.* The supervisor concludes the conference by checking that both parties agree to the action and details. The supervisor might do this verbally—"Could you repeat what you understand

the plan to be and then I'll repeat my understanding"—or in writing—"Let's write this down together so that we are clear on what we've agreed to do."

Issues in Collaborative Supervision

Our work with collaboration has shown that it is a deceptively simple set of behaviors for supervisors to understand. The reason is that collaboration appears to be the democratic way of doing things. Most of us have been schooled in equality and democracy, and collaboration appears to be democracy in action. Therefore, it seems apparent that we should ask others for input and that decisions should be made by the majority. However, collaboration with an individual or a group involves more than the mechanical procedures of democracy. The purpose of collaboration is to solve problems through a meeting of minds of equals. True equality is the core of collaboration.

One difficulty in working collaboratively occurs when the teacher (or group) believes a supervisor is manipulating the decision when in fact he or she is not. The teacher appears to concur with the supervisor's ideas and suggestions not because of their merit but because the teacher believes the supervisor is really giving a directive. The underlying message the teacher perceives is: "This is my supervisor telling me what she thinks I should do. Even though she says we are making a joint decision, I know I had better do what she says." How does the supervisor know whether a teacher's agreement is sincere or mere compliance? The supervisor might confront the issue by asking the teacher whether he or she is agreeing or only pretending to agree with the supervisor's idea. Acknowledging that the supervisor suspects something is amiss brings the issue out into the open. A teacher who responds, "I don't believe you really are going to let me have equal say" can be dealt with more easily than when a supervisor must guess at the teacher's hidden feelings.

Teachers who refuse to disclose their feelings probably have a history of being mistreated by supervisors. Until the supervisor can demonstrate consistently that he or she really means to be collaborative, no progress will be made. The teacher is not going to believe the supervisor is being collaborative until there is proof. True intent can be demonstrated by refusing to allow decisions to be made without teacher feedback. With nonresponsive and readily acquiescing teachers, a supervisor might say: "I don't know if you're agreeing with me because you like the idea or because of some power I hold over you. We won't carry out any action unless we both agree with that action. I want to be collaborative because I believe you have as much expertise on this matter as I do. Together we can make a better decision than separately. I'm uncertain why you are agreeing with me. Please tell me what you think."

A supervisor cannot find out what a teacher thinks without asking. As they continue to meet, the supervisor should begin by encouraging teachers to offer their own thoughts about the problem and suggestions for action. The supervisor should try to withhold any ideas of his or her own. Once the teacher's ideas are forthcoming, the supervisor can offer his or her ideas. When negotiating a final decision, the supervisor should let teachers take the lead. If teachers continue to be unresponsive or overly compliant with the supervisor after he or she has confronted the issue of perception and encouraged teacher initiative, then, after several unsuccessful attempts, the supervisor might consider another approach.

When to Use Collaborative Behaviors

There are circumstances in which a supervisor definitely should use collaborative behaviors. We will leave more detailed instructions for Chapter 12, but, for now, collaboration should be used

1. When teachers are functioning at moderate or mixed developmental levels
2. When the teacher(s) and supervisor have approximately the same degree of expertise on the issue, or if the supervisor knows part of the problem and teachers know the other part
3. When the teacher(s) and supervisor will both be involved in carrying out the decision, or if the teacher(s) and supervisor will be held accountable for showing results to someone else (say, parents or the superintendent)
4. When the teacher(s) and supervisor are both committed to solving the problem or if teachers want to be involved and leaving them out will lead to low morale and distrust

Moving from Collaborative toward Nondirective Behaviors

The developmental supervisor attempts gradually to move from collaborative toward nondirective interpersonal behaviors. As the teacher or group increases expertise, problem-solving capacity, and motivation, the supervisor hands over more and more decision-making responsibility. An example of a transitional phase between the collaborative and nondirective approach would be to use collaborative behaviors while assisting a teacher or group to decide on an instructional improvement goal, then shift to nondirective behaviors as the teacher or group decides on actions to reach the goal. Nondirective behaviors are discussed in the following chapter.

Collaboration and Cooperation

The supervisor using collaborative interpersonal behaviors jointly shares decision-making responsibility with the teacher or group. Collaborative supervision should not be confused with supervisor-teacher cooperation. To *cooperate* is "to work or act together toward a common end or purpose," according to the 2000 *American Heritage Dictionary*. The supervisor should strive for cooperation with the teacher or group regardless of his or her supervisory approach. Supervisors and teachers can maintain positive professional relationships and work together toward the common purpose of instructional improvement whether the supervisor uses controlling directive, informational directive, collaborative, or nondirective behaviors, provided the supervisor selects and effectively implements the correct approach.

Critical Reflection on Collaborative Supervision

Questions to foster the supervisor's critical reflection on collaborative behaviors include the following:

- Beyond my mechanical use of collaborative behaviors, have I really given the individual or group equal decision-making power regarding the problem to be solved?
- Have I verified that the teacher or group perceives the decision-making process to be collaborative?
- Have I accepted conflict and reassured the teacher or group that disagreement is part of the decision-making process?
- Have I continued the collaborative process toward a solution acceptable to both the teacher or group and me?

SUMMARY

Collaborative supervision is premised on participation by equals in making instructional decisions. Its outcome is a mutual plan of action. Collaborative behaviors consist of clarifying, listening, reflecting, presenting, problem solving, negotiating, and standardizing. Collaboration is appropriate when teachers and supervisors have similar levels of expertise, involvement, and concern with a problem. The key consideration for a supervisor is the fact that collaboration is both an attitude and a repertoire of behaviors. Unless teachers have the attitude that they are equal, collaborative behaviors can be used to undermine true equality.

REFERENCES AND RECOMMENDED READINGS

Blumberg, A. 1980. *Supervisors and teachers: A private cold war* (2nd ed.). Berkeley, CA: Mc-Cutchan.

Bryk, A. S., and Schneider, B. L. 2002. *Trust in schools: A core resource for improvement.* New York: Sage.

Cogan, M. 1973. *Clinical supervision.* Boston: Houghton Mifflin.

Gordon, T. 1977. *Leader Effectiveness Training, L.E.T.: The no-lose way to release the produc-tive potential of people.* New York: Wyden Books.

Harris, T. 1967. *I'm OK—You're OK: Practical guide to transactional analysis.* New York: Harper & Row.

Wagner, A. 1981. *Transactional manager: How to solve people problems with transactional analysis.* Englewood Cliffs, NJ: Prentice Hall.

Wiles, K. 1967. *Supervision for better schools* (3rd ed.). Englewood Cliffs, NJ: Prentice Hall.

Nondirective Behaviors

Teacher: (barging into supervisor's office) This damn place is a zoo! I can't stand it any longer. These kids are a bunch of ingrates! I've had it.

Supervisor: (looking at the teacher) Wow, you are angry! Tell me what's going on. Have a seat.

Teacher: (refusing to sit) I get no help around here from you or the administration. The students know that they can act any way they damn please and get away with it. I'm not going to put up with it anymore.

Supervisor: What have they been doing?

Teacher: Just now, I went back into the class after being called out for a message and they were jumping all over the place, running around, throwing papers, and being totally obnoxious. I can't leave them for a minute.

Supervisor: What did you do?

Teacher: What do you think? I screamed my bloody head off at them and after it all, Terence had the nerve to laugh at me.

Supervisor: Terence laughed at you?

Teacher: Yeah, that little snot! He always has the last word. He's so defiant it drives me mad!

Supervisor: Is he always like that?

Teacher: He sure is. Terence is my number one problem; if I could get him to behave and learn, the rest of the class would be no problem.

Supervisor: So the main problem is Terence. What do you do when he misbehaves?

Teacher: I've been sending him out of the room but that doesn't work. He couldn't care less about school and will only work when forced to. He really gets to me.

Supervisor: He's a lot to handle.

Teacher: He sure is! That kid is a bundle of jumping nerves. He doesn't pay any attention to what goes on in class.

Supervisor: He must really keep you hopping! Does Terence do anything right in class?

Teacher: Hardly! He's just not excited about anything in school. If he could live in a world of rock videos and football games, he'd be just fine.

Supervisor: (joking) Well, maybe we need a flashing movie room of video and football highlights to keep him entertained!

Teacher: (laughing and calming down) Oh, I don't know. He just drives me nuts. He's not a bad kid.

Supervisor: Could we capitalize on his interests to improve his classroom behavior?

Teacher: I need to sit down with him and talk to him one on one. I really want to find something in class that would interest him and keep him out of my hair.

Supervisor: What might that be?

Teacher: Students get to do special history projects in class. Maybe I could tie his love for music or sports into a history project, or maybe make a contract with him about his good behavior so that he could earn time to listen to music? Let me talk to him.

Supervisor: Sorry about your class today. It sounds to me as if Terence is the key and you have some ideas. Are there ways that I could help?

Nondirective Continuum of Behaviors

Nondirective supervision is based on the assumption that an individual teacher knows best what instructional changes need to be made and has the ability to think and act on his or her own. The decision belongs to the teacher. The role of the supervisor is to assist the teacher in the process of thinking through his or her actions.

As the foregoing hypothetical script shows, the supervisor behaves in ways that keep the teacher's thinking focused on observation, interpretation, problem identification, and problem solutions. Notice how in the example the nondirective approach allowed the teacher to move from an angry outburst about the entire class to an analytical focus on Terence's behavior. Rarely will a teacher move this rapidly from anger to reflection, but the pattern of the supervisor helping the teacher to come to his or her own conclusions is characteristic of a nondirective approach. The supervisor does not interject his or her own ideas into the discussion unless specifically asked. All verbalizations by the supervisor are intended as feedback or to extend the teacher's thinking; they do not influence the actual design.

Refer to the supervisory behavior continuum to understand how nondirective behaviors are used. Read carefully, because the misuse of listening, clarifying, encouraging, reflecting, problem-solving, and presenting behaviors can result in a decision that is not really the teacher's.

Figure 11.1 shows a typical pattern of supervisory interpersonal behaviors used in a nondirective conference, beginning with listening and ending with asking the teacher to present his or her decision. The sequence of behaviors between start and finish can vary, but the end should be the same—a noninfluenced teacher decision.

1. Listening: *Wait until the teacher's initial statement is made.* Face and look at the teacher; concentrate on what is being said. Avoid thinking about how you see the problem or what you think should be done. It is not easy to restrain your mind from galloping ahead, but your job is to understand what the teacher initially has said.

2. Reflecting: *Verbalize your understanding of the initial problem.* Include in your statement the teacher's feelings and perceived situation: "You're angry because students don't pay attention." Wait for an acknowledgment of accuracy from the teacher: "Yes, I am, but . . ." Do not offer your own opinion; your job is to capture what the teacher is saying.

3. Clarifying: *Probe for the underlying problem and/or additional information.* You now ask the teacher to look at the problem in some different ways and to consider new information that might be contributing to the problem. Clarifying is done to help the teacher further identify, not solve, the problem. Questions such as "Do you mean that you are really fed up with school?" "Is it a particular student who is getting to you?" and "When has this happened before?" are appropriate information-seeking questions. Avoid questions that are really solutions in disguise. Such questions as: "Have you thought about taking up yoga to relax?" and "Maybe you could suspend that student for a few days, what do you think?" are inappropriate. Such leading or suggestive questions are attempts to influence the teacher's final decision.

4. Encouraging: *Show willingness to listen further as the teacher begins to identify the real problems.* Show that you will continue to assist and not leave the discussion incomplete. Statements such as "I'm following what you're saying, continue on," "Run that by me again," and "I see where you're coming from" are correct. Saying "I like that idea," "Yes, that will work," or "Ah, I agree with that" are, even unintentionally, influencing behaviors. A teacher, like any other person, cannot help but be influenced by the judgments a supervisor is making on what he or she says. Encouraging keeps the teacher thinking; praise, on the other hand, influences the final decision.

1 Listening	2 Clarifying	3 Encouraging	4 Reflecting	5 Presenting

T
_____

s

1. Wait until the immediate message is finished

2. Verbalize inital problem—feeling and situation

3. Probe for underlying problem and/or additional information

4. Show willingness to listen further

5. Constantly paraphrase understanding of teacher's message

8. Ask teacher for commitment to a decision

10. Restate the teacher's plan

Key:	T = Maximum teacher responsibility	S = Maximum supervisor responsibility
	t = Minimum teacher responsibility	s = Minimum supervisor responsibility

FIGURE 11.1 *The Supervisory Behavior Continuum: Nondirective Behaviors*

5. Reflecting: *Constantly paraphrase understanding of the teacher's message.* Throughout the discussion, check on the accuracy of what you understand the teacher to be saying. When the teacher adds more information to the perceived problem, or explains different sources of the problem, considers the possible actions, and finally makes a decision, the supervisor should paraphrase. First, whenever you are uncertain of what the teacher is saying, you should paraphrase with a statement such as: "I think you're saying . . ." or

6 *Problem Solving*	7 *Negotiating*	8 *Directing*	9 *Standardizing*	1 0 *Reinforcing*

t

S

6. Ask teacher to think
of possible actions

7. Ask teacher to con-
sider consequences
of various actions

9. Ask teacher to set
time and criteria
for action

FIGURE 11.1 *Continued*

"I'm not sure but do you mean . . ." Then you can sit back and allow the teacher to affirm or reject your understanding. Second, when the teacher has come to a halt in thinking about the problem, the paraphrase should be used to jog the teacher's mind to reflect on what has already been said and what more needs to be done. For example, after a considerable pause in the teacher's talk, the supervisor might say, "Well, let me see if I can summarize what has been said so far . . ." or "So this is where you are—you're angry because . . ." Comprehensive summarizing allows the teacher to rest, mentally stand off from himself or herself, and think about what has been said. Usually, such paraphrasing will stimulate the teacher to interject, add, and continue. Reflecting should not become mechanical or artificial, with the supervisor paraphrasing every teacher statement. Instead, it should be used judiciously when the supervisor is not completely clear about what has been said or when there is a long pause in the conversation. Incessant interjections of "I hear you saying . . . ," without aid or purpose, make teachers skeptical about the supervisor's concern.

6. Problem solving: *Ask the teacher to think of possible actions.* After the teacher has finished identifying the problem and you are clear about his or her perception of the problem, your responsibility shifts to helping the teacher generate possible solutions. You can do this by asking straightforward questions: "What can you do about this?" "What else could be done?" "Think hard about actions that might help." "Let me see if you can come up with three to four possible solutions." It is helpful to allow the teacher to think for a minute or two about possible actions before verbalizing them. After actions have been proposed, you should reflect on the proposals, check on their accuracy, and probe for others. Regardless of whether the teacher proposes only a few or many possibilities, if further probing is not successful, then you should move the conference on.

7. Problem solving: *Ask the teacher to consider consequences of various actions.* The moment of truth is almost at hand. Your emphasis is on having the teacher move from possible to probable solutions. Taking each solution in order, ask: "What would happen if you did . . . ?" "Would it work?" "What problems would be associated with it?" Finally, after having the teacher explore the advantages and disadvantages of each action, he or she should be asked to compare the various actions: "Which would work best?" "Why do you think so?" "How would that be better than the others?"

8. Presenting: *Ask the teacher for a commitment to a decision.* After you have explored possible actions and the teacher has compared their likelihood of success, you must emphasize that the teacher should select actions that are within his or her resources *(do-able),* can be implemented in a short period of time *(feasible),* and are concrete *(accountable).* A simple question—"Well, what will you do now that is likely to improve the situation?"—should cut quickly to the heart of the matter.

9. Standardizing: *Ask the teacher to set time and criteria for action.* The teacher is assisted in monitoring his or her own decision about future improvement by specifying the time period during which the action will be implemented, when various parts of the plan will be done, what resources are needed, and how the teacher will know the decision is working. A further series of supervisor questions to accomplish this purpose would be: "Now tell me what you are going to do." "What will be done first, next, last?" "What do you need in order to do it?" "How will you know it's working?" "When will it be done?" When the teacher can answer these questions, the conference is near completion.

10. Reflecting: *Restate the teacher's plan.* Before leaving, repeat the teacher's entire plan with "So you're going to do . . ." After the teacher verifies the restated plan, the session is over.

Initiating Nondirective Supervision

While facilitating a workshop, one of the authors decided to illustrate the non-directive approach with an unstructured simulated conference, with the author taking the role of a supervisor and a volunteer participant assuming the role of a teacher. The focus of the conference was a real-world problem that the volunteer, a mentor-teacher, was experiencing. After a successful simulation in which the author used nondirective behaviors to facilitate the teacher's reflection on the problem, consideration of alternative solutions, and an action plan for solving the problem, the author congratulated the volunteer on a simulation well done. The teacher responded, "I don't feel as if I did a very good job. I didn't know what you were trying to get me to say. Was my solution the one you were looking for?" The author explained that there was no preconceived solution to the problem, that the "supervisor" in the role play was not trying to elicit any particular responses from the teacher. The teacher, who had been selected by his district as a mentor of other teachers because of his outstanding teaching and leadership, explained that he simply did not know how to respond to such supervision because in his many years of teaching he had never been exposed to a nondirective approach.

The above story illustrates the point that supervisors seldom use nondirective behaviors with teachers; indeed, the supervisory approach most often used is directive (Gordon, 1989). Moreover, supervisors sometimes create the illusion of using nondirective behaviors when in fact they are manipulating a supervisory conference or group meeting toward a predetermined decision. When this happens often enough, teachers realize that the supervisor is attempting to manipulate them. Without any experience with authentic nondirective supervision, then, it's no wonder that teachers are leery of the supervisor who is trying to use that approach with them for the first time.

What's the solution when a teacher is perfectly capable of solving his or her own instructional problems but who, because of past experience, is likely to become confused or suspicious of the supervisor's first use of nondirective supervision? One technique is to simply explain to the teacher or group what nondirective supervision is, what specific behaviors are involved, and why the supervisor believes the teacher or group can benefit from the nondirective approach. Even when the supervisor has provided a rationale for nondirective supervision, some teachers may still be reluctant to identify problems, consider actions, commit to decisions, or establish criteria for success. When this happens, the supervisor should not automatically assume that the nondirective approach is inappropriate for the teacher or group. Rather the supervisor should continue to build trust and rapport through active listening, probe for problems and related information, and encourage the teacher or group to describe situations and feelings. Eventually, the teacher or group should reach a stage of trust and self-confidence that will enable them to consider alternatives and generate an improvement plan. Supervisor commitment to teacher self-direction, along with the use of appropriate interpersonal behaviors, will ultimately lead to teacher-driven instructional improvement.

Nondirective, Not Laissez-Faire, Supervision

Some educators have criticized nondirective supervision by arguing that supervisors who use nondirective behaviors are abdicating their responsibility to assist teachers improve their instructional performance. This is a valid argument against laissez-faire supervision, which advocates minimal supervisor involvement in the instructional improvement process. However, under our definition of nondirective supervision, the supervisor is actively involved in instructional improvement, clarifying, encouraging, reflecting, and facilitating teacher decision making at each stage of the improvement process. Also, in developmental supervision the nondirective approach is used only with those teachers who are operating at high levels of abstraction, motivation, and expertise. The developmental supervisor uses one of the other three supervisory approaches with teachers who are not ready to assume full decision-making responsibility.

Issues with Nondirective Supervision

Based on numerous skill-training sessions conducted with school leaders on employing nondirective behaviors, some common issues and practical questions have arisen:

1. Can a supervisor really remain nonjudgmental and not influence the teacher's or group's decision?
2. What happens if the teacher or group desires the supervisor's input?
3. What does a supervisor do with a teacher or group that is reluctant or not capable of generating solutions?

Whether a supervisor can really remain nonjudgmental is a legitimate concern. Even when one is consciously avoiding praise, not interjecting one's own ideas, and not offering solutions in the guise of questions, some influencing probably will take place. Studies by Mears, Shannon, and Pepinsky (1979) analyzing the tapes of counseling sessions conducted by the most renowned expert on nondirectiveness, psychologist Carl Rogers, revealed a definite pattern to his interrupting the patient and to which statements he selected to paraphrase. It is apparent that any interaction between humans is bound to be influential. Frequency of eye contact, timing of questions, facial expressions, and ways of paraphrasing can always be interpreted by a teacher as approving or disapproving. There is no way to avoid influencing through unconscious supervisory responses. The best one can do is to minimize those behaviors that knowingly influence. One should not knowingly offer ideas, praise, or directions that will influence the teacher's decision.

What if the teacher or group asks for the supervisor's suggestions? The answer to this question centers on timing. If the suggestions are asked for and given in the initial stages of a conference or meeting before the teacher or group has been required to think through the issue, then such feedback will structure the stream of subsequent thought and heavily influence the decision. If the suggestions are given after the teacher or group has already narrowed its own choices of actions, however, a supervisor's answer will not be as influential. Ideally, it is better to refrain completely from giving one's own ideas. If asked, the supervisor might respond, "I'm sorry, but I don't want to answer that. Instead, I want you to think through what can be done. Only you know your own situation. Therefore, what *I* think is not as important as what *you* think."

Being nondirective with an individual or group that is reluctant or not capable of generating solutions is tricky. Reluctance and capability are not necessarily inversely related. If the teacher is reluctant but capable, the worst possible response would be for the supervisor to take over decision making for the teacher. Such a move might reinforce the teacher's reluctance to speak his or her own mind. Reluctance usually stems from a disbelief that one will be listened to or allowed to act on one's own initiative. The supervisor must be patient and persistent, giving constant encouragement. Patience is shown by listening and waiting, encouragement by accepting what the teacher says, and persistence by not allowing the teacher to rest without making a decision. A supervisor can be persistent by asking questions, by taking breaks from the conference, and by giving the teacher time for further reflections.

Capability is a different matter. What if a teacher or group is incapable of making a decision? If they continually insist they do not know what the problem is or have no ideas about what could be done, and if every supervisory prompt is met by vacant stares and shrugs of shoulders, then patience, encouragement, and persistence on the part of the supervisor will create further frustration and perhaps antagonism. If they simply don't know, no matter how nondirective the supervisor is, no decisions will be forthcoming. Obviously, if lack of capability is the source of nonresponsiveness, then the nondirective approach is an unwise choice of supervisory behaviors.

When to Use Nondirective Behaviors

When and with whom should nondirective behaviors be used? A supervisor should consider using a nondirective approach

1. When the teacher or group is functioning at high developmental levels
2. When the teacher or group possesses most of the knowledge and expertise about the issue and the supervisor's knowledge and expertise are minimal ("If you don't know anything about it and they do, let them solve it")

3. When the teacher or group has full responsibility for carrying out the decision and the supervisor has little involvement ("If they are going to be accountable for it and you aren't, let them solve it")
4. When the teacher or group is committed to solving the problem but the problem doesn't matter to the supervisor ("If they want to act and you couldn't care less, let them decide")

There are special circumstances in which initial use of nondirective behaviors are appropriate even if the above criteria are not met. Regardless of teacher developmental level, expertise, responsibility, or commitment, when a teacher or group has become extremely emotional over a problem, rational problem solving using any of the four supervisory approaches may be unproductive. What may be more beneficial in such situations is the initial use of the nondirective behaviors of listening, clarifying, encouraging, and reflecting as the teacher or group describes the problem and expresses the anger, frustration, fear, resentment, or other feelings the problem has generated. Once the teacher or group has had the opportunity to vent emotions in the presence of an empathetic listener, the supervisor can then shift to a problem-solving mode, using the criteria of developmental level, expertise, responsibility, and commitment to select the appropriate supervisory approach for the problem-solving phase of the conference or meeting.

Nondirective Supervision, Teacher Collaboration

Although nondirective supervision can be a valuable means of assisting individual teacher development, we see its greatest potential in the supervisor facilitating expert teachers' collaboration with each other for classroom and school-wide instructional improvement. An example of nondirective supervision of teacher collaboration at the classroom level would be the supervisor facilitating a teacher-driven peer-coaching program. An example of nondirective supervision for schoolwide instructional improvement would be the supervisor assisting a group of teachers as the group plans, implements, and evaluates a series of integrated instructional units cutting across several content areas. The ultimate goal of developmental supervision is for the supervisor to be facilitating a self-actualized teaching staff engaged in collaborative and continuous instructional improvement.

Critical Reflection on Nondirective Supervision

The supervisor can consider the questions below when reflecting on the use of nondirective behaviors:

- Is the teacher or group reluctant to assume decision-making responsibility? If so, what might be the reason for that reluctance?

- In addition to using overt nondirective behaviors like clarifying, encouraging, and reflecting, do I avoid influencing the teacher or group through subtle comments or nonverbal behaviors?
- If the teacher or group asks for my input, do I respond appropriately?
- Am I actively facilitating the teacher or group's decision making, or do I sometimes slip into laissez-faire supervision?

SUMMARY

Supervisors can use nondirective behaviors in helping teachers determine their own plans. Such supervisory behaviors consist of listening, reflecting, clarifying, encouraging, and problem solving. When individuals and groups of teachers are functioning at high developmental levels and possess greater expertise, commitment, and responsibility for a particular decision than the supervisor does, then a nondirective approach is appropriate. Important considerations for a supervisor when using nondirectiveness are attempting to be nonjudgmental, hesitating in response to teachers' wishes for more supervisor input, and adjusting one's behavior when teachers demonstrate reluctance to generate solutions. The purpose of nondirective supervision is to provide an active sounding board for thoughtful professionals.

REFERENCES AND RECOMMENDED READINGS

Carkhuff, R. R. 1969. *Helping and human relations: A primer for lay and professional helpers. Vol. 2: Practice and research.* New York: Holt, Rinehart and Winston.

Combs, A., Avila, D. L., and Purkey, W. H. 1979. *Helping relationships: Basic concepts for the helping professions* (2nd ed.). Boston: Allyn and Bacon.

Gazda, G. M., Asbury, R. R., Balzer, F. J., Childers, W. C., and Walters, R. P. 1977. *Human relations development: A manual for educators* (2nd ed.). Boston: Allyn and Bacon.

Gordon, S. P. 1989. *The theory of developmental supervision: An investigation of the critical aspects.* Unpublished Ed.D. dissertation, University of Georgia.

Gordon, S. P. 1990. Developmental supervision: An exploratory study of a promising model. *Journal of Curriculum and Supervision, 5,* 293–307.

Mears, N. M., Shannon, J. W., and Pepinsky, H. B. 1979. Comparison of the stylistic complexity of the language of counselor and client across three theoretical orientations. *Journal of Counseling Psychology, 26*(3), 181–189.

Mosher, R. L., and Purpel, D. E. 1972. *Supervision: The reluctant profession.* Boston: Houghton Mifflin.

Rogers, C. R. 1951. *Client-centered therapy: Its current practice, implications, and theory.* Boston: Houghton Mifflin.

Developmental Supervision
Theory and Practice

Thus far in Part III we have introduced the supervisory behavior continuum, provided an overview of developmental supervision, and explained each of the four supervisory approaches (directive control, directive informational, collaborative, and nondirective). This chapter provides an in-depth discussion of developmental supervision as an integrated model. The first part of the chapter presents the underlying rationale for developmental supervision. The second part explains how the model can be applied in practice.

Rationale for Developmental Supervision

One aspect of developmental supervision is the match of initial supervisory approach with the teacher's or group's developmental levels, expertise, and commitment. In Chapter 4, we described characteristics of teachers functioning at various stages of adult and career development. Teachers functioning at generally low developmental levels were described as performing at the concrete operations stage of cognitive development, low conceptual levels, the preconventional level of moral reasoning, the fearful stage of ego development, the durable category level of consciousness, and the self-adequacy stage of concern. Teachers or groups of low developmental levels, expertise, and commitment seem well matched to directive supervision. They have difficulty defining problems, have few ways of responding to problems, and are unlikely to accept decision-making responsibility. They clearly are in need of the structure and intensive assistance provided by directive supervision. For most teachers in need of direction, an informational directive approach is appropriate. For teachers functioning at extremely low levels of development, expertise, and commitment, and with serious instructional problems, a controlling directive approach might be necessary.

Teachers of generally moderate developmental levels were described as functioning at the formal operations stage of cognitive development, moderate conceptual levels, the conventional level of moral reasoning, the conforming stage of ego development, the cross-categorical level of consciousness, and the teaching tasks stage of concern. Teachers or groups at moderate developmental levels, expertise, and commitment are usually best served by a collaborative supervisory approach. They can generate some possible solutions to an instructional problem, but still need some assistance in examining all options and developing a comprehensive plan for instructional improvement. The brainstorming inherent in collaborative supervision allows the teacher or group to share perceptions and offer some possible alternatives for future action, but also receive the benefit of supervisor perceptions and proposals. Negotiated action plans made during collaborative supervision allow teachers to meet needs of emerging independence while receiving the moderate guidance needed to assure that the plan will lead to instructional improvement.

Teachers functioning at generally high developmental levels were described in Chapter 4 as being at the postformal operations stage of cognitive development, high conceptual levels, the postconventional level of moral reasoning, the autonomous stage of ego development, the systems or trans-systems level of consciousness, and the teaching impact stage of concern. Teachers or groups functioning at generally high developmental levels, expertise, and commitment are ready for the self-direction fostered by the nondirective supervisory approach. They are autonomous, explorative, and creative. They can think of a problem from many perspectives, generate a variety of alternative actions, think through each step of an action plan, and follow the plan through to completion.

The Problem of Variability

The fact that the criteria for selecting a supervisory approach may fluctuate means that choosing the best approach can become more complicated than the broad guidelines just discussed might suggest. The following possibilities must be kept in mind:

1. Individual or group levels of development, expertise, and commitment may vary. For example, a teacher might be functioning at high levels of consciousness as well as cognitive, conceptual, and moral development but at only moderate levels of ego development, concern, and commitment. In addition, a group might include teachers of low, moderate, and high developmental levels. Some general guidelines are to use a controlling directive approach if most characteristics of an individual or group indicate an

extremely low decision-making capacity, informational directive supervision if most attributes point to a fairly low capacity, a collaborative approach if most characteristics indicate a moderate capacity, and nondirective supervision if most attributes point to a high capacity for decision making. When working with an individual or group with widely fluctuating characteristics, a collaborative approach would probably be most effective.

2. Characteristics of teachers and groups might change in certain situations. For example, a teacher who has successfully taught general science to middle school students for 10 years might regress to lower levels of development, expertise, or commitment after being transferred to a senior high school to teach chemistry and physics. Similarly, a faculty at a former junior high school might regress to lower levels of group development, expertise, or commitment after the campus has been converted to a middle school. In short, the developmental supervisor sometimes must change supervisory behaviors in order to adapt to a change in the teacher's or group's situation.

Research on adult and teacher development can suggest guidelines for determining the best supervisory approach. The tremendous variability of teacher characteristics, however, means that the supervisor must choose his or her approach on a case-by-case basis, relying on the knowledge base on teacher characteristics, recent observations of and interactions with the teacher or group, and analysis of the current situation. One way to describe developmental supervision is to say that it provides teachers with as much initial choice as they are ready to assume, then fosters teachers' decision-making capacity and expanded choice over time.

SuperVision for Teacher Development

The long-term goal of developmental supervision is teacher development toward a point at which teachers, facilitated by supervisors, can assume full responsibility for instructional improvement. There are several reasons why we believe that teacher development should be a critical function of supervision. First, as described in Chapter 4, teachers functioning at higher developmental levels tend to use a wide variety of instructional behaviors associated with successful teaching. Second, teachers who have themselves reached high stages of cognitive, conceptual, moral, and ego development are more likely to foster their own students' growth in those areas. In a democratic society, it is vital that students learn to think reflectively, function at high stages of moral reasoning, and be autonomous decision makers. Finally, teachers at higher levels of adult development, expertise, and commitment are more likely to embrace "a cause beyond oneself" and participate in collective action toward schoolwide instructional improvement—a critical element found in the effective schools research. This section has focused on the *why* of developmental supervision. The remainder of the chapter is concerned with *how* developmental supervision can be applied in the real world of schools and teachers.

Applying Developmental Supervision

Chapter 7 introduced the three phases of developmental supervision. To review, they are (1) choosing the best entry-level supervisory approach, (2) applying the chosen approach, and (3) fostering teacher development while gradually increasing teacher choice and decision-making responsibility. Our discussion of applying developmental supervision addresses each of these three phases.

Phase 1: Choosing the Best Approach

There are two primary ways to assess a teacher's developmental levels, expertise, and commitment, all of which should be considered when choosing the supervisory approach to be used. One way is to observe the teacher teaching or working with other teachers. Another way is to discuss with the teacher his or her ideas about students, teaching, and instructional improvement. The supervisor can use discussions with the teacher to find answers to the following questions:

1. Is the teacher aware of improvements that can be made in the classroom? Can the teacher identify those needs?
2. Has the teacher considered possible causes of the instructional needs? Does the teacher gather information from multiple sources about the instructional needs?
3. Can the teacher generate several possible solutions? How carefully does the teacher weigh the merits of each solution? Does the teacher consider what he or she can do to reach the goal without looking unrealistically for outside help?
4. Can the teacher be decisive in choosing a course of action? Does the teacher commit himself or herself to an implementation procedure?
5. Does the teacher do what he or she says?

Teacher responses to questions like these can provide clues to the appropriate supervisory approach.

Some cautions need to be made here concerning the organizational relationship between the individual providing supervision and the teacher or group receiving supervision. Generally, directive control supervision should be used only by supervisors in line relationships with teachers (supervisors who have been given formal authority by the school district over teachers they are supervising). Informational directive supervision should be used only by those who are acknowledged by the organization to have special expertise. Examples of individuals with acknowledged expertise include supervisors in line or staff relationships with teachers, lead teachers, mentors of beginning teachers, and so on. Collaborative and nondirective behaviors can be used by supervisors in line or staff relationships, teachers designated as instructional leaders, and teachers in reciprocal helping relationships, such as peer coaches. Table 12.1 provides a review of supervisory approaches normally appropriate for use by those carrying out some

TABLE 12.1   *Supervisory Roles and Approaches*

Supervisory Roles	Approaches Appropriate for Particular Supervisory Roles			
	Directive Control	Directive Informational	Collaborative	Nondirective
Line supervisor	X	X	X	X
Staff supervisor		X	X	X
Lead teacher		X	X	X
Designated mentor		X	X	X
Peer coach			X	X

common supervisory roles. The task of the person in a particular supervisory role is to choose the best approach from those appropriate for his or her role.

Phase 2: Applying the Chosen Approach

Previous chapters provided scenarios of supervisors using each of the four supervisory approaches. But can a supervisor shift from one approach to another when working with teachers and groups at different developmental levels? Stated differently, can the same supervisor effectively use directive informational, directive control, collaborative, and nondirective behaviors? The question of *supervisor flexibility* was addressed by Gordon (1989, 1990) during a study in which he trained supervisors in developmental supervision, then asked each supervisor to work with separate teacher triads. The supervisors attempted informational directive supervision with one teacher, collaborative supervision with a second teacher, and nondirective supervision with a third teacher (supervisors based their decisions on supervisory approach on earlier observations of and conferences with teachers). When supervisors attempted the different approaches, their conferences with teachers were audiotaped. The taped conferences were analyzed to determine if attempted approaches were effectively used. The investigator found that 93 percent of the supervisors were able to implement informational directive supervision, 100 percent were able to engage in collaborative supervision, and 70 percent were able to use nondirective supervision. An implication of this study is that supervisors being trained to use developmental supervision must receive their most intensive training in nondirective supervision, which seems to be the most difficult approach for many to use.

What if a supervisor in the early stages of working with a teacher or group—even after preliminary observation and discussion—is not sure which supervisory approach to use? A good rule of thumb in such cases is to *prepare to use a collaborative approach, but be ready to shift to a nondirective or directive approach if necessary.* When preparing to use a collaborative approach a supervisor determines possible improvement goals, actions, and criteria to be considered and potentially integrated with goals, actions, and criteria suggested by the teacher or group. However, if during the early phases of the conference or meeting it becomes apparent that the teacher or group will be able to identify an appropriate goal and action plan on their own, then the supervisor can forget about his or her possible suggestions and shift to nondirective behaviors as a means of facilitating self-directed teacher planning. If, on the other hand, the teacher or group is unable to identify an obvious problem, any of its underlying causes, or any possible solutions, the supervisor can shift to a directive mode, mandating (directive control) or suggesting (directive informational) a goal, actions, and improvement criteria.

One type of *supervisor flexibility* is the ability to plan and implement different supervisory approaches with different teachers and groups. The ultimate supervisor flexibility, however, is the ability to "shift supervisory gears," so to speak, and effectively use an approach not originally planned because of new discoveries about teachers or the situation at hand. Like successful teachers, successful supervisors must be able to think on their feet and flex accordingly (Zellermayer and Margolin, 2005).

Phase 3: Fostering Teacher Development

Simply matching the best supervisory approach to the teacher's or group's current developmental levels can promote some degree of teacher development. For example, Siens and Ebmeier (1996) found that teachers assisted by supervisors trained to tailor their conference approaches to teachers' levels of motivation, analytical skill, and knowledge experienced significantly more growth on a measure of reflective thinking than did a control group of teachers receiving only the regular supervision provided at their schools. Previous chapters in this text have discussed facilitating teacher development by gradually decreasing supervisor control and increasing teacher control over the decision-making process. There are additional strategies that supervisors can use to stimulate teacher development. One method is to introduce teachers to new information about students and learning, innovative teaching strategies, and novel ways to frame and solve problems. Initially, new ways of thinking and acting that teachers are invited to explore should be linked to their existing knowledge, experience, and values. Gradually, teachers can be exposed to a broader spectrum of theory and practice.

Another method is to assign teachers to decision-making teams or learning groups in which most of the other members are functioning at slightly higher developmental levels. Significant, ongoing professional interaction with teachers of somewhat higher development will tend to pull the teacher of lower development toward the group's functioning level. Unfortunately, the reverse is also true. Teachers of higher developmental levels assigned to groups in which the majority of teachers are functioning at lower developmental levels tend to be "pulled down" to the group's level.

Lois Thies-Sprinthall (1984) has identified five conditions necessary to promote psychological/cognitive growth:

1. Role-taking experiences
2. Careful and continuous guided reflection

3. Balance . . . between real experience and discussion/reflection
4. Both personal support and challenge
5. Continuity (programs should be at least six months in length with meetings at regular intervals) (p. 54)

Phillips and Glickman (1991) studied a peer-coaching program that incorporated Thies-Sprinthall's five conditions for psychological/cognitive growth. The researchers measured participants' conceptual levels before and after the program, and found that a significant increase in teachers' conceptual levels had occurred by the end of the program. Exploratory studies such as the study reported by Phillips and Glickman indicate that stimulation of teacher growth toward higher developmental levels is possible.

Not Algorithms, But Guideposts for Decisions

Eventually, we must discuss, question, and ask each other (in a supervisor-supervisee relationship) which supervisory approach has been most helpful in the past, which will be most helpful in the present, and which approach we should be striving for

---

BOX 12.1   Scenario and Discussion: Inappropriate Use of Interpersonal Behaviors?

Megan Janson, a teacher at Lakeside High School, has come to instructional supervisor Jim Autry with a concern. Several female teachers have complained that Jim seems to be overly directive with them during conferences focused on instructional supervision. These same teachers have told Megan that they have heard from a number of male colleagues that Jim is nondirective when conferring with the male teachers.

Megan, a close friend of Jim, tells him she wanted him to know this so he could reflect on the situation and decide what, if anything, to do about it. Jim has been using different supervisory approaches with different teachers and groups lately, but has been trying to use collaborative supervision with most teachers and has been intentionally directive informational with only one female teacher and intentionally nondirective with only one male teacher. He is surprised and disturbed at the comments from female teachers reported by Megan.

What advice would you give Jim on each of the following issues:

1. How can Jim determine whether he is using directive behaviors with females better matched with a different approach, and/or being nondirective with males better matched with a different approach?

2. If Jim concludes that he really is using unintended interpersonal behaviors with some teachers, how can he explore possible reasons for such unintended behaviors?

3. If Jim eventually concludes that he has been engaging in unconscious gender bias in his supervisory conferences, what can he do to correct the situation? How can he verify improvement in this area?

in the future. With the exception of emergency situations, this is the responsibility of both parties.

Life in the school world is ragged and complex. This chapter offers a great deal of information to ponder about available behaviors, human motivation, types of environments, and characteristics of individuals and groups. There are no algorithms to provide exactly correct responses to human behavior. Such formulas as "if individual X exhibits characteristics A, B, and C, then supervisor Y should do D, F, and G" do not and should not exist. Such algorithms are useful only in mechanically and technically controlled systems (such as computer operations, assembly production, or chemical alterations). Algorithms work in technical but not human endeavors, and it would be misleading to suggest that such supervision formulas are available. Instead, what is available is information about ourselves and others that can serve as guideposts to suggest what *might* be of use. Such developmental guideposts can help reduce some of the infinite complexity of the school world so that supervision can be a purposeful and thoughtful function for improving instruction.

SUMMARY

This chapter explored the theory and practice of developmental supervision in detail. We discussed the rationale for matching various supervisory approaches with different teacher characteristics, as well as the problem of variability of those characteristics. We argued that the long-term goal of supervision should be to foster teacher growth toward higher levels of development, expertise, and commitment.

In the second part of the chapter, we discussed the application of developmental supervision. We suggested observations of and discussions with teachers as ways to assess teacher characteristics, and made recommendations for matching supervisory approach to teacher or group characteristics. We discussed long-term programs designed to stimulate teacher development. Finally, we proposed that the supervisor needs to use his or her own decision-making abilities to determine the most appropriate interpersonal approaches to use with his or her staff.

REFERENCES AND RECOMMENDED READINGS

Cawelti, G. 1976. "Selecting appropriate leadership styles for instructional improvement." Videotape. Alexandria, VA: Association for Supervision and Curriculum Development.

Clark, C. M., and Joyce, B. R. 1976. *Teacher decision making and teacher effectiveness.* Paper presented at the annual meeting of the American Educational Research Association, San Francisco.

Clinton, B. C., Glickman, C. D., and Payne, D. A. 1982. Identifying supervision problems: A guide to better solutions. *Illinois School Research and Development, 9*(1).

Drucker, P. 1973. *Management.* New York: Harper and Row.

Gates, P. E., Blanchard, K. H., and Hersey, P. 1976. Diagnosing educational leadership problems. *Educational Leadership, 33*(February), 348–354.

Gordon, S. P. 1989. *The theory of developmental supervison: An investigation of the critical aspects.* Unpublished Ed.D. dissertation, University of Georgia.

Gordon, S. P. 1990. Developmental supervision: An exploratory study of a promising model. *Journal of Curriculum and Supervision, 5,* 293–307.

Hunt, D. E., and Sullivan, E. V. 1974. *Between psychology and education.* Hinsdale, IL: Dryden Press.

Kohlberg, L. 1969. Stage and sequence: The cognitive developmental approach to socialization. In D. Goslin (Ed.), *Handbook of socialization theory and research.* Chicago: Rand McNally.

Levine, D. V. 1991. Creating effective schools: Findings and implications from research and practice. *Phi Delta Kappan, 72*(5), 389–393.

Piaget, J. 1965. *The moral judgements of the child.* New York: Free Press/Macmillan.

Phillips, M. D., and Glickman, C. D. 1991. Peer coaching: Developmental approach to enhancing teacher thinking. *Journal of Staff Development, 12*(2), 20–25.

Porter, A. C., and Brophy, J. 1988. Synthesis of research on good teaching: Insights from the work of the Institute for Research on Teaching. *Educational Leadership, 45*(8), 74–85.

Riley, J. F. 1980. Creative problem solving and cognitive monitoring as instructional variables for teaching training in classroom problem solving. Unpublished Ed.D. dissertation, University of Georgia.

Siens, C. M., and Ebmeier, H. 1996. Developmental supervision and the reflective thinking of teachers. *Journal of Curriculum and Supervision, 11*(4), 299–319.

Suzuki, S. 1970. *Zen mind, beginner's mind.* New York: Weather Hill.

Thies-Sprinthall, L. 1984. Promoting the developmental growth of supervising teachers: Theory, research programs, and implications. *Journal of Teacher Education, 35*(3), 53–60.

Zellermayer, M., and Margolin, I. 2005. Teacher educators' professional learning described through the lens of complexity theory. *Teachers College Record, 107*(6), 1275–1304.

Technical Skills

The supervisor who knows about characteristics of successful schools, the norms that mediate against success, and the ways teacher development contrasts with optimal adult development can begin to formulate a supervisory belief system that becomes a reality when interpersonal and technical skills of supervision are applied in practice.

The previous section matched directive, collaborative, and nondirective interpersonal skills in working with developmental levels of individuals and groups of teachers. Part IV deals with the technical supervisory skills needed in working with teachers to assess, plan, observe, research, and evaluate. Understanding schools and relating well to teachers are necessary components, but technical skills are equally important for accomplishing the tasks of supervision.

Assessing and Planning Skills

Assessing and planning are two sides of the same coin. *Assessing* involves determining where you and your staff have been and where you and your staff currently are. *Planning* includes deciding where you want to go and choosing the path you and your staff hope to traverse in order to reach that destination. Until you are certain of the origination and destination of your travel, a map is useless. Once you are certain, a route can be created.

Assessing and Planning within the Organization

We might think of assessing and planning as a recipe (Bruce and Grimsley, 1979). A plan for direct assistance, professional development, curriculum development, or group development has the same elements as a cooking recipe. *We decide our objective:* "to bake a sweet potato soufflé" (thanks to Ms. Donna Bell for providing this culinary example). Knowing our family's previous history of food preferences, we are confident that if we cook the soufflé correctly, they will enjoy it and we will be held in positive regard for at least 10 minutes. Next, *we determine the activities and when they will take place.*

Activity 1: Mash 6 cups of cooked sweet potatoes.

Activity 2: Beat into the mashed potatoes: 4 eggs, 1 cup butter, 2 cups sugar, 1 cup milk, 1 teaspoon vanilla.

Activity 3: Spread out in unbuttered pan.

Activity 4: Mix in a separate bowl: 1 cup brown sugar, 2/3 cup flour, 1 cup butter, 1 cup chopped pecans.

Activity 5: Spread this mix (Activity 4) evenly over the potatoes (Activity 3).

Activity 6: Bake at 350° for 1 hour.

With the activities and times determined, *we need to identify resources.* Equipment resources are an oven, measuring cups, measuring spoons, a large bowl, a pan, a mixing fork, and a spreading knife. Food resources are sweet potatoes, eggs, butter, sugar, vanilla, brown sugar, flour, pecans, and milk.

Finally, *we will evaluate the success* of our cooking endeavor by the following criteria: Everyone in our family will eat the sweet potato soufflé. At least two of the three members will ask for seconds. All of them will tell us we're wonderful cooks, and they will volunteer to wash the dishes.

If the supervisor tries acting as a gourmet of instructional cookery and planning recipes for success, all staff members will delight in the soufflé of instructional improvement. The food analogy has run its course (by now, you are probably heading for the refrigerator), and we can turn to assessing and planning within the school context. For purposes of illustration, let's take an example of an elementary reading supervisor who is responsible for developing revised curriculum guides in reading.

Ways of Assessing Need

The first question for the reading supervisor is: What do we hope to accomplish with a new curriculum guide? To answer this question, we need to collect information about the past and present state of reading instruction. The supervisor can use multiple ways of assessing need: (1) eyes and ears, (2) systematic classroom and school observations, (3) official records, (4) review of teacher and student work products, (5) third-party review, (6) written open-ended survey, (7) check and ranking list surveys, (8) the Delphi technique, and (9) nominal group technique.

Eyes and Ears

Talk to teachers, administrators, aides, and anyone else who works directly with the task under consideration. In this case, the supervisor would want to ask teachers and aides individually and in small groups what they believe are the strengths and weaknesses of the curriculum guide. How is it being used? Is it helpful, and in what ways? Where does it break down? When is it not useful?

Systematic Classroom and School Observations

This type of assessment goes beyond informal discussions and observation. It consists of the systematic gathering of quantitative or qualitative observation data. Chapter 14 provides a variety of classroom observation instruments. Such instruments can be used to assist the individual teacher, but also can be used to gather data from many classrooms and identify schoolwide instructional needs. For example, in a schoolwide needs assessment one of the authors coordinated, observers used the same observation instrument to gather data on instructional methods used in classrooms throughout the school. The observers found that most of the teachers in the school relied on lecture and independent seatwork as their primary instructional methods. It was concluded that there was a need for teachers to develop a wider variety of instructional methods. Observations also can be carried out in common areas of the school. In one school experiencing disruptive student behavior during lunch periods, the teachers gathered a variety of observation data on student behaviors in the cafeteria, and based on that data identified needed changes in the school's lunch procedures.

Official Records

Look at any documents that indicate the current use and effect of the task under consideration. In this case, what do reading achievement test scores show? How about diagnostic reading tests? Are students mastering reading skills, or are there certain areas (comprehension, fluency, vocabulary) that are consistently out of line with others? What about the curriculum guide itself? When was it last revised? What recent knowledge about writing curriculum guides, instructional approaches to reading, and reading topics are not reflected in the current curriculum?

Review of Teacher and Student Work Products

Assessors can review teacher and student work products to assess need. Examples of teacher work products are unit and lesson plans, videos of teaching, and teacher portfolios. Examples of student work products include daily assignments, videos of student presentations, student projects, and student portfolios. Samples of work produced by several teachers or students can be reviewed to identify common instructional needs. In some schools, teachers build classroom and school portfolios that can be reviewed to analyze representative teacher and student work products.

Third-Party Review

Having a neutral outside person review the task area can be helpful. The supervisor might contact a university or central office consultant, a graduate doctoral student, or some other person with expertise to do an investigation and write a report. The third-party person should be given a clear description of the task (to look at the strengths and weaknesses of the reading curriculum guides), and care should be taken not to bias the third-party person's judgment. The report can then serve as an additional source of objective knowledge, not tied to any special interest in the forthcoming project.

Written Open-Ended Survey

To document and add to the information already received through eyes and ears and official records, a written survey can be administered. Send out a brief questionnaire that asks teachers, aides, administrators, and parents what they think about the current reading curriculum. Keep the survey brief, and word the questions simply, without education jargon. An example of a survey is found in Figure 13.1.

Check and Ranking List Surveys

After gathering ideas of the strengths and weaknesses of the task at hand from many sources, the supervisor can ask staff to rank the ideas. The supervisor can then compile a group frequency and numerical priority for each idea previously mentioned. For example, if—through eyes and ears, official documents, and open-ended surveys—the supervisor has collected a list of ideas about perceived weaknesses of the current reading program, he or she then could disseminate the list back to teachers, aides, and others. The disseminated form might be as shown in Figure 13.2. The supervisor can meet with the staff and show the frequency of numbers assigned to each idea and the average score for each item. Those items receiving frequent low scores and/or with the lowest average scores would be the first to focus on when discussing curriculum revisions. The ranking list can be further refined by having the participants do two separate rankings—first, to see how all the ideas rank, and second, to rerank a shortened list of prioritized ideas.

Explanation: As you may know, this year we are determining changes to be made in our reading curriculum. Please take a few minutes to respond to the following questions. We will use the information to rewrite our curriculum guides. Please be frank!

Question 1. What do you think about the current reading curriculum?

Question 2. What are the strengths of the current reading curriculum?

Question 3. What are the weaknesses of the current reading curriculum?

Question 4. What changes do you believe would improve the reading curriculum?

FIGURE 13.1 *Survey of Reading Curriculum*

Directions: The following are the ideas for possible changes that you have suggested. Please prioritize this list by placing the number 1 next to the idea needing the greatest attention, number 2 next to the item needing the next most attention, and so on, until all items are ranked.

_____ Format of the guides.

_____ Readability of the guides.

_____ Activities to go with curriculum objectives.

_____ Objectives and units dealing with reading newspapers.

_____ Objectives and units dealing with reading in other subject areas.

_____ More phonic and word recognition objectives.

_____ Cross-reference units with materials in the classrooms.

_____ Cross-reference objects with fourth-grade competency-based reading test.

FIGURE 13.2 *Ranking Ideas for Improving Reading Curriculum*

Delphi Technique

Another written way to prioritize needs is the Delphi technique, developed by the Rand Corporation (Hostrop, 1975; Weaver, 1971; Wilhelm, 2001). The technique, originally intended to forecast future trends, is often used for needs assessment. It is a combination of open-ended survey and ranking. The supervisor sends around a problem statement to staff: "We are looking at revisions in the reading curriculum. Write down what you believe needs to be done." The supervisor retrieves the written comments, reproduces everyone's comments, and returns all the comments to the participants. They read the comments and then individually write a synthesis of the various ideas. The supervisor then collects everyone's syntheses and makes a new list of all synthesized ideas. The new list goes back to the participants for ranking. The supervisor collects and computes average and frequency of ratings and then returns the tallies to participants to rerank. This procedure continues until clear priorities emerge.

Nominal Group Technique

The nominal group technique, made popular by Delbecq, Van de Ven, and Gustafson (1975), is an effective way to involve all individuals within large groups of stakeholders in needs assessment and goal setting. The process is outlined here in eight steps:

1. The large group is divided into small groups. Each small group is assigned a facilitator to explain and coordinate the process.
2. Each individual within a small group silently generates and writes perceived needs.

3. In round-robin manner, participants orally share with their small group one perceived need at a time. The facilitator records each idea on a flip chart. At this point, there is no discussion—only listing of perceived needs.

4. Small-group discussions of each perceived need are led by the facilitators. The purpose of the discussion is clarification of the perceived needs, not debate on their validity.

5. Individuals within each small group rate all of the perceived needs that were listed in step 3. This step usually takes the form of participants assigning each perceived need a numerical value. For example, the facilitator might instruct group members to rate each need from 1 to 5, with an item assigned a value of 1 considered to be unimportant and an item rated a 5 perceived to be an extremely important need.

6. Each small-group facilitator collects all group members' ratings and calculates a mean for each perceived need. The facilitator rewrites the perceived needs in rank order by mean and shares the results with the small group.

7. Each small group submits its top-ranked needs (often its top five needs) to the large group.

8. A lead facilitator then takes the large group through steps 4 through 6. In the large-group version of step 4, any participant can ask for clarification of any perceived need, with the appropriate small-group facilitator providing the requested clarification. In the whole-group version of step 5, each participant rates all perceived needs presented to the large group. The product of the large-group version of step 6 is a list of organizational needs in rank order.

Analyzing Organizational Needs

Some organizational needs are easily understood and addressed by supervisors and teachers. Others are more complicated. They require analysis to determine their underlying causes before a plan can be formulated. For decades, W. Edwards Deming argued for the use of data displays to examine factors that may contribute to organizational needs and problems. In this section we'll discuss a few types of charts suggested by Deming and his colleagues. We'll do this by applying each chart to a school situation. The words of Mary Walton (1986) should allay any anxiety concerning the use of such charts that the reader without expertise in complex data analysis might be experiencing:

> Some of the most useful statistical tools are neither difficult nor complicated to master. The level of mathematics necessary is no more than a seventh or eighth grader might learn. Several of the basic tools are merely ways of organizing and visually displaying data. In most cases, employees can collect the data and do much of the

interpretation, and they are happy to do so because it gives them more responsibility. (p. 94)

Cause and Effect Diagrams

Figure 13.3 is an example of a cause and effect diagram, often referred to as a *fishbone diagram.* In our example, a newly formed staff-development committee has received feedback from teachers throughout the district that recent staff-development programs have been ineffective. Based on a series of interviews with representative groups of teachers, the committee constructed the cause and effect diagram in Figure 13.3.

Four general causes were identified for the ineffective professional development: (1) poor planning, (2) low-quality staff-development sessions, (3) inadequate support for the program, and (4) unsatisfactory program evaluation. Contributing causes within the poor planning category included failure to involve teachers in the planning process, the fact that the professional development plan was not based on teacher needs, and the absence of alternatives for staff from different grade levels, content areas, and specialty areas.

The poor quality of the staff-development sessions was ascribed to the fact that too many teachers were present, each session was a one-shot workshop unrelated to the other workshops in the program, and the workshop presentations were of poor quality. The workshops were perceived to be substandard because the outside presenters did not have a good understanding of the school culture or the purposes of the program, and their presentations were too abstract to evoke teacher interest.

Problems with support included a lack of funds to purchase instructional materials necessary to implement ideas introduced in the workshops and a failure to provide support for teachers attempting to transfer workshop concepts to the classroom. Finally, the committee found that the district's evaluation of the program had been inadequate. The evaluation forms used by the district were the same ones used for all staff-development workshops; they were not relevant to the specific content of the workshops being assessed. Additionally, the wording of the evaluation questions was so general that teachers were not sure what the questions were asking. Since no formal analysis of evaluation data took place, no information on program outcomes was available and no program revisions were made. The "anatomy of a failure" depicted in Figure 13.3 is not the most pleasant project the planning committee could have undertaken. Yet, the completed diagram was a valuable tool in planning future professional-development programs.

Flowcharts

A flowchart can be used to review a process when either the process or conflicting perceptions of the process are resulting in unmet needs. When different parties involved in a process draw their own flowcharts, the charts often are dissimilar. Figure 13.4 shows a flowchart tracking what happens from the time a student is

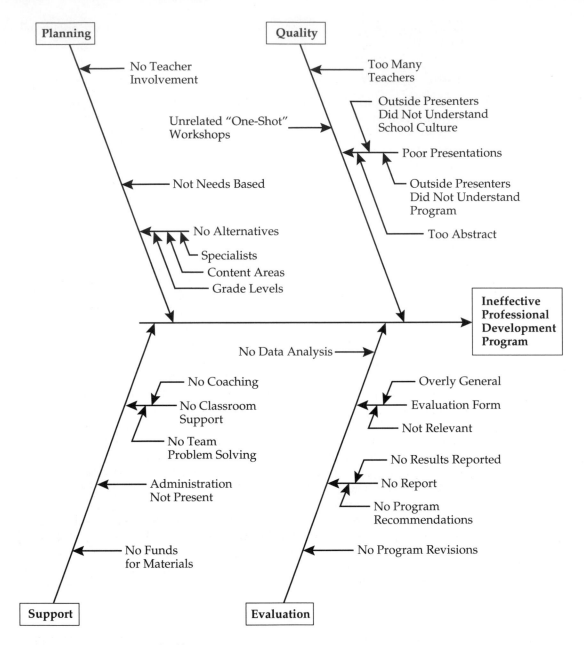

FIGURE 13.3 *Cause and Effect Diagram*

sent to the office for misbehavior until the student returns to class. This chart was drawn by the principal's secretary. Flowcharts of the same process drawn by the principal, the teacher, and the student might be very different from the secretary's and each other!

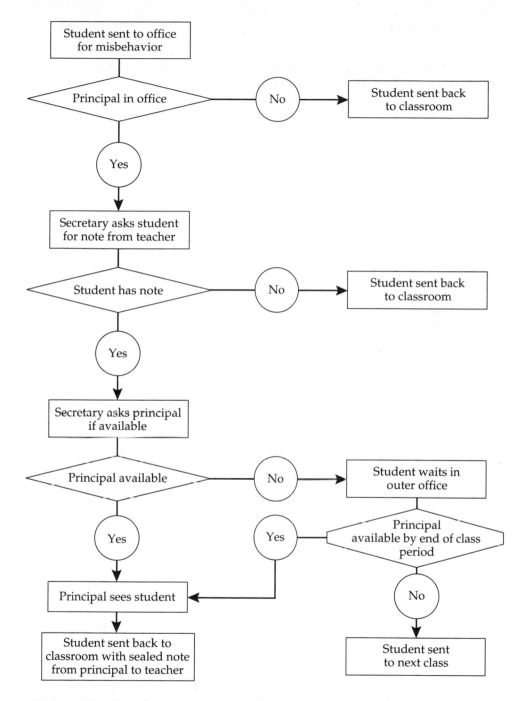

FIGURE 13.4 *Flowchart*

Pareto Charts

A Pareto chart illustrates in descending frequency of size those factors that cause a need or problem. Displaying the relative impact of causal factors gives planners information to help them set priorities and allocate resources. Figure 13.5 illustrates a Pareto chart with bars showing the percentage of students dropping out of a senior high school for each of several reasons. Above the bars, a cumulative percentage line runs across the chart. This data would be valuable to a planning team designing a dropout prevention program.

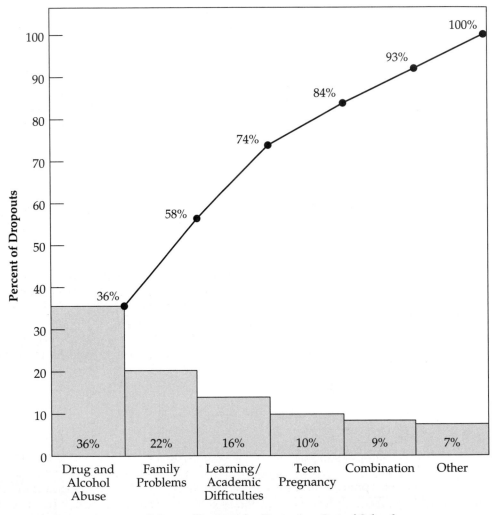

Primary Reasons for Dropping Out of School

FIGURE 13.5   *Pareto Chart*

Planning

After assessing and prioritizing needs and identifying causes, planning proceeds. Techniques of planning discussed in this section include affinity diagrams, impact analysis charts, and Gantt charts.

Affinity Diagrams

Let us assume that a needs assessment has identified a number of specific needs, with many of those needs appearing to be related to each other. An affinity diagram is a way of clustering needs and identifying broad goals that address a set of related needs. One way to begin the building of an affinity diagram is to list each identified need on a separate card or Post-it. Figure 13.6 displays results of a curriculum needs assessment. In the assessment, teachers, parents, and community members stated that students should attain each of the outcomes in Figure 13.6. The affinity diagram in Figure 13.7 clusters the curriculum needs and identifies a broad goal common to each cluster. Enfolding specific needs within larger categories enables the planning team to focus on a few broad goals, while retaining information on specific needs.

Impact Analysis Charts

Impact analysis charts are usually constructed early in the planning process. Their purpose is to assist planners in projecting who and what a potential program or change will affect and what the effects might be. In Figure 13.8, triangles represent people and things a revised reading curriculum would impact. Predicted effects are symbolized by rectangles. Impact analysis charts can become far more complex than the example in Figure 13.8 (the more ambitious the goals, the more extensive the chart). Building and discussing impact analysis charts can help planners to create a "conceptual map" of areas they want to address during the planning process. They can also help planners to include objectives, activities, and evaluation procedures in their formal plan that they might otherwise neglect.

Gantt Charts

A Gantt chart is simply a graph that portrays the beginning and completion dates of each activity involved in completing the overall task (Bishop, 1976). As shown in Figure 13.9, the activities for revising the curriculum guides are placed on the left-hand side of the chart. The beginning and ending time for each activity is shown by a black solid bar across the time line. The supervisor can refer to the chart at any time to check on the progress of the project and be reminded of what groups and what subtasks should be receiving his or her attention.

FIGURE 13.6   *Curriculum Needs, to Be Clustered in Affinity Diagram*

Models Combining Assessment and Planning

Thus far we have considered assessment and planning as separate entities. Three models that combine these functions are force field analysis, the PDSA cycle, and strategic planning. All three models attempt to address the dynamic, unpredictable

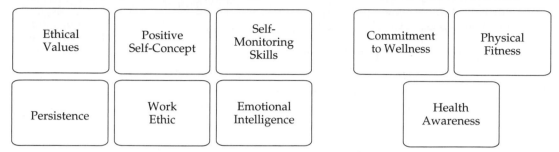

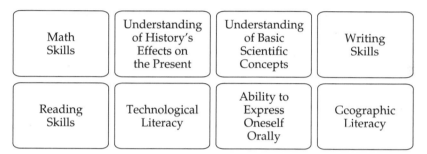

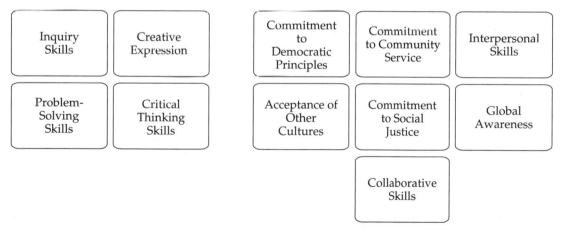

FIGURE 13.7 *Affinity Diagram*

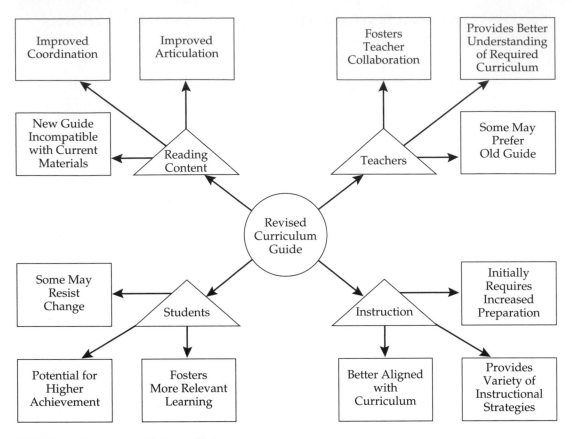

FIGURE 13.8   *Impact Analysis Chart*

nature of complex organizations. In recent years these three models have been applied to education.

Force Field Analysis

This process can help educators define goals, analyze competing forces, and plan how to bring about needed change. A force field analysis consists of ten phases.

1. Describe the desired state of affairs (what should be).
2. Describe the current state of affairs (what is).
3. Describe the gap between the desired and current state of affairs.
4. Describe the restraining forces: those forces that resist movement toward the desired state.
5. Describe the driving forces: those forces that can assist movement toward the desired state.

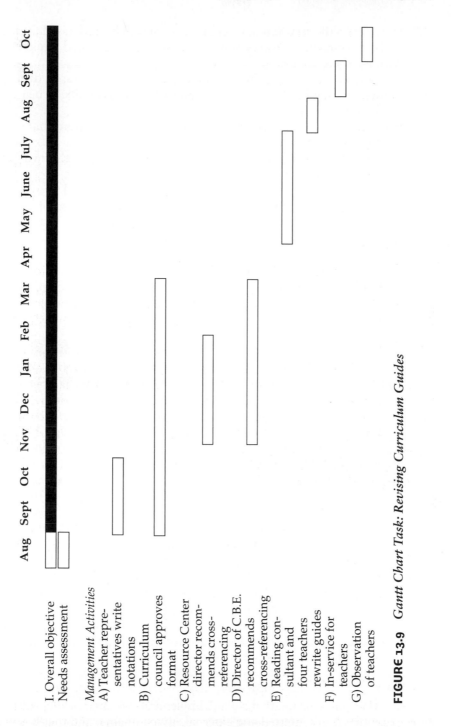

FIGURE 13-9 *Gantt Chart Task: Revising Curriculum Guides*

6. Select from the restraining forces those that will be addressed during change efforts. Restraining forces that both are important and capable of being weakened are chosen.
7. Select from the driving forces those that will be addressed during change efforts. Driving forces that are both important and capable of being strengthened are those chosen.
8. For each restraining force chosen in phase 6, identity actions that will weaken the restraining force.
9. For each driving force chosen in phase 7, identify actions that will strengthen the driving force.
10. Integrate and sequence the actions chosen in phases 8 and 9 to create a comprehensive action plan for moving from the current state of affairs to the desired state of affairs. Include a plan for evaluating the effects of the action plan and a timeline for implementing the action plan and evaluation.

A force field analysis is most effective if the descriptions of the desired and current state of affairs as well as restraining and driving forces are based on data gathered during the force field analysis, rather than the planners' perceptions alone.

PDSA Cycle

W. Edward Deming's popular "14 points for managers," "seven deadly sins," and data-based approach to quality control (see Walton, 1986) have had enormous impact in Japan and North America. Educators have jumped on the total quality management (TQM) bandwagon, adapting the ideas of Deming and others associated with TQM to teaching and school leadership (see Bonstingl, 1992a, 1992b; Brandt, 1992). Full discussions of Deming's management method and TQM are beyond the scope of this chapter. However, one process with its origins in the total quality movement is especially relevant to our discussion of assessment and planning. That process is the PDSA cycle (alternative versions of the process are referred to as the *Shewhart, Deming,* or *PDCA cycle*).

The PDSA cycle consists of *planning, doing, studying,* and *acting.* The cyclical relationship of these four stages is illustrated in Figure 13.10. In the *planning* stage, assessment and planning take place. In the *doing* stage, the plan is implemented, usually on a small scale. In the *studying* stage, data are collected on the implementation process and its effects. In the *acting* stage, the data are analyzed and conclusions about strengths and weaknesses of the plan and its implementation are drawn. A new cycle then begins with the formulation of a revised plan. The PDSA cycle is the heart and soul of "continuous quality improvement."

Strategic Planning

Strategic planning assumes that a plan's implementation and results will be affected by the organization's internal and external environments, and that it is impossible to completely predict and control the future in our rapidly changing world. There

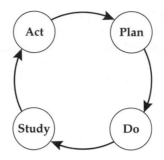

FIGURE 13.10   *PDSA Cycle*

are many versions of strategic planning (see, for example, Dyson, 1990; Kaufman, 1991) as well as applications to education (Cook, 1990; Kaufman, 1992; Shapiro and Nunez, 2001; Moore, 2004). A nine-step strategic planning process is presented below:

1. *Identify common beliefs.* This first stage of strategic planning becomes the foundation of everything that follows. Cook (1990) discusses the statement of beliefs:

   > It is a formal expression of the organization's fundamental values: its ethical code, its overriding convictions, its inviolate commitments. Essentially, it describes the moral character of the organization. That means that the statement of beliefs of an organization must represent a composite, a distillation, of the personal values of those who make up the organization. (p. 89)

2. *Identify the organization's vision.* The organization's vision is its scenario of what *should be* in the future. For a school district or school, this includes such things as the abilities and attitudes graduates should possess. A vision statement should focus on intended outcomes, not processes. One common visioning strategy the authors have found successful is to ask planners what characteristics they would like their next kindergarten class to possess when those students graduate from high school.

3. *Identify the organization's mission.* A mission statement is a summary (usually one sentence in length) of the organization's purpose. The mission is based on the organization's beliefs and vision. It becomes the focus of all remaining phases of the strategic planning process.

4. *Formulate policies.* In relationship to strategic planning, policies are ground rules that will apply to the remaining phases of the planning process, the content of the strategic plan, and its implementation. An example of a strategic policy is "All action plans will be based on the best interests of the school district's students." Another example is "No new curricula or instructional programs will be established without the agreement of at least three-fourths of the teachers who will have responsibility for implementing

the new curriculum or program." Strategic policies become the boundaries within which future planning and change take place.

5. *Conduct external analysis.* This phase consists of analysis of demographic, economic, political, social, and technological factors in the external environment. Current conditions and predicted futures concerning each of these five factors are analyzed. The purpose of external analysis is to identify external *threats* to the organization's mission as well as *opportunities* for external assistance or collaboration in carrying out the mission. Threats or opportunities within each of the five factors are identified.

6. *Conduct internal analysis.* The internal analysis consists of examination of such factors as school governance, culture, leadership, staff expertise and commitment, curriculum and instruction, student characteristics, and student achievement. As with external analysis, both current conditions and future predictions within each factor are examined. The purpose of internal analysis is to determine the organization's *strengths* and *weaknesses,* especially in respect to its mission.

7. *State objectives.* The objectives are tied directly to the organization's mission. In other words, if all of the organization's objectives are met, then in all probability the mission will be achieved. Like the vision statement, the objectives focus on outcomes, not processes. Strategic objectives should be student centered, few in number, specific, measurable, and clearly stated.

8. *Develop and analyze alternative strategies.* At this point in the strategic planning process, action teams can be formed for each objective. After reviewing decisions made during the first seven phases of the process, action teams develop and analyze alternative strategies for reaching their assigned objective. Alternative strategies are then compared. One type of comparison is carried out by testing each strategy for consistency with the organization's beliefs, vision, mission, and policies. Another type of comparison involves considering the feasibility of each strategy in light of external threats and opportunities as well as internal strengths and weaknesses. A third way to compare strategies is to create scenarios of each strategy being implemented, projecting the strategic effects on the organization and its mission.

9. *Design action plans.* Based on the analysis from phase 8, action teams choose the strategies most likely to achieve the objectives, and sequence those strategies into action plans. The action plans involve time lines for implementation as well as provisions for monitoring progress and outcomes. Since the effects of any plan are not completely predictable, strategic action plans have built-in contingencies—back-up plans enabling adaptation to changing external or internal conditions. During implementation of action plans, periodic reviews are carried out to determine if alternative strategies are needed.

Strategic plans can be comprehensive district or school-based plans (macroplans) or specific programs (microplans). In school-based strategic planning, care must be taken to assure that the school and district's beliefs, visions, missions, and policies (phases 1–4) are consistent. Specific program planning begins with a review of the organization's existing beliefs, vision, mission, and policy, with actual program planning beginning in phase 5.

Cautions Concerning Planning

Postmodern theory warns us that the rational analyses, predictions, controls, and measurements that make up conventional planning often are inconsistent with the multiplicity of realities and competing interests that make up the real world. Chaos theory reminds us that, unlike traditional plans, complex systems like schools do not consist of simple cause and effect relationships, are affected by seemingly unrelated variables inside and outside the system, and are subject to unpredictable events and changes (a full discussion of chaos theory and its implications for schools is presented in Chapter 21).

Do these cautions mean that we throw out the planning tools discussed in this chapter and simply "wing it" regarding instructional improvement? No, but they do mean that we change our traditional concept of planning to provide for

- Planning that is centered on people—students, teachers, parents and community members—not on planning tools and documents (the tools and documents should be used in the service of people)
- Decentralized planning in which the supervisor becomes the coordinator of stakeholder teams actively involved in the planning process
- Diversity, in terms of both the groups represented and the ideas considered in the planning process
- Regular interaction among planners and between planners and those who will be affected by the plan
- A recognition by planners of the complexity, multiplicity, and nonlinearity inherent in the school organization
- The consideration of alternative futures for the school community
- Improvement plans with built-in flexibility, allowing a fair degree of spontaneity and exploration during implementation
- Provisions for continuous and critical assessment of the plan during implementation
- An understanding that the important thing is the goal the plan is intended to reach, not the plan itself, and a willingness to revise the plan when appropriate

SUMMARY

This chapter has explained the complementary nature of assessment and planning for realizing a vision of instructional improvement. The first topic was assessing and planning organizational change. Assessment techniques discussed were eyes and ears, systematic classroom and school observations, official records, review of teacher and student work products, third-party review, written open-ended surveys, check and ranking list surveys, the Delphi technique, and the nominal group technique. Ways of determining the underlying causes of needs discussed were cause and effect diagrams, flowcharts, and Pareto charts. Planning techniques discussed were affinity diagrams, impact analysis charts, and Gantt charts. Techniques described as combining assessment and planning were force field analysis, the PDSA cycle, and strategic planning. The last section discussed cautions concerning planning. Assessing and planning skills are generic; they help us to organize our own professional life as well as organize instructional improvement programs that involve many people. Assessing and planning enable us to take stock of present conditions, analyze consequences, and choose events, activities, and resources.

REFERENCES AND RECOMMENDED READINGS

Bennis, W. G., Benne, K. D., and Chin, P. 1985. *The planning of change.* New York: Holt, Rinehart and Winston.

Bishop, L. J. 1976. *Staff development and instructional development: Plans and procedures.* Boston: Allyn and Bacon.

Bostingl, J. J. 1992a. The total quality classroom. *Educational Leadership, 49*(6), 67.

Bostingl, J. J. 1992b. *Schools of quality: An introduction to total quality management in education.* Alexandria, VA: Association for Supervision and Curriculum Development.

Brandt, R. (Ed.). 1992. *Educational Leadership, 50.* Theme issue on "Improving School Quality."

Bruce, R. E., and Grimsley, E. E. 1979. Course supplementary reading—Introduction to supervision. Unpublished manuscript, University of Georgia.

Clark, D., Lotto, L., and Astuto, T. 1984. Effective schools and school improvement: A comparative analysis of two lines of inquiry. *Educational Administration Quarterly, 20,* 41–68.

Cook, W. J. 1990. *Bill Cook's strategic planning for America's schools* (rev. ed.). Arlington, VA: American Association of School Administrators.

Delbecq, A. L., Van de Ven, A. H., and Gustafson, D. H. 1975. *Group techniques for program planning.* Glenview, IL: Scott, Foresman.

Deming, W. E. 1986. *Out of the crisis.* Cambridge, MA: Massachusetts Institute of Technology.

Dyson, R. G. 1990. *Strategic planning: Models and analytical techniques.* Chichester, UK: John Wiley and Sons.

Goodlad, J. I. 2000. Educational renewal and the arts. *Arts Education Policy Review, 101*(4), 11–14.

Hostrop, R. W. 1975. *Managing education for results* (2nd ed.). Homewood, CA: ETC Publications.

Kaufman, R. 1991. *Strategic planning: An organizational guide.* Glenview, IL: Scott, Foresman.

Kaufman, R. 1992. *Mapping educational success: Strategic thinking and planning for school administrators.* Newbury Park, CA: Corwin.

Moore, E. A. 2004. Strategic planning during times of uncertainties and opportunities. *The Agricultural Education Magazine, 77*(3), 23–25.

Schmoker, M. J., and Wilson, R. B. 1993. *Total quality education: Profiles of schools that demonstrate the power of Deming's management principles.* Bloomington, IN: Phi Delta Kappa.

Shapiro, L. T., and Nunez, W. J. 2001. Strategic planning synergy. *Planning for Higher Education, 30*(1), 27–34.

Walton, M. 1986. *The Deming management method.* New York: Putnam.

Weaver, W. T. 1971. The Delphi forecasting method. *Kappan, 52,* 267.

Wilhelm, W. J. 2001. Alchemy of the oracle: The Delphi technique. *Delta Pi Epsilon Journal, 43*(1), 6–26.

Observing Skills

- ▶ **Formative Observation Instruments Are Not Summative Evaluation Instruments**
- ▶ **Ways of Describing**
- ▶ **Quantitative Observations**
- ▶ **Qualitative Observations**
- ▶ **Tailored Observation Systems**
- ▶ **Types and Purposes of Observation**
- ▶ **Cautions Concerning Observation**
- ▶ **Summary**

Consider the classroom shown in Figure 14.1. If you were an observer of this classroom, what would you say is happening? Of course, one illustration is not a sufficient basis for an observation, but pretend you are seeing this episode for an entire class period. Could you say that the students have behavior problems, discipline is lax, the teacher is not responding to the students' interests, or the teacher is lecturing too much?

If your observations are similar to those listed here, then you have fallen into the *interpretation trap*, which is the downfall of most attempts to help people improve their performance. How would you respond if your evaluator—say, the superintendent of schools—observed you conducting a faculty meeting and later told you that teachers lack respect for you? Your response probably would be a combination of defensiveness ("It isn't so"), confusion ("What do you mean?"), and quiet hostility ("Who are you to say that to me?"). The superintendent has inadvertently turned you against him or her, and compliance on your part will be grudging at best.

Observation is a two-part process—first *describing* what has been seen and then *interpreting* what it means. The mind almost simultaneously processes a visual image, integrates that image with previously stored images related to satisfactory and unsatisfactory experiences, and ascribes a value or meaning to that image. If a student yawns, our mind signals "boredom." If a teacher yells at students, our mind registers "losing control." A judgment derives from an image or a description of events. We must be aware of splitting that almost simultaneous

FIGURE 14.1   *Classroom Picture*

process, of separating description from interpretation. When we lose the description of the event and retain only the interpretation, we create communication difficulties and obstacles to improvement. Sharing the description of events is the forerunner of professional improvement. Interpretation leads to resistance. When both parties can agree on what events occurred, they are more likely to agree on what needs to be changed.

Remember that if the goal of supervision is to enhance teachers' thought and commitment about improving classroom (and school) practice, observations should be used as a base of information to create an instructional dialogue between supervisor and teacher. Using description first when talking to a teacher about his or her classroom creates an instructional dialogue. Providing interpretations and evaluative statements first ushers in defensiveness, combativeness, or resentment in the teacher and stifles discussion (see Glickman and Jones, 1986).

Differentiating description from interpretation in observation is so crucial for instructional improvement that we need to refer back to our original illustration of the classroom (Figure 14.1). Look at the picture again and tell what you now see going on. You might say that there are three students looking away from the teacher and talking to each other while the teacher stands in front of the room calling on a student in the front row. Can we agree that this is happening?

Probably so, and thus we can *later* judge the rightness or wrongness of the event in regard to student learning. The teacher can more readily change the events of three students talking to each other and two others looking away than he or she can change being "a poor classroom manager."

Formative Observation Instruments Are Not Summative Evaluation Instruments

A formative observation instrument used to describe what is occurring in a classroom (consistent with what teacher and supervisor agreed to focus on and later discuss) is a means for professional growth and instructional improvement. Therefore, the use of a formative observation instrument is conditioned on prior agreement about what is most worthy of learning by that teacher in that classroom—whether the interest is derived from a desire to know more about himself or herself as a teacher, attempting a particular instructional model, experimenting with a new practice or strategy, or struggling with a problem or weakness. A summative evaluation instrument, on the other hand, is an externally imposed, uniformly applied measure, intended to judge all teachers on similar criteria to determine their worthiness, merit, and competence as employees.

Ways of Describing

There are many ways to record descriptions. At the end of this chapter, there are multiple references to various observation methods and instruments. An observation instrument is a tool for organizing and recording different categories of classroom life. It can be as simple as a single category or as complex as a matrix of dozens of possible coded combinations. For example, an instrument can be used to count the displays on a classroom wall or to record the hundreds of students' and teachers' verbal and nonverbal interactions.

We will first look at quantitative observations, including categorical instruments, performance indicator instruments, visual diagramming, and space utilization. The second section will deal with qualitative observations, including verbatim, detached open-ended narrative, participant observation, focused questionnaire observation, and educational criticism. Finally, we will discuss tailored observations—quantitative or qualitative observations designed to gather data on specific teacher concerns.

Quantitative Observations

Quantitative observations are ways of measuring classroom events, behaviors, and objects. Definitions and categories must be precise. Eventually, the observations can be used for statistical operations.

Categorical Frequency Instrument

A categorical instrument is a form that defines certain events or behaviors that can be checked off at frequency intervals and then counted. There is nothing mysterious about it. Almost any aspect of classroom life can be isolated and counted. Figure 14.2 is a categorical instrument that measures the frequency of different types of questions asked by the teacher. The seven categories of teacher questions are based on Bloom's taxonomy (the taxonomy is explained in Chapter 19). By dividing the number of questions in each category by the total number of questions asked by the teacher during the lesson, the observer can calculate the percent of total questions each category represents.

Other classroom topics can be observed with categorical instruments. For example, one can focus on on-task and off-task behavior. To complete the instrument in Figure 14.3, the observer begins a sweep of the classroom every five minutes. During each sweep, the observer focuses on each student for approximately 20 seconds, then records that student's behavior. During a 40-minute lesson, eight sweeps can be made. The instrument allows the observer to record specific on-task and off-task behaviors listed in the key at the bottom of the chart.

Performance Indicator Instruments

A performance indicator instrument records whether or not actions listed on the observation instrument have been observed. With some instruments, a third option—"not applicable" (N/A)—is included. Performance indicator instruments may also include space for the observer to add supplemental notes concerning the presence or absence of the action. Figure 14.4 is a performance indicator instru-

Question Category	Tally	Total	Percent
Evaluation		0	0
Synthesis	*I*	1	5
Analysis	*I*	1	5
Application	*II*	2	10
Interpretation	*III*	3	15
Translation	*IIII*	4	20
Memory	*THI IIII*	9	45
Total of Questions Asked = 20			

FIGURE 14.2 *Teacher Questions*

Student	Time When Sweep Began							
	9:00	9:05	9:10	9:15	9:20	9:25	9:30	9:35
Andrew	A	C	D	E	E	A	B	B
Shawn G.	A	A	D	E	E	A	C	B
Maria	A	A	D	E	E	C	B	B
Sam	I	F	F	E	F	A	B	C
Barbara	H	F	D	E	E	F	F	B
Angie	C	G	G	C	E	G	G	G
Jeff	A	A	C	E	E	A	B	B
Jessica	F	F	D	E	E	A	B	E
Shawn L.	A	A	D	E	H	H	B	B
Chris	F	F	D	E	E	A	B	C
Michele	A	A	D	E	H	H	B	B
Mark	A	I	I	F	I	I	I	F
Melissa	C	A	D	E	E	C	H	B
John	J	A	J	I	J	J	J	J
Rolanda	A	C	D	E	E	A	B	F

Key

A = on task, listening / watching
B = on task, writing
C = on task, speaking
D = on task, reading
E = on task, hands-on activity

F = off task, passive
G = off task, doing work
   for another class
H = off task, listening to others
I = off task, disturbing others
J = off task, playing

FIGURE 14.3 *Student On-Task and Off-Task Behavior*

ment used to record the presence or absence of the elements in Madeline Hunter's lesson design model, a model well suited for direct instruction. Figure 14.5 is an instrument to assess whether or not each of the basic elements of a cooperative learning lesson are present.

The instrument in Figure 14.6 lists indicators of an authentic constructivist lesson, and Figure 14.7 lists indicators of culturally sensitive teaching. Since the indicators in Figures 14.6 and 14.7 are more open to interpretation than indicators in many instruments of this type, it is especially important for the observer to

Elements	Response	Comments
Anticipatory set	Yes ___ No ___ N/A ___	_____ _____ _____
Statement of objective and purpose	Yes ___ No ___ N/A ___	_____ _____ _____
Input	Yes ___ No ___ N/A ___	_____ _____ _____
Modeling	Yes ___ No ___ N/A ___	_____ _____ _____
Checking for understanding	Yes ___ No ___ N/A ___	_____ _____ _____
Guided practice	Yes ___ No ___ N/A ___	_____ _____ _____
Independent practice	Yes ___ No ___ N/A ___	_____ _____ _____

FIGURE 14.4 *Hunter Model Performance Indicators*

describe in the comments column specific classroom behaviors that are the basis for the observer's responses.

Remember that performance indicators used for observation purposes should not imply an absolute standard. The fact that a teacher does not perform all of the activities listed on the observation instrument may or may not be a cause of concern. Only after the supervisor and teacher have discussed the circumstances surrounding the teacher's instructional procedures can they be properly interpreted.

Visual Diagramming

Visual diagramming is another way to portray what is occurring in a classroom. Videotaping a classroom captures the closest representative picture of actual occurrences. Without videotapes, however, there are other ways to portray observations, such as verbal interactions among teachers and students and how a teacher uses space. After diagramming the occurrence, the supervisor and the teacher can view the picture and then analyze the events.

Elements	Response	Comments
Explanation of academic and social objectives	Yes ___ No ___ N/A ___	_____ _____ _____
Teaching of necessary social skills	Yes ___ No ___ N/A ___	_____ _____ _____
Face-to-face interaction	Yes ___ No ___ N/A ___	_____ _____ _____
Positive interdependence	Yes ___ No ___ N/A ___	_____ _____ _____
Individual accountability	Yes ___ No ___ N/A ___	_____ _____ _____
Group processing	Yes ___ No ___ N/A ___	_____ _____ _____

FIGURE 14.5 *Cooperative Learning Performance Indicators*

Classroom verbal interactions can be charted by drawing arrows symbolizing verbal statements between members in a classroom (see Figure 14.8). The observer can use six separate sheets of this diagram and fill out one sheet for each time sample of five minutes spaced throughout the hour. Each arrow drawn on the diagram would indicate a full statement directed to another person. The arrows are numbered in the sequence of statements. After diagramming, the observer would then have information on the frequency of individual student interaction, the amount of interaction with different areas of the room, which students triggered interactions among others, and which students were excluded. For illustration purposes, if the diagram was a sample consistent with the other five samples of the classroom period, the observer would be able to state some of the following conclusions:

1. Interaction is mainly directed toward the left aisle and front row.
2. There is almost no attention to the last two rows in the back of the room or the two rows on the right.
3. Of 14 interactions, 12 included the teacher and 2 were between students.

Such diagramming is easier to follow with small groups and when students are not moving around the classroom. Class activities such as teacher lecturing

Indicators	Response	Comments
Co-planned by teacher and students	Yes ___ No ___ N/A ___	_____ _____ _____
In-depth explanation of big idea	Yes ___ No ___ N/A ___	_____ _____ _____
Student-initiated questions	Yes ___ No ___ N/A ___	_____ _____ _____
Problem-centered	Yes ___ No ___ N/A ___	_____ _____ _____
Use of primary material	Yes ___ No ___ N/A ___	_____ _____ _____
Students test own hypotheses	Yes ___ No ___ N/A ___	_____ _____ _____
Dialogue fostered	Yes ___ No ___ N/A ___	_____ _____ _____
Active learning	Yes ___ No ___ N/A ___	_____ _____ _____
Collaborative learning	Yes ___ No ___ N/A ___	_____ _____ _____
Students construct knowledge	Yes ___ No ___ N/A ___	_____ _____ _____
Self and group reflection on constructions	Yes ___ No ___ N/A ___	_____ _____ _____
Learning assessed by teachers and students	Yes ___ No ___ N/A ___	_____ _____ _____
Assessment of process and product	Yes ___ No ___ N/A ___	_____ _____ _____

FIGURE 14.6 *Indicators of a Constructivist Lesson*

Indicators	Response	Comments
The Teacher		
Displays understanding of diverse cultures	Yes ___ No ___	_____ _____ _____
Displays personal regard for all students	Yes ___ No ___	_____ _____ _____
Uses instructional materials free of cultural bias	Yes ___ No ___	_____ _____ _____
Uses examples and materials that represent different cultures	Yes ___ No ___	_____ _____ _____
Promotes examination of concepts and issues from different cultural perspectives	Yes ___ No ___	_____ _____ _____
Facilitates higher-level learning for all students	Yes ___ No ___	_____ _____ _____
Adopts materials and instruction to different student learning styles	Yes ___ No ___	_____ _____ _____
Provides equitable opportunities for student participation	Yes ___ No ___	_____ _____ _____
Provides individual assistance, when necessary, for all students	Yes ___ No ___ N/A ___	_____ _____ _____
Intervenes to address acts of student intolerance	Yes ___ No ___ N/A ___	_____ _____ _____
Uses "teachable moments" to address cultural issues	Yes ___ No ___ N/A ___	_____ _____ _____
Reinforces student acts of respect for diverse cultures	Yes ___ No ___ N/A ___	_____ _____ _____

FIGURE 14.7 *Indicators of Culturally Sensitive Teaching*

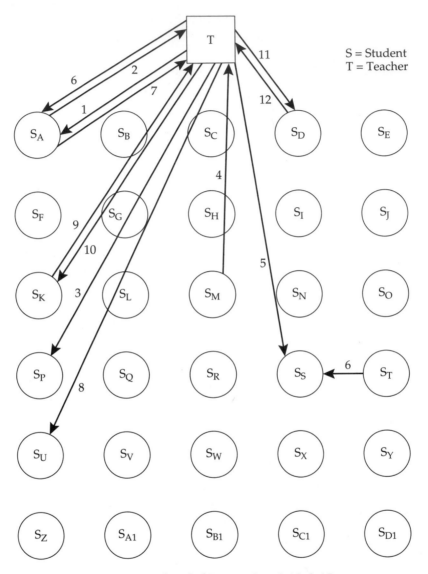

FIGURE 14.8 *Diagram of Verbal Interaction, 9:10–9:15*

interspersed with questions and answers or classroom discussions would be in-structional sessions appropriate for diagramming. Another type of diagramming is flowcharting teacher space utilization, which follows the teacher's movement throughout the classroom. A sketch of the physical classroom is done first; then the observer follows the teacher by using arrows on the sketch. Figure 14.9 illustrates a period of reading instruction. The arrow follows the teacher with each movement and is labeled with the time on the clock. After a class period, the observer and the teacher can see where the teacher has been and for how long. Such information

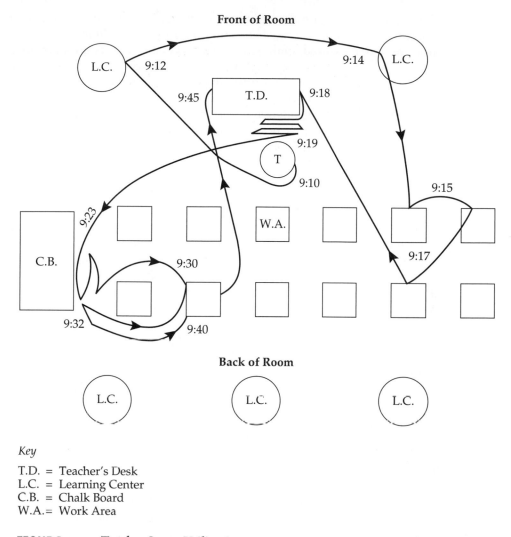

Front of Room

Back of Room

Key

T.D. = Teacher's Desk
L.C. = Learning Center
C.B. = Chalk Board
W.A.= Work Area

FIGURE 14.9 *Teacher Space Utilization*

might help make a teacher aware of the relationship of his or her space utilization to concerns of classroom management and instruction. For example, in Figure 14.9 there is much physical presence in the front and on the left side of the classroom, with no presence at the rear learning centers or the middle work area.

Qualitative Observations

There are alternative means of observing based on not knowing exactly what is to be recorded. These are called qualitative or descriptive forms of observation.

The observer goes into the classroom with a general focus, or no focus at all, and records events as they occur. The events are not made to fit into a specific category, nor are they measured. Only after the recording of events does the observer rearrange his or her observations into themes. Such recording of observations defies the use of an instrument (an instrument is technically a measurement device). Instead, qualitative observations record the complexity of classroom life. There are several types of qualitative observations. We will look at verbatim, detached open-ended narrative, participant observation, and focused questionnaire observation. These observations can be used by a supervisor to provide a broad and complex recording of classroom life.

Verbatim and Selected Verbatim

The observer taking verbatim notes (sometimes called scripts) records all verbal interaction taking place in the classroom. Verbatim notes allow the observer and teacher to identify patterns of interpersonal behavior during a lesson. Verbatim also provides specific examples of teacher-student or student-teacher interactions. For more efficient recording, the observer may abbreviate words and leave out words that add no meaning to the transcript. Despite these time-savers, verbatim can be an arduous process requiring the observer to spend every moment taking notes, with no time for attention to anything else going on during the lesson. One alternative to verbatim is *selected verbatim,* in which the observer records only those interactions that relate to a particular focus agreed to by the observer and teacher prior to the observation. Figure 14.10 provides an excerpt from selective verbatim notes focused on teacher responses to students who initially gave incorrect or partially correct answers to teacher questions.

Detached Open-Ended Narrative

Detached open-ended narrative occurs when the supervisor steps into a classroom and records every person, event, or thing that attracts his or her attention. At the start, the pages are empty, without questions, indicators, or categories. The heading might simply say:

Open-Ended Narrative

Observation Teacher: _____ Time: _____ Observer: _____

The recorder then has the task of writing, writing, and more writing. A sample of such an observation might read:

Students begin arriving at 10:13; the teacher is at his desk correcting papers. The bell rings at 10:15 to begin third period. Students keep arriving. Mr. X gets up from his desk to begin class at 10:25. In the meantime, students have put away their school

```
C = Chris D.                                    10:20
T = Teacher

T.  C, what are 3 branches of fed. Govt.?
C.  President, House, Senate
T.  What branch fed. Govt. is pres. head of?
C.  Ah, I don't know
T.  The president is Chief _____.
C.  Executive! Executive branch!
T.  The House and Senate are both part of what branch?
C.  Legislative
T.  Legislative branch, but both mean same thing. That's 2
    branches, exec. and leg. What is the third branch?
C.  The Courts.
T.  What branch is made of Sup. Ct and other fed. cts.
C.  Judicial
T.  Right!
```

FIGURE 14.10 *Excerpt from Selective Verbatim Notes*

Source: Originally published in S. Gordon (1990). *Assisting the entry-year teacher: A leadership resource.* Columbus, OH: Ohio Department of Education.

bags and are awaiting instruction, except three girls in the back corner who are talking, combing their hair, and spreading the contents of their pocketbooks on their desks. Five minutes after Mr. X begins, he talks to them and they put away combs and pocketbooks. Mr. X describes the activities for the day but then cannot find his prepared handouts. After two minutes of looking, he finds the papers in his desk drawer.

The intercom comes on at 10:30 with two announcements by the principal. Mr. X gives the assignments, and the class begins to read at 10:33. Two students are reprimanded for talking, and occasional student talk can be heard as Mr. X moves around and reviews yesterday's homework with students. He talks with 12 students before asking for class attention at 10:45. He then lectures on the classification of insects. The PowerPoint slide is difficult for students in the back to read. One student asks if he can darken the lights. . . .

With practice, the observer can write in shorthand to keep up with the flow of events. It is impossible to record all that could possibly be seen and heard in a classroom. The observer must constantly scan the entire classroom and decide what is significant.

Participant Open-Ended Observation

Participant open-ended observation occurs when the supervisor becomes a functioning part of the classroom (Spradley, 1980). He or she assists in the instruction, helps students with questions, uses classroom materials, and talks with the teacher and students. Being involved in the classroom gives the supervisor an inside-out view of the classroom different from that of the detached observer who tries to be invisible and keep away from students and teachers. Obviously, events cannot be written down as they occur if the supervisor is engaged in talking, moving, and assisting. Instead, he or she must write between pauses in the action. The observation form can be carried on a clipboard so that notes can be taken on the run.

The participant observer takes sketchy notes (catch phrases and words) during classroom time so that afterward he or she can write in greater detail. These quick notes serve to remind the observer of the situation that will be described more fully after the observation period is over. The following is an example of such short notes.

Teacher X directs students into study groups.

John B. does not understand the assignment. I work with him on organizing the theme of a play.

Sally T. and Ramona B. are wandering around. I ask them if they need help; they say no and leave the room (ask teacher about this).

Sondra and her group are ready to role-play their theme. I listen as they read through their parts.

Steven's group is stuck; he doesn't know how to find materials on historic buildings. I suggest calling the town historic society.

Susan is not participating at all—looking at *Teen Magazine.* The rest of the group just leaves her alone. (I wonder why?)

The filmstrip shown has everyone's attention.

Teacher B dismisses the class. I overhear a student say, "This class goes so quickly. I wish other classes were as much fun."

These are some notes from a 50-minute classroom period. Much more happened in the classroom than is noted, but the observer picks up insights from his or her involvement. The supervisor can later fill in details—the two girls leaving the classroom, the specifics of John's confusion about the theme, Susan's absorption in *Teen Magazine,* and so on.

Focused Questionnaire Observation

Qualitative observation can be done in a more focused manner by having general topics to use in recording events. An observer seeks information about specific questions. In order to answer the questions, the observer writes pertinent evidence.

Topic 1: Classroom
How is the classroom made attractive?

Topic 2: Teacher
What shows that the teacher has a warm, friendly relationship with the pupils?

Topic 3: Pupil
What indicates that pupils know what they are doing and why they are doing it?

Topic 4: Lesson
How do classroom and homework assignments indicate that consideration is given to, and use made of, resources of the community and real-life situations of pupils?

FIGURE 14.11   *Focused Questionnaire*

For example, Harris (1975, pp. 364–376) has developed a detached observation questionnaire that has as its topics: (1) classroom, (2) teacher, (3) pupil, and (4) lesson. Figure 14.11 shows sample questions taken from each category.

An observer enters the classroom with questions in hand and looks for the answers. For example, the question "What shows that the teacher has a warm, friendly relationship with pupils?" could be answered by participant observation, such as: "Overheard three students saying how nice Ms. Y is. Noticed how Ms. Y put her hand on the shoulders of five different students when speaking to them." It is the task of the observer to respond to these questions with descriptions of the evidence.

Tailored Observation Systems

Supervisors often observe lessons to collect data on unique instructional concerns or improvement efforts. If no observation system exists that is capable of gathering the desired data, the supervisor and teacher can design a tailored observation system. Tailored observation systems can be quantitative, qualitative, or a combination of both. Figure 14.12 is a system designed to collect four specific types of data. The teacher in this example requested that the observer collect data on (1) how often the teacher called on each student; (2) whether each student's response was correct or incorrect; (3) whether the teacher drew out correct student responses through encouragement or prompting, especially after a student's initial response was incorrect; and (4) how often the teacher provided positive feedback to students making correct responses. In Figure 14.12, codes symbolize both student responses (−, +, ×) to teacher questions, and teacher reactions (→, o) to student responses. Several codes on the same line indicate verbal behaviors that were part of the same series of interactions. Codes on different lines indicate separate series of interactions.

In another example, teacher Simmons was concerned about the conduct of one of his students and asked the supervisor to collect data on the student's behaviors, Simmons' responses, and the effects of those responses on the student.

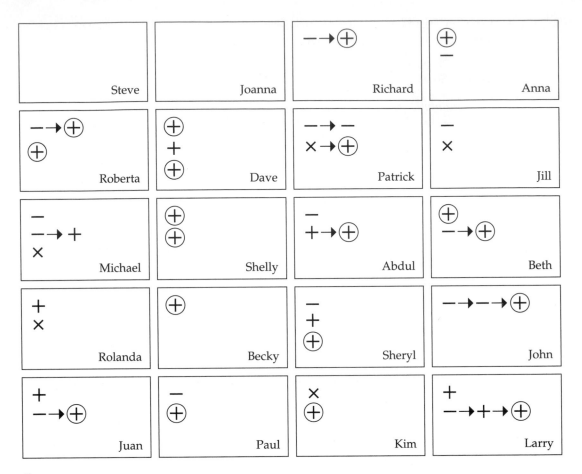

Key

— Incorrect response

→ Teacher prompt or encouragement

+ Correct response

✕ Response cannot be classified as correct or incorrect

◯ Positive teacher feedback following student response

FIGURE 14.12   *Tailored Question–Response Instrument*

Figure 14.13 is the observation chart completed by the supervisor. Arrows point to immediate responses of the teacher to selected student behaviors and immediate responses of the student to relevant teacher behaviors. Some of the most meaningful and helpful classroom observation data we have viewed has been collected with instruments designed by supervisors and teachers focused on specific teacher concerns.

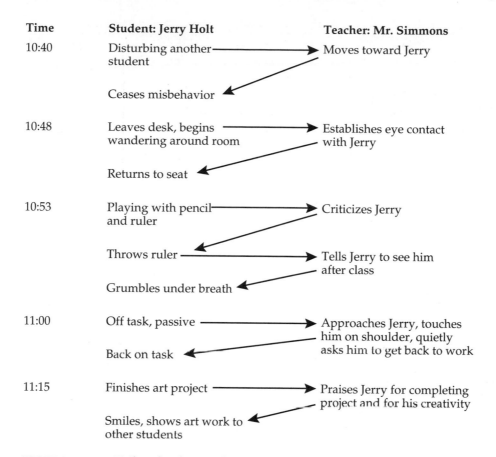

FIGURE 14.13   *Tailored Behavior–Response Observation*

Types and Purposes of Observation

Figure 14.14 illustrates the types of observation available to a supervisor. The purpose of the observation should determine the type, method, and role of observation. The categorical-frequency observation is a quantitative method used by a detached observer for the purpose of counting, totaling, and statistically analyzing behaviors. The performance-indicator observation is quantitatively used by a detached observer to record evidence of human behavior. Visual diagramming is a quantitative observation used by a detached observer for the purpose of depicting verbal interaction. Human space utilization observation is a quantitative measure used by a detached observer for the purpose of depicting the length and pattern of physical movement. Verbatim is a qualitative method in which the observer records all verbal interaction. The detached open-ended narrative is a qualitative observation used by a detached observer for recording events as they unfold. Participant open-ended observation is a qualitative technique used to record how

Type	Method		Role of Observer		Purpose
	Quantitive	*Qualitative*	*Detached*	*Participant*	
Categorical frequency	x		x		Count behaviors
Performance indicator	x		x		Evident or not
Visual diagramming	x		x		Picture verbal interaction
Space utilization	x		x		Picture movement
Verbatim		x			Script of verbal interaction
Detached open-ended narrative		x	x		Attention to unfolding event
Participant open-ended observation		x		x	Inside-out view
Focused questionnaire		x	x or	x	Focus on particular events
Tailored	x or	x	x or	x	Address unique concerns

FIGURE 14.14   *Observation Alternatives*

people and events unfold to one involved in the classroom. The focused questionnaire is another qualitative method that can be used by a detached or participant observer for the purpose of gathering evidence according to general questions about classroom topics. Finally, tailored observation systems cut across the different categories previously discussed. They are designed by the supervisor and teacher to collect data on specific teacher concerns when there is no existing observation system for collecting such data. They may be quantitative or qualitative and may be used by a detached or participant observer.

Cautions Concerning Observation

Quantum physics informs us that a phenomenon cannot be measured without the measurement process interacting with the phenomenon and thus affecting the measurement (Greene, 2004). Closer to home for those of us who are educators, the constructivist epistemology holds that, rather than identifying a fixed reality through objective observation, we construct knowledge by interacting with our environment and with others. One implication for classroom observation is our need to realize that our observations are affected by our personal experiences and values, our presence in the classroom during the observation, the observation instrument we use, our skill at recording data, and so on. Another implication is that the interpretation of what the observation data means is a construction, and in most cases is best co-constructed with the teacher. Observation data, thus, should be an entry point for teacher–supervisor dialogue and co-interpretation during a post-observation conference. Clinical supervision, discussed in Chapter 16, provides a structure for teacher–supervisor dialogue on classroom observation.

SUMMARY

There are many ways to observe classrooms. The choice of a particular type of observation depends on the purpose and focus of the observation. Observation enables a supervisor to put a mirror of the classroom up to the teacher, who can then attend to matters previously unknown. Several studies (Brophy and Good, 1974, pp. 297–328) have shown that teachers often change instructional behaviors on their own after their classrooms have been described to them by an observer. The mirror can often be the stimulus for change. The observer must be careful in using interpretations, because such value judgments can actually cloud the mirror and prevent the teacher from seeing his or her own image. At all times, the observer needs to distinguish description from interpretation when recording and explaining events to the teacher.

REFERENCES AND RECOMMENDED READINGS

Brophy, J. E., and Good, T. L. 1974. *Teacher-student relationships: Causes and consequences.* New York: Holt, Rinehart and Winston.

Glickman, C. D., and Jones, J. W. 1986. Research in supervision: Creating the dialogue. *Educational Leadership, 44*(3), 83.

Greene, B. 2004. *The fabric of the cosmos: Space, time and the texture of reality.* New York: Vintage Books.

Harris, B. M. 1975. *Supervisory behavior in education* (2nd ed.). Englewood Cliffs, NJ: Prentice Hall.

Hyman, R. T. 1975. *School administrator's handbook of teacher supervision and evaluation methods.* Englewood Cliffs, NJ: Prentice Hall.

Simon, A., and Boyer, E. C. 1967. *Mirrors of behavior: An anthology of classroom observation instruments.* 6 vols. Philadelphia: Research for Better Schools.

Spradley, J. P. 1980. *Participant observation.* New York: Holt, Rinehart and Winston.

Research and Evaluation Skills

15

In schools and districts that improve instruction, evaluation and research are not perfunctory paper assignments done by a particular person or division to fulfill district or state requirements. Rather, evaluation and research are seen as the basis for determining professional actions as to the what and the how of improving learning for students. Knowledgeable decision making about instruction comes from intense and critical study of the consequences of the common work of teachers: teaching. Including teachers in determining the criteria, procedures, and use of evaluative data in schools is not simply a nice thing to do—*it is essential to do*. If teachers are to extend their own thinking and commitment about collective instruction, they have to be part of the research and evaluation process. Without their involvement, policy makers have denied teachers the intellectual engagement of viewing teaching as a collective activity—"a cause beyond oneself."

Such engagement, in itself, enhances thinking and decisions about individual practice. In a high school in the Southeast, during the year when teachers and administrators in the school began to collect data on profiles of high school dropouts, the dropout rate decreased by more than 12 percent (Glickman, 1989). This was *before* the school had determined what interventions to make. One teacher said, "It simply never occurred to me, until we researched and evaluated our school, that we had a problem with dropouts. I and most of my peers have certainly changed our attitudes toward average students. The dropout rate is coming down right now because of our awareness. I can't wait until next year when we implement new programs!"

Alternative Approaches to Research and Evaluation

Research on and evaluation of instructional programs is based on methodology derived from one of two broad approaches to research, or in some cases a combination of both approaches. These two approaches are *quantitative* and *qualitative*. The difference between quantitative and qualitative research goes way beyond the fact that quantitative results are reported numerically and qualitative results are reported through narrative. The two approaches are based on different conceptions of reality, the purpose of research, the researcher's role, the role of values in research, the relationship between researcher and subject, and appropriate research methodology. Let's begin this discussion by outlining the major differences between these two alternatives.

Quantitative and Qualitative Research Compared

A number of scholars have compared quantitative and qualitative research in relation to critical research issues (Bogdan and Biklen, 1992; Borg and Gall, 1989; Fang, 1995; Hathaway, 1995; Lincoln and Guba, 1985; Shank, 1994; Anfara, Brown, and Mangione, 2002; Creswell, 2001; Nastasia and Schensul, 2005). The assumptions of quantitative and qualitative researchers regarding seven such issues are discussed below.

What Is the Nature of Reality and Knowledge?   Quantitative research is based on the assumption that there is a single, external reality. Knowledge consists of objective measurements of phenomena that are part of that reality. Complex phenomena can be broken down into simple variables that can be studied independently. Eventually, the study of component variables leads to an overall understanding of a phenomenon, which in turn can lead to prediction and control of the phenomenon.

Qualitative research is based on the assumption that the world consists of multiple realities that are constructed by individuals or groups. Knowledge comes with understanding of an individual's or group's assumptions, relationships, intentions, actions, perceptions, and feelings within a given context. A phenomenon can only be studied holistically. Since each phenomenon is unique, prediction and control of future phenomena are unlikely.

What Are the Goals of Research?   The goals of quantitative research are to identify relationships between variables, explain causes, predict and control phenomena, and develop knowledge that is *generalizable* to other contexts. The goals of qualitative research are to describe phenomena from the perspective of participants, discover multiple realities, and develop a holistic understanding of individual phenomena within particular contexts. This is done through a continuous cycle of intense observation and in-depth description, formation of working hypotheses, more observation and description, and so on.

What Is the Researcher's Role?   In quantitative research the researcher assumes the role of the detached observer. The purpose of detachment is to avoid bias. This detachment extends to the researcher's relationship with the *subjects* of the study. The researcher is to have as little interaction with the subjects as possible. Quantitative research methods are designed to minimize the effects of any unavoidable interaction between the researcher and the study or subjects.

Qualitative research assumes that the researcher and the study will interact and affect each other. In fact, the qualitative researcher intentionally becomes deeply involved with the phenomenon being studied. The researcher attempts to develop empathy, trust, and even friendship with the study's *participants*. The researcher documents interactions with the study and its participants, critically examining his or her effects on the research and results.

What Is the Importance of Context in Research?   Context is the setting or framework within which the phenomenon being studied exists. The quantitative view is that a phenomenon can be studied independently of its context. Indeed, quantitative research attempts to develop context-free generalizations. Qualitative research assumes that a phenomenon is greatly influenced by its particular context. The whole is greater than the sum of its parts. This is why a qualitative study places so much emphasis on describing context, and usually will not attempt to generalize results to other contexts.

What Place Do Values Have in Research?   Both quantitative and qualitative research admit that values can affect research. Quantitative research responds to the values issue by attempting to make the research as value free as possible through the use of objective research methods. Qualitative research is based on the assumption that the researcher, participants, context, and research methodology all possess values that will inevitably influence the study, and so it is best to describe those values and their effects as part of the study.

What Is the Relationship of Cause and Effect?   Quantitative research assumes that every *effect* can be explained by a preceding *cause* or combination of causes. It attempts to identify cause-effect relationships. Qualitative research assumes that the variables of a phenomenon are mutually and simultaneously affecting each other. Thus it is impossible to separate causes from effects.

How Should Research Studies Be Designed?   Shank (1994) compares the quantitative approach to manufacturing: A blueprint for the study is created, and then quality control ensures that production takes place according to the blueprint. A hypothesis is stated. A research design, such as correlational, experimental, or quasi-experimental, is chosen. Formal data-collection instruments such as inventories, questionnaires, or tests are selected or developed. Subjects are identified and grouped according to precise procedures (random selection, stratified samples, experimental and control groups, and so on). Only after all of the above have been completed does data collection begin; and after data collection is complete, data analysis begins. Analysis involves the use of statistical techniques intended to reduce bias and error and control for extraneous variables in order to determine whether or not the hypothesis is correct and indicate to what extent results can be generalized.

Shank (1994) compares qualitative research to *hunting and gathering*—the qualitative researcher is not trying to test a predetermined hypothesis, but is searching for evidence and understanding of processes and relations. The qualitative research design is broad, emergent, and flexible. The research sample is small and hand-picked to meet the purpose of the study. Data-collection methods include long-term observation, participation, open-ended interviews, gathering of documents and artifacts, videotaping, and photography, to name a few. The most important data-collection instrument is the *researcher*. Data analysis consists of reviewing, inductive coding, comparing, integrating, and constructing themes, concepts, hypotheses, and models. Data-collection and data analysis are cyclical and interactive; initial data collection and data analysis may lead to the formulation of a working hypothesis that then calls for a new round of data collection and analysis. The aim of this continuously evolving research design is to develop a body of in-depth knowledge concerning the particular phenomena being studied.

Table 15.1 summarizes our comparison of quantitative and qualitative research.

Can Quantitative and Qualitative Methods Be Used in the Same Study?

Is it desirable or even possible to effectively use both quantitative and qualitative methods in the same research or evaluation study? There are a number of positions on this issue taken by different experts. One position, taken by some quantitative and some qualitative proponents, is that the approach they embrace is not only incompatible with the other approach, but is so superior to it that the approach they favor should be the only one used in any serious study. A second group of experts agrees with the first group's contention that quantitative and qualitative research are incompatible, but does not endorse one approach as superior to the other. This group takes the position that quantitative research is the more appropriate methodology for some studies, but that qualitative research is more appropriate for others.

A third group of experts believes that quantitative and qualitative research are compatible and that the best studies combine the two approaches. This view may seem curious in light of the comparison of quantitative and qualitative research provided above. But proponents of mixing the two approaches point out that each approach can generate types of information that the other cannot, that only quantitative and qualitative perspectives used together can form a complete picture of the phenomenon being studied, and that the results of one method can help to explain and validate the results of the other (Piontek, 1992; Chatterji, 2005).

TABLE 15.1   *Comparison of Quantitative and Qualitative Research*

Research/Issue	Quantitative Research	Qualitative Research
Nature of Reality and Knowledge	A single, external reality; Knowledge consists of objective measures	Multiple realities; Knowledge comes with understanding of these realities
Goals of Research	Explain causes; Predict and control; Develop generalizable knowledge	Describe phenomena; Discover multiple realities; Holistic understanding
Researcher's Role	Detached observer	Interact and become involved with phenomenon being studied
Importance of Context	Phenomenon can and should be studied separate from context	Phenomenon is greatly influenced by its context; They must be studied together
Values in Research	Make research objective (value free)	Describe values and their inevitable effects
Cause and Effect	Each effect has preceding cause; Identify cause-effect relationships	Variables mutually and simultaneously affect each other
Research Design	Correlational, experimental or quasi-experimental; Formal instruments; Precise procedures; Statistical techniques; Determine if predetermined hypothesis is correct, if results are generalizable	Broad, emergent, and flexible; Long-term observation, participation; Data collection and analysis are cyclical and interactive; Formulate working hypothesis, developing in-depth knowledge of particular phenomena

As the reader of previous chapters in this text may have already predicted, the authors adhere to a fourth, eclectic view concerning the quantitative-qualitative debate. First, we do not agree that quantitative and qualitative research are in all cases incompatible, or that either approach is inherently superior to the other. Based on our own experience as researchers and evaluators, we believe that:

- For *some* studies, using quantitative methods is the best approach.
- For *some* studies, using qualitative methods is the best approach.
- For *many* studies, a combination of quantitative and qualitative methods is the best approach.

The following criteria are recommended for determining whether a quantitative, qualitative, or combined approach is the most appropriate methodology for a research or evaluation study:

1. The context of the study (school history, demographics, culture, climate, and so on)
2. The goals of the study
3. The values and skills of the person or group conducting the study
4. The resources available for the study

5. The values of those who will participate in the study (principals, teachers, students, parents), as well as the time and effort participants are able and willing to contribute (qualitative studies often require more participant time and effort than quantitative studies)
6. The values and needs of the audience to whom the study will be reported

In the remainder of this chapter we'll examine individual program evaluation and evaluation of the overall instructional program. The following pages will provide examples of how quantitative and qualitative methods can be applied to each of these types of evaluation.

Judgments

How do we know our instructional programs are successful? Should we continue with the same curriculum, instructional methods, scheduling, and grouping practices, or should changes be made? Evaluating is the act of making such a judgment. How do we decide whether something is good or bad? Frequently, we make judgments with statements such as, "What a great reading program," "What a lousy classroom," or "What wonderful students." How do we really know if something is great, lousy, or wonderful? Wolfe (1969) has offered a tongue-in-cheek classification of five typical methods by which we make such judgments:

Cosmetic method: You examine the program, and if it looks good it is good. Does everybody look busy? The key is attractive and full bulletin boards covered with projects emanating from the project.

Cardiac method: No matter what the data say, you know in your heart that the program was a success. This is similar to the use in medical research of sub-clinical findings.

Colloquial method: After a brief meeting, preferably at a local watering hole, a group of project staff members conclude that success was achieved. No one can refute a group decision.

Curricular method: A successful program is one that can be installed with the least disruption of the ongoing school program. Programs that are truly different are to be eschewed at all costs.

Computational method: If you have to have data, analyze it to death. Whatever the nature of the statistics, use the most sophisticated multivariate regression discontinuity procedures known to humans.

Wolfe's humor aside, let's look at reasonable, valid ways of evaluating. In the turbulence of instructional change, it is useful to know whether the new practice is going to be any better than the old. If not, then we may be investing large amounts of energy without a justifiable increase in instructional benefits to students. As discussed in Chapter 13 (assessing and planning), if we are to make a commitment to instructional change, we must also make a commitment to evaluating that instructional change. If not, then we truly do not know what we are doing.

Evaluating Specific Instructional Programs

How does one make a judgment of worth? When assessing specific instructional programs, there are six components of a comprehensive program evaluation:

1. *Evaluation of needs assessment:* The most basic question that program evaluators can ask is: Was there a need for the program? At first glance, this might seem like an unnecessary evaluation component. Why would a school expend resources to adopt a program unless there is clear evidence of need? Yet after studying innovations in urban secondary schools, Nelson and Sieber (1976) concluded that schools often adopted innovations because of good salesmanship, the innovation's transportability, or the publicity value of the innovation rather than a desire for educational reform. Also, Berman and McLaughlin (1976) found that schools often adopted innovations in order to receive external funding rather than to respond to locally identified needs. Many new programs, of course, are adopted as a result of genuine needs assessments. In these cases, the needs assessment process (data gathering, data analysis, conclusion drawing) should be reviewed to determine if the assessment was valid—if it identified actual educational needs.

2. *Evaluation of program design:* In Chapter 13 we saw that program planning can take a variety of different forms. For educational programs, some type of coherent, written plan should be made. A second component of program evaluation is to review the written plan. Evaluations should determine whether program goals and objectives are consistent with the needs the program was created to meet (if the goals and objectives are met, will the needs be met?) and whether program activities are consistent with program goals and objectives (if the activities are effectively carried out, will the objectives and goals be met?). Finally, evaluators need to determine if adequate human and material resources have been committed to the program.

3. *Evaluation of readiness:* No matter how critical a need or how logical a plan, programs often fail because some stakeholders (principals, teachers, students, parents, other community members) are not prepared to support implementation. For instance, a sex education program that has been extremely successful in other school districts might be a complete failure in a conservative district if stakeholders are not provided with extensive information about the program and opportunities to have their concerns addressed. Likewise, a peer-coaching program, by itself, is not likely to be successful in a school with a history of teachers exhibiting distrust and animosity toward each other. Extensive communication and trust-building activities would have to precede the peer-coaching program. To

carry out this component, evaluators determine if stakeholders were ready for the program, and, if not, whether effective readiness activities were carried out prior to program implementation.

4. *Implementation evaluation:* Key questions evaluators need to answer in this component are: Was the program implemented as planned? If not, why not? and if not, how did the program's implementation differ from the original plan? Three phases of implementation need to be examined: (1) program initiation, (2) program continuation over time, and (3) program integration with the school culture. Implementation evaluation is important because many programs have "failed" because they were never actually implemented as intended, or because initial implementation was followed by a gradual loss of program fidelity. One aspect of implementation that evaluators are wise to examine is the level of administrative support for the program. (In our own work as program evaluators, we have found that a key aspect of effective implementation is continued, coordinated support by central office administrators, supervisors, and principals.)

5. *Evaluation of outcomes:* There are two types of outcomes or products that evaluators can measure. *Intended outcomes* are the program goals and objectives. *Unintended outcomes* are unforeseen results of the program. Unintended outcomes can be positive or negative.

6. *Cost-benefit analysis:* In cost-benefit analysis, evaluators compare the costs of the program (human and material resources expended, unintended negative outcomes) to its benefits (intended and unintended positive outcomes). This component, used infrequently in educational program evaluations, takes us beyond whether or not program goals were met to judgments about the relative worth of the program.

The authors' observation and review of program evaluations in education have caused us to conclude that most schools do not engage in comprehensive evaluations involving these six components. Rather, typical evaluations tend to include only component 5: evaluation of outcomes. The number of components included in an evaluation will depend on the school's resources, the size of the program to be evaluated, and the purpose of the evaluation. However, a study including all six components will provide those with program decision responsibilities (school committees, curriculum councils, superintendents, school boards, state and federal agencies) the most thorough and informative evaluation results.

Key Decisions in the Program Evaluation Process

Regardless of how many of the six components are included in a program evaluation, a number of key decisions must be made. We will examine each of these decisions.

What Is the Purpose of the Evaluation?

There are two broad purposes of educational evaluation. *Formative evaluation* is intended to improve a program. It is carried out while the program is in progress and can be ongoing throughout the life of the program. *Summative evaluation* results in a definitive judgment about the value of a program. It is carried out after a program has been in existence for a period of time. A summative evaluation is usually the basis for a decision about whether the program will continue, undergo major revisions, or be terminated. Formative and summative program evaluations are not always mutually exclusive. For instance, data gathered for formative evaluations might be reanalyzed later as part of a summative evaluation.

Who Will Evaluate?

Whether the supervisor, a team of faculty members, central office personnel, or private consultants should have major control over evaluation depends on the particular school's resources and the purpose of the evaluation. However, it is critical that teachers be involved in evaluation of instructional programs and the overall instructional effectiveness of their schools and district. All stakeholders (those affected by the decisions from the evaluation) should not only be subjects of the study, but also co-investigators. As Greene (1986) has noted, there exists a "consensus on the need for stakeholder participation" (p. 1), and such participation is defined as "shared decision making, rather than just advising or providing input" (p. 9).

What Questions Need to Be Answered?

Specific questions can be formulated for each of the six components of a comprehensive evaluation discussed earlier in this chapter. Evaluation questions will depend on the nature of the program and what members of the evaluation's audience wish to learn about the program. Let's say that a new social studies curriculum is to be evaluated. An *implementation* question might be: To what extent has the new curriculum been implemented at the classroom level? An *outcomes* question might be: What changes in students' knowledge, skills, and attitudes have resulted from the new curriculum? Once the evaluation questions have been formulated, they become the basis for the remainder of the evaluation.

What and How Will Data Be Gathered?

Data sources are persons, places, things, events, or processes from which data needed to answer evaluation questions can be gathered. Examples of data sources are students, teachers, principals, parents, teaching episodes, student products, and school records. *Data-gathering methods* are ways to collect data from sources. Examples include testing, observations, content analysis, case studies, review of records, administration of rating scales and surveys, and interviewing. Our bias is toward using multiple sources of data and multiple data-collection methods for each evaluation question. Later in this chapter, we will provide examples of program and school evaluations using multiple sources and methods.

How Will the Data Be Analyzed?

Data analysis is largely determined by the evaluation questions and types of data. Decisions to be made include how to organize, summarize, and display data, and how to reach conclusions based on the data. Central office, university, or private experts may be necessary to assist with complex quantitative or qualitative analysis. Stakeholders, however, can make valuable contributions to data analysis, especially by reviewing results and suggesting explanations, implications, and conclusions.

How Will the Evaluation Be Reported?

After collecting and analyzing the results of tests, observations, surveys, interviews, and testimonials, how should the evaluation be reported? The answer is largely determined by the audience. Most school board members and superintendents will not read a 200-page technical report on the raw data, statistical treatments, and evaluation methodologies. They are interested in the results and conclusions. The technical report should be available to decision makers as a reference to the summarized paper. Any reader of the condensed paper who is confused or desires more information about certain parts of the paper can check the complete technical report.

On the other hand, if the audience for the evaluation report consists of people with sophisticated evaluation skills, a complete technical report would be in order. In a study of violations of evaluation standards (Newman and Brown, 1987, p. 9), among the most frequent violations were "those concerning the evaluator's lack of knowledge of the audience."

Regardless of the audience, there are certain types of information included in most evaluation reports (again, these components will vary in length and technical sophistication depending on the audience). Typical evaluation reports include discussions of

1. The purpose of the evaluation
2. A description of the program being evaluated
3. Evaluation questions or objectives
4. Methodology: data sources, data-gathering methods, and data analysis methods
5. Results and conclusions, including the strengths and weaknesses of the program
6. Recommendations for the future

Multiple Sources and Methods

Now that we've taken a close-up look at components and key decisions in program evaluations, let's explore the idea of using multiple data sources and multiple data-gathering methods to a comprehensive evaluation of a science program that has been in place for two years. In the first evaluation component, *evaluation of needs assessment,* data sources might be school records of student achievement in science prior to the new program, teachers who used the old science program, and data from the needs assessment administered to science teachers prior to the school's decision to adopt the new program. Data-gathering methods could include interviews of teachers and review of student achievement and needs assessment data.

For the second component, *evaluation of program design,* data sources might be the new science curriculum (goals, objectives, activities, resources and materials, assessment) and the original needs assessment. Data would be collected from both of these two sources in order to compare identified needs with the new curriculum for consistency.

The third component, *evaluation of readiness,* could include the following as sources: the science supervisor, teachers, and records of professional-development activities intended to prepare teachers to implement the new program. Data-gathering methods might be interviews, rating scales asking the supervisor and teachers to rate teacher readiness for the new program, and document review.

In the fourth component, *evaluation of implementation,* we would determine whether the new science curriculum was being used as intended. Data sources could be teachers, science lessons, and reports on material utilization. Corresponding data-gathering methods might be teacher self-reports and surveys, classroom observations, and document review.

For the fifth component, *evaluation of outcomes,* data sources could be test scores, grades, exhibits, awards, extracurricular science activities, students, teachers, and parents. Data-collection methods might include review of school records and student products, classroom observations, interviews, and surveys.

Finally, the sixth component, *cost-benefit analysis,* would involve reviewing the data from component 5 as well as the human and material resources expended on the program, and listing program costs and benefits for review by decision makers.

Overall Instructional Program Evaluation

Evaluating a school's overall instructional program is different from evaluating specific programs. In this section, we'll outline an evaluation model that we have used when serving as consultants to schools wishing to evaluate the quality of their instruction with an eye toward comprehensive, schoolwide instructional improvement. We always recommend extensive participation by the school community in planning the evaluation, developing data-collection methods, analyzing data, and drawing conclusions about current quality and needed change.

Phase One: Selecting Areas to Be Examined

The evaluation process begins with a meeting with the school's administration and an evaluation steering committee representing key stakeholders from the school community. At that meeting we recommend the following broad areas for evaluation, based on the rationale that each of these areas is significantly related to the success of the school's overall instructional program:

1. Community characteristics
2. School culture and climate
3. School governance
4. Student characteristics
5. Teacher characteristics
6. Parent characteristics
7. Instructional supervision
8. Curriculum and curriculum development process
9. Classroom teaching practices
10. Student assessment methods
11. Student achievement
12. Professional development programs
13. Parent and community involvement programs
14. Relationships with other schools, central office, and external organizations

Of course it's up to the school district or school to decide which areas to evaluate, and the steering committee may wish to delete or add evaluation areas. However, most steering committees agree that a comprehensive evaluation needs to examine all of the above areas. At this initial meeting we also propose the remainder of the evaluation process outlined here, with the understanding that the actual evaluation plan will result from a collaborative effort of the consultants and steering committee with input from all of those who will be affected by the evaluation.

Phase Two: Identifying Specific Evaluation Questions

The second phase of the process begins with a large-group session attended by administrators, teachers, other staff members, parents, and other community members. After a general session to review the areas to be examined in the evaluation, the group splits up into small planning teams. The number of planning teams is equal to the number of areas to be examined. To the extent possible, each of the stakeholder groups listed above is represented within each planning team. Each team is assigned one of the areas for evaluation decided on in phase one and the task of recommending specific evaluation questions for their area. For example, the *community characteristics* planning team agrees on a set of evaluation questions about the community that it believes should be answered by the evaluation, the *school culture and climate* team proposes a set of evaluation questions concerning their assigned area, and so on. A *community characteristics* evaluation question might be "To what extent are community resources used to enhance teaching and learning in our school?" A *school culture and climate* question might be "Is our school culture consistent with the research on successful school cultures?"

After all planning teams agree on proposed evaluation questions for their broad area, each team presents and explains its recommendations to a general session. Suggestions for deleting, adding, or revising questions are made by general session participants and then considered by the appropriate teams. After each planning team has had the opportunity to revise proposed questions, each team presents its final recommendations to another general session. At this final general session, the entire body of participants votes on whether to include each proposed evaluation question in the evaluation. After the large-group session is completed, the consultants and steering committee rewrite the evaluation questions for each area, so that the questions can be presented in a common format. Although the language of a question may be revised, the basic content of the question must remain as it was approved at the general session.

Phase Three: Designing the Evaluation

Phase three consists of consultants, the steering committee, and planning teams collaborating to design the evaluation proper. Teams propose sources (persons, places, things, events, processes) from which data necessary to answer each of their evaluation questions can be gathered, as well as data-gathering methods (testing, observations, content analysis, case studies, record review, rating scales, surveys, interviews, and so on). For reasons of coordination and efficiency, however, it is the evaluation steering committee that makes the final decisions on data sources and data-gathering methods.

After identifying sources and methods, it is time to select or design data-gathering instruments such as tests, classroom observation systems, written surveys, interview guides, and so on. Planning teams make suggestions for specific test items, survey and interview questions, classroom behaviors to be observed, and so on, and then the consultants and steering committee construct the instruments. With the wide variety of areas to be assessed, efficiency becomes critical. For example, let's assume that six planning teams each propose several teacher survey questions aimed at gathering data for their assigned areas and research questions. Rather than constructing six different surveys, the consultants and evaluation committee might design a single survey divided into six sections, with the questions within each section designed to gather data sought by a different evaluation team. Figure 15.1 provides a matrix for planning an evaluation of a school's overall instructional program. The grid is used to develop an overview of data sources and data-gathering methods relative to each area to be assessed.

Phase Four: Gathering and Analyzing Data

Teachers, supervisors, and consultants can all assist in gathering data needed to answer evaluation questions. For example, teachers can interview or survey

Data Sources and Data-Gathering Methods

Areas to Be Assessed	Students				Teachers				School Leadership				Parents				Community				Central Office				Written Curriculum				School Records			
	R	O	S	I	R	O	S	I	R	O	S	I	R	O	S	I	R	O	S	I	R	O	S	I	R	O	S	I	R	O	S	I
Community Characteristics																																
School Culture & Climate																																
School Governance																																
Student Characteristics																																
Teacher Characteristics																																
Parent Characteristics																																
Instructional Supervision																																
Curriculum																																
Classroom Teaching																																
Student Assessment																																
Student Achievement																																
Professional Development																																
Parent-Community Involvement																																
External Relations																																

Key   R =   Review of existing data (demographic data, student achievement data, etc.)
        O =   Observation or videotaping
        S =   Written survey, rating scale, etc.
        I =   Interview

Checks (✓) are placed in appropriate cells to indicate the relationship of areas to be assessed, data sources, and data-gathering methods.

FIGURE 15.1 *Planning Grid for Evaluating Overall Instructional Program*

students, gather representative student work, or videotape sample lessons. Supervisors can conduct classroom observations, interview or survey parents, or gather schoolwide student achievement data. Consultants can provide technical assistance, interview or survey teachers, or conduct qualitative case studies. The best matches of personnel with data-gathering assignments will depend on the nature of the data to be collected and the skills and interests of participants, and thus will vary from school to school. In any evaluation, however, it is essential to clearly define (1) who will be responsible for collecting each type of data, and (2) the data-gathering procedures they will follow. Teachers and other staff who will collect data may need staff development to acquire necessary data-gathering skills.

Teachers can also work with supervisors and consultants to analyze evaluation data. Although it may be necessary for consultants to perform more complex statistical or qualitative analysis, teachers can engage in a variety of data analysis activities. They can assist in organizing, reviewing, comparing, and interpreting most types of data, and can participate in data-based decisions concerning needed improvements in the school's instructional program.

Data gathering and data analysis need not be treated as discrete activities. Analysis of data gathered early in the evaluation process may indicate the need to collect additional data in order to adequately answer an evaluation question. Data gathering and analysis thus can be viewed as an interactive cycle rather than a linear process. The data-gathering and analysis process is coordinated by the consultants and steering committee. Figure 15.2 contains an example of a chart that can be used to coordinate gathering and analysis of data for each evaluation question.

Phase Five: Preparing and Presenting the Evaluation Report

Due to the variety of areas addressed in an evaluation of the overall instructional program, this type of evaluation report will be more extensive than an evaluation report on a specific program. The report should address not only each area that was assessed, but also *relationships* between those areas. For example, if most teachers report that the school culture (one area assessed) affects their classroom teaching (another area), observed effects should be discussed in the report. Conclusions made in the report should be based on data gathered during the study and collaborative interpretation of that data.

Recommendations for improving the school's overall instructional program should be directly related to the study's results and conclusions. Some recommendations for improvement will be for specific areas (school governance, curriculum, classroom teaching, and so on), but others will be comprehensive, involving suggested changes that will impact several or all of the areas that have been assessed. Since implementation of all recommendations may not be feasible, they should be prioritized. Like reports on specific programs discussed earlier, the depth and length of the report on an evaluation of the overall instructional program should

Evaluation Question	Coordinator	Evaluation Team Members	Data Sources	Data-Gathering Methods	Data Analysis Methods	Evaluation Timeline	Resources Needed
1)							
2)							
3)							
4)							
5)							
6)							

FIGURE 15.2 *Chart for Planning Data Gathering and Analysis*

be tailored to the intended audience, with different audiences receiving different types of reports. Finally, just as we have argued that teachers and other stakeholders should be involved in planning and carrying out the evaluation, we also recommend that representatives of these various groups participate in scheduled presentations of results to the central office, school board, and community groups.

Program Evaluation and Teacher Empowerment

Fetterman (1996) uses the term "empowerment evaluation" to describe program participants evaluating their own program. Empowerment evaluation has two purposes: improving the program and fostering self-determination. Fetterman describes five stages of empowerment evaluation that can be applied to supervisors working with teachers to evaluate instructional programs.

- *Training:* The supervisor teaches teachers how to conduct program evaluations.
- *Facilitation:* The supervisor coaches teachers as they plan and implement the program evaluation.
- *Advocacy:* the supervisor seeks support for the self-evaluation from the administration, parents and community. If the evaluation results show the need for program changes, the supervisor advocates that teachers be allowed to change the program accordingly.
- *Illumination:* As a result of the evaluation, teachers tend to develop new understanding of the program, their roles, and their relationships with others.
- *Liberation:* Empowerment evaluation often serves to free teachers from previous constraints and roles and enables teachers to become more self-directed.

Empowerment evaluation does not replace program evaluation by external evaluators, but can complement traditional evaluation by providing rich data to outside evaluators. Since most external evaluations are one-time snapshots of instructional programs, self-evaluations have benefits not typically provided by external evaluations, such as ongoing program improvement and teacher development.

Teacher Evaluation

Although teacher evaluation involves some of the same skills as program evaluation (e.g., data gathering, data analysis), it is essentially a separate process requiring different strategies and techniques. In this section we will compare summative and formative teacher evaluation, propose that these two types of evaluation be carried out separately, and discuss self-evaluation.

Comparing Summative and Formative Teacher Evaluation

Summative and formative are two broad categories of teacher evaluation. *Summative teacher evaluation* is an administrative function intended to meet the organizational need for teacher accountability. It involves decisions about the level of a teacher's performance. Summative evaluation always seeks to determine if the teacher has met minimum expectations. If the teacher has not met his or her professional responsibilities, the summative process documents inadequate performance for the purpose of remediation and, if necessary, termination. Sometimes summative evaluation also gathers data to determine if a teacher is eligible for rewards provided by the district for outstanding performance.

Summative evaluation is based on policies that mandate its purpose, frequency, and procedures. Teacher performance is usually documented on an evaluation form. On the form, an administrator completes checklists, rating scales, or narratives indicating the extent to which the teacher has met performance criteria. Evaluation forms usually are standard (same criteria for all teachers) and global (general enough to apply to teachers with different responsibilities). Evaluation forms judge teachers on the quality of their instruction, including such areas as classroom climate, planning, the teaching act, and classroom management (Danielson and McGreal, 2000). But evaluation criteria usually include noninstructional areas as well, such as compliance with school regulations, cooperation with colleagues, completion of extracurricular assignments, and so on.

Evaluation instruments must be valid (accurate) and reliable (consistent). Valid instruments are those that include all criteria considered essential for effective performance, exclude criteria considered extraneous to effective performance, and weight relevant criteria in proportion to their importance (Haefele, 1993; Danielson and McGreal, 2000). Reliable instruments include low-inference (as nearly objective as possible) rather than high-inference (requiring a high level of evaluator subjectivity) indicators. For example, *"teacher clarity"* is an example of a high-inference indicator, and *"uses examples when explaining"* is an example of a low-inference indicator (Haefele, 1993, p. 25). Reliability also requires that administrators be properly trained in the use of the evaluation instrument, so that they become aware of rating errors to avoid and develop a high level of interevaluator reliability (agreement with experts and other administrators in their ratings of the same teacher).

In addition to validity and reliability of individual evaluations, experts suggest that evaluations be done several different times during the evaluation period rather than relying on a one-shot visit to a teacher's classroom. Also recommended are a preevaluation conference in which the administrator and teacher discuss the evaluation process, and a postevaluation conference in which the administrator reviews the results of the evaluation. Finally, legal and ethical considerations require that when a teacher's performance has been judged to be inadequate, the teacher be notified of deficiencies, given an opportunity to respond, provided a remediation plan and support for implementing the plan, and be reevaluated (Sutton, 1989).

Formative teacher evaluation is a supervisory function intended to assist and support teachers in professional growth and the improvement of teaching. It is focused on the needs of teachers rather than on the organization's need for accountability. Unlike summative evaluation, which usually considers teacher behavior inside and outside the classroom, formative evaluation is focused only on teaching and learning. While summative evaluation is concerned with a summary of performance over a specific time period, formative evaluation is ongoing and concerned with continuous improvement. Rather than relying on standardized evaluation instruments that gather data on all essential performance criteria, formative evaluation is usually based on *systematic observation,* which is limited to a single aspect of classroom process (e.g., questioning techniques, student participation, classroom movement, and so on). Thus, the observation systems described in Chapter 14 are well suited for formative evaluation.

McGreal (1989) recommends that, in addition to classroom observation data, classroom artifacts be analyzed to evaluate teaching. Artifacts include such things as assignments, experiments, practice activities, projects, quizzes, and tests. Although artifacts could be used as summative evaluation data, their variety and idiosyncrasy mean that comparing many of them to standardized criteria is difficult if not impossible. Artifacts are more useful for formative evaluation. Analysis of artifacts can help supervisors and teachers identify specific areas for instructional improvement as well as plan and monitor improvement efforts. Analysis of systematic observation data and artifacts together increases the value of formative evaluation.

Because it is not concerned with standardized, global criteria, formative evaluation can concentrate on particular contexts and needs of individual teachers. Since its purpose is helping teachers, not judging them, formative evaluation is not concerned with legal issues like due process. Rather, it is concerned with building trust and rapport, developing a collegial relationship between evaluator and teacher, and addressing teacher needs and concerns. Although some have recommended that students, peers, and parents participate in summative evaluation, administrators and teachers have resisted such involvement. However, student, peer, and parent feedback is much more likely to be offered and accepted if done as part of formative evaluation, purely for the purpose of helping the teacher to improve his or her instruction.

Table 15.2 summarizes our comparison of summative and formative teacher evaluation.

Why Summative and Formative Evaluation Should Be Separate

Most school districts have a single evaluation system and maintain that their system meets both summative and formative needs. However, when schools attempt to carry out summative and formative evaluation simultaneously, they tend to place primary emphasis on summative goals, and formative evaluation is reduced to secondary status. "Too often school districts espouse a strong growth-oriented

TABLE 15.2 *Comparison of Summative and Formative Teacher Evaluation*

	Summative	*Formative*
Function	Administrative	Supervisory
Purpose	Accountability; Judgment on teacher performance; Employment decisions	Assistance; Professional development; Improvement of teaching
Scope	Instruction; Compliance with regulations; Extracurricular responsibilities; Personal qualities	Instruction
Focus	Evaluation form	Any classroom data (observation, artifacts, etc.) relevant to the teacher's instructional concerns and needs
Duration	Set period (usually one academic year)	Ongoing (aimed at continuous improvement)
Concerns	Standardization, validity, reliability, due process	Building trust, rapport, collegiality; Understanding context; Understanding and addressing teacher concerns and needs
Evaluator	Usually an administrator; Final decision by administrator	Administrator, supervisor, self, peers, students, sometimes parents

position but the evaluation system constructed does not reflect that stance" (McGreal, 1989, p. 38).

Evaluation systems that purport to combine summative and formative evaluation while relying on rating scales alone are particularly suspect. "A school system that relies solely on periodic evaluations of teacher performance through rating scales *may* capture data suited for in-system summative purposes but will be handicapped in pursuing formative/developmental objectives" (Allison, 1981, p. 15; emphasis in original). One reason for this is that summative rating scales are designed to be standardized, global, legally defensible, efficiently completed and processed, and include many non-instructional criteria. This means not only that the ratings have little value for formative evaluation, but also that the richest, most meaningful data for formative assessment is precluded (Allison, 1981; Stiggins and Bridgeford, 1984).

It is widely recognized that summative evaluation, while necessary to make employment decisions, does not lead to instructional improvement for most teachers (Stiggins and Bridgeford, 1984). In fact, summative evaluation can actually discourage improvement by promoting "negative feelings about evaluation which, in turn, lead to a lack of participation and a lower likelihood of teachers being willing to alter classroom behavior" (McGreal, 1982, p. 303). Successful formative evaluation depends on trust and open communication between the teacher and evaluator. Yet summative evaluation is potentially punitive (Sutton, 1989). The possibility of a bad performance rating is always lurking in the background. It's no wonder that the two types of evaluation don't mix.

We're not arguing that summative evaluation should be eliminated in favor of formative evaluation. Both types of evaluation are necessary. Like Popham (1988), we maintain that since they have entirely different purposes, they need to be kept separate. With McGreal (1982), we argue that the likelihood that either type of evaluation system will succeed is greater if both systems are internally consistent, which can only be accomplished by the two systems being kept separate. If separated, can the two systems coexist? Yes, but only if the purpose of each is clearly defined, they are perceived by teachers as distinct, and the integrity of each is protected (Allison, 1981).

How to Separate Summative and Formative Evaluation

One way to separate the two types of evaluation is to use different evaluators. For example, first-year teachers (who clearly need to have both types of evaluation) could have their summative evaluation carried out by an administrator and formative evaluation by an experienced teacher assigned as their mentor. Experienced teachers could receive summative evaluation from the principal and formative evaluation from an assistant principal for instruction, lead teacher, or peer coach. There are many different combinations of summative and formative evaluators. The important thing is to make clear to everyone who is responsible of each type of evaluation and to have each evaluator carry out their assessment separately from the other.

Another way to separate summative and formative evaluations relates to the time period when each is carried out. For example, all summative evaluations could be carried out in the fall of each school year, leaving the remainder of the year for formative assessment. When this strategy is used, the same person or persons can perform both types of evaluation. This strategy does not work as well if formative evaluation is carried out in the fall and summative evaluation takes place throughout the rest of the year. This is because the teacher involved in formative evaluation during the fall realizes that summative evaluation is looming on the horizon. That knowledge may affect the willingness of the teacher to engage in open and honest communication about his or her need for instructional improvement. Better to get the summative evaluation out of the way early in the year, give the teacher his or her "seal of approval," and then allow the teacher and supervisor to engage in non-judgmental assessment for the remainder of the school year. A long-term variation of the "separate time periods" strategy is to conduct summative evaluation throughout the first year of a multiyear cycle, and then focus on formative evaluation for the next two to three years, returning to a summative year at the beginning of the next three- to four-year cycle. Should serious problems with a teacher's performance develop during a formative assessment year, that teacher could be shifted back to a summative evaluation-remediation track until the problem is resolved.

A third way of separating summative and formative evaluation has been suggested by Thomas McGreal (1983). Under McGreal's model, a clear and visible set of minimum performance expectations would be developed, including administrative, personal, and instructional expectations. Teacher performance regarding these minimal expectations would be continuously, informally monitored, but no special procedures or evaluation instruments would be established. If a problem occurred with a teacher's performance, the administrator would remind the teacher of minimum expectations. If the problem continued to occur, the administrator would issue to the teacher a written notice of the teacher's deficiency, with a copy placed in the teacher's file. If serious violations continued even after the formal notice, the administrator would recommend more serious administrative action. Beyond the contingencies outlined above, there would be no standard summative evaluation process or annual write-up. This would take care of summative evaluation. Most of the time and energy spent on evaluation would be for formative assessment, including goal setting, a focus on teaching, systematic classroom observation, and collecting and analyzing additional classroom data. This additional data could include peer, parent, student, and self-evaluation, as well as student performance and classroom artifacts (McGreal, 1983).

Which strategy for separating summative and formative evaluation is the best for a district or school? This will depend on the level of administrative and supervisory expertise, the size of the staff, teacher preference, and available resources. The important thing is that they be kept separate. Doing so will mean that both summative and formative evaluation are carried out more effectively.

Self-Evaluation

Self-evaluation can be an important part of the formative evaluation process for teachers functioning at moderate or high levels of development, expertise, and commitment. Self-assessment can take a variety of forms, including any of the following:

- Visits to the classrooms of several expert teachers for the purpose of comparing expert teaching to one's own teaching and identifying self-improvement goals based on such comparison
- Videotaping one's own teaching across several lessons, then analyzing teaching performance while reviewing the videotape
- Designing or selecting and analyzing results of surveys or questionnaires administered to students or parents
- Interviewing supervisors, peers, students, or parents about effective teaching and learning or about one's own instructional performance
- Keeping a journal of teaching experiences, problems, and successes, accompanied by critical reflection for the purpose of instructional improvement
- A comprehensive review of student achievement on traditional tests as well as student projects, presentations, portfolios, social behavior, and so on

- The development of a teaching portfolio for the purpose of self-reflection and analysis. Danielson (1996) recommends a variety of items for possible inclusion in a portfolio, including unit and lesson plans, knowledge of students and resources, videotapes of teaching, examples of student work, written reflections on lessons taught, and logs on professional service, growth, and research. Langer (Teaching for Performance, 1996) argues for a more focused approach, in which the teacher's portfolio documents a process in which the teacher defines a problem, sets an improvement goal, designs a plan to reach the goal, implements the plan, collects data on professional growth, and reflects on results. Both Danielson's broad approach and Langer's focused approach go beyond the documentation of teaching accomplishments (the purpose of portfolios used in summative teacher evaluation) by providing teachers with opportunities for self-assessment as the basis for instructional improvement.

It's important to note that self-evaluation of teaching need not be done in isolation. Videotapes, survey or interview results, journals, student achievement data, and teacher portfolios can be analyzed and discussed collaboratively with a supervisor or peers, and in some cases with students or parents. The process is called self-evaluation because the teacher assumes full responsibility for decision making regarding planning and implementing the evaluation as well as the instructional improvement plan that results (Keller and Duffy, 2005). Once the teacher has completed the self-evaluation, she or he may select from a number of vehicles for meeting instructional improvement goals. The teacher might request clinical supervision from a formally designated supervisor, become part of a peer coaching program (see Chapter 16), or begin an individualized professional development program (see Chapter 18).

SUMMARY

Educational program evaluation has been influenced heavily by educational research design. The attention to school performance has stimulated multiple data sources, research designs, and compositions of evaluation teams. A consensus on the need for involving stakeholders in program evaluation has developed. We must be cautious in selecting instruments that measure what we truly wish to find out about a program. Various types of educational evaluations are used for specific programs and for the overall instructional program. It is not sufficient to know intuitively that a program is good or bad. Rather, decisions about revising, improving, or discarding need to be made with multiple sources of information. The school as a collective enterprise must center its work on questions of educational value and use answers to those questions as guidance for instructional change. Finally, summative and formative teacher evaluation are both necessary but need to be separate. Formative evaluation is more likely to lead to the improvement of instruction.

REFERENCES AND RECOMMENDED READINGS

Allison, D. J. 1981. *Process evaluation: Some summarizing and integrating notes on the organizational implications of this form of teacher evaluation.* (ERIC ED 235 580)

Anfara, V. A., Brown, K. M., and Mangione, T. L. 2002. Qualitative analysis on stage: Making the research process more public. *Educational Researcher, 31*(7), 28–38.

Behuniak, P. 2002. Consumer-referenced testing. *Phi Delta Kappan, 84*(3), 199–207.

Berman, P., and McLaughlin, M. 1976. Implementation of educational innovation. *Educational Forum, 40*(31), 345–370.

Bogdan, R. C., and Biklen, S. K. 1992. *Qualitative research for education: An introduction to theory and methods* (2nd ed.). Boston: Allyn and Bacon.

Borg, W. R., and Gall, M. D. 1989. *Educational research: An introduction* (5th ed.). New York: Longman.

Chatterji, M. 2005. Evidence on "what works": An argument for extended-term mixed-method (ETMM) evaluation designs. *Educational Researcher, 34*(5), 14–24.

Coladarci, R. 2002. Is it a house or a pile of bricks? Important features of a local assessment system. *Phi Delta Kappan, 83*(10), 772–774.

Creswell, J. 2001. *Educational research: Planning, conducting, and evaluating quantitative and qualitative research.* Upper Saddle River, NJ: Prentice Hall.

Danielson, C. 1996. *Enhancing professional practice: A framework for teaching.* Alexandria, VA: Association for Supervision and Curriculum Development.

Danielson, C., and McGreal, T. L. 2000. *Teacher evaluation: To enhance teacher professional practice.* Alexandria, VA: Association for Supervision and Curriculum Development.

Eisner, E. W. 1983. Anastasia might still be alive, but the monarchy is dead. *Educational Researcher, 12*(5), 23–24.

Fang, Z. 1995. On paradigm shift in reading/literacy research. *Research Psychology, 16*, 215–260.

Fetterman, D. M. 1996. Empowerment evaluation: An introduction to theory and practice. In D. M. Fetterman, S. J. Kaftarian, and A. Wandersman (Eds.), *Empowerment evaluation: Knowledge and tools for self-assessment and accountability* (pp. 3–46). Thousand Oaks, CA: Sage.

Glickman, C. D. 1989. *The story of Ogelthorpe County High School: Five years of shared decision making.* Athens, GA: Monographs in Education.

Greene, J. C. 1986. *Participatory evaluation and the evaluation of social programs: Lessons learned from the field.* Paper presented to the annual meeting of the American Educational Research Association, San Francisco, April.

Haefele, D. L. 1993. Evaluating teachers: A call for change. *Journal of Personnel Evaluation in Education, 7*(1), 21–31.

Hall, G. E., and Hord, S. M. 1987. *Change in schools: Facilitating the process.* Albany: State University of New York Press.

Hathaway, R. S. 1995. Assumptions underlying quantitative and qualitative research: Implications for institutional research. *Research in Higher Education, 36*(5), 535–562.

Keller, C. L., and Duffy, M. L. 2005. "I said that?" How to improve your instructional behavior in just 5 minutes per day through data-based self-evaluation. *Teaching Exceptional Children, 37*(4), 36–39.

Lincoln, Y. S., and Guba, E. G. 1985. *Naturalistic inquiry.* Beverly Hills: Sage.

McGreal, T. L. 1982. Effective teacher evaluation systems. *Educational Leadership, 39*(4), 303–305.

McGreal, T. L. 1983. *Successful teacher evaluation.* Alexandria, VA: Association for Supervision and Curriculum Development.

McGreal, T. L. 1989. Necessary ingredients for successful instructional improvement initiatives. *Journal of Staff Development, 10*(1), 35–41.

Nastasia, B., and Schensul, S. 2005. Contributions of qualitative research to the validity of intervention research. *Journal of School Psychology, 43*(3), 177–195.

Nelson, M., and Sieber, S. 1976. Innovations in urban secondary schools. *School Review, 84*, 213–231.

Newman, D. C., and Brown, R. D. 1987. *Violations of evaluation standards: Frequency and seriousness of occurrence.* Paper presented at the annual meeting of the American Educational Research Association, Washington, DC, April.

Patton, M. Q. 1980. *Qualitative evaluation methods.* Beverly Hills, CA: Sage.

Piontek, M. E. 1992. *Synthesized approaches: Expanding the perspectives and impact of qualitative and quantitative evaluation.* Paper presented at the annual meeting of the American Evaluation Association, Seattle, November.

Popham, J. 1988. The dysfunctional marriage of formative and summative evaluation. *Journal of Personnel Evaluation in Education, 1,* 269–273.

Popham, W. J. 1975. *Educational evaluation.* Englewood Cliffs, NJ: Prentice Hall.

A practical guide to measuring project impact on student achievement. Number 1 in a series of monographs on evaluation in education. Under contract OEC-0 = 73-6662, U.S. Office of Education, Washington, DC.

Shank, G. 1994. Shaping research in educational psychology. *Contemporary Educational Psychology, 19,* 340–359.

Shipman, V. 1983. *New Jersey Test of Reasoning Skills.* Upper Montclair, NJ: IAPC Test Division, Montclair State College.

Spray, M. 1993. State assessment programs: Images of state reform. *R and D Preview, 8*(6), 4–5.

Stiggins, R. J. 2002. Assessment crisis: The absence of assessment for learning. *Phi Delta Kappan, 83*(10), 758–765.

Stiggins, R. J., and Bridgeford, N. J. 1984. *Performance assessment for teacher development.* Portland, OR: Northwest Regional Educational Lab Center for Performance Assessment.

Sutton, J. H. 1989. *Evaluation: A prime for teachers.* (ERIC ED 310 146)

Teaching for performance: New assessments help reshape classroom practice (1996, December). *Education Update, 38*(8), 1, 6.

Wise, A. 1988. *Restructuring schools.* Presentation to the Annual Georgia Leadership Institute, Athens, GA, June.

Wolfe, R. 1969. A model for curriculum evaluation. *Psychology in the Schools, 6,* 107–108.

PART V

Tasks of SuperVision

If one has responsibility for the improvement of instruction, what does one do? We've accounted for what the supervisor needs to possess in terms of knowledge, interpersonal skills, and technical skills. What are the tasks of supervision that can bring about improved instruction? A supervisor can facilitate improved instruction by direct assistance to teachers, group development, professional development, curriculum development, and action research.

Direct assistance: The supervisor can provide or facilitate one-to-one feedback with teachers to improve instruction.

Group development: The supervisor can provide for instructional problem-solving meetings among teachers to improve instruction.

Professional development: The supervisor can provide learning opportunities for teachers to improve instruction.

Curriculum development: The supervisor can provide for changes in teaching content and instructional materials to improve instruction.

Action research: The supervisor can provide teachers with ways to evaluate their own teaching to improve instruction.

Each of these tasks is directly related to improved instruction. A supervisor needs to take responsibility for these tasks if a school is to become increasingly effective. Part V will detail how these tasks can be performed so that teachers take individual and collective responsibility for instructional improvement.

Direct Assistance to Teachers

Direct assistance to help teachers improve instruction can come from different sources. This book has contended that someone needs to take responsibility for the supervisory function of direct assistance to ensure that teachers receive feedback, are not left alone, and are involved as part of a collective staff. Research by Dornbush and Scott (1975) and Natriello (1982) has shown that teachers who receive the most classroom feedback are also most satisfied with teaching. Other research studies have shown that teachers in need of assistance tend to seek out first fellow teachers and second supervisory or administrative personnel (Lortie, 1975, pp. 75–77). Direct assistance to teachers is one of the crucial elements of a successful school (Little, 1982; Rosenholtz, 1985; DuFour, 2002; Glickman, 2002; Davenport and Smetana, 2004). Keeping the frequency and source of direct assistance in mind, we will look at an established structure for assisting teachers and then at some alternative ways of implementing the structure.

Clinical Supervision

Although there are multiple ways of observing, the model for conducting observations with teachers is relatively standard and accepted, with a respectable research base (Sullivan, 1980; Adams and Glickman, 1984; Pavan, 1985; Nolan, Hawkes, and Francis, 1993; Glickman, 2002). The model, commonly referred to as *clinical supervision,* is derived from the pioneering work of Morris Cogan with supervisors of intern teachers at Harvard University. Cogan's *Clinical Supervision* (1973) and Robert Goldhammer's book, also entitled *Clinical Supervision* (1969), are publications resulting from this pioneer work. Since then, numerous refinements and alterations of clinical supervision have been made (Goldhammer, Anderson, and Krajewski, 1993; Acheson and Gall, 1992; Costa and Garmston, 1985; Anderson and Snyder, 1993; Pajak, 1993, 2002). Those desiring an in-depth study of the research and development of clinical supervision can find references at the end of this chapter.

Clinical supervision is both a concept and a structure. Goldhammer, Anderson, and Krajewski (1993) reviewed nine characteristics of clinical supervision as a concept:

1. It is a technology for improving instruction.
2. It is a deliberate intervention into the instructional process.
3. It is goal-oriented, combining school needs with the personal growth needs of those who work within the school.
4. It assumes a professional working relationship between teacher(s) and supervisor(s).
5. It requires a high degree of mutual trust, as reflected in understanding, support, and commitment to growth.
6. It is systematic, although it requires a flexible and continuously changing methodology.
7. It creates a productive (i.e., healthy) tension for bridging the gap between the real and the ideal.
8. It assumes that the supervisor knows a great deal about the analysis of instruction and learning and also about productive human interaction.
9. It requires both preservice training (for supervisors), especially in observation techniques, and continuous in-service reflection on effective approaches. (pp. 52–53; parenthetical explanation provided)

The structure of clinical supervision can be simplified into five sequential steps:

1. Preconference with teacher
2. Observation of classroom
3. Analyzing and interpreting observation and then determining conference approach
4. Postconference with teacher
5. Critique of previous four steps

Step 1. At the *preconference,* the supervisor sits with the teacher and determines (1) the reason and purpose for the observation, (2) the focus of the observation, (3) the method and form of observation to be used, (4) the time of observation, and (5) the time for postconference. These determinations are made before the actual observation, so that both supervisor and teacher are clear about what will transpire. The purpose of the observation, as mentioned in Chapter 14, should provide the criteria for making the remaining decisions on focus, method, and time of observation.

Step 2.   The next step, *observation,* is the time to follow through with the understandings of the preconference. The observer might use any one observation or combinations of observations. Methods include categorical frequencies, performance indicators, visual diagramming, space utilization, verbatim reports, detached open-ended narratives, participant observation, focused questionnaire, and tailored observation systems. The observer should keep in mind the difference between *descriptions* of events and *interpretations.* Interpretation should follow description.

Step 3.   The *analysis* and *interpretations* of the observation and determination of approach are now possible. The supervisor leaves the classroom with his or her observations and seeks solitude in an office or corner. He or she lays out the recorded pages of observations and studies the information. The task might be counting up frequencies, looking for recurring patterns, isolating a major occurrence, or discovering which performance indicators were present and which were not. Regardless of the instrument, questionnaire, or open-ended form used, the supervisor must make sense out of a large mass of information. Then the supervisor can make interpretations based on the analysis of the description. Figure 16.1 is a form that can be used to organize this task.

A. Analysis: Write the major findings of your observation. Write down only what has been taken directly from your observation.
   1.
   2.
   3.
   4.
   5.

B. Interpretations: Write below what you believe is desirable or not desirable about the major findings.
   1.
   2.
   3.
   4.
   5.

FIGURE 16.1   *Worksheet for Analysis and Interpretation of Data*

A case study might help to clarify this worksheet. Supervisor A has completed a verbal interaction instrument for students and teacher. She reviews the 10 sheets, tallies the columns, and writes in the worksheet under analysis:

1. The teacher asked 27 questions and received 42 answers.
2. Out of 276 total verbal moves, 6 were student to student; the other 270 were teacher to student or student to teacher.
3. . . .

The supervisor, knowing that the purpose of the lesson was to encourage student involvement, now makes interpretations on the worksheet *corresponding* to the analysis:

1. The teacher encouraged students to answer questions.
2. There was little interaction among students.
3. . . .

Note the relationship between analysis 1 and interpretation 1. There is clear documentation of evidence leading to the supervisor's judgment.

Let's examine one more case, this time of supervisor B doing a participant observation. The supervisor reads through his brief classroom notes, picks out the most significant events, and writes under analysis:

1. James, Tyrone, Felix, and Sondra asked me about the assignment they were supposed to be doing.
2. Kirk and Felipe were talking with each other about sports the three times I overheard them.
3. . . .

From this analysis, the supervisor makes the following interpretation:

1. The teacher was not clearly communicating the directions to some students.
2. At least a couple of students were not interested in the classwork.
3. . . .

Although one could argue with the supervisor's interpretation, it is readily apparent how it was logically derived from the recorded descriptions.

The last determination for the supervisor to make in step 3 of the clinical structure is to choose the interpersonal approach to use with the teacher in the postconference. The directive informational, collaborative, and nondirective approaches to supervision were explained in Chapters 9, 10, and 11, respectively. Should the supervisor use a directive informational approach by presenting his or her observations and interpretations, asking for teacher input, setting a goal, and providing teachers with alternative actions to choose from? Should the supervisor be collaborative by sharing the observation, allowing the teacher to present his or her own interpretations, and negotiating a mutual contract for future improvement? Should the supervisor be nondirective by explaining his or her observations and encouraging the teacher to analyze, interpret, and make his or her own plan? The supervisor must consider the individual teacher's level of development, expertise, and commitment as explained in Chapter 12. When working with a teacher who is best matched with a collaborative or nondirective approach and who has experience with clinical supervision, some supervisors provide the teacher with the observation data prior to the postconference. This allows the teacher to review the data in advance and bring his or her preliminary interpretations to the postconference.

Step 4.   With the completed observation form, completed analysis, and interpretation form, and with the chosen interpersonal approach, the supervisor is ready to meet with the teacher in a *postconference*. The postconference is held to discuss the analysis of the observation and, finally, to produce a plan for instructional improvement.

The first order of business is to let the teacher in on the observation—to reflect back to the teacher what was seen. Then the supervisor can follow the chosen approach—directive informational, collaborative, or nondirective. The responsibility for developing a future plan may reside with the supervisor, be equally shared, or belong to the teacher. The conference ends with a plan for further improvement. Figure 16.2 can be used to develop such a plan.

Postconference Date _____   Observed Teacher _____

Time _____   Supervisor _____

Objective to be worked on:

Activities to be undertaken to achieve objectives:

Resources needed:

Time and date for next preconference:

FIGURE 16.2 *Plan for Instructional Improvement*

The *objective* is a statement of what the teacher will attain for the next observation: "I will improve student-to-student interaction by 50 percent in group discussions." *Activities* are the listed preparation points to accomplish the objective: (1) Practice pausing at least three seconds before answering a student response. (2) Practice using open-ended questions. (3) Set up ongoing mini-debates. *Resources* are the materials and/or people needed to do the activities: (1) Read a book on *Leading Discussion Groups*. (2) Attend a workshop on "Involving Students." (3) Observe Mr. Filler when he holds a science discussion. *Date* and *time* specify when the teacher will be ready to display his or her improvement. Such a plan—whether designed by the teacher, the supervisor, or both—should be clearly understood by both parties before they leave the postconference.

Step 5. The *critique* of the previous four steps is a time for reviewing whether the format and procedures from preconference through postconference were satisfactory and whether revisions might be needed before repeating the sequence. The critique might be held at the end of the postconference. It need not be a formal session but can be a brief discussion, consisting of questions such as: What was valuable in what we have been doing? What was of little value? What changes could be suggested? The critique has both symbolic and functional value. It indicates that the supervisor is involved in an improvement effort in the same way as the supervisee. Furthermore, the feedback from the teacher gives the supervisor a chance to decide on what practices to continue, revise, or change when working with the teacher in the future.

The five steps are now complete, and a tangible plan of future action is in the hands of the teacher. The supervisor is prepared to review the plan in the next preconference and reestablish focus and method of observation.

Comparing Clinical Supervision with Teacher Evaluation

In Chapter 15 we discovered the differences between summative and formative evaluation. Clinical supervision is consistent with formative evaluation; it provides nonjudgmental assistance aimed at improving the teacher's instruction. Indeed it has been equated by some with formative evaluation. Clinical supervision actually includes but goes beyond formative evaluation by helping the teacher to design and implement an action plan to meet instructional improvement goals.

Clinical supervision is *not* consistent with summative evaluation; it is not intended to gather data to make judgments about whether teachers are meeting performance criteria for continued employment. Some school districts have confused the two processes by calling their summative evaluation cycle clinical supervision. At one level this is understandable. Both clinical supervision and summative evaluation can take place within similar structures, including a preconference, classroom visit, and postconference. To understand the difference between the two concepts we must look beyond the structure to the purpose and principles of clinical supervision, which clearly are not consistent with summative evaluation. The two processes need to be separate, for the same reasons that summative and formative evaluation should be separate (see Chapter 15).

Integrating Clinical Supervision and Developmental Supervision

As discovered in Part III, developmental supervision calls for the supervisor to match one of four interpersonal approaches—directive control, directive informational, collaborative, or nondirective—with teachers' developmental levels, expertise, and commitment. Are all four of these interpersonal approaches consistent with clinical supervision? The answer to this question depends to some extent on the model of clinical supervision being considered. Goldhammer's (1969) text on clinical supervision emphasizes a nondirective interpersonal approach. Cogan's (1973) clinical cycle reflects a collaborative orientation. Hunter's (1980, 1983, 1984, 1986) clinical model supports a directive approach. Our own view is that directive informational, collaborative, and nondirective supervisory approaches are all consistent with the clinical model.

Using a directive informational approach, the supervisor can suggest and explain two or three alternative observation foci and data collection methods in the preconference, and ask the teacher to select from the options provided. In the postconference, the supervisor can help the teacher to interpret observation data and ask the teacher to choose from a limited range of possible improvement objectives, activities, and follow ups. The supervisor and teacher engaged in a collaborative preconference can consider observation alternatives and select a mutually agreeable observation focus and data-collection method. In the collaborative postconference, the supervisor and teacher can share decision-making responsibility as they build an action plan for instructional improvement. The supervisor using nondirective behaviors in a preconference can ask the teacher to choose the focus of the observation and facilitate the teacher as he or she chooses or creates an observation system that the supervisor would feel comfortable using. In the postconference, the supervisor would clarify, encourage, and reflect as the teacher designed his or her own improvement plan.

Although directive control behaviors are necessary in rare situations, we do not consider those behaviors to be consistent with the purpose and principles of clinical supervision. Directive control should be used only in short-term crisis situations, not as part of a normal clinical cycle.

Peer Coaching

Since teachers naturally turn to each other for help more often than to a supervisor, and since supervision is concerned primarily with improving instruction rather than with summative evaluation (renewal of contracts), teachers helping teachers has become a formalized and well-received way of assuring direct assistance to every staff member. With the advent of extended responsibilities for career-ladder teachers, mentor teachers, master teachers, grade-level chairpersons, team leaders, and department heads, the time and resources for peer assistance have increased. Keedy (1987) recommends that principals and supervisors provide instructional leadership through the coordination of instructional specialists like those listed above, rather than by attempting on their own to provide direct assistance to all teachers in the school. If teachers become proficient in observation skills and the format of clinical supervision, the supervisor can take on the role of clarifier, trainer, scheduler, and troubleshooter—clarifier by determining the purpose; trainer by preparing the teachers for the task; scheduler by forming teams or trios of teachers who take responsibility for preconferencing, observing, and postconferencing with each other; and troubleshooter by consulting with teams of teachers who are experiencing difficulties and with individual teachers who need more specialized attention. The use of teachers helping teachers through clinical supervision has been labeled *peer supervision* or *peer coaching*. If direct assistance is a worthy task for instructional improvement but a supervisor cannot provide it on a regular basis, the choice is either to have teachers provide help to each other or simply not to offer the help.

Obviously, the way to begin such a program is not to call a staff meeting and announce, "Since I can't see each of you as much as I would like, why don't you start to visit each other? Go to it!" Without planning and resources, disaster is inevitable. To be successful, peer coaching needs components addressing purpose, preparation, scheduling, and troubleshooting. Let's take each in turn.

Purpose

A peer-coaching program devoid of articulated definition and purpose has no rudder for steering and selecting the training, scheduling, and troubleshooting essential for success. Instead, it becomes another fad, exciting in that it's on the "cutting edge" of school change, but lacking substance in terms of what is to be accomplished. If there is a lack of direction in peer-coaching programs, well-intentioned teachers will have a vague sense of having done something pleasant but little sense of accomplishment (see Little, Galagaran, and O'Neal, 1984). Therefore, the first step is to meet with teachers to discuss how a proposed peer-coaching program would fit into a school's or district's instructional goals and then to decide on the specific purposes of the program. For example, if the purpose is simply to acquaint teachers with each other's teaching strategies, less preparation is needed than if the purpose is to provide teachers with feedback on their teaching and assist them to develop action plans for instructional improvement. The next subsection provides some training guidelines for proceeding with a peer-coaching program that is focused on the purpose of reflective decision making.

Preparation

Before implementation, preparation of teachers would include training on (1) understanding the purpose and procedures of peer coaching, (2) conducting a preconference for determining the focus of observations, (3) conducting and analyzing an observation to distinguish between observing and interpreting classroom events, and (4) conducting two postconferences with different approaches for developing action plans—one using a nondirective approach, the other using a collaborative approach.

A standard form for writing instructional improvement plans in the postconference should be reviewed. The form should be simple and easy to fill out. Each peer member should understand that a completed plan is the object of the first four clinical steps and the basis for beginning the next round of supervision. For purposes of training, you may use the forms found in this chapter and in Chapter 14.

Training sessions of about six hours should provide the minimum knowledge and skills to begin peer coaching. After peers have gained some familiarity with the process through demonstrations, modeling, and practice in the workshop setting, they will be anxious but ready to begin a coaching cycle. For the initial attempts, perfection is not expected, of course. After the first cycle of implementation, a follow-up meeting should be held to discuss what has occurred and what revisions need to be made before beginning the second cycle. It is often convenient to review the past cycle and conduct the preconference for the next cycle during the same meeting. This gives participants a sense of sharing and learning from each other, enables the trainer to answer questions, allows for observation schedules to be arranged, and eliminates the need to meet another time to hold the preconference. From this point on, follow-up meetings concluding and beginning further cycles can be held every two to three weeks until the agreed-on number of peer cycles have been finished. For the first year, it is recommended that at least four cycles be conducted—two times being the coach and two times being coached.

Toward the end of the year, a culminating meeting should be held to summarize the advantages and disadvantages of using peer coaching and to make a recommendation on whether to continue the program for the following year.

Let's emphasize that the program should be based on *agreement* and *volunteerism*. If an entire staff is willing to be involved, that's fine, but if only three teachers are willing, it is still a beginning and a previously unavailable source of help for those three teachers.

Scheduling

A teacher will have a more difficult time becoming enthusiastic about a project if it means increasing the amount of personal time and energy expended beyond an already full day. Because peer coaching will require additional time, the program should be voluntary, at least in the beginning. Greater participation of teachers is likely if the supervisor can schedule time for peer coaching during the school day. For example, placing teachers together in teams that share the same planning or lunch periods would allow for pre- and postconferences during the school day. Hiring a few substitutes for two days, twice a year, would allow teachers to be relieved of class duties so that they can observe their peers. One substitute could relieve six classroom teachers for one period at a time. Relief could also be found by having the supervisor (we mean you!) occasionally substitute for a teacher for one class period. This would enable the teacher to observe and would also give the supervisor a glimpse into the operating world of the classroom. Another way of freeing time for peer observations is for teachers to release each other by periodically scheduling a video, lecture, or some other large-group instruction so that two classes can be taught by one teacher. Whatever the actual schedule used to release teachers for peer coaching, preplanning by supervisor and teachers is needed to ensure that teachers can participate without extreme personal sacrifice. Research on lasting classroom change has shown that scheduling released time for teachers during the school day is critical (Humphries, 1981; Ballinger, 2000).

Another issue is arranging teams of teachers. As in most issues in education, there are no hard and fast rules. Generally, teachers should be grouped with each other so that they are comfortable together but not necessarily at identical levels of experience and/or competence. It may be useful to put experienced teachers with new ones, superior teachers with adequate ones, or adequate teachers with struggling ones.

Troubleshooting

The third component of establishing a peer-coaching program is the close monitoring of peer progress. The supervisor should be available to peer teams as a resource person. For example, what happens when the preconference concludes with an agreement to observe a teacher's verbal interaction in the classroom, and the peer coach is at a loss about where to find such an observation instrument? The training program should answer such questions, but orientation meetings cannot cover all possible needs. The supervisor must therefore monitor the needs of peer teams and be able to step in to help.

An elaborate monitoring device is not necessary. The supervisor might simply wander around the halls and check with peer coaches every few weeks. At periodic faculty meetings, he or she might ask peer coaches to write a note on their team progress. The supervisor should be sure that books, videos, and methods/instruments for observations are catalogued and available to teachers in the professional library.

Now that the supervisor can attend to *purpose, training, scheduling,* and *troubleshooting,* a peer-coaching supervision program can be implemented. The initial implementation of such a program undoubtedly will create more work for the supervisor. However, the initial work is less than would be necessary for providing clinical supervision to every teacher two or three times a year. If it is important enough to supervisor and staff, the time spent at the start in preparing for the program will pay off with ongoing instructional improvement of teachers.

Other Forms of Direct Assistance

Clinical supervision and peer coaching are currently two of the most popular forms of direct assistance in schools, but a variety of other forms are available. A few additional examples of direct assistance follow:

• *Demonstration teaching:* The supervisor or expert peer can be a guest teacher, demonstrating a new teaching model or method for the teacher requesting assistance. Alternatively, the teacher seeking to learn new skills can visit an expert peer's classroom for a demonstration lesson. A demonstration teaching cycle can include a preconference in which the demonstrator previews the lesson, and a postconference in which the demonstrator and observer analyze the completed lesson and discuss how the model or methods can be adapted to the observer's teaching.

• *Co-teaching:* The supervisor or expert peer and the teacher seeking assistance together can plan, teach, and evaluate a lesson. Co-teaching establishes trust and rapport, and fosters the collegiality, dialogue, and mutual reflection that foster teacher growth.

• *Assistance with resources and materials:* An unglamorous but vital supervisory activity is providing, explaining, and demonstrating instructional resources and materials. All of us in education are aware of teachers who make little or no use of particular instructional resources and materials (from manipulatives to new computer software) because of a lack of awareness or expertise. Many teachers would benefit greatly from the effective use of such resources and materials, but they need individualized assistance for technical mastery and adaptation to teaching content and students.

• *Assistance with student assessment:* There is a clear trend within the educational reform movement toward alternative forms of student assessment, especially authentic assessment (Clark and Clark, 2000; Coladarci, 2002; Stiggins, 2002). In the coming years, teachers will likely need considerable direct assistance from supervisors in developing criteria and skills for assessing such things as student portfolios, "real-world" performances, and integrative projects. No doubt, authentic assessment techniques will be introduced to teachers through group in-service sessions. However, adapting new assessment techniques to particular content areas, grade levels, and individual students will, we believe, require individualized assistance.

• *Problem solving:* Teachers experience a variety of professional problems that can be solved in one-to-one conferences and without classroom observation. Once a relationship of openness, trust, and rapport has been established, a supervisor can assist a teacher through a problem-solving process involving (1) identification of the problem, (2) generation and weighing of alternative actions, (3) selection of the most appropriate actions, and (4) planning follow-up to assess the results of chosen actions.

• *Mentoring:* In schools, mentoring typically is direct assistance provided by an experienced teacher to a beginning teacher. The mentor might provide any of the forms of direct assistance discussed previously—expert coaching, demonstration teaching, co-teaching, and so on. The heart of mentoring, however, goes beyond any specific form of direct assistance to the ongoing relationship of mentor and beginner. This trusting, helping relationship can make the difference between a successful and a failed entrance to the profession. The formal supervisor has a significant role to play in mentoring programs, helping to select and prepare mentors, assisting with the matching of mentors with beginners, and providing ongoing support for mentors.

Beyond Technical Assistance: Improving Classroom Culture

A great deal of direct assistance is for the purpose of improving teachers' instructional skills or solving immediate instructional problems. As important as these goals are, direct assistance can help teachers reach deeper goals based on democratic and moral purpose. The classroom can be viewed as both a microcosm of the larger culture and as a vehicle for transforming that culture. By modeling and encouraging adherence to democratic and moral values in the classroom, the teacher fosters a democratic and moral society.

The teacher and supervisor can begin the process of improving classroom culture by asking questions like the following:

• Are students treated equitably by the teacher and by each other?
• Do the teacher and students follow democratic principles appropriate to the students' ages and maturity levels?
• Do the teacher and students demonstrate compassion to those in need?
• Do students feel physically and emotionally safe?
• Are all cultures respected, valued, and celebrated?

Processes such as clinical supervision and peer coaching can be used to answer questions like these. Quantitative observation data can be gathered in this arena (for example, data can be gathered on whether the teacher gives students response opportunities, assistance, or praise in an equitable manner), but often rich narrative is needed to adequately describe classroom culture. The teacher and supervisor can work together to interpret the meaning of data on classroom culture and to develop action plans for cultural improvement. Because classroom culture is so complex, teacher-supervisor conferral and action planning for cultural improvement will be more complicated than conferral and planning for technical improvement, and cultural improvement will take much longer than implementing a new teaching skill. However, if a critical goal of education is a more democratic society, then the increased complexity and longer duration of cultural improvement efforts are well justified.

SUMMARY

Regardless of how or where the responsibilities reside, no school or school system can hope to improve instruction if direct assistance is not provided to teachers. To leave classroom teachers alone and unobserved in their classrooms, without professional consultation and without school resources tailored to their unique needs, is a statement (intended or not) that teaching is unimportant. The message to teachers is that what is important is keeping your class quiet, your doors shut, and your problems to yourself. Assuredly, this is not the message we want to give.

A different message can be given by arranging for observation, feedback, and discussion of classroom improvement. Within the structure of clinical supervision, peer coaching is a recognizable structure for assistance that teachers can use to help each other. Furthermore, supervisors can be accessible, facilitate self- and group evaluation, arrange contact times, and refer specialists to teachers. Direct assistance, separated from summative evaluation, will help teachers confide, improve, and move with each other toward collective action.

REFERENCES AND RECOMMENDED READINGS

Acheson, A. A., and Gall, M. D. 1992. *Techniques in the clinical supervision of teachers* (3rd ed.). New York: Longman.

Adams, A., and Glickman, C. D. 1984. Does clinical supervision work? A review of research. *Tennessee Educational Leadership, 11*(11), 38–40.

Anderson, R. H., and Snyder, K. J. (Eds.). 1993. *Clinical supervision: Coaching for higher performance.* Lancaster, PA: Technomic Publishing.

Ballinger, J. 2000. Programs aim to stop teacher washout. *Journal of Staff Development, 21*(2), 28–33.

Barbknecht, A., and Kieffer, C. W. 2001. *Peer coaching: The learning team approach.* Arlington Heights, IL: Skylight.

Clark, D. C., and Clark, S. N. 2000. Appropriate assessment strategies for young adolescents in an era of standards-based reform. *The Clearing House, 73*(4), 201–204.

Coe, E. E. 1985. Towards collegial inquiry: A case study in clinical supervision. (ERIC Document ED 281 847)

Cogan, M. 1973. *Clinical supervision.* Boston: Houghton Mifflin.

Coladarci, R. 2002. Is it a house or a pile of bricks? Important features of a local assessment system. *Phi Delta Kappan, 83*(10), 772–774.

Costa, A. L., and Garmston, R. 1985. Supervision for intelligent teaching. *Educational Leadership, 42*(5), 70–80.

Davenport, J., and Smetana, L. 2004. Helping new teachers achieve excellence. *The Delta Kappa Gamma Bulletin, 70*(2), 18–22.

Dornbush, S. M., and Scott, W. R. 1975. *Evaluation and the exercise of authority.* San Francisco: Jossey-Bass.

DuFour, R. 2002. How deep is your support system? *Journal of Staff Development, 23*(4), 72–73.

Educational Leadership. 1987. Theme issue: Progress in Evaluating Teaching, 44(7).

Egelson, P. 1994. *Teacher evaluation plans that support professional growth.* Paper presented at The Third Annual National Evaluation Institute, Gatlinburg, TN, July. (ERIC ED 026 286)

Garmston, R. J. 1987. How administrators support peer coaching. *Educational Leadership, 44*(5), 71–78.

Glatthorn, A. 1984. *Differentiated supervision.* Alexandria, VA: Association for Supervision and Curriculum Development.

Glickman, C. D. 2002. *Leadership for learning: How to help teachers succeed.* Alexandria, VA: Association for Supervision and Curriculum development.

Glickman, C. D., and Esposito, J. P. 1979. *Leadership guide for elementary school improvement* (pp. 233–250). Boston: Allyn and Bacon.

Goldhammer, R. 1969. *Clinical supervision: Special methods for the supervision of teachers.* New York: Holt, Rinehart and Winston.

Goldhammer, R., Anderson, R. H., and Krajewski, R. J. 1993. *Clinical supervision: Special methods for the supervision of teachers* (3rd ed.). Fort Worth, TX: Harcourt Brace Jovanovich.

Harris, B. M. 1975. *Supervisory behavior in education* (2nd ed.). Englewood Cliffs, NJ: Prentice Hall.

Hazard, W. R. 1993. *Legal aspects of teacher evaluation.* Paper presented at the Annual Convention of the National Organization on Legal Problems in Education, Philadelphia, November. (ERIC ED 377 182)

Humphries, J. D. 1981. Factors affecting the impact of curriculum innovations on classroom practice: Project complexity, characteristics of local leadership and supervisory strategies. Unpublished Ed.D. dissertation, University of Georgia.

Hunter, M. 1980. Six types of supervisory conferences. *Educational Leadership, 37,* 408–412.

Hunter, M. 1983. Script-taping: An essential supervisory tool. *Educational Leadership, 41*(3), 3.

Hunter, M. 1984. Knowing, teaching, and supervising. In P. L. Hosford (Ed.), *Using what we know about teaching.* Alexandria, VA: Association for Supervision and Curriculum Development.

Hunter, M. 1986. Let's eliminate the preobservation conference. *Educational Leadership, 43*(6), 69–70.

Keedy, J. L. 1987. Principals as instructional leaders: A realistic definition. *ERS Spectrum: Journal of School Research and Information, 5*(1), 3–7.

Little, J. W. 1982. Norms of collegiality and experimentation: Work place conditions of school success. *American Educational Research Journal, 19*(3), 325–340.

Little, J. W., Galagaran, P., and O'Neal, R. 1984. Professional development roles and relationships: Principles and skills of "advising." (Contract 400-83-003.) San Francisco: Far West Laboratory for Educational Research and Development.

Lortie, D. C. 1975. *School teacher: A sociological study.* Chicago: University of Chicago Press.

McColskey, W., and Egelson, P. 1993. *Designing teacher evaluation systems that support professional growth.* Greensboro, NC: Southeastern Regional Vision for Education, School of Education, University of North Carolina at Greensboro. (ERIC ED 367 662)

McGreal, T. L. 1982. Effective teacher evaluation systems. *Educational Leadership, 39*(4), 303–305.

Natriello, G. 1982. *The impact of the evaluation of teaching on teacher effect and effectiveness.* Paper presented at the annual meeting of American Educational Research Association, New York, March.

Nolan, J., Hawkes, B., and Francis, P. 1993. Case studies: Windows into Clinical Supervision. *Educational Leadership, 51*(2), 52–56.

Oliva, P. F. 1976. *Supervision for today's schools.* New York: Harper & Row.

Pajak, E. 1993. *Approaches to clinical supervision: Alternatives for improving instruction.* Norwood, MA: Christopher-Gordon.

Pajak, E. 2002. Clinical supervision and psychological functions: A new direction for theory and practice. *Journal of Curriculum and Supervision, 17*(3), 189–205.

Pavan, B. N. 1985. *Clinical supervision: Research in schools utilizing comparative measures.* Paper presented at the annual meeting of the American Educational Research Association, Chicago, April.

Popham, W. J. 1988. The dysfunctional marriage of formative and summative teacher evaluation. *Journal of Personnel Evaluation in Education, 1,* 269–273.

Rosenholtz, S. J. 1985. Effective schools: Interpreting the evidence. *American Journal of Education, 93,* 352–388.

Stiggins, R. J. 2002. Assessment crisis: The absence of assessment for learning. *Phi Delta Kappan, 83*(10), 758–765.

Sullivan, C. G. 1980. *Clinical supervision: A state of the art review.* Alexandria, VA: Association for Supervision and Curriculum Development.

Group Development

- A vertical team at Highlands Elementary School is using action research to improve student literacy.
- The Level Six team at M. L. King Middle School is developing a new interdisciplinary curriculum.
- A teacher task force at Edwards High School is examining strategies for assisting students placed at risk.

The teams described above are different in terms of school level and purpose, but they also have much in common. Each of the groups has a task it is expected to complete that will involve making a number of decisions along the way. Each group needs to be concerned about maintaining positive interpersonal relationships. Each group is almost certain to face some level of conflict and some types of dysfunctional behavior along the way. There are myriad teams with myriad purposes operating at schools across the nation, but they all possess some common roles, developmental phases, and challenges. This chapter will discuss task and personal roles needed by all groups, dysfunctional roles that can impede any group, and general approaches to conflict management and decision making. There are, of course, differences among groups, including differences in group purposes, ability, and commitment. This chapter also will address changing group leadership style to match group readiness for the situation at hand.

Learning the skills of working with groups to solve instructional problems is a critical task of supervision. Just as cooperative learning with students has been found to produce significant gains in academic and social outcomes (Cooper,

2002; King, 2002; Slavin, 1987), so have collegial adult groups been shown to produce higher adult achievement and performance than individualistic or competitive learning (Johnson and Johnson, 1987b; Yorks and Kasl, 2002; Kasl and Yorks, 2002). This chapter covers knowledge, skills, and procedures for developing productive instructional improvement groups: using group observations, changing group leadership styles, dealing with dysfunctional members, resolving conflict, and preparing for meetings.

Professional people who are brought together to deal with pressing mutual problems have the right to expect results. Meetings that drag on, with seemingly endless and unfocused discussion, are morale breakers. Participants become reluctant, apathetic, and sometimes hostile toward future meetings. They might even suspect that the group leader is deliberately leading them astray, so that the group's inability to decide can be used as an excuse for the leader to do whatever he or she wishes. Regardless of whether the leader is actually trying to create confusion or truly desires a group decision, the lack of clear results erodes unity and common purpose. We already know how important unity, common purpose, and involvement are in developing a cause beyond oneself related to school success.

Groups that work productively, efficiently, and harmoniously generally have a skillful leader. Unfortunately, since being part of a group is such an everyday occurrence in professional, personal, and social life, we seldom stop to think about what makes some groups work well and others fail. It is unrealistic for the leader of a new group to expect the group to proceed naturally in a professional manner. A leader needs to be conscious of the elements of a successful group, select clear procedures for group decision making, be able to deal with dysfunctional behavior, use conflict to generate helpful information, and determine appropriate leadership style.

Dimensions of an Effective Group

There are two dimensions of an effective professional group (Bales, 1953): the task dimension and the person dimension. The *task* dimension represents the content and purpose of the group meeting. The task is what is to be accomplished by the end of the meetings. Typical tasks of professional groups might be deciding on a new textbook, writing a new instructional schedule, coordinating a particular curriculum, or preparing a professional development plan. An effective group, obviously, accomplishes what it sets out to do. The *person* dimension of an effective group comprises the interpersonal process and the satisfaction participants derive from working with each other. Concern and sensitivity to participants' feelings create a climate of desiring to meet with each other from week to week to accomplish and implement the group task.

Let's explain these two dimensions in a different way. Specific task behaviors are clarifying the group's purpose, keeping discussions focused, setting time limits, and appraising group progress toward the goal. A leader who says, "We're getting off the track; let's get back to discussing textbooks," is exhibiting a task behavior.

Specific person behaviors seen in a group include recognizing people for their contributions, smiling, injecting humor, and listening attentively. A leader who says, "Fred, I'm following what you've been saying; it's a point worth considering," would be demonstrating a person behavior. Imagine a group that exhibits only task behaviors. The meeting would be formal, cold, and tense. People would not receive feedback, would not be encouraged, and probably would swallow hard before addressing the unsmiling, staring faces. Such a group would accomplish its task quickly, with little mutual support. The decision would be quick because participants would wish to remove themselves from the tense environment as soon as possible. The formality of the sessions would prevent in-depth discussions of feelings, attitudes, and differences of opinion. Decisions would be made on the basis of incomplete information and commitment from group members. The implementation of the decision would be problematic at best.

Next, imagine a group that exhibits only person behaviors. There would be much personal chatter, humorous storytelling, and frequent backslapping and touching. People would be smiling and laughing. The image of a raucous cocktail party might characterize a group with all person behaviors and no task behaviors, and the morning-after hangover is also analogous to the sense of accomplishment after a meeting devoid of task behaviors. People would enjoy each other's company for its own sake; everyone would have a wonderful time, but little would be done.

Group Member Roles

First, the leader needs to determine what behaviors are indicative of roles already in existence. Are some members displaying task roles and/or person roles? What roles are ongoing? Are certain roles lacking? Remember that both task and person roles are functional to group performance. Another set of roles and behaviors, called *dysfunctional,* distract a group from task and person relations. Dysfunctional roles, unlike functional roles, are a concern when present. After listing and briefly describing the most common functional member roles, we will examine dysfunctional roles.

Task Roles

The following descriptions are adapted from those listed by Benne and Sheats (1948):

> *Initiator-contributor:* Proposes original ideas or changed ways of regarding group problem, goal, or procedure. Launches discussion, moves group into new areas of discussion.
>
> *Information seeker:* Asks for clarification in terms of factual adequacy. Seeks expert information and relevant facts.

Opinion seeker: Asks for clarification of values pertinent to the group undertaking or to proposed suggestions. Checks on others' attitudes and feelings toward particular issues.

Information giver: Provides factual, authoritative information or gives own experience relevant to the issue.

Opinion giver: Verbalizes his or her own values and opinions on the group problem; emphasizes what the group should do.

Elaborator: Picks up on others' suggestions and amplifies with examples, pertinent facts, and probable consequences.

Coordinator: Shows the link between ideas and suggestions, attempts to pull diverse proposals together.

Orienter: Clarifies the group's position, gives a state-of-the-scene review. Summarizes what has been discussed, points out where discussion has departed from the goal, and reminds the group of their ultimate goal.

Evaluator-critic: Evaluates the proposals of the group against a criteria of effectiveness. Assesses whether proposals are "reasonable," "manageable," "based on facts," and derived through fair procedures.

Energizer: Focuses the group to move toward decisions. Challenges and prods group into further action.

Procedural technician: Facilitates group discussion by taking care of logistics. Sees that the group has the necessary materials for the task (paper, pencils, chalk, and so on).

Recorder: Writes down the group's suggestions and decisions. Keeps an ongoing record of what transpires in the group.

A group needs these member roles to keep moving toward accomplishing its task. A leader can use these descriptions to figure out what roles are missing. Additional roles might need to be assigned to group members or incorporated by the leader. For example, if a group has many opinion givers but no information givers, then decisions would be made on the basis of feelings, without regard to actual experience or knowledge. A leader would need to consider ways to add more information giving. Perhaps he or she could assign people to gather more knowledge or ask outside experts for assistance. Likewise, if a group has many opinion givers and information givers but lacks orienters and coordinators, the members may be talking past each other. There would be a lack of direction and a lack of synthesis of the relationships among members' ideas. The leader would need to plan ways to coordinate discussions. As a final example, a group might contain most of the task roles except for a procedural technician or recorder. Such a group probably would converse easily but would bog down on recalling what has been said. The leader who knows what roles are needed can ask for a volunteer to be a recorder and summarizer. Knowledge of task roles and behaviors enables a leader to assess what roles are evident and what further roles need to be assigned. The leader might take on some of the missing roles, assign them to others, or add particular persons to a group.

Person Roles

The knowledge of person roles and behaviors provides a guide to the group leader. Consider the following descriptions:

> *Encourager:*   Affirms, supports, and accepts the contribution of other members. Shows warmth and a positive attitude toward others.
>
> *Harmonizer:*   Conciliates differences between individuals. Looks for ways to reduce tension between members through nonthreatening explanations and humor.
>
> *Compromiser:*   Offers to change his or her proposals for the good of the group. Willing to yield position or to acknowledge own errors by meeting other opposing ideas halfway.
>
> *Gatekeeper or expediter:*   Regulates flow of communication by seeing that all members have a chance to talk. Encourages quiet persons to speak and puts limits on those who dominate the conversation. Proposes new regulations for discussions when participation becomes unbalanced.
>
> *Standard setter/ego ideal:*   Appeals to group's pride by not letting group members give up when trouble occurs. Exudes confidence that the group is a good one and can make sound decisions.
>
> *Observer and commentator:*   Monitors the working of the group. Records who speaks to whom, where and when most roadblocks occur, and the frequency and length of individual members' participation. Provides feedback when the group wishes to evaluate its procedures and processes.
>
> *Follower:*   Is willing to accept the decisions of the group and follow them even though he or she has not been active or influential in those decisions. Serves as a listener to group discussion.

The seven person roles provide human satisfaction and group cohesiveness. People feel positive about meeting and talking with each other and comfortable enough to express their ideas. As a result, meetings are seen as pleasant times to continue the group's work. When person roles are missing, a group may face severe difficulties in making acceptable and committed decisions. Without person behaviors and roles, only the strongest, most assured, and vocal members will speak. Decisions might be made that more timid persons strongly reject but the group may not know that such strong disapproval exists. Again, it is the group leader's responsibility to see if people roles are evident. If roles are missing, then he or she can confront the group with their absence, pick up the role(s) himself or herself, quietly suggest particular roles to existing members, or add to the group other individuals who more naturally play such roles. *Both task and person roles, when not already in existence, need to be added.*

Dysfunctional Roles

Dysfunctional roles and behaviors are those that are conspicuous in their presence. Such roles and behaviors disrupt the progress toward a group goal and weaken group cohesiveness. Consider the following:

Aggressor: Personally attacks the worth of other members. Belittles and deflates the status, wisdom, and motivation of others. Examples of such verbal attacks are: "That's the most ridiculous thing I've ever heard," "You must be crazy to suggest . . ."

Blocker: Sees all opinions and suggestions by group members as negative. Opposes any decision being made and stubbornly refuses to propose alternatives. Examples of such blocking statements are: "That's a terrible idea," "I don't want to do that," "It's futile to do anything."

Recognition-seeker: Uses the group setting to receive personal attention. Examples of such behaviors are dropping books, scattering papers, coughing incessantly, pretending to be asleep, raising hand and then forgetting intended comment.

Self-confessor: Uses the group to ventilate personal feelings not related to the group's tasks. Talks about personal problems or feelings of inadequacy whenever he or she can see ways to slip such confessions into the group discussion. Examples of self-confessing statements are: "This discussion reminds me of when I was a little child and the weight problem I had," or when the group is talking about differences of opinion, "You should hear my son and me fight; I don't know what to do about him."

Playboy or playgirl: Lacks interest and involvement by using the group setting to have a merry time. Distracts other members from the group's purpose. Tells private jokes, passes notes, makes faces at others, plays cards, and so on.

Dominator: Asserts superiority in controlling group discussion and dictates what certain members should do. Claims to know more about the issue under discussion and have better solutions than anyone else. Has elaborate answers to almost every question and monopolizes the discussion.

Help-seeker: Tries to gain group's sympathy by expressing feelings of inadequacy or personal confusion. Uses such self-derogation as reason for not contributing: "This is all too confusing for me," "I can't make a decision on my own," "Why ask me? I can't help."

Special-interest pleader: Has no opinion or suggestions of his or her own but instead speaks for what others would say or do. Cloaks own bias by using an outside group: "We couldn't do that. Do you know what the school board would think?" "If those parents down in the local restaurant ever heard that we were going to change . . ."

Dysfunctional roles are fairly self-evident in a group. The leader's responsibility is to reduce or eliminate such dysfunctional roles before they severely harm the morale and efficiency of the group. He or she might try to understand the dysfunctional member's reason for acting as an aggressor, playboy, special interest pleader, and so on, and then might either confront the person privately or provide changes within the group to satisfy the unmet needs that are leading to the dysfunctional behavior. Methods for dealing with dysfunctional behaviors will be discussed shortly, but first let's focus on leadership styles matched with maturity levels of groups.

Changing Group Leadership Style

If a group lacks either task or person behaviors, the leader can choose a style that will fill the void. A group that exhibits much initiative, information, and competitiveness (high task) as well as hostility, aggression, and bitterness (low person) could benefit from a leadership style that is encouraging, praising, harmonizing, and humorous (high person). A group that exhibits much positive camaraderie (high person) but is being uninterested, apathetic, or uninformed (low task) could benefit from a leadership style that presses for information, sets goals, and enforces procedures (high task).

The work of Hersey and Blanchard (1969, 1988) on what they call the "life-cycle theory of leadership," also known as *situational leadership,* is a comprehensive theory of leadership style in response to group characteristics. Hersey and Blanchard identified four styles of leadership based on the relative emphasis on task and relationship (person) behavior:

Style 1 (S1): High task, low relationship. This is an autocratic style, whereby the leader tells the group members what is to be done, when, and by whom. The leader makes decisions for the group. This style is similar to directive supervision, discussed in Chapters 8 and 9. One word that describes this style is *telling.* The leader determines both the process and the content of decision making.

Style 2 (S2): High task, high relationship. This is a democratic style whereby the leader actively participates with the group both as a facilitator of the decision-making process and an equal member contributing his or her own ideas, opinions, and information. This style is similar to collaborative supervision, explained in Chapter 10. One word that describes this influencing style is *selling.* The leader attempts to influence both the processes and the content of decision making by being a persuasive equal.

Style 3 (S3): High relationship, low task. This is an encouraging and socializing style whereby the leader promotes cohesion, open expression, and positive feelings among the members but does not influence or interfere with the actual decision. (The leader's role is one of clarification, encouragement, and reflection.) The style is similar to nondirective supervision, described in Chapter 11. Note that the leader participates by helping members express their ideas, opinions, and needs but does not participate in the sense of offering his or her own ideas, opinions, and needs. The leader participates in the process but not in the content of decision making.

Style 4 (S4): Low relationship, low task. This is a hands-off or laissez-faire style whereby the leader turns the task over to the group and does not participate in any manner. The leader tells the group what the task is and then physically or mentally removes himself or herself from any further involvement. One word that describes this style is *delegating.* The leader is involved in neither the process nor the content of decision making.

Hersey and Blanchard (1988) stated that effective leadership is based on matching leadership style to the readiness of the group. The readiness of a group depends on the particular task; the same group could be of high readiness for one task and low readiness for another. Readiness can be assessed according to the characteristics of ability and willingness.

Ability is the knowledge, skills, and experience to achieve without the need for outside assistance.

Willingness is the degree of motivation, confidence, and interest in accomplishing certain tasks.

The leader can assess the readiness of individuals and a group according to these levels (Hersey and Blanchard, 1988, pp. 176–177).

- *Readiness Level One (R1)*
    Unable and unwilling
    Unable and insecure
- *Readiness Level Two (R2)*
    Unable but willing
    Unable but confident
- *Readiness Level Three (R3)*
    Able but unwilling
    Able but insecure
- *Readiness Level Four (R4)*
    Able and willing
    Able and confident

Situational leadership matches leadership style to the readiness level of the group (see Figure 17.1 on matching and directionality of a developing group). An R1 group is best matched with a *telling,* autocratic style (S1). An R2 group is best matched with a *selling,* democratic style (S2). An R3 group is best matched

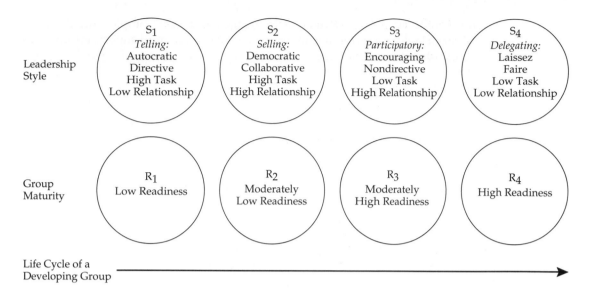

FIGURE 17.1 *Matching and Directionality of a Developing Group*

with a *participating,* encouraging style (S3). An R4 group is best matched with a *delegating,* laissez-faire style (S4).

Hersey and Blanchard's theory was originally called *life-cycle leadership* but is now more commonly referred to as *situational leadership*. This is an unfortunate change in terminology, because *life cycle* connotes development or growth in both leader and group behaviors, an implication that is missing from the term *situational*. Groups are complex human entities that respond to the gradual shifting of a group leader's external control in the same manner that an individual teacher will respond to gradual shifting of supervisory control. In other words, an R1 (low readiness) group with an S1 (telling and autocratic) leadership style will not develop until the leader gradually allows them to gain greater internal control. An unmotivated group might work most efficiently with S1 leadership at first. As the group gains experience, as members become acquainted with each other, and as the group acquires expertise, the leader should be alert to those signals of increasing readiness and provide for greater group involvement by shifting to an S2 leadership style. It is conceivable that a group working on a long project might complete the entire life cycle by beginning with S1 (telling) leadership and concluding with S4 (delegating) leadership. A group leader might work toward eliminating his or her control over the group. The ultimate goal should be for a group to provide its own task and person behaviors and not be dependent on formal leadership.

Applying Developmental Supervision to Groups

Developmental supervision, when applied to groups, has much in common with situational leadership but also has some key differences. Let us first review how developmental supervision is used with groups, and then compare the developmental model with situational leadership. The developmental supervisor matches one of the four supervisory approaches to the group's characteristics:

- **Directive control behaviors** are used with a group functioning at very low developmental levels, lacking the expertise needed to act on the problem, and without any commitment to its resolution, or in an emergency situation. In group meetings, a supervisor uses directive control behaviors to give a clear message about what changes are expected. The supervisor *presents* by stating his or her understanding of the problem, *clarifies* by asking group members if they have any perceptions to add, *listens* to input, and then *problem solves* by reassessing the problem and possible solutions. She or he then *directs* by stating what is to be done, *clarifies* by asking for additional input, *standardizes* by laying out a specific timeline and expectations, and *reinforces* by monitoring the expected group performance. The supervisor moves away from directive control and toward directive informational behaviors as soon as possible.

- **Directive informational behaviors** are used with a group functioning at fairly low developmental levels, with little expertise, and little commitment. The supervisor *presents* by stating his or her understanding of the problem, *clarifies* by asking group members for input, *listens* to their perceptions of the problem, and *problem solves* by formulating two or three alternative solutions. He or she *directs* by stating the alternatives, *listens* after asking the group for input, and *directs* by reformulating and stating final choices. The supervisor *clarifies* by asking the group to choose from alternatives, *standardizes* by suggesting a timeline and criteria for success, and *reinforces* by suggesting ways to follow up.

- **Collaborative behaviors** are used when the group is functioning at moderate or mixed levels of development, the supervisor and group have the same degree of expertise concerning the problem, and both the supervisor and group are committed to solving the problem. The supervisor *clarifies* by asking group members for their perceptions of the problem, *listens* to group perceptions, and *reflects* by verifying group perceptions. The supervisor *presents* by adding his or her perceptions, *clarifies* by determining if the group understands supervisor perceptions, *problem solves* by exchanging suggested solutions, *encourages* by accepting conflict, and *negotiates* a mutually acceptable solution. Finally, the supervisor *reflects* by summarizing the collaborative plan.

- **Nondirective behaviors** are used when the group is functioning at high developmental levels, possesses extensive expertise, and is highly committed to solving the problem. The supervisor *listens* as group members provide their perceptions of the problem, *reflects* by paraphrasing group members' perceptions and feelings, *probes* the group for additional information on the problem's underlying causes, *listens* further to teacher perceptions, and *reflects* further by continuing to paraphrase group members' comments. The supervisor *problem solves* by asking the group to think of possible actions and to consider the consequences of potential actions, *presents* by asking the group to commit to a plan of action, *standardizes* by asking the group to establish a timeline and criteria for success, and *reflects* by restating the group's plan.

The long-term goal of the developmental supervisor is to foster the group toward higher levels of development, expertise, and commitment. This can be accomplished through training in collaborative skills (communication, decision making, problem solving, and so on), providing observer feedback on group behaviors, facilitating self-study, facilitating reflection on group process, and a variety of other strategies for group development. As the group develops, the supervisor gradually shifts from directive to collaborative or from collaborative to nondirective behaviors.

Comparing Developmental Supervision with Situational Leadership

Situational leadership and developmental supervision with groups have several commonalities. Both begin with the leader assessing group characteristics. In situational leadership, ability and willingness are assessed; and in developmental supervision, adult development levels, expertise, and commitment are assessed. Both models match alternative leadership approaches with group characteristics. The situational leader matches a telling approach (high task, low relationship) to groups of low readiness, and a developmental supervisor matches directive control or directive informational behaviors to low readiness groups. Unlike developmental supervision, situational leadership does not distinguish between controlling and informational "telling."

Both the developmental and situational models call for using high-task, high-relationship leadership with groups of emerging readiness. In developmental supervision this approach is referred to as *collaborative,* and in situational leadership it is called *selling.* Developmental supervision's nondirective approach is similar to situational leadership's participatory style: both involve low-task, high-relationship leadership. A major difference between the two leadership models is that, unlike situational leadership, developmental supervision does not include a "delegating" (laissez-faire) approach. The developmental model holds that laissez-faire supervision is inappropriate even when working with groups functioning at the highest readiness levels. For the developmental supervisor, nondirective supervision of highly developed groups still includes forming or maintaining a strong relationship with the group and active group facilitation through listening, clarifying, encouraging, and reflecting.

Critical to both developmental supervision and situational leadership is leadership to assist the group toward higher levels of readiness and performance, with increasing decision-making responsibility handed over to the group as it grows in its capacity to assume responsibility.

Dealing with Dysfunctional Members

The fact that a group is made up of individuals with varying temperaments and motivations is important when thinking about ways to work with groups. Dealing with individuals, particularly those who display dysfunctional behaviors, is an additional responsibility of a group leader.

If the leader has observed the group at work and has determined that his or her own leader behaviors are appropriate for most members of the group, yet there continue to be a few dysfunctional members, then individual treatment might be in order. The procedure for treating a dysfunctional member is (1) observe the member, (2) try to understand why the member is acting unproductively, (3) communicate with the member about the behavior, (4) establish some rules for future behavior, and (5) redirect the unfavorable behavior (Corey and Corey, 1982; Kemp, 1970). Each step of this procedure will be amplified.

1. *Observe the member:* When and with whom does the dysfunctional behavior occur? What does the group member do, and how do others respond? For example, a dominator might start monopolizing the conversation as soon as he or she walks into the meeting. Other people might be interested in the dominator's talk for the first few minutes of the meeting but become increasingly annoyed as the dominator continues. They might roll their eyes, yawn, fidget, or make comments to each other.

2. *Try to understand the member:* Why does the member persist with dysfunctional behavior? Does he or she know the behavior is unproductive? Is the behavior being used to mask some underlying emotion? For example, a playboy might be insecure about his own worth and pretend not to care rather than exposing inner thoughts to the scrutiny of the group.

3. *Communicate with the member:* What can you communicate about the group member's behavior and the situation? Describe the situation and the behavior to the member without denigration. Instead of saying, "You're being an aggressive son of a gun," say, "I've noticed that you speak loudly and angrily to Sara. At the last meeting, you told her to keep her mouth shut." Tell the dysfunctional member the effect of the behavior on you as group leader: "When you tell Sara to shut up and tell Bob that he's stupid, it starts an argument that takes time away from the meeting. I can't complete the agenda on time when those arguments take place" (see Gordon, 1980).

4. *Establish some rules for future behaviors:* Either ask the member to suggest some rules that he or she can abide by in the future, or tell the member your future rules, or establish them jointly. Regardless of which tactic is chosen, the leader should think of rules that would minimize further disruptions to the group. For example, the leader might say to a self-confessor, "The next time you have a personal problem, come speak to me privately about it," or to a dominator, "I'm going to enforce a two-minute limit on every member's participation," or to a blocker,

"If you don't think we're on the right course, tell us your objection once and only once."

5. *Redirect the unfavorable behavior:* Pick up on the group member's dysfunctional behavior, and try to make it functional. A dominator can be assigned the role of recorder, summarizer, or time keeper. A playboy can be given an opening time for sharing a funny story to relax the group before starting official business. An aggressor can be asked to play devil's advocate and argue the position of an adversary.

The five steps outlined here will help the meeting leader understand and deal with individual dysfunctional behavior. The steps are predicated on the leader confronting the dysfunctional member in private. Dysfunctional behaviors that occur infrequently and in isolated situations might simply be ignored. The leader can respond to infrequent misbehaviors or make light of them: "Sara, I guess you really got wound up today; perhaps we might hear from someone else now." Only incessant behaviors that distract the entire group need to be dealt with via direct confrontation. Confrontation is not easy but is necessary at times for the sake of the group. Role Play 17.1 provides a demonstration of how to deal with a dysfunctional group member.

Resolving Conflict

The key to a productive group is the way ongoing conflict is resolved. Conflicts are particular disagreements that occur between two or more members at a particular time. *Conflict is not necessarily dysfunctional.* In fact, research has shown that successful groups exhibit much conflict (Johnson and Johnson, 1987a; Fullan, 2000). As Roger Johnson stated, "A critical moment of truth in a . . . group is when two teachers disagree strongly with each other and argue" (Brandt, 1987). A group can make wise decisions only when there is a wealth of information and ideas to consider. Information and ideas are generated through conflict. To suppress conflict is to limit the group's decision-making capacity. Therefore, the leader should encourage conflict, not stifle it. Of course, conflict, if not handled correctly, can degenerate into adversarial and harmful relations. It is not conflict that is bad; it is the way the leader deals with it that determines its value.

Conflict occurs when there is a disagreement over ideas. The leader should keep the disagreement focused on the ideas rather than on the personalities of the members. The following procedure for handling conflict serves as a ready reference for the group leader:

1. Ask each member to state his or her conflicting position.
2. Ask each member to restate the other's position.
3. Ask each member if conflict still exists.
4. Ask for underlying value positions: Why do they still stick to their positions?

ROLE PLAY **17.1**   **Dealing with a Dysfunctional Group Member**

Context.   The purpose of this role play is for a subgroup of four to provide a demonstration to the remainder of the group on how to effectively deal with a dysfunctional group member. Participants will need approximately 20 minutes of preparation time away from the rest of the group. In the role play, a "supervisor" and three "teachers" are members of a committee meeting to discuss a schoolwide instructional issue. In their preparation for the role play, the role players may choose the school level (elementary, middle, or high school), the issue to be discussed, and any other details of the fictional situation that they need to agree on to perform an effective role play. The group is assigned or chooses a dysfunctional role that one member of the group will assume during the role play. The role play is presented in three scenes.

Scene 1 (10 minutes).   The supervisor and three teachers begin the meeting. Throughout the scene, one of the teachers assumes a dysfunctional role that is clearly impeding the rest of the group's efforts to resolve the issue. The supervisor observes the teacher's dysfunctional behaviors. This scene ends with a break in the meeting, with the issue unresolved. During the break the other two teachers leave to get a cup of coffee, and the supervisor and teacher are left alone.

Scene 2 (10 minutes).   In a private discussion with the dysfunctional teacher during the break, the supervisor uses techniques suggested under this chapter's heading "Dealing with Dysfunctional Group Members" to address the teacher's behaviors. The specific discussion will depend on the dysfunctional role that the teacher has been playing. The discussion culminates with an agreed on plan for minimizing future disruptions.

Scene 3 (10 minutes).   The other teachers return and the meeting resumes. Due to the agreements worked out during the break and the supervisor's support during the second part of the group meeting, the teacher's dysfunctional behaviors are greatly reduced. The group is able to resolve the issue under discussion.

Whole-Group Processing (10 minutes). The entire group discusses what the dysfunctional role was, specific behaviors that indicated the dysfunctional role, and effects of the dysfunctional role on the group in Scene 1. Next, the group discusses the techniques used by the supervisor in Scenes 2 and 3 to deal with the dysfunctional role and the effects of those techniques on the teacher and group.

5. Ask other members of the group if there is a third position that synthesizes, compromises, or transcends the conflict. If not, reclarify the various positions. Acknowledge that there exists no apparent reconciliation, and move the discussion to other matters.

The following is an application of conflict-resolution procedures to a high school meeting:

The supervisor from the central office has called a meeting of the English high school department heads to discuss possible changes in the tenth-grade English curriculum. The topic of composition writing comes up, and two department heads begin to argue. Mrs. Strick of Toofarback High School says, "We need to require three technical compositions each semester from each tenth grader. Each composition should be graded according to spelling, punctuation, and format. I'm sick and tired of seeing kids coming into the eleventh grade without being able to put a sentence together!"

Mr. Ease of Space High School objects: "Are you serious? Three technical compositions a year should just about kill any remaining interest that tenth graders have in writing. That is a ridiculous idea!"

The language supervisor, Mr. Cool, is now aware of a conflict and wants to capitalize on these varying points of view in providing information to the group. At the same time, he is aware of emotional intensity in this conflict (words such as "sick and tired" and "ridiculous") and wishes to soften the emotion and promote the ideas. So he uses step 1 and asks the two members to state their conflicting positions.

"Mrs. Strick and Mr. Ease, you both have definite ideas about the requirements of technical compositions. We are interested in fully understanding what you think. Would you each take a few minutes and further explain your positions?"

After Mrs. Strick and Mr. Ease have stated their positions, the supervisor moves to step 2 by asking each member to restate the other's position.

"Now that you have stated your position, I want to make sure that you fully understand each other. Mrs. Strick, would you please paraphrase Mr. Ease's position, and Mr. Ease, would you repeat Mrs. Strick's position." Mrs. Strick says, "Mr. Ease thinks that technical writing assignments are a waste of time and students lose interest." Mr. Ease replies, "No, I didn't say they are a waste of time; but if such assignments are frequent, students learn to hate English class." Mr. Ease then restates Mrs. Strick's position: "You're saying that tenth graders need skills in the basics of writing. Required compositions would ensure proper spelling, grammar, and format." Mrs. Strick replies, "Yes, that's what I'm saying."

Now that both positions have been made and paraphrased, Supervisor Cool goes to step 3 and asks if conflict still exists.

He asks Mrs. Strick and Mr. Ease: "Are you both still far apart about composition requirements for tenth-grade English?" Mrs. Strick nods, but Mr. Ease says, "Well, not as far apart as at the beginning. I'm not against some technical writing requirements. It's the number, three for each semester, that hangs me up. I could accept one per semester." Mrs. Strick replies, "Well, I can't. If they are going to write correctly, they must do it frequently. Three compositions a semester is just the minimum!"

Mr. Cool, knowing that Mrs. Strick is adamant about her position, goes to step 4, asking for the underlying value:

Mr. Cool asks Mrs. Strick: "Could you explain why technical composition writing is important to you?" Mrs. Strick says, "Kids today don't get any basics in writing. Everything is creativity, expression, write it like you speak it in the streets! I was taught standards of good manners and proper English. If these kids are to succeed in later life, they have to know how to write according to accepted business and professional standards. I'm not being hardnosed for my own sake. It's them I'm concerned about!" Mr. Cool turns to Mr. Ease and says, "What about you? Why do you disagree?" Mr. Ease replies, "I don't completely disagree, but I'm against making tenth-grade English class a technical writing drill. Writing should be a vehicle for expression and students should love, not dread, it. They should be able to write personal thoughts, juggle words and formats, and not worry about every comma and dotted *i*. Let them play with words before pushing standards at them. I don't write letters with one-and-a-half-inch margins to my friends or in my diary—why should kids have to? Sure, there is a need for them to learn to write formally, but not at the expense of hating to write!"

Mr. Cool restates the conflict to the group: "We have an obvious disagreement between Mrs. Strick and Mr. Ease. Mrs. Strick believes there should be at least three technical compositions per semester in the tenth grade. Mr. Ease believes there should be less emphasis on technical writing and more on expressive writing."

Supervisor Cool goes to step 5: *Asking other members of the group if there is a third position that can be taken.* Some members might side with one over the other, suggest a compromise (one technical composition in the first semester, two in the second semester), or offer a new alternative (let's require a three-week minicourse of technical writing and let each school decide the type of work and assignments). If the conflict between Mrs. Strick and Mr. Ease does not resolve itself, the supervisor acknowledges that the conflict remains: "We understand the difference of opinion that you both have, and we can't find a ready solution." Then he moves to other matters: "Eventually the committee will have to decide or vote on what to do about required assignments. For now, we'll leave this particular issue and discuss the tenth-grade testing program."

Conflict cannot and should not be avoided. Conflict, if encouraged and supported, will enable a group to make better decisions. It is the group leader's handling of conflict that makes the difference. The group should have the feeling that it is all right to disagree and that anyone who does disagree will be able to make his or her full position known. Role Play 17.2 provides demonstrations of the right way and the wrong way to deal with conflict within a group.

Preparing for Group Meetings

A group can proceed more easily with its task if the leader has made certain preparations. Shelton and Bauer (1994) suggest that premeeting planning should involve decisions about whether a meeting is necessary, who should attend the meeting, setting, agenda, and preparation. Figure 17.2 includes specific questions that Shelton and Bauer recommend planners consider when preparing for a meeting. Some especially important aspects of preparing for a meeting include planning an agenda, establishing ground rules, and writing guided discussion questions.

ROLE PLAY **17.2**   **Resolving Conflict**

Context. The purpose of this role play is for a subgroup of five to provide a demonstration to the remainder of the group on how to effectively resolve conflict within a group. Participants will need approximately 20 minutes of preparation time away from the rest of the group. In the role play, a "supervisor" and four "teachers" are members of a committee meeting to discuss a schoolwide instructional issue. In their preparation for the role play, the role players may choose the school level, the issue to be discussed, and any other details of the fictional situation that they need to agree on to perform an effective role play. The group is assigned or chooses a conflict to be played out between two members of the group during the meeting. The role play is presented in two scenes.

Scene 1: Wrong Way (10 minutes). Soon after the beginning of the meeting, a conflict breaks out between two of the "teachers." The supervisor and the other teachers in the group deal with the conflict poorly, and the meeting deteriorates rapidly. The meeting breaks up with neither the interpersonal conflict nor the original issue resolved.

Scene 2: Right Way (10 minutes). This scene involves the same group, the same setting, and the same issue. The same conflict breaks out between the same two teachers. This time, however, the supervisor and teachers in the group use procedures discussed under this chapter's topic "Resolving Conflict" to facilitate a resolution of the conflict and the original issue by the end of the meeting.

Whole-Group Processing (10 minutes). The entire group discusses the nature of the conflict, the failed efforts to resolve it, and effects of the conflict on the group in Scene 1. Also discussed are the techniques used to resolve the conflict and the effects of the conflict resolution process in Scene 2.

Agendas

A group has to be clear on its task and purpose. Why are they meeting? What are they to accomplish? Is there to be a product? An agenda distributed several days before the actual meeting will inform members of the reasons for the meeting and what will be accomplished. The agenda need not be elaborate. See Figure 17.3 as a sample agenda. Notice how the agenda includes a brief explanation and a breakdown of items. Time limits for each item provide members with a sense of priorities as well as the assurance that the leader plans to end on time. Keeping to starting and ending times displays respect for group members' personal schedules.

Establishing Ground Rules

Participants will need to know not only agenda items like the meeting's purpose, place, time, and topics, but also behaviors that are expected of them at

Should We Meet?
1. Can a memo be used instead of holding a meeting?
2. Is there a goal for the meeting?

Who Should Attend the Meeting?
3. Who needs to come to the meeting?
4. Will there be less than 15 participants?

The Setting
5. Where will the meeting be held?
6. Is the site convenient to participants?
7. Will a circular table arrangement be used?
8. Is the room temperature comfortable?
9. Have refreshments been arranged?

The Agenda
10. Have all participants been asked for agenda input?
11. Are the "For Information" items stated in sentence format?
12. Are the "For Discussion" items stated in question format?
13. Has the draft agenda been proofed?
14. Has the agenda been distributed, with at least 2 days' lead time?

The Preparation
15. Have possible "troublesome items" been thought through?
16. If problem solving is a goal of the meeting, has the problem been adequately explained to meeting participants?
17. Has someone been asked to take minutes?
18. Has a follow-up on the previous evaluations been done?
19. Have evaluation forms (Blips) been distributed?

FIGURE 17.2 *Shelton and Bauer's Premeeting Planner*

Source: Maria M. Shelton and Laurie K. Bauer, *Secrets of Highly Effective Meetings*, p. 43. Copyright © 1994 by Corwin Press. Reprinted by permission of Sage Publications, Inc.

the meeting. Ground rules can be established in advance concerning any of the following:

- Type of participation expected (sharing of information, professional dialogue, choosing from established alternatives, brainstorming, problem solving, conflict resolution, and so on)
- Roles to be assigned (coordinator, timekeeper, information giver, recorder, etc.)
- Interpersonal expectations (everyone contributes, use active listening, criticize ideas but not people, consider each person's views, use agreed-on conflict management strategies, and so on)
- Decision-making method (decision by averaging individuals' opinions, majority vote, consensus, etc.)
- Type of follow-up expected (assigned tasks, continued dialogue, classroom implementation, follow-up meeting, and so on)

To: All physical education teachers
From: Morris Bailey, athletic director
Subject: Agenda for the meeting of February 23 in Room 253, 3:30–5:00

Next Thursday will be the last meeting before voting on the revisions of
our student progress forms. Remember, bring any progress forms you
have collected from other school systems. Sally and Bruce are to report
on the forms provided by the State Department. At the conclusion of the
meeting, we are to make specific recommendations of changes.

Agenda

I.	Review purpose of meeting	3:30–3:40
II.	Report from Sally and Bruce on State Department forms	3:40–4:00
III.	Report on other school system forms	4:00–4:20
IV.	Discussion of possible revisions	4:20–4:40
V.	Recommendations	4:40–5:00

See you Thursday. Please be on time!

FIGURE 17.3   *Sample Agenda*

Guided Discussion

When meeting with a small group to discuss an issue, it is helpful to have in mind
the type of questions to ask. Typically, questions to be asked will shift during a
meeting. At the beginning of the meeting, the leader usually spends time clarifying
the topic for discussion. During the meeting, the leader uses open-ended questions that allow for seeking, elaborating, and coordinating of ideas, opinions,
and information. At the conclusion of the meeting, the leader asks questions that
summarize what has been accomplished and what remains to be done.

Some discussion questions that might help as a reference are presented in Figure 17.4. Prior to a meeting, the leader might review the questions in Figure 17.4
and write down specific questions concerning the topic to have in front of him
or her. When the discussion stalls, the leader can look at his or her notes and ask
one of the preselected questions. A discussion guide helps the leader ensure that
the topic will be thoroughly examined.

SUMMARY

This chapter examined the knowledge and skills needed to help professional
groups develop. Particular emphasis was put on the supervisor's role in terms of
behaving, confronting dysfunctional members, resolving conflict, and preparing
for meetings.

The theme of looking at professional groups in a developmental manner
should be familiar by now. As a group works together, the leader needs to practice

*Questions Designed to
Open Up Discussion*

1. What do you think about the problem as stated?
2. What has been your experience in dealing with this problem?
3. Would anyone care to offer suggestions on facts we need to better our understanding of the problem?

*Questions Designed to
Broaden Participation*

1. Now that we have heard from a number of our members, would others who have not spoken like to add their ideas?
2. How do the ideas presented so far sound to those of you who have been thinking about them?
3. What other phases of the problem should be explored?

*Questions Designed
to Limit Participation*

1. To the overactive participant: We appreciate your contributions. However, it might be well to hear from some of the others. Would some of you who have not spoken care to add your ideas to those already expressed?
2. You have made several good statements, and I am wondering if someone else might like to make some remarks?
3. Since all our group members have not yet had an opportunity to speak, I wonder if you would hold your comments until a little later?

*Questions Designed
to Focus Discussion*

1. Where are we now in relation to our goal for this discussion?
2. Would you like to have me review my understanding of the things we have said and the progress we have made in this direction?
3. Your comment is interesting, but I wonder if it is germane to the chief problem that is before us.

*Questions Designed to Help
the Group Move Along*

1. I wonder if we have spent enough time on this phase of the problem. Should we move to another aspect of it?
2. Have we gone into this part of the problem far enough so that we might now shift our attention and consider this additional area?
3. In view of the time we have set for ourselves, would it be appropriate to look at the next question before us?

*Questions Designed to Help
the Group Evaluate Itself*

1. I wonder if any of you have a feeling that we are blocked on this particular question? Why are we tending to slow down?
2. Should we take a look at our original objective for this discussion and see where we are in relation to it?
3. Now that we are nearing the conclusion of our meeting, would anyone like to offer suggestions on how we might improve our next meeting?

*Questions Designed to Help
the Group Reach a Decision*

1. Am I right in sensing agreement at these points? (Leader then gives brief summary.)
2. Since we seem to be tending to move in the direction of a decision, should we consider what it will mean for our group if we decide the matter this way?
3. What have we accomplished in our discussion up to this point?

*Questions Designed to Lend
Continuity to the Discussion*

1. Since we had time for partial consideration of the problem at the last meeting, would someone care to review what we covered then?
2. Since we cannot reach a decision at this meeting, what are some of the points we should take up at the next one?
3. Would someone care to suggest points on which we need further preparation before we convene again?

FIGURE 17.4 *Questions for Use in Leadership Discussion*

Source: Produced in group development course at the University of Georgia.

skills that enable the group to become more cohesive, responsible, and autonomous. Eventually the leader would hope to lessen his or her own control and influence so that the group becomes a wise and autonomous body.

REFERENCES AND RECOMMENDED READINGS

Bales, R. F. 1953. The equilibrium problem in small groups. In T. Parsons, R. F. Bales, and E. A. Shils (Eds.), *Working papers in the theory of action* (pp. 111–161). Glencoe, IL: Free Press.

Benne, D. D., and Sheats, P. 1948. Functional roles of group members. *Journal of Social Issues, 4*(2), 41–49.

Brandt, R. 1987. On cooperation in schools: A conversation with David and Roger Johnson. *Educational Leadership, 45*(3), 14–19.

Cooper, S. M. 2002. Classroom choices for enabling peer learning. *Theory into Practice, 41*(1), 53–57.

Corey, G., and Corey, M. 1982. *Groups: Process and practice.* Monterey, CA: Brooks/Cole.

Fullan, M. 2000. *Change forces: The sequel.* Philadelphia: George H. Buchanan.

Gordon, T. 1980. *Leadership effectiveness training— L.E.T.* New York: Bantam Books.

Hare, A. P. 1982. *Creativity in small groups.* Beverly Hills, CA: Sage.

Hersey, P., and Blanchard, K. H. 1969. Life-cycle theory of leadership. *Training and Development Journal, 23*(5), 26–34.

Hersey, P., and Blanchard, K. H. 1988. *Management of organizational behavior: Utilizing human resources* (5th ed.). Englewood Cliffs, NJ: Prentice Hall.

Johnson, D. W., and Johnson, R. T. 1987a. *Joining together: Group theory and group skills* (3rd ed.). Englewood Cliffs, NJ: Prentice Hall.

Johnson, D. W., and Johnson, R. T. 1987b. Research shows the benefits of adult cooperation. *Educational Leadership, 45*(3), 27–30.

Kasl, E., and Yorks, L. 2002. Collaborative inquiry for adult learning. *New Directions for Adult and Continuing Education, 94,* 3–11.

Kemp, C. G. 1970. *Perspectives on the group process: A foundation for counseling with groups* (2nd ed.). Boston: Houghton Mifflin.

King, A. 2002. Structuring peer interaction to promote high-level cognitive processing. *Theory into Practice, 41*(1), 33–39.

Shelton, M. M., and Bauer, L. K. 1994. *Secrets of highly effective meetings.* Thousand Oaks, CA: Corwin Press.

Slavin, R. E. 1987. Cooperative learning and the cooperative schools. *Educational Leadership, 45*(3), 7–13.

Yorks, L., and Kasl, E. 2002. Learning from the inquiries: Lessons for using collaborative inquiry as an adult learning strategy. *New Directions for Adult and Continuing Education, 94,* 93–104.

18

Professional Development

Bob Jeffries, director of professional development, calls six school principals into his office to plan for the upcoming in-service day. He begins by explaining that the in-service program will start with a morning session, attended by the entire school system faculty, in the high school auditorium. The afternoon will consist of individual school activities, with the principal being responsible for whatever transpires. Mr. Jeffries asks the principals, "What might we do for the morning session?" One principal suggests that at this time of year teachers could use an emotional lift and that an inspirational speaker would be good. Another principal adds that she had heard a Dr. Zweibach give a great talk entitled "The Thrill of Teaching" at a national principals' conference last summer. She thinks he would be a terrific speaker. Bob Jeffries likes these suggestions and tells the principals he will call Dr. Zweibach and make arrangements for his appearance.

On the in-service day, 238 teachers file into the auditorium and fill all but the first eight rows of seats. Mr. Jeffries makes a few introductory remarks about how fortunate "we" are to have Dr. Zweibach with "us" and then turns the session over to Dr. Zweibach. A rumpled, middle-aged university professor walks to the microphone and launches into his talk on the thrill of teaching. Within 10 minutes, signs of restlessness, boredom, and bitterness are evident throughout the audience. It seems that 12 of the teachers are sitting through a talk they had heard Dr. Zweibach deliver verbatim two years earlier at a teacher convention; 15 others are thinking about the classroom work they could be doing to prepare for next semester and wondering, "Why in the world are we sitting through this talk?" Another 22 teachers have become impatient with Dr. Zweibach's continual reference to the academic high school settings where he found teaching thrills. Their own work settings are vocational, special education, and elementary; they can't relate what he is saying about high schools to their world. Eventually, some teachers begin to correct papers, read, or knit; a few appear to fall asleep. On the other hand, nearly half the members of the audience remain attentive and give Dr. Zweibach a rousing ovation when he concludes. The other half appear relieved that the talk is finally over and they can return to their own schools. On leaving the auditorium, one can overhear such remarks as "What a great talk!" and "Why do we have to put up with all this staff-development crap?"

This depiction of an in-service day is typical of many school systems. Some teachers find it valuable, but many do not. Staff development has been referred to as "the slum of American education, neglected and of little effect" (Wood and Thompson, 1980). Professional development is often viewed by supervisors, administrators, and teachers as a number of days contracted for in the school calendar that simply need to be endured. Three crucial questions will shape this chapter: (1) Why is professional development needed? (2) How should it be planned and conducted? (3) Are teachers to be the objects or the agents of professional development?

Why the Need for Professional Development?

Over 85 percent of a total school budget is used to pay employee salaries. Education is a human enterprise. The essence of successful instruction and good schools comes from the thoughts and actions of the professionals in the schools. So if one is to look for a place to improve the quality of education in a school, a sensible place to look is the continuous education of educators—that is, professional development. Virtually any experience that enlarges a teacher's knowledge, appreciation, skills, and understandings of his or her work falls under the domain of professional development.

When one of the authors gave a presentation to a Michigan school board to explain the need to allocate more money for professional development, he used an analogy to the automobiles made in Detroit. When a customer purchases a new car costing upwards of $30,000, he or she brings it in every 5,000 miles for preventive maintenance and fine-tuning. The customer continues to put additional money into the car to prolong its life and performance. Simply to run the car into the ground would be a dumb way to protect such an investment! In education, the school board is the customer, who purchases more than a new car with its $30,000 initial investment—it purchases a living and breathing professional! Without resources for maintaining, fine-tuning, and reinvigorating the investment, the district will run teachers into the ground. This is far more consequential than a neglected car. The district will lose teachers, physically and/or mentally. The real losers will be the students of these teachers.

Professional development has gathered increased attention in both research and resource allocation across the nation. States have dramatically increased their expenditures for professional development in local districts and schools since the series of national reports issued in the mid-1980s. The National Staff Development Council has become the fastest-growing educational organization in the United States. Until 1957, only about 50 studies had been conducted on professional development in schools (Showers, Joyce, and Bennett, 1987). Now several times that number of studies are being conducted every year.

Since professional development should be a responsibility of those who supervise, the research and application discussed here will focus on the use of successful professional development to improve instruction. According to a study of teachers and administrators in New York state (Tetenbaum and Mulkeen, 1987, p. 11), the primary criticisms of professional development programs are that the activities are "one-shot deals" and that there is "no integration with a comprehensive plan to achieve school goals." Let's see how these criticisms can be avoided.

Characteristics of Successful Professional Development Programs

A considerable knowledge base exists on successful professional development, including original research and reviews of research and best practice (Loucks-Horsley et al., 1987; Orlich, 1989; Wood and Thompson, 1993; Guskey, 1994; Corcoran, 1995; U.S. Department of Education, 1996; Hawley and Valli, 1996; Joyce, Calhoun, and Hopkins, 1999; Fullan, 2000; Gordon, 2000; Zech, Gause-Vega, Bray, Secules, and Goldman, 2000; Bernauer, 2002; Harris, 2002). Although these reports do not agree on all factors, there are a number of common characteristics:

1. Involvement of participants in planning, implementing, and evaluating programs
2. Programs that are based on schoolwide goals, but that integrate individual and group goals with school goals
3. Long-range planning and development
4. Programs that incorporate research and best practice on school improvement and instructional improvement
5. Administrative support, including provision of time and other resources as well as involvement in program planning and delivery
6. Adherence to the principles of adult learning (see Chapter 4)
7. Attention to the research on change, including the need to address individual concerns throughout the change process (see Chapter 21)

8. Follow-up and support for transfer of learning to the school or classroom
9. Ongoing assessment and feedback
10. Continuous professional development that becomes part of the school culture

As you review the characteristics listed here, think of a professional development program that you are familiar with. How many of the ten characteristics are present in that program?

Integrating Schoolwide, Group, and Individual Professional Development

One characteristic of effective professional development listed is the integration of schoolwide, group, and individual goals. How does a school go about doing this? To begin, it is critical that all members of the school community provide input into schoolwide professional development goals. The schoolwide goals should be broad enough to allow groups and individuals to set their own goals, consistent with school goals.

For an example of integrating schoolwide and group professional development, let us assume that a middle school has identified improved student discipline as a schoolwide professional development goal. Different grade level or instructional teams, all committed to improved discipline, might identify different group goals relative to the school goal. One group might decide that they need to focus their professional development on improving students' respect for others. Another group might determine that their primary need is to improve students' on-task behavior during class. A third group may wish to focus on finding ways to encourage self-discipline so that students take more responsibility for their homework, studying for tests, and asking for assistance.

Different groups also may decide that they prefer different professional development formats. One group may decide that they prefer to form a study group that will share readings, visit other schools to see how they address student discipline, and discuss how exemplary practices can be adapted to their students. The second group may decide that they wish to attend a training program on effective discipline, followed up by peer coaching at the classroom level. The third group might prefer to follow an action research format, gathering classroom data to find out more about the problem, designing an action plan, implementing the plan, and gathering evaluation data to determine effects. Although it is important that various groups within the school be allowed to adapt schoolwide goals to group needs, it also is important that each group show how its particular goals relate to and support the schoolwide goals.

A faculty is made up of individuals, and schoolwide professional development cannot take place without individual development. Thus, it is important to integrate individual professional development goals with group and schoolwide goals. Let us return to our example of the schoolwide goal of improved student discipline. You will recall that one possible group goal was improving students' respect for others. Even this more focused goal would have different meanings to different teachers within the group that chose the goal. For one teacher it might mean helping students to work together in cooperative groups. For another teacher it could mean students respecting other students from different cultures. For a third teacher it might mean working with students who are disrespectful to authority figures. Thus, even within the group goal of increased respect for others there should be opportunities for teachers to identify individual goals consistent with group and school goals. Since adults, like students, have different experiences and learning styles, teachers within the study group might pursue different learning activities and make different contributions to the group. One teacher might bring to the group reports from visits to other schools, another teacher might share journal articles related to the topic of student respect for others, and so forth. The individual teacher can connect individual goals to group and schoolwide goals in a manner that allows the same professional development activities to serve all three types of goals.

Alternative Professional Development Formats

We are rapidly moving away from the era when professional development usually means either a 60-minute speech by an outside consultant or a "one-shot" workshop. A variety of new formats for professional development have emerged over the last several years. Some examples follow:

• *Beginning teacher assistance programs:* The new teacher is provided ongoing, intensive assistance throughout at least the first year of teaching. This support includes such things as an assigned mentor; an orientation to the school and community; assistance from a support team including the mentor, other teachers, and a supervisor; training in classroom management and effective teaching; and support seminars focused on beginning teachers' concerns.

• *Skill development programs:* This might consist of several workshops over a period of months and classroom coaching between workshops to assist teachers to transfer new skills to their daily teaching.

• *Teacher centers:* Teachers can meet at a central location to engage in professional dialogue, develop skills, plan innovations, and gather or create instructional materials.

• *Teacher institutes:* Teachers participate in intensive learning experiences on single, complex topics over a period of consecutive days or weeks.

• *Collegial support groups:* Teachers within the same school engage in group inquiry, address common problems, jointly implement instructional innovations, and provide mutual support.

- *Networks:* Teachers from different schools share information, concerns, and accomplishments and engage in common learning through computer links, newsletters, fax machines, and occasional seminars and conferences.

- *Teacher leadership:* Teachers participate in leadership preparation programs and assist other teachers by assuming one or more leadership roles (workshop presenter, cooperating teacher, mentor, expert coach, instructional team leader, curriculum developer). The teacher–leader not only assists other teachers but also experiences professional growth as a result of being involved in leadership activities.

- *Teacher as writer:* This increasingly popular format has teachers reflect on and write about their students, teaching, and professional growth. Such writing can be in the form of private journals, essays, or reaction papers to share with colleagues, blogs, or formal articles for publication in educational journals.

- *Individually planned professional development:* Teachers set individual goals and objectives, plan and carry out activities, and assess results.

- *Partnerships:* Partnerships between schools and universities or businesses, in which both partners are considered equal, have mutual rights and responsibilities, make contributions, and receive benefits. Such partnerships could involve one or more of the previously described formats (Moore and Seeger, 2004).

There can be considerable overlap between various professional development formats (not to mention between professional development and the other four tasks of supervision!). Our own experience as staff developers and researchers has led us to conclude that many of the most successful professional development programs combine multiple formats. Next, we will describe several professional development programs, each including a combination of formats.

Examples of Effective Professional Development Programs

We will describe several model professional development programs, including two districtwide programs, one site-based program, and two individualized programs. Each of the examples is either an actual program or a composite based on several actual programs.

Districtwide Professional Development Programs

The *St. Mary's Achievement Related Teaching (SMART) program* was based on a written needs assessment of all district teachers conducted by the district's professional development planning committee, comprising a majority of teachers. During the first year of the program, a group of 18 volunteer instructional leaders (14 teachers, 3 building administrators, and 1 central office supervisor) chosen by the committee participated in professional development leadership preparation.

The leadership preparation was conducted by a team of professors from a nearby university that had entered into a formal partnership with the district. Leadership preparation addressed the following areas:

I. Generic Instructional Skills
   A. Classroom Management
   B. Lesson Design
   C. Student Assessment
   D. Teacher Expectations
   E. Questioning Skills
   F. Student Motivation
II. Instructional Models
   A. Concept Attainment
   B. Compare and Contrast
   C. Cooperative Learning
   D. Concept Mapping
III. Coaching and Leadership
   A. An Overview of Peer Coaching
   B. Systematic Observation of Instruction
   C. Conferencing Skills
   D. Professional Relationships
   E. Matching Coaching to Teacher Concerns

Leadership training consisted of 12 workshops over the course of a year. Between workshops, doctoral students from the university visited the school district and provided coaching to the staff developers as they implemented new instructional strategies and models in actual classroom lessons. This expert coaching was intended to (1) assist the staff developers to master strategies and models they would be conducting workshops on the following year and (2) allow the staff developers to observe effective coaches in action.

During subsequent years, the staff developers became workshop presenters as small groups of regular teachers (groups of approximately 15) were cycled through the instructional strategies and models components of the program. Just as they had been coached by doctoral students in their leadership preparation, the district's staff developers provided coaching between workshops to assist new participants to transfer skills to their classrooms.

Buckeye School District's efforts to support beginning teachers began with the design of a beginning teacher assistance program by a planning committee made up of administrators, supervisors, and teachers. A key component of the program is a pool of experienced mentor teachers. Volunteer mentors are selected by a screening committee. Selection criteria include years of experience in the school system, effective teaching performance, interpersonal skills, past commitment to the profession, flexibility, and willingness to spend time helping beginning teachers. The selected teachers take part in an intensive mentor-preparation program, including the following elements:

- Introduction to the knowledge base on problems of beginning teachers, beginning teacher assistance programs, and mentoring
- Overview of the district's beginning teacher assistance program
- Research on effective classroom management
- Research on effective teaching
- Principles of adult learning
- Adult and teacher development
- Goal setting and action planning
- The coaching of teaching, including conferencing skills and observation skills
- Action research

A number of variables are considered when assigning mentors to beginning teachers, including grade level and content area, classroom location, and philosophical and personal compatibility of mentor and beginner. An attempt is made to make an overall "best match" of mentor and beginner.

Prior to the beginning of the school year, a special orientation for beginners is attended by novices and their mentors. During this orientation, new teachers are walked through key information about the community, district policies and procedures, and the curriculum they will be responsible for teaching. Later in the orientation, they are given tours of their schools and meet with building administrators and instructional leaders. Their mentors review building policies and procedures and provide them with a profile of the school, its staff, students, and parents.

The orientation is only the beginning of assistance for the beginning teacher in Buckeye School District. Ongoing support is provided throughout the school year. For each beginner, a support team is formed, consisting of a building administrator, department chairperson or instructional team leader, and mentor. The team meets on a regular basis. Continuous assistance is based on written needs assessments and discussions with support teams. Workshops are provided for beginners on such topics as classroom management, effective teaching, and working with parents. Mentors visit beginners' classrooms on a regular basis to provide nonevaluative assistance, including expert coaching following the five-step model presented in Chapter 16. Beginners visit the classrooms of mentors and other effective teachers to observe best practice. Mentors are available on a daily basis to provide beginners with psychological support, information, and instructional assistance.

Mentors too are given support by the district in the form of follow-up workshops, support seminars, tuition reimbursement for relevant university coursework, released time, and stipends. Their contributions to beginners and the district are recognized during faculty meetings, in district publications, and at an annual recognition dinner.

Buckeye School District's support program includes a partnership with a nearby university. Professors from the university collaborated with Buckeye School District in the design of its support program. The same professors assist with mentor preparation and offer course credit for mentors willing to do additional academic work beyond the mentor workshops. Finally, the professors assist in the delivery of several of the workshops for beginning teachers. To summarize, although mentoring is the heart and soul of Buckeye School District's beginning teacher assistance program, other formats—such as skill development programs, collegial support groups, and partnerships—are part of the overall program.

Site-Based Initiatives

There are numerous recent examples of staff development planned and implemented by school councils and school task forces as part of site-based initiatives to address the educational priorities of the particular school. Faculty and parents assess their current instructional programs, establish learning goals for students, and then decide whether the expertise to conduct staff development programs lies within or outside the school. The various school renewal networks—such as the League of Professional Schools, the Coalition of Essential Schools, the Accelerated Schools, and the Comer Schools—have many powerful examples of decentralized staff development plans derived by faculty interested in learning new methods of instruction (such as models of teaching, cooperative learning, conflict mediation, service learning, Socratic discussions, interdisciplinary curriculum, higher-order thinking, nongraded schedules, team teaching, and technology integration). The schools plan their own retreats, staff development days, and summer institutes. The results of many of these efforts have been major improvements in student achievement and attitudes, higher attendance, and lower incidence of discipline and vandalism (see Levin, 1994; Glickman, 1992, 2002; Gursky, 1990).

Ponticell (1995) provides a description of a site-based professional development program in an *inner-city Chicago high school.* The aim of the program was instructional improvement based on collegial learning and support. The program was supported by a grant from a nearby university and facilitated by a professor from the university. The program began with a professional retreat where teachers engaged in reflective dialogue about teaching and began to build collaborative relationships.

Following the retreat, the teachers began to read and discuss research on effective teaching and professional development alternatives. Next, the teachers developed a cycle of monthly professional development activities including the following phases:

1. Teachers identified an instructional concern, read current research addressing that concern, selected ideas that made sense, developed a strategy for classroom implementation, and created a checklist of planned teacher behaviors.

2. Teachers videotaped themselves implementing improvement strategies, analyzed their own videotapes, and compared their actual behaviors to the checklist of anticipated behaviors.
3. Peer coaching, focused on the month's strategy, with a coaching cycle consisting of a preconference, observation, and postconference.
4. End-of-month group meetings in which teachers met to share video clips, discussed what aspects of the month's strategy had worked and not worked, reflected on what they had learned, and determined the topic of study for the following month.

Based on pre- and postinventories, direct observation, analysis of audiotapes of group discussions, and interviews with participants, Ponticell (1995) found that the site-based program had increased collegiality, improved self-analysis of teaching, enabled teachers to learn new ways of collaboratively observing and discussing each other's teaching, and fostered learning and experimenting with new teaching strategies.

Individually Planned Professional Development

An individually planned professional development program at *Holidaysburg Area School District* (Wilshire, 1991) consisted of five phases:

1. *Invitation:* Interested teachers were invited to a meeting to discuss the program. After an overview of the program was provided, teachers who wished to participate completed biographical data sheets. The biographical information was used to match the volunteer teachers to facilitators from a nearby university. The role of the facilitators was to aid professional planning.
2. *Assessment:* Facilitators audiotaped individual interviews with participating teachers. Interview questions were designed to determine individual teachers' needs, interests, and preferred professional development formats. Facilitators reviewed interview transcripts and generated potential professional development projects or learning activities in which individual teachers might be interested.
3. *Validation–Negation:* In a second meeting with individual teachers, facilitators shared interview data and data-based professional development options. Teachers could select from options presented by their facilitators, propose their own options, or decide to reflect further on various options. Eventually, teachers, assisted by facilitators, developed their own written professional development plans, including goals, objectives, activities, assessment, and needed resources and materials.
4. *Disclosure:* During a group meeting of facilitators and participants, the teachers shared their individual plans with each other. Collaboration was encouraged when two or more plans were similar.

5. *Implementation:* After a meeting with a district administrator to approve the individual plans, implementation began. Teachers had two years to complete their self-directed programs. Facilitators remained available to assist the participants as they carried out their plans. Participants were required to provide the district with products developed during their self-directed programs, which became resources for the district and its teachers.

Individual plans in the Holidaysburg program included developing new curricula, learning and using new instructional strategies, engaging in interdisciplinary team teaching, and collecting information about successful educational practices to share with school personnel. The Holidaysburg model and other individually planned programs open the door for individual teachers to become involved in any of the staff development formats discussed earlier in this chapter, including *group staff development* to help them to reach their *individual goals.*

A second example of individually planned professional development can be found at *Leander (Texas) Middle School.* Individual improvement plans are tied to the school's annual improvement plan. Individual projects follow the PDSA cycle (Plan, Do, Study, Act) and are documented in teacher portfolios. In the *planning phase,* teachers gather a variety of self-assessment data (videotapes of lessons, student achievement data, peer observations, and so on), analyze the data, and design individualized professional development plans. The individual plans include objectives, learning activities, needed resources, and plans for self-evaluation.

The teacher implements the improvement plan during the *doing* phase. Professional development activities might include attending workshops or conferences, observing other teachers, peer coaching, participation in study groups, and so on. The teacher's portfolio documents learning activities, support received from colleagues, and changes in practice.

The *studying* phase involves gathering data to evaluate the plan's effectiveness. Data is gathered on the teacher's professional growth as well as changes in student learning. Evaluation data might include the teacher's reflective writing, classroom observation data, student achievement data, or artifacts of student work.

The *acting* phase consists of a portfolio conference with the teacher's supervisor. During the conference, the teacher reflects on activities completed, learning that has taken place, and future directions for professional growth. In Leander, all adults—teachers, supervisors, and staff—implement individual development plans and construct portfolios. Each spring, all members of the school community share their individual projects at a "portfolio fair."

In this section, we have presented examples of various levels (district, school, individual) and formats for professional development. In the next section, we will discuss stages of professional development that apply to any long-term professional development program.

Stages of Professional Development

Professional development typically involves three stages of learning: (1) orienta-tion, (2) integration, and (3) refinement. To illustrate these three stages, we will re-late them to staff development on the cooperative learning instructional model.

In the *orientation stage,* benefits, responsibilities, and personal concerns about involvement in the staff development are addressed. Next, participants en-gage in learning necessary for initial "real-world" application. In our cooperative learning example, orientation topics might include the following:*

- Differences between cooperative, competitive, and individual learning
- Differences between cooperative learning and traditional group work
- Research on cooperative learning
- Basic elements of cooperative learning (teaching social skills, positive in-terdependence, face-to-face interaction, individual accountability, group processing)
- Forming cooperative groups
- Standard cooperative learning structures (think-pair-share, jigsaw, student teams achievement divisions ([STAD], teams-games-tournaments [TGT], group investigation, and so on)
- Planning cooperative lessons

Failure to take teachers beyond the orientation stage is one reason why many staff development programs are ineffective. Teachers are given rudimentary knowledge or skills and then are left to fend for themselves.

In the *integration stage,* teachers are assisted as they apply previous learning in their classrooms and schools. One aspect of integration is learning to adapt general learning to specific situations. In the cooperative learning example, this would mean learning to alter cooperative teaching strategies to make them appro-priate for different learning content and students. A related aspect of integration is regular and effective use of the new learning. This would mean, for example, the teacher develops enough competence and confidence in cooperative learning methods to make them part of his or her standard repertoire of instructional strategies.

In the *refinement stage,* teachers move from basic competence to expertise through continuous experimentation and reflection. In the refinement stage of staff development on cooperative learning, teachers would become expert at a wide range of cooperative learning strategies and at mixing and matching those strategies for optimal student learning. Teachers in the refinement stage synthesize

---

*Outlining a complete professional development program on cooperative learning is beyond the scope of this text. Some critical topics are listed to provide examples of the types of learning in each stage of professional development. Sources of cooperative learning professional development topics are Johnson, Johnson, and Holubec (1991) and Kagan (1992).

different types of previous learning in order to create new learning. In our cooperative learning example, a teacher at this stage might combine aspects of two or more standard cooperative learning structures to create a more complex structure. For another example, a teacher at the refinement stage might synthesize whole language and cooperative learning strategies to create an entirely new teaching strategy. Perhaps the best thing that a supervisor can do when teachers have reached this stage is to sign them up as teacher-staff developers!

The Nuts and Bolts

Professional development does not always need to take place in group sessions, but groups remain a major component of the majority of staff development formats and programs. The best planning for a group session is useless if the supervisor forgets the nuts and bolts. What value is an excellent speaker who lectures in a room where the acoustics garble every word? What good is a fast-paced microteaching demonstration if it conflicts with other teacher meetings so that few can attend? What good is an exciting role-playing activity whose participants have had no chance to eat, unwind, or use the restroom during the previous two hours? If one is going to the trouble to plan professional development, then one should go the extra step to ensure an environment that enables participants to be responsive and comfortable. Here are six important considerations:

1. *Prepare speakers by telling them exactly what they are expected to do.* If a speaker is invited to conduct an activity, make sure he or she understands the assignment. Speakers will do whatever they normally do unless someone tells them otherwise. Most speakers have their own topics, their own rehearsed presentations, and their own formats. If a speaker is expected to demonstrate a particular skill (for example, asking higher-order questions) or to include role-playing, *tell him or her so.* Speaker and participants are both in an embarrassing situation when the speaker, through no fault of either party, is not doing what the participants have been led to expect.

2. *Check the facility beforehand for seating arrangements, media, and acoustics.* Make sure the facility is appropriate to the activity. For example, small-group discussions in an auditorium give teachers stiff necks and a stiffer attitude toward the next in-service. See that all equipment is operating correctly. Check projectors and sound systems. Move around the room to see if displays on screen or walls can be viewed clearly by everyone. Have at hand spare bulbs and replacement equipment in case of an equipment failure.

3. *Provide refreshments and transition time at the beginning.* Tell participants where the restrooms are. Provide drinks and snacks. Informally greet the participants at the door and tell them when the session will begin. When formally beginning, inform participants when other breaks are scheduled.

4. *Check the comfort of the room.* Beforehand, check whether the room will maintain a comfortable temperature. Find out if the heating or cooling system is turned off at the time of the meeting and, if so, arrange to have the system operating. Estimate the temperature of the room when it is full. A room that feels comfortable when only a few people are present can become oppressively hot when full to capacity.

5. *Have materials run off and a plan for easy dissemination to participants.* Prior to the session, check with the leader of the activity to make sure all desired materials will be prepared. Also before the session, figure out a distribution system for materials. Often it is sufficient to place a table next to the entrance with collected materials and make one person responsible for telling entrants to pick up the materials.

6. *Have evaluation forms for participants to fill out after the session.* Asking participants to evaluate the session allows existing problems to be corrected before the next session. A simple form to be filled out anonymously by participants can be seen in Figure 18.1.

Extending the Concept of Professional Development

Professional development for much of its history focused primarily on the development of pedagogical skills. Pedagogical development remains a critical purpose of professional development, but in recent years the field has expanded to include a variety of other purposes.

> *Personal development* entails helping teachers to move toward better understanding of their own adult life cycle, transition events, and roles, as well as improving teachers' self-concept and self-efficacy.
>
> *Career development* supports teachers as they move through phases of the teaching career from induction to retirement, helping teachers to address concerns as well as providing new professional opportunities and rewards during each career phase. Career development includes assisting teachers to assume various types of teacher-leadership roles as their careers progress.
>
> *Moral development* enables teachers to model the principles of compassion, equality, and justice that they hope to instill in their students. Every word a teacher speaks and every action a teacher takes during the school day has moral implications, and professional development can enhance teachers' moral insight and decision making in ways that foster students' overall well-being.
>
> *School improvement* is a to a large part dependent on professional development. Almost any significant change in the school organization, curriculum, or instructional program is dependent on professional development to provide teachers with the capacity to implement the change. It is difficult

We would like your feedback to plan future professional development sessions. Please circle the number closest to your feelings and provide comments in the space provided on the form. If you need more space, feel free to use the back of the sheet. As you leave, please drop this form in the box on the back table.

Professional Development Topic _____

Date _____

	Poor 1	Satisfactory 2	Good 3	Excellent 4
1. The session today was Comments	1	2	3	4
2. The organization of the session was Comments	1	2	3	4
3. The meeting room was Comments	1	2	3	4
4. The materials were Comments	1	2	3	4

Suggestions for future meetings: _____

FIGURE 18.1 *Professional Development Evaluation*

to imagine *any* school improvement effort succeeding without professional development.

Improvement of the teaching profession has become a national goal in recent years, and professional development is the engine driving this movement. Although much of the impetus for improving the profession has come from national certification boards, associations, and networks, professional development for meeting and applying new standards often takes place at the local level.

Teachers as Objects or Agents in Professional Development

A superintendent remarked that he had been at a national conference and attended a presentation on "Elements of Effective Instruction." He decided that this was exactly what the teachers needed. As a result, the district was off and running with a three-year commitment to training all principals and teachers in "elements." Highly paid national consultants were brought in; personnel were identified for advanced training and traveled during the summer to faraway sites; and virtually all contracted in-service time and school supervision was devoted to "elements." It was not long before a new evaluation instrument was established to check that every teacher was using the training in effective instruction in the same prescribed manner. Over the three years, expenditures by the school district exceeded $300,000, not including the cost of participants' time. What have been the results? No appreciable gain in student achievement, considerable grumbling by a core of "malcontent" teachers, enthusiasm by the chosen core of teachers who received special training and compensation, and a firm claim by the superintendent that "we now have focused long-term professional development on scientifically derived principles, and our teaching is more effective."

In recent years, education has been bombarded by packaged programs on "effective teaching," "effective schools," "effective supervision," and "effective discipline." All claim to be derived from research and to have documented success, and all use the components and sequence of transfer of training that have been sorely lacking in traditional professional development programs. The programs provide for explanation, demonstration, modeling, role-playing, practice, and coaching. They are not one-shot programs—they are focused and they are classroom based. The only problem is that the people who think these programs are worth the cost and effort are the same people who have a personal investment and commitment to use them (see Garman and Hazley, 1988; DiBernardo and Stiles, 1988). If the programs are not as successful as predicted, the decision makers do not blame the program but rather the lack of enough training to ensure that teachers "do it right" (Lambert, 1988). Schools, districts, and states that have committed themselves to such programs come to the ludicrous conclusion that they need more training, more money, and greater enforcement to see that all teachers will finally learn to teach as prescribed more frequently and correctly. This is an incredible rationalization by policy makers that their initial decision was right, regardless of the effect that the program is having on teachers and students.

This rationale underscores the point that was made about adult development earlier in the book. Motivation is premised on two dimensions: one is choice and the other is responsibility to make knowledgeable decisions about one's work. That's why the superintendent wants so badly to see this program on "effective elements" work. The superintendent had the choice and took responsibility for making the decision. The selected core of teachers also want to see this program work, because they were given choice and responsibility in making decisions on how to train others. Yet most teachers and principals were not given any choice or responsibility in these decisions about the needs of their students and themselves. Instead, they were treated as objects rather than as agents of professional development, without due regard for their capacity to make wise decisions in the interest of students and teaching. Without choice or responsibility to make knowledgeable decisions about their work, they have little motivation or commitment to somebody else's program.

To use knowledge about sequencing training for transfer of learning, without an awareness of the need truly to involve teachers as decision makers in professional development, will leave us where we currently are. We will be more sophisticated in teaching teachers how to follow someone else's program, but we will find little commitment on the part of teachers or little stimulation to increase teachers' own collective and critical capacities to make lasting changes.

SUMMARY

For professional development to be meaningful to teachers and to lead to teacher renewal and instructional improvement, it must operate at two levels. First, teachers as individuals should have a variety of learning opportunities to support their pursuit of their own personal and professional career goals. Second, teachers as part of a school and district organization should together define, learn, and implement skills, knowledge, and programs that achieve common goals of the organization. Professional development must be geared to teachers' needs and concerns. Research on successful professional development programs has shown an emphasis on involvement, long-term planning, problem-solving meetings, released time, experimentation and risk taking, administrative support, small-group activities, peer feedback, demonstration and trials, coaching, and leader participation in activities. Consideration for individual and group characteristics can help make professional development more relevant to the participant. Teachers move through three stages of professional development: orientation, integration, and refinement. Nuts-and-bolts considerations—informing speakers, checking facilities, and providing refreshments, materials, and evaluation—can increase the comfort and attentiveness of teachers. It is time to change the perception that professional development is a waste of teachers' time to the perception of professional development as time well spent. Viewing teachers as the agents rather than the objects of professional development will be the impetus for such change.

REFERENCES AND RECOMMENDED READINGS

Bernauer, F. 2002. Five keys to unlock continuous school improvement. *Kappa Delta Pi Record,* 38(2), 89–92.

Corcoran, T. B. 1995. *Helping teachers teach well: Transforming professional development.* CPRE Policy Briefs, RB-16-June. New Brunswick, NJ: Rutgers University, Consortium for Policy Research in Education.

DiBernardo, G., and Stiles, D. 1988. The Madeline Hunter and Lee Canter teacher improvement packages: What every school needs? *Democratic Schools,* 3(2), 1–9.

ERIC. 1980. ERIC Research Action Brief—Clearinghouse on Educational Management, No. 10. Eugene, OR: University of Oregon. (ERIC ED 021 256)

Fullan, M. 2000. *Change forces: The sequel.* Philadelphia: George H. Buchanan.

Garman, N. B., and Hazley, H. M. 1988. Teachers ask: Is there life after Madeline Hunter? *Kappan,* 69(9), 669–672.

Glickman, C. D. 1992. The essence of school renewal. *Educational Leadership,* 50(1), 87–97.

Glickman, C. D. 2002. The courage to lead. *Educational Leadership,* 59(8), 41–44.

Gordon, S. P. 2000. *Professional development for teacher and school renewal: Alternative pathways, common characteristics.* Paper presented at the University Council for Educational Administration Annual Convention, Albuquerque, NM, November.

Gursky, D. 1990. A plan that works. *Teacher* (June/July), 46–54.

Guskey, T. R. 1994. *Professional development in education: In search of the optimal mix.* Paper presented at the annual meeting of the American Educational Research Association, New Orleans, April. (ERIC 369 181)

Hall, G. H., and Hord, S. M. 1987. *Change in schools: Facilitating the process.* Albany: State University of New York Press.

Harris, A. 2002. *School improvement: What's in it for schools?* New York: Routledge Falmer.

Harris, B. M. 1975. *Supervisory behavior in education* (2nd ed.). Englewood Cliffs, NJ: Prentice Hall.

Harris, B. M. 1980. *Improving staff performance through in-service education.* Boston: Allyn and Bacon.

Hawley, W. D., and Valli, L. 1996. *The essentials of effective professional development: A new consensus.* Paper presented at the AERA Invitational Conference on Teacher Development and School Reform, Washington, D.C.

Johnson, D. W., Johnson, R. T., and Holubec, E. J. 1991. *Cooperation in the classroom.* Edina, MN: Interaction Book Company.

Joyce, B., Calhoun, E., and Hopkins, D. 1999. *The new structure of school improvement: Inquiring schools and achieving students.* Philadelphia: Open University Press.

Kagan, S. 1992. *Cooperative learning.* San Juan Capistrano, CA: Kagan Cooperative Learning.

Karst, R. R. 1987. *New policy implications for in-service and professional development programs for the public schools.* Presentation to the annual meeting of the American Educational Research Association, Washington, DC, April.

Lambert, L. 1988. Staff development redesigned. *Kappa, 69*(9), 665–668.

Lead Teacher Centers of Pennsylvania. No date. *Pennsylvania lead teachers: Enhancing the teaching profession.* Harrisburg: Pennsylvania Department of Education.

Levin, H. M. 1994. Learning from accelerated schools. In S. H. Block, S. T. Evertson, and T. R. Guskey (Eds.), *Selecting and integrating school improvement programs.* New York: Scholastic Books.

Loucks-Horsley, S., Harding, C. K., Arbuckle, M. A., Murray, L. B., Dubea, C., and Williams, M. K.

1987. *Continuing to learn: A guidebook for teacher development.* Andover, ME: The Regional Laboratory for Educational Improvement of the Northeast and Islands.

McLaughlin, M. W., and Marsh, D. D. 1978. Staff development and school change. *Teachers College Record, 80*(1), 69–94.

Moore, R., and Seeger, V. 2004. Validating teaching and learning communities for teacher education reform. *The Teacher Educator, 40*(2), 116–132.

Newlove, B. W., and Hall, G. E. 1976. *A manual for assessing open-ended statements of concern about an innovation.* Austin: Research and Development Center for Teacher Education, University of Texas.

Oja, S. N. 1981. *Adapting research findings in psychological education: A case study.* Presentation at the annual meeting of the American Association of Colleges for Teacher Education, Detroit, February.

Orlich, D. C. 1989. *Staff development: Enhancing human potential.* Boston: Allyn and Bacon.

Ponticell, J. A. 1995. Promoting teacher professionalism through collegiality. *Journal of Staff Development, 16*(3), 13–18.

Rubin, L. (Ed.). 1978. *The in-service education of teachers.* Boston: Allyn and Bacon.

Showers, B., Joyce, B. R., and Bennett, B. 1987. Synthesis of research on staff development: A framework for future study and a state of the-art analysis. *Educational Leadership, 45*(3), 77–80.

Tetenbaum, T. J., and Mulkeen, T. A. 1987. *Prelude to school improvement: Understanding perceptions of staff development.* Presentation to the annual meeting of the American Educational Research Association, Washington, DC, April.

Thies-Sprinthall, L. 1981. Promoting the conceptual and principled thinking level of the supervising teacher. Unpublished research funded by St. Cloud State University, 1978 and 1979. Reported in *Educating for teacher growth: A cognitive developmental perspective.* Paper presented at the annual meeting of the American Educational Research Association, Los Angeles, April.

U.S. Department of Education. 1996. National Center for Education Statistics. *Measures of inservice professional development: Suggested items for the 1998–1999 Schools and Staffing Survey.* Working Paper No. 96-25, Washington, DC: Author.

Wilsey, C., and Killion, J. 1982. Making staff development programs work. *Educational Leadership, 40*(1), 36–38, 43.

Wilshire, D. K. 1991. Teachers in transition: An exploratory study of self-selected change and educational planning in professional development. Unpublished doctoral dissertation, Pennsylvania State University.

Wood, F. W., and Thompson, S. R. 1980. Guidelines for better staff development. *Educational Leadership, 37*(5), 374–378.

Wood, F. W., and Thompson, S. R. 1993. Assumptions about staff development based on research and best practice. *Journal of Staff Development, 14*(4), 52–57.

Zech, L. K., Gause-Vega, C. L., Bray, M. H., Secules, T., and Goldman, S. R. 2000. Content-based collaborative inquiry: A professional development model for sustaining educational reform. *Educational Psychologist, 35*(3), 207–217.

Curriculum Development

"**T**eaching is a moral activity that implies thoughts about ends, means, and their consequences" (Zeuli and Buchmann, 1988, p. 147). Moral activity is explicitly expressed in a school's curriculum. To be an effective school is of little matter unless the personnel within an organization first have defined what is meant by a good school—what should students learn in order to be well educated? The institutional job then becomes one of effectively achieving that definition of goodness. As Sergiovanni (1987) remarked, "It's not important to do things right, unless we are doing the right things!" Curriculum is the moral deliberation on what is "right" for students to be taught.

Hirsch, in *Cultural Literacy: What Every American Needs to Know* (1987), attacked American education as abandoning the essential literature, ideas, and facts of the national culture. Bloom, in *The Closing of the American Mind* (1987), likewise indicted schools for abandoning the core programs of traditional liberal arts education. In *What Do Our 17-Year-Olds Know?* (1987), educators Ravitch and Finn wrote that a large proportion of high school students don't know such basic facts as in what half-century the Civil War took place. Hirsch, Bloom, Ravitch, and Finn believe it is both necessary and right to reduce the school curriculum to a focus on predetermined, essential knowledge.

Yet the National Assessment of Educational Progress (NAEP), in its report card on high school students' knowledge of literature and U.S. history, suggests that students' inadequate knowledge may be because "the typical course relies heavily on a textbook . . . students regularly are expected to memorize important information, and are tested frequently . . . class time is spent listening to the teacher lecture" (Applebee, Langer, and Mullis, 1987). Indeed, what is taught and how it is taught according to the NAEP study of literature and history is no different from what Goodlad found in his national study of schooling. Goodlad (1984) found that nearly 90 percent of teaching across all subjects and grade levels is up-front teaching—lecturing, with students passively listening except for an occasional opportunity to answer questions. On one side, academic essentialists argue that the problem with curriculum is that too much stress is placed on process skills (problem solving, inquiry, and critical thinking) to the detriment of straight, old-fashioned teaching of content and basic skills. Social activists and experimentalists such as Goodlad reply that such teaching is what already exists and is to blame for inadequate student comprehension. Their argument is that there should be less memorization and facts and more active problem solving and conceptual understanding.

Sizer (1984) reasoned that schools are too concerned with teaching all subjects superficially. Instead, schools should teach fewer subjects, topics, and skills more thoroughly—"teach less, better" rather than "teach more, quicker." Others argued that curriculum should expose students to a vast array of educational experiences. Howard Gardner, a noted cognitive psychologist, stated (in Brandt 1988b) that his research on human intelligence indicates that elementary and middle schools should not be concerned with subjects; instead, curriculum should focus on long-term core projects that integrate rather than separate learning of language, mathematics, science, reading, art, and physical education.

How does one make sense of these topsy-turvy controversies about curriculum? How can so many esteemed experts have so many contradictory ideas? It comes down to a matter of educational philosophy (as discussed in Chapter 5). Curriculum experts are human too! They possess the same ideological, philosophical, and political biases as the rest of us. They may argue more eloquently and have better support for their claims than we do, but at the bottom of their discourse are philosophical premises and assumptions about education no different from ours. Ultimately, decisions about a good school, appropriate curriculum, and needs of students should be made by those closest to students. After considering the available experts, research, readings, and articulated conflicts, people in the schools, districts, and local communities should ultimately decide what is worthy to teach. However, by default, pressure, and abdication, curriculum decisions have generally been made by those farthest from the classroom action.

Sources of Curriculum Development

Curricula can be developed at many levels—by outside specialists, school district specialists, school curriculum teams, and teachers alone. At the national level, commercial materials such as textbooks, learning kits, and audiovisual materials are developed mainly by outside specialists. The No Child Left Behind Act of 2001 (Public Law 107-110) introduced unprecedented federal controls over K–12 school curricula in the 50 states. At the state level, departments of education have become increasingly active in curriculum development. Many states have legislated statewide competency tests for student promotion and graduation and have developed curriculum guides for local schools to ensure the teaching of those competencies. At the local level, many school systems have written their own curriculum guides for coordinating instruction across grade levels. This is done either by having curriculum specialists at the district level write the guides themselves, or by having such specialists work with representative teams of teachers (perhaps with community and student representation). Rarely do local schools turn curriculum development over entirely to teachers.

We can think about sources of curriculum development as shown by Figure 19.1 (see Oliva, 1992). Much curriculum is developed at the state, federal, and commercial levels. In other words, most curricula are produced far away from the local teacher and the local schools.

Curriculum Development as a Vehicle for Enhancing Collective Thinking about Instruction

It is a shame that most educators view curriculum as something given that they must follow. Books about curriculum development are widely neglected. Coursework in educational leadership programs gives curriculum short attention (at best, one required course). The criteria for assessing school leaders' performance largely ignores curriculum work as an important aspect of leadership responsibilities. Instead, assessment criteria emphasize "the monitoring of teachers using the district curriculum."

Why is it that curriculum is no longer a province for school inquiry and action, but rather a matter of complying with external mandates? The reason is that in the era of legislated learning, teachers and school leaders are seen as incapable of knowing what their students should be taught. State-mandated curricula and high-stakes achievement tests have taken the place of locally developed curricula.

The tragedy of curriculum being simply a response to state tests is the loss of a powerful vehicle for creating a broader instructional dialogue in a school or district that could enhance teachers' individual and collective thinking about the following questions: What is worth teaching? How shall we teach? How shall we assess? Most teachers—when trusted, when given time and money, and when given the assistance, choice, and responsibility to develop

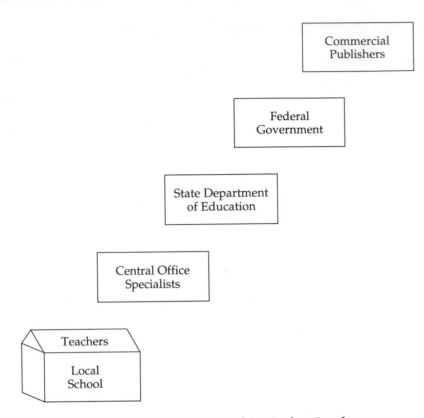

FIGURE 19.1 *Illustration of Sources of Curriculum Development*

curricula—will make extraordinarily sound decisions about what students should be taught. Often, their decisions will be far superior to those made in central offices, state departments, or commercial publishing firms (McEvoy, 1986; McNeil, 1988).

Teachers who are involved in making decisions about school curriculum go through changes in their own thinking about teaching. To discuss, debate, and finally come to an agreement with peers about what is important for students to know is an intellectually challenging experience.

It is clear that in order for schools to be successful, teachers need to be involved in curriculum development and focused on the following issues:

1. What should be the purpose of the curriculum?
2. What should be the content of the curriculum?
3. How should the curriculum be organized?
4. In what format should the curriculum be written?
5. At what level of curriculum development should teachers be involved?

Forthcoming sections will discuss each of these issues.

What Should Be the Purpose of the Curriculum?

Alternative beliefs about the purpose of the curriculum are described by Miller and Seller (1985) as orientations to curriculum. They describe three "metaorientations" or positions:

- In the *transmission position* the function of education is to transmit facts, skills, and values to students. Specifically, this orientation stresses mastery of traditional school subjects through traditional teaching methodologies. (pp. 5 and 6)
- In the *transaction position* the individual is seen as rational and capable of intelligent problem solving. Education is viewed as a dialogue between the student and the curriculum in which the student reconstructs knowledge through the dialogue process. The central elements in the transaction position are an emphasis on curriculum strategies that promote problem solving . . . application of problem solving skills within social contexts in general and within the context of the democratic process . . . and development of cognitive skills within the academic disciplines. (pp. 6 and 7)
- The *transformation position* focuses on personal and social change. It encompasses . . . teaching students skills that promote personal and social transformation . . . (and) a vision of social change as movement toward harmony with the environment rather than an effort to exert control over it. (p. 8)

If Miller and Seller's three orientations to curriculum sound vaguely familiar, it may be due to your review of educational philosophies in Chapter 5. The transmission curriculum orientation is related to the educational philosophy of essentialism. The transactional curriculum orientation is based largely on the philosophy of experimentalism. Finally, aspects of the transformation orientation are related to the philosophy of existentialism. In Chapter 5, we found that our educational beliefs help to shape our definition of effective teaching and instructional improvement. Similarly, curriculum orientations drive the curriculum-development process and affect curriculum purpose, content, organization, and format. Therefore, it is important that early in the curriculum design process the curriculum-development team examines alternative curriculum orientations and clarifies its own orientation. The most basic decision the team needs to make (with input from all stakeholders) is whether the purpose of the curriculum will be to transmit, transact, transform, or accomplish some combination thereof.

What Should Be the Content of the Curriculum?

Curriculum, for purposes of this book, is the *what* of instruction—what is intentionally taught to students in a district, school, or classroom. The elements of curriculum are sequence and continuity, scope, and balance (Doll, 1989). *Sequence* is the ordering of learning experiences, and *continuity* is the length or duration of such experiences. *Scope* is the range of learning experiences to be offered. *Balance* is the degree and amount of topics, subjects, and learning experiences that adequately prepare students. A curriculum is developed by deciding (1) What should students learn? (2) What is the order of content for the student to follow? (3) How is the learning to be evaluated? (See Firth and Newfield, 1984; Glatthorn, 1987; Brandt, 1988a; Clark and Clark, 2000; Gandal and Vranek, 2001.)

Decisions about curriculum content are influenced by priorities of state and federal governments, values of professional educators and local community, knowledge of student development, current economics, and future societal conditions. Underlying all decisions about curriculum content are curriculum orientations (transmission, transaction, or transformation), which ultimately are derived from educational philosophies (essentialism, experimentalism, or existentialism).

Benjamin Bloom's taxonomy of learning might serve as a guide for determining types of learning within or across content areas (Table 19.1). His lower-level learnings—(1) memory and (2) translation—are based on students recalling and demonstrating known answers. Curriculum objectives calling for memory and translation tend to dominate a curriculum with the purpose of transmission. Bloom's intermediate levels of learning—(3) interpretation, (4) application, and (5) analysis—are based on students using logic to discover relationships, solve

TABLE 19.1 *Bloom's Taxonomy*

Category Name	*Description*
1. Memory	Student recalls or recognizes information.
2. Translation	Student changes information into a different symbolic form or language.
3. Interpretation	Student discovers relationships among facts, generalizations, definitions, values, and skills.
4. Application	Student solves a life problem that requires the identification of the issue and the selection and use of appropriate generalizations and skills.
5. Analysis	Student solves a problem in the light of conscious knowledge of the parts and forms of thinking.
6. Synthesis	Student solves a problem that requires original creative thinking.
7. Evaluation	Student makes a judgment of good or bad, right or wrong, according to standards designated by student.

Source: G. Manson and A. A. Clegg, Jr., "Classroom Questions: Keys to Children's Thinking?" *Peabody Journal of Education, 47,* No. 5 (March 1970), 304–305. Reprinted by permission of Lawrence Erlbaum Associates, Inc.

problems, and reflect on their own thought processes. Curriculum objectives at the interpretation, application, and analysis levels are emphasized in a curriculum with the purpose of transaction. Finally, Bloom's higher levels of learning— (6) synthesis and (7) evaluation—are based on combining various facts, skills, knowledge, and logic to make unique personal judgments. Curriculum objectives at the synthesis and evaluation levels are prevalent in a curriculum with the purpose of transformation. By examining a written curriculum, then, we can ascertain whether its purpose (and the curriculum developers' underlying orientation) is transmission, transaction, or transformation.

How Should the Curriculum Be Organized?

Three broad approaches to organizing curriculum content are discipline based, interdisciplinary, and transdisciplinary. A *discipline-based curriculum* is described by Jacobs (1989):

> The discipline-based content design option focuses on a strict interpretation of the disciplines with separate subjects in separate time blocks during the school day. No attempt for integration is made, in fact, it is avoided. Traditional approaches to subjects such as language arts, mathematics, science, social studies, music, art, and physical education are the usual fare. In secondary programs, these general academic and arts areas break down into more specific fields, such as algebra under mathematics or American history under social studies. There are some variations of block scheduling and the way the week or cycle is programmed. Nevertheless, knowledge is presented in separate fields without a deliberate attempt to show the relationships among them. (p. 14)

Because of its emphasis on breaking learning down into discrete segments of traditional content to be learned in specified blocks of time, the discipline-based approach is best suited to a curriculum with the purpose of transmission. This approach clearly has been the dominant curriculum organization pattern in the United States.

In an *interdisciplinary curriculum,* common themes connect traditional content areas. For instance, different aspects of an instructional unit on transportation might be taught in science, math, social studies, language arts, art, music, and physical education. Or a set of common concepts or skills (for example, technology or problem-solving skills) might connect different subject areas throughout the year. Figure 19.2 illustrates an interdisciplinary curriculum. A curriculum organization of this type requires extensive team planning. Since the interdisciplinary approach encourages students to discover relationships and make applications across existing content areas, it is most appropriate for a curriculum with the purpose of transactional learning (Jenkins, 2005).

In a *transdisciplinary curriculum,* traditional disciplines do not exist. The entire curriculum is organized around common themes, skills, or problems. Daily learning activities are built around the topic being studied rather than conforming

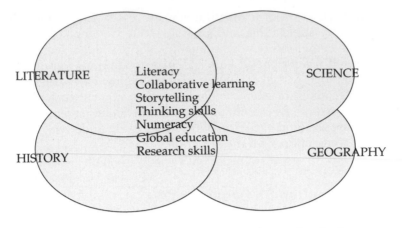

FIGURE 19.2 *Illustration of an Interdisciplinary Curriculum*

Source: S. M. Drake, J. Bebbington, S. Laksman, P. Mackie, N. Maynes, and L. Wayne (1992). *Developing an Integrated Curriculum Using the Story Model,* p. 4. Ontario: The Ontario Institute for Studies in Education Press. Reprinted with permission of University of Toronto Press.

to academic disciplines or class schedules. For example, while studying the concept of commerce, students could spend all of their school time developing, managing, and analyzing their own in-school "marketplace." Students might study selected content from economics, math, sociology, communication, politics, ethics, history, and other academic disciplines, but only as such content became relevant to the commercial community they were developing. Transdisciplinary curricula usually begin with very broad intended learning outcomes. The integration into the curriculum of contemporary problems from the real world and students' interests and concerns become part of an ongoing curriculum development process. This type of curriculum organization can be successful only if teachers are willing to totally reconceptualize their concept of the school curriculum. A transdisciplinary curriculum organization requires students to synthesize knowledge and skills from various content areas and encourages student creativity and self-direction. Such an organizational pattern is most consistent with a curriculum whose purpose is transforming teaching and learning.

In What Format Should the Curriculum Be Written?

This section will discuss various formats used in writing curriculum. Behavioral-objective, webbing, and results-only formats will be described. Like the content and organization of curriculum, the format it is written in reflects a curriculum's orientation. Behavioral-objective formats reflect a transmission orientation. Webbing formats reflect a transaction orientation. Results-only formats reflect a transformation orientation.

Behavioral-Objective Format

Predetermined knowledge, facts, and skills are written in curriculum guides in a linear cause-and-effect format. The curriculum developers determine what is to be learned, state the learning as a behavioral objective, specify the teaching/learning activities, and conclude with a posttest to see if the objective has been achieved. The progression is

Objective   Activity   Evaluation

Figure 19.3 is an example of a behavioral-objective guide written for a fifth-grade social studies class. Curriculum developers break their unit into the most important facts or skills that cover the subject. They write behavioral objectives for each fact or skill. Each behavioral objective is the basis for a sequence of activities and evaluation. The teacher who uses such a curriculum guide is expected to follow the sequence of activities and administer the evaluation. Recycling activities might be included in the guide for those students who do not pass the evaluation. Each behavioral-objective plan is tightly sequenced so that one objective is mastered before a student moves to the next (for example, after identifying and spelling the original 13 American colonies, the next objective might be identifying and spelling those states that came into the Union from 1776 to 1810).

Most school curricula that have been written in the last two decades follow a behavioral-objective format. It is particularly easy to use in subjects such as mathematics and physical sciences, where skills are obvious and facts are clear. (For example, 2 plus 2 is always 4, but is war always justifiable?)

Webbing

Curriculum can be written in a format that shows relationships of activities around a central theme. William Kilpatrick popularized this type of curriculum in writing about the work unit (Kilpatrick, 1925). Instead of predetermining the knowledge

---

Behavioral objective: At the end of the week, students will recall and spell the original 13 colonies at a 100 percent level of mastery.

Activities:

1. Lecture on 13 colonies.
2. Students fill in map of 13 colonies.
3. Students read pp. 113–118 of text and do assignments on p. 119 as homework.
4. Call on students at random to spell the various colonies.

Evaluation: Ask students to recall the names and spell correctly each of the 13 original colonies on a sheet of paper.

FIGURE 19.3 *Behavioral-Objective Format*

or skills, the curriculum developer determines the major theme, related themes, and then possible student activities, as shown in Figure 19.4a.

After the activities have been written, the curriculum developers write possible learning outcomes: "Students will be able to identify four major environmental issues." "Students will be able to argue and give evidence for both the pro and con sides of each issue." "Students will take a personal stance on each issue." In planning activities, developers consider multimodes of learning via reading, writing, listening, and constructing, and then integrate many fields of knowledge around a central theme. Notice how the theme of environmental issues integrates activities in sociology, mathematics, economics, history, journalism, physics, and biology.

A webbing curriculum guide would contain a blueprint of the web followed by sections for each related theme with activities, possible outcomes, and resources needed (see Figure 19.4b). Notice that the webbed curriculum includes possible outcomes and allows for the possibility of others. In a behavioral-objective curriculum, activities are controlled toward predetermined ends. In a webbed curriculum, activities lead to possible and unanticipated learning.

Results-Only Format

A results-only format for curriculum provides teachers with the widest latitude for using materials, activities, and methods. Such a curriculum specifies the goals and general learning about a subject, theme unit, or course. The guide might include ways to evaluate the learning. For example, a results-only guide in elementary reading might specify the following skills to be learned:

Comprehension

1. Develops powers of observation
2. Classifies by name, color, shape, size, positions, use
3. Anticipates endings to stories
4. Discriminates between fact and fantasy
5. Understands who, what, when, where, how, and why phrases
6. Recalls a story sequence

2. Related theme
3. Activities
4. Possible outcomes

2. Related theme
3. Activities
4. Possible outcomes

1. SUBJECT THEME

2. Related theme
3. Activities
4. Possible outcomes

2. Related theme
3. Activities
4. Possible outcomes

FIGURE 19.4a *Webbing Format*

7. Reads to find the main ideas of a story
8. Reads to draw a conclusion
9. Compares and contrasts stories

It is then left to the teacher to determine when and how to teach these skills. The teacher is held accountable only for the results, not for the procedures used.

Curriculum Format as Reflective of Choice Given to Teachers

The less specificity and detail a curriculum has, the greater the choice given to teachers to vary instruction according to the situation. Figure 19.5 illustrates the enlargement of teacher choice by curriculum.

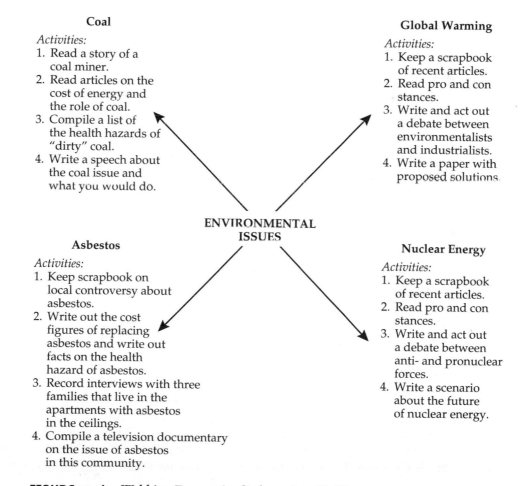

Coal

Activities:
1. Read a story of a coal miner.
2. Read articles on the cost of energy and the role of coal.
3. Compile a list of the health hazards of "dirty" coal.
4. Write a speech about the coal issue and what you would do.

Global Warming

Activities:
1. Keep a scrapbook of recent articles.
2. Read pro and con stances.
3. Write and act out a debate between environmentalists and industrialists.
4. Write a paper with proposed solutions.

ENVIRONMENTAL ISSUES

Asbestos

Activities:
1. Keep scrapbook on local controversy about asbestos.
2. Write out the cost figures of replacing asbestos and write out facts on the health hazard of asbestos.
3. Record interviews with three families that live in the apartments with asbestos in the ceilings.
4. Compile a television documentary on the issue of asbestos in this community.

Nuclear Energy

Activities:
1. Keep a scrapbook of recent articles.
2. Read pro and con stances.
3. Write and act out a debate between anti- and pronuclear forces.
4. Write a scenario about the future of nuclear energy.

FIGURE 19.4b *Webbing Format Applied to a Specific Theme*

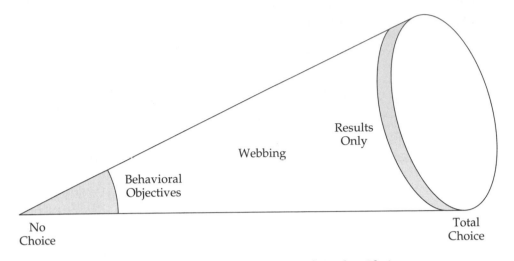

FIGURE 19.5   *Curriculum Format as a Reflection of Teacher Choice: The Curriculum Cone*

Picture being in a curriculum cone where, at the behavioral-objective bottom, a teacher can barely budge. As the teacher moves toward the webbing area, he or she finds room to move hands, feet, elbows, and knees. At the results-only end of the cone, the teacher can extend fully. If the teacher is allowed to step out of the curriculum cone, there are no limits on where and how he or she can move. Behavioral-objective formats predetermine the *what* and *how* of teaching as much as possible in a loosely coupled organization. Webbing formats focus on themes and relationships of possible activities for teachers but give them a choice of actual activities, duration of activities, and evaluation methods. A results-only format focuses on generalized learning and gives teachers the latitude to proceed as they wish.

It would appear relatively easy to match teacher stages of development to curriculum formats. It is not so easy, however; further examination of type and degree of involvement in curriculum development is necessary.

If a school has decided to use a behavioral-objective format, that does not necessarily mean that classroom teachers have little choice about how to teach. Perhaps the teachers have chosen to use that format; perhaps they wrote the curriculum themselves. Also, an elaborately detailed behavioral-objective curriculum could be presented to teachers as a reference guide to use as they wish. Simply knowing the format of the curriculum would not tell us how much choice was given to teachers. Although behavioral curricula usually are used as prescriptive teaching and can be equated with limiting choice, this is not always so. Therefore, before completing the picture of curriculum and teacher choice, it is necessary to consider how curricula are developed, interpreted, and implemented.

Relationship of Curriculum Purpose, Content, Organization, and Format

In previous sections we have proposed logical links between curriculum purpose, content, organization, and format. To review, a curriculum with the purpose of transmission is logically matched with memory and translation learning content, discipline-based curriculum organization, and behavioral-objective format. A curriculum with the purpose of transaction is well matched with interpretation, application, and analysis learning content; interdisciplinary curriculum organization; and webbing format. A curriculum with the purpose of transformation is consistent with synthesis and evaluation learning content, a transdisciplinary curriculum organization, and a results-only format. Table 19.2 illustrates logical relationships of curriculum purpose, content, organization, and format.

The "natural matches" we've outlined, of course, don't occur in all curricula. For instance, not all webbing formats are found within interdisciplinary curricula. The webbing format in Figure 19.4b, for example, could be part of a science course within a discipline-based curriculum. For another instance, a results-only curriculum format could focus on learning content at the lower and intermediate as well as the higher levels of Bloom's taxonomy, or could be part of a discipline-based or interdisciplinary rather than a transdisciplinary curriculum. In general, however, our own reviews of K–12 curricula indicate that the logical matches in Table 19.2 tend to hold true in most schools.

Levels of Teacher Involvement in Curriculum Development

Tanner and Tanner (1980) wrote of teachers and local schools functioning in curriculum development at one of three levels: imitative maintenance, mediative, or generative. Teachers at Level I are concerned with maintaining and following the existing curriculum. Teachers at Level II look at development as refining the existing curriculum. Teachers at Level III are concerned with improving and changing the curriculum according to the most current knowledge about learning and societal conditions. Tanner and Tanner explained these three levels according to Table 19.3.

TABLE 19.2 *Logical Relationships of Curriculum Purpose, Content, Organization, and Format*

Curriculum Purpose:	Transmission	Transaction	Transformation
Curriculum Content:	Memory Translation	Interpretation Application Analysis	Synthesis Evaluation
Curriculum Organization:	Discipline Based	Interdisciplinary	Transdisciplinary
Curriculum Format:	Behavioral Objective	Webbing	Results Only

TABLE 19.3   *Levels of Teacher Involvement in Curriculum Development*

Level	*Locus*	*Tasks and Activities*	*Principal Resources*

Level I: Imitative maintenance	Microcurriculum
	Established
	  conditions
	Segmental treatment
		Rudimentary
		Routine
		Adoptive
		Maintenance of
		  established practice
			Textbook, workbook, syllabi (subject by subject), segmental adoption of curriculum packages, popular educational literature, school principal

Level II: Mediative	Microcurriculum
	Established
	  conditions
	Segmental treatment
	Awareness of:
	  emergent conditions
	  aggregate treatment
	  macrocurriculum
		Interpretive
		Adaptive
		Refinement of
		  established practice
			Textbook, courses of study (subject by subject with occasional correlation of subjects), multimedia, adaptation of segmental curriculum packages, professional literature on approved practice

			Pupils, teacher colleagues, helping teacher, supervisor, curriculum coordinator, parents, community resources, school principal, in-service courses

Level III: Generative	Macrocurriculum
	Emergent conditions
	Aggregate treatment
		Interpretive
		Adaptive
		Evaluative:
		  problem-diagnosis
		  problem-solving
		Improvement of
		  established practice
		Search for
		  improved practice
			Textbook, courses of study (across subjects and grade levels), alternative modes of curriculum design, professional literature on research and approved practice, multimedia, projects

			Pupils, teacher colleagues, helping teacher, supervisor, curriculum coordinator, parents, community resources, school principal, in-service courses, outside consultants, experimental programs, professional conferences and workshops

Source: Daniel Tanner and Laurel N. Tanner, *Curriculum Development: Theory into Practice* (2nd ed.), p. 637. Copyright © 1980. Reprinted by permission of Pearson Education, Inc., Upper Saddle River, New Jersey.

Level I: Imitative Maintenance

Teachers operating at Level I rely on textbooks, workbooks, and routine activities, subject by subject. Skills are treated as dead ends rather than as means of generating further learning. Readymade materials are used without critical evaluation, resulting in a multiplicity of isolated skill-development activities. (The already segmental curriculum is further fragmented.) The imagination of the teacher does not go beyond maintaining the status quo. This teacher would like to think that he or she has less freedom than he or she may actually have for curriculum improvement. In the secondary school, concern for curriculum development is largely confined to each departmental domain.

When change is made, it is made on the adoption level, without adaptation to local needs. As shown in Table 19.3 curriculum development at this level is plugging in the package to the existing situation without attention to the resulting interactions. Teachers at this level tend to be left alone to struggle with innovations that are handed to them from above. Schools are turned inward, with the principal as the sole resource for classroom assistance.

Level II: Mediative

Teachers at Level II are aware of the need to integrate curriculum content and deal with emergent conditions. (Societal problems such as the energy crisis and children's questions about things that interest and concern them are examples of emergent conditions.) Although teachers at this level may have an aggregate conception of curriculum, implementation does not go beyond the occasional correlation of certain subjects. The focus of curriculum remains segmental; theory remains divorced from practice; curriculum improvement remains at the level of refining existing practice.

Yet teachers at the second level of curriculum development do not blindly plug in an innovation or curriculum package to the existing situation. The necessary adaptations, accommodations, and adjustments are made [see Table 19.3] of and capitalize on a range of resources for curriculum improvement, including pupils, parents, and peers; and they utilize resources beyond the local school. Teachers are consumers of professional literature on approved practices and tap the resources of the university through in-service courses. The mediative level is a level of awareness and accommodation. Teachers are attracted to, and can articulate, new ideas but their efforts to improve the curriculum fall short of the necessary reconstruction for substantive problem solving.

Level III: Creative-Generative

As shown in [Table 19.3] teachers at Level III take an aggregate approach to curriculum development. Ideally, the curriculum is examined in its entirety by the teacher and the whole school staff, and questions of priority and relationship are asked. While individual teachers can and should be at the generative-creative level, a macrocurricular approach requires cooperative planning for vertical and horizontal articulation.

Granted that teachers as individuals usually cannot create new schoolwide curricula, an individual teacher can establish continuities and relationships in his or her own teaching and with other teachers. Teachers at Level III use generalizations and problems as centers of curriculum organization. They stress the broad concepts that specialized subjects share in common, and they use and develop courses of study that cross subject fields. These are aggregate treatments.

Teachers at the third level of curriculum development think about what they are doing and try to find more effective ways of working. They are able to diagnose their problems and formulate hypotheses for solutions. They experiment in their classrooms and communicate their insights to other teachers.

Teachers at this level are consumers of research and seek greater responsibility for curriculum decisions at the school and classroom levels. They exercise independent judgment in selecting curriculum materials and adapt them to local needs. They regard themselves as professionals and, as such, are continually involved in the problems of making decisions regarding learning experiences. To this end, their antennae are turned outward to a wide range of resources.*

Integrating Curriculum Format with Developers and Levels of Development

To integrate what has been said about curriculum format, developers, and development, refer to Figure 19.6. When the developers are either outside the school

*Daniel Tanner and Laurel N. Tanner, *Curriculum Development: Theory into Practice,* 2nd ed., pp. 636, 638–639. Copyright © 1980. Reprinted by permission of Pearson Education, Inc., Upper Saddle River, New Jersey.

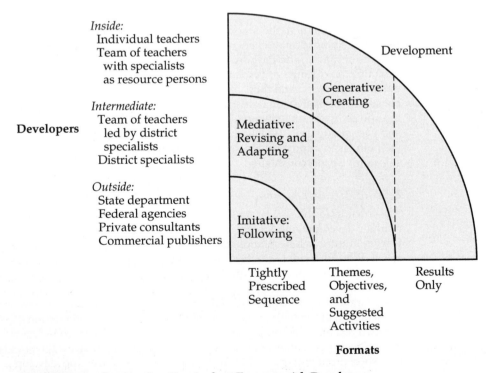

FIGURE 19.6 *Integrating Curriculum Format with Developers and Levels of Development*

system or from the district level and the curriculum is in a tightly prescribed format, development will be primarily *imitative,* characterized by teachers following the course of study. When the developers are intermediate teams of teachers led by district specialists and the curriculum is written with objectives and suggested activities, development will be primarily *mediative,* characterized by teachers revising and adapting the course of study to their immediate situation. When curriculum developers are teams of teachers using specialists as resource persons or individual teachers with a results-only curriculum format that identifies what students should learn and leaves activities to the teacher, then development is *generative,* characterized by ongoing creativity.

Matching Curriculum Development with Teacher Development

A progression of curriculum development matched with teacher development might look like Table 19.4. The supervisor might think of his or her staff in terms of the commitment, thinking, and expertise they currently bring to curriculum and then determine whether the current curriculum is appropriately matched

TABLE 19.4 *Progression of Curriculum Matched with Characteristics of Staff*

Staff Characteristics	Low	Moderate	High
Commitment to curriculum change	Low commitment to change	Would like to make change	Eager to make change
Level of thinking about curriculum	Low ability to think about possible changes	Can think of some possible changes	Has many suggestions
Expertise in curriculum procedures	Low expertise in how to proceed	Does not know how to write curriculum	Knows how to proceed
Curriculum Characteristics			
Developers	Outside developers	Outside developed but substantially revised by team of teachers led by specialists	Internally developed by team of teachers with specialists as resource
Format	Behavioral-objective, highly structured	Webbing	Results-only, with suggested activities
Development	Imitative, with allowance for minor revisions	To be mutually adapted	To be discussed and changed continually

with the teachers' level of curriculum functioning. If the present curriculum is inappropriate to teachers' development, readjustments to the curriculum would be in order.

A staff that has a low level of curriculum functioning—as displayed by little commitment to change, little ability to suggest possible changes, and little curriculum expertise—*initially* would be matched with an outside-developed, behavioral-objective, and imitative curriculum. They should be allowed to make minor revisions in adapting the curriculum to their classrooms. On the other hand, a staff that has a moderate level of curriculum functioning (as displayed by a desire to change, ability to think of possible changes, but a lack of expertise in writing curriculum) would be appropriately matched with a curriculum originally developed by outside experts but substantially revised by an internal team of teachers led by a curriculum specialist. The format of the curriculum might be webbing. Throughout the development and implementation, teachers should have problem-solving meetings for purposes of curriculum adaptation. Finally, a staff that is at a high level of curriculum functioning (as displayed by initiating and suggesting ways to change and knowing how to proceed in creating curriculum) would be appropriately matched with an internally developed curriculum. The format should emphasize "results only" with *suggested* activities, and should be continuously open to revision.

The supervisor should keep in mind the question: How does one increase teacher control over curriculum making? If a staff has been appropriately matched—for example, low-functioning staff with an imitative curriculum—and successful implementation is occurring, then the supervisor should plan for the next cycle of curriculum development to give teachers additional responsibilities by serving on decision-making teams under the leadership of a curriculum specialist. This would lead to more mutually adaptive curriculum and at the same time continue to stimulate and increase teacher commitment, development, and expertise.

The supervisor wishing to facilitate changes in curriculum purpose, content, organization, and format must remember that successful change will be based on teachers changing their conceptions of curriculum and their level of involvement in curriculum development. Changes in teachers *and* curriculum are more likely to be successful if done in an incremental manner. For example, rather than announcing that the school will be moving from a discipline-based to interdisciplinary curriculum organization, the supervisor could initially encourage small teams of teachers functioning at moderate to high levels of development, expertise, and commitment to plan and teach a few interdisciplinary units of instruction throughout the school year. In another school already operating at an interdisciplinary level, movement toward a transdisciplinary curriculum could begin with a group of teachers operating at high levels of development, expertise, and commitment forming a "broad field." A *broad field* results from the fusion of two or more separate disciplines. Courses or subjects (rather than departments) with titles like "humanities," "social science," and "natural science" usually reflect a broad-field approach. The formation of one or more broad fields involving a subset of faculty and curricula would not represent a fully transdisciplinary curriculum, but would be a major step in that direction.

Large-scale teacher-driven changes in curriculum content, organization, and format will not take place unless teachers change their curriculum orientations or beliefs about the purpose of curriculum. Yet teachers are not likely to change their orientations unless their levels of understanding of and involvement in curriculum development gradually increase. Supervisor openness and trust building, staff development in curriculum design, and time, support, and rewards for teacher involvement can all foster teacher *and* curriculum development. Throughout the curriculum-development process, the supervisor must remember that if he or she has a curriculum orientation or favors a curriculum content, organization, or format different from teachers, he or she is not necessarily right and the teachers wrong. Government mandates, the community, the school's mission and culture, parents, teachers, and students must all be considered when deciding which direction curriculum development should take and at what rate it should proceed.

The Curriculum and Cultural Diversity

There are a variety of reasons why the curriculum should be culturally diverse. First, students from nondominant cultures are not likely to reach their learning potential if the curriculum ignores their culture. Second, a society cannot offer democracy, equal opportunity, and justice for all unless it experiences, understands, and respects the variety of cultures that make up the society. Third, communities and societies that recognize the value of diversity and invite citizens from different cultures to participate in their development enjoy more educational, economic, and social success; the quality of life for all citizens improves. A culturally diverse curriculum, then, benefits all students, as well as the community and society.

How do schools integrate multicultural and ethnic content into their curriculum? James Banks (2005) describes four approaches to integration. Banks presents the approaches as four levels of integration, with Level 1 the least effective and Level 4 the most effective. Level 1, the *contributions approach,* calls for inserting minority culture heroes, holidays, and elements (food, dances, music, art) into the curriculum alongside mainstream content. This is the easiest approach to implement, but it leaves the curriculum virtually unchanged. Level 2, the *additive approach,* adds concepts and perspectives from other cultures to the mainstream curriculum without changing the curriculum's basic structure. This approach might include adding books by minority authors, a few units of instruction, or a single course to the curriculum. Level 3, the *transformation approach,* changes the fundamental structure of the curriculum by enabling students to consider concepts, issues, and problems from several different cultural perspectives rather than from only the dominant culture's perspective. Finally, level 4, the *social action approach,* includes all aspects of the transformation approach but also requires students to engage in critical inquiry about cultural issues and problems and to take action for social change. Figure 19.7 summarizes the four approaches.

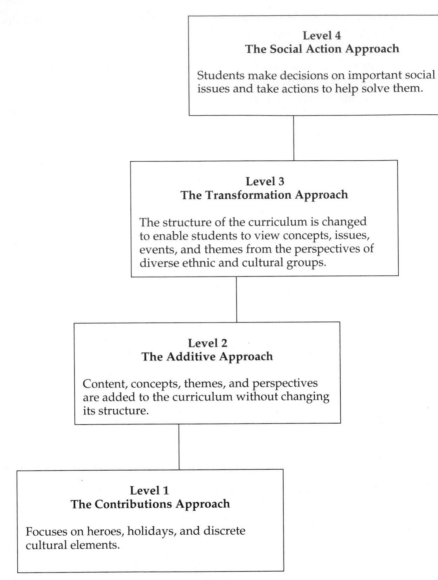

FIGURE 19.7 *Levels of Integration of Ethnic Content*

Source: J. A. Banks, "Approaches to Multicultural Curriculum Reform." In J. A. Banks and C. A. Mc-
Ghee Banks (Eds.), *Multicultural Education: Issues and Perspectives* (5th ed.), p. 246. Copyright © 2005
by John Wiley & Sons, Inc.

Other scholars support Banks's assertion that transformative and social action approaches are more effective at integrating multicultural content into the
curriculum than the contributions or additive approaches (Bennett, 2003; Gay,
1995; Nieto, 2000). Unfortunately, many school curricula have not gone beyond

the contributions approach. Why the gap between scholarship on multicultural curriculum and practice? Geneva Gay (2005) offers an explanation:

> Most school teachers and administrators have good intentions about implementing the ideas and proposals suggested in the scholarship on multicultural education. Unfortunately, many do not have the knowledge base and pedagogical skills needed. Others are still struggling with how to resolve what they see as inherent tensions between the national ideals of the United States embedded in the motto *E Pluribus Unum* and recognizing, accepting, and promoting diversity in schools and society. Confusion is still rampant over calls for diversity, equity, and excellence in education. Too many educators continue to believe that to treat students differently based on their cultural heritages, ethnic identities, and background experiences are synonymous to discrimination, and to promote diversity is to compromise high-quality performance and standards of excellence. This confusion drives some educators to question the merits of education for diversity, to judge it divisive and counterproductive, and to redefine it in ways that reaffirm their comfort levels and serve their own proposes. These reactions have different consequences on efforts to implement multicultural education, but in general they produce distortions, inaccuracies, and misconceptions that are not consistent with the thinking, research, and writing of multicultural education scholars. (pp. 109–110)

Gay (2005) proposes that we begin to close the gap between scholarship and practice by developing well-articulated guidelines for translating theoretical principles into practice, establishing performance standards for educators, and providing professional development to help educators meet those standards. The professional development Gay proposes would be long-term, assisting educators to develop self-understanding, cultural knowledge, and multicultural education skills.

SUMMARY

Teachers will implement curriculum successfully if they have been involved in its development and can adapt it to their specific classroom and school situation. The failure of the teacher-proof curriculum movement should remind us that imposing curriculum from outside is useless. Instead, the questions for supervisors to consider have to do with type and degree of curriculum development. The supervisor can pick from six arenas. The first arena includes sources of development, ranging from teachers to district-level personnel, state and federal experts, and commercial writers. The second arena involves the purpose of the curriculum, based on one of three curriculum orientations: transmission, transaction, or transformation. The third arena consists of the content emphasis of curriculum: the lower, middle, or higher levels of Bloom's taxonomy. The fourth arena involves curriculum organization, including discipline-based, interdisciplinary, and transdisciplinary curricula. The fifth arena is curriculum format, including behavioral-objective, webbing, and results-only formats. Finally, the sixth arena consists of levels of teacher involvement, including imitative-maintenance, mediative, and creative-generative levels. The supervisor and teachers should work together to select curriculum purpose, content, organization, and format that (1) is most appropriate for the students and (2) increases teachers' choice and commitment to curriculum implementation. Curriculum, when treated as a task for school action, is a powerful, relatively nonthreatening intervention for enhancing collective thought and action about instruction.

REFERENCES AND RECOMMENDED READINGS

Applebee, A. N., Langer, S. A., and Mullis, V. S. 1987. *Literature and U.S. History: The instructional experience and factual knowledge of high school juniors. The nation's report card.* Princeton, NJ: Educational Testing Service.

Banks, J. A. 2005. Approaches to multicultural curriculum reform. In J. A. Banks and C. A. McGhee Banks (Eds.), *Multicultural education: Issues and perspectives* (5th ed., pp. 242–264). Hoboken, NJ: Wiley.

Bennett, C. I. 2003. *Comprehensive multicultural education: Theory and practice* (5th ed.). Boston: Allyn and Bacon.

Bloom, A. 1987. *The closing of the American mind.* New York: Simon and Schuster.

Brandt, R. S. (Ed.). 1988a. Content of the curriculum, 1988. In *ASCD Yearbook.* Alexandria, VA: Association for Supervision and Curriculum Development.

Brandt, R. S. 1988b. On assessment in the arts: A conversation with Howard Gardner. *Educational Leadership, 45*(4), 30–34.

Brubaker, D. L. 1982. *Curriculum planning: The dynamics of theory and practice.* Glenview, IL: Scott Foresman.

Clark, D. C., and Clark, S. N. 2000. Appropriate assessment strategies for young adolescents in an era of standards-based reform. *The Clearing House, 73*(4), 201–204.

Cornbleth, C. 1981. Curriculum materials can make a difference. *Educational Leadership, 38*(7), 567–568.

Cremin, L. A. 1976. *Public education.* New York: Basic Books.

Doll, R. C. 1989. *Curriculum improvement: Decision making and process* (6th ed.). Boston: Allyn and Bacon.

Drake, S. M., Bebbington, J., Laksman, S., Mackie, P., Marnes, N., and Wayne, L. 1992. *Developing an integrated curriculum using the story model.* Toronto: The Ontario Institute for Studies in Education.

Driscoll, M. 1988. Transforming the "under achieving" math curriculum. *ASCD Curriculum Update* (January), p. 6.

Eisner, E. W., and Vallance, E. 1974. *Conflicting conceptions of curriculum.* Berkeley, CA: McCutchan.

Firth, G. R., and Newfield, J. W. 1984. Curriculum development and selection. In J. M. Cooper (Ed.), *Developing skills for instructional supervision.* New York: Longman.

Gandal, M., and Vranek, J. 2001. Standards: Here today, here tomorrow. *Educational leadership, 59*(1), 6–13.

Gay, G. 1995. Bridging multicultural theory and practice. *Multicultural Education, 3,* 4–9.

Gay, G. 2005. Standards for diversity. In S. P. Gordon (Ed.), *Standards for instructional supervision: Enhancing teaching and learning.* Larchmont, NY: Eye on Education.

Glatthorn, A. A. 1987. *Curriculum renewal.* Alexandria, VA: Association for Supervision and Curriculum Development.

Glickman, C. D. 1999. *School based authority and responsibility.* Unpublished invited report to the Georgia Governor's Education Reform Study Commission. Atlanta, GA: The Office of the Governor of Georgia.

Goodlad, J. 1984. *A place called school.* New York: McGraw-Hill.

Hirsch, E. D., Jr. 1987. *Cultural literacy: What every American needs to know.* Boston: Houghton Mifflin.

Jackson, P. W. 1969. Technology and the teacher. In Committee for Economic Development, *The school and the challenge of innovation.* New York: McGraw-Hill.

Jacobs, H. H. 1989. *Interdisciplinary curriculum: Design and implementation.* Alexandria, VA:

Association for Supervision and Curriculum Development.

Jenkins, R. A. 2005. Interdisciplinary instruction in the inclusion classroom. *Teaching Exceptional Children, 37*(5), 42–48.

Kilpatrick, W. H. 1925. *Foundations of method.* New York: Macmillan.

Kirst, M., and Walker, D. 1971. An analysis of curriculum policy-making. *Review of Educational Research, 41*(5), 479–509.

Manson, G., and Clegg, A. A., Jr. 1970. Classroom questions: Keys to children's thinking? *Peabody Journal of Education, 47*(5), 304–305.

McEvoy, B. 1986. *"Against our better judgements." Three teachers' enactment of mandated curriculum.* Paper presented at the annual meeting of the American Educational Research Association, San Francisco.

McNeil, L. N. 1988. Contradictions of control, Part 2. Teachers, students and curriculum. *Kappan, 69*(6), 432–438.

Miller, J. P., and Seller, W. 1985. *Curriculum: Perspectives and practice.* New York: Longman.

Nieto, S. 2000. *Affirming diversity The sociopolitical context of multicultural education.* New York: Longman.

Oliva, P. F. 1992. *Developing the curriculum* (3rd ed.). New York: HarperCollins.

Ravitch, D., and Finn, L. E., Jr. 1987. *What do our 17-year-olds know? A report of the First National Assessment of History and Literature.* New York: Harper and Row.

Rutter, M., Maughan, B., Mortimore, P., Ouston, J., and Smith, A. 1979. *Fifteen thousand hours: Secondary schools and their effects on children.* Cambridge, MA: Harvard University Press.

Saylor, J. G., Alexander, W. M., and Lewis, A. 1981. *Curriculum planning for better teaching and learning* (4th ed.). New York: Holt, Rinehart and Winston.

Sergiovanni, T. 1987. *Introduction to the Breckinridge Conference on Restructuring Schools.* San Antonio, TX: August.

Sizer, T. R. 1984. *Horace's compromise: The dilemma of the American high school.* Boston: Houghton Mifflin.

Tanner, D., and Tanner, L. W. 1980. *Curriculum development: Theory into practice* (2nd ed.). Upper Saddle River, NJ: Pearson Education.

Weick, K. E. 1976. Educational organizations as loosely coupled systems. *Administrative Science Quarterly, 21,* 1–19.

Zeuli, J. S., and Buchmann, M. 1988. Implementation of teacher thinking research as curriculum deliberation. *Journal of Curriculum Studies, 20*(2), 141–154.

20

Action Research
The School as the Center of Inquiry

Why should our schools not be staffed, gradually if you will, by scholar-teachers in command of the conceptual tools and methods of inquiry requisite to investigating the learning process as it operates in their own classrooms? Why should our schools not nurture the continuing wisdom and power of such scholar-teachers? (Schaefer, 1967, p. 5)

The famous social scientist, Kurt Lewin, devoted his career to studying democracy and the relationships of individuals within groups. His contributions ushered in the school of gestalt psychology, group dynamics, and the concept of action research. He argued that social research should be based on the actions groups take to improve their conditions. Social research should not focus on controlled experiments, removed from real conditions. As people plan changes and engage in real activities, fact-finding should determine whether success is being achieved and whether further planning and action are necessary (Lewin, 1948, p. 206).

Stephen Corey applied Lewin's concept of action research to education. He argued that traditional research is done mainly by researchers outside the public school and has little influence on school practice. Corey wrote:

Learning that changes behavior substantially is most likely to result when a person himself tries to improve a situation that makes a difference to him . . . when he defines the problem, hypothesizes actions that may help him cope with it, engages in these actions, studies the consequences, and generalizes from them, he will more frequently internalize the experience than when all this is done for him by somebody else, and he reads about it. . . . The value of action research . . . is determined primarily by the extent to which findings lead to improvement in the practices of the people engaged in the research. (1953, p. 9)

Thus, action research in education is study conducted by colleagues in a school setting to improve instruction. Although an individual teacher can conduct action research, in most cases it is best done as a cooperative endeavor by faculty attempting to improve on a common instructional concern (see Calhoun, 2002).

As Richard Sagor (1993) wrote, "By turning to *collaborative* action research . . . we can renew our commitment to thoughtful teaching and also begin developing an active community of professionals" (p. 10). Action research implies that the practitioners are the researchers. The objectivity and rigor of research methodology can be questioned by classical researchers, but the benefits of the process for students and teachers seem to outweigh the loss of experimental purity.

In addressing the power of teacher-led research, Hubbard and Power (1993, p. xiii) wrote: "Teachers throughout the world are developing professionally by becoming teacher-researchers, a wonderful new breed of artists-in-residence. Using our own classrooms as laboratories and our students as collaborators, we are changing the way we work with students as we look at our classrooms systematically through research." Table 20.1 compares traditional research with action research.

How Is Action Research Conducted?

In the first phase of action research, a focus area is selected—an area of teaching and learning in need of improvement. Second, a needs assessment gathers data on

TABLE 20.1 *Comparison of Traditional Research and Action Research*

	Traditional Research	*Action Research*
Usually led by	Outside expert	Practitioners
Purpose	Develop new knowledge	Solve practical problem, improve practice
Types of data gathered	Quantitative or qualitative	Quantitative or qualitative
Purpose of gathering and analyzing data	Gain better understanding of phenomenon, develop or test hypotheses	Explore practical problem, guide action planning, evaluate results
Standard for quality research	Peer review of methods and results	The research results in desired change
Primary audience(s)	Other researchers, the profession, government or private agencies	Members of the school community

the focus area. The purposes of data gathering at this stage are to understand the problem and how it might be solved and to gather baseline data to help with the evaluation of improvement efforts. The third phase of action research is to design an action plan for solving the problem. The plan includes activities for evaluating the success of improvement efforts. The fourth phase is the implementation of the plan. The fifth phase of action research is the evaluation; data on the action plan's effects are gathered and analyzed. Based on the evaluation, action plan objectives and activities may be continued, expanded, revised, or discontinued.

If these five phases sound suspiciously similar to the development of action plans with individual teachers in Chapter 16 (direct assistance), you have won the first round of the supervision concentration game. The aim of direct assistance to teachers is to promote increased thought, choice, and responsibility in individual teachers, and this can be done through cycles of classroom action research. The supervisor's role is to determine what type of assistance the individual teacher needs (directive informational, collaborative, or nondirective), depending on the developmental levels of the teacher with respect to the particular topic. Figure 20.1 depicts the five phases of action research.

A Developmental Approach to Action Research

The developmental model we have discussed throughout this text can be applied to action research. Of the four supervisory approaches discussed in Part III, the

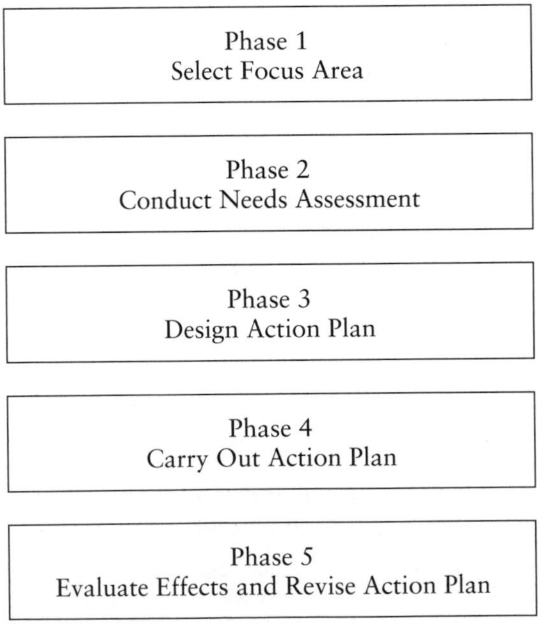

Phase 1
Select Focus Area

Phase 2
Conduct Needs Assessment

Phase 3
Design Action Plan

Phase 4
Carry Out Action Plan

Phase 5
Evaluate Effects and Revise Action Plan

FIGURE 20.1   *Five Phases of Action Research*

directive informational, collaborative, and nondirective approaches are appropriate for supervising action research. Since teacher action research involves teachers making their own decisions about inquiry and instructional improvement, controlling directive supervision is inappropriate for such research.

Teachers of *very* low levels of development, expertise, and commitment are probably not ready to engage in action research. They will need to receive intensive direct assistance and staff development to help them develop the minimal decision-making capacity and motivation necessary for successful action research. They might be asked to read and discuss articles about action research, shadow a teacher or group engaged in research, or attend a workshop to develop action research skills. For teachers of *fairly* low levels of development, expertise, and commitment, the supervisor can use directive informational supervision while suggesting alternative goals, data-collection and analysis methods, and action plans, and then asking teachers to choose from the alternatives. Since this type of action research involves limited teacher decision making, the supervisor will wish to move toward collaborative action research as soon as teachers are ready to assume more decision-making responsibility (McBee, 2004).

The supervisor can engage in collaborative action research with teachers of moderate or mixed levels of development, expertise, and commitment. In this approach, the supervisor engages in joint decision making with teachers during the goal identification, action planning, implementation, evaluation, and revision phases of action research. Even collaborative action research is a transitional form of teacher inquiry. The ultimate goal is for teachers to reach levels of development, expertise, and commitment that allow teacher-driven research, in which the supervisor uses nondirective supervision to facilitate teacher decision making during each of the five phases of action research. Houser (1990) described full-fledged "teacher-researchers": "They initiate every aspect of the research project. They are responsible for formulating the questions, selecting the (research) tools, and collecting, analyzing, and interpreting the data" (p. 58).

Decisions about Action Research

Collective action research can integrate direct assistance, group development, professional development, and curriculum development. Prior to the beginning of action research, the supervisor chooses an appropriate entry strategy for working with an action research team. The choice of interpersonal approach is shown in Table 20.2.

First, the team conducts a needs assessment of faculty and collects baseline data to determine common goals for improvement of instruction. Techniques for conducting a needs assessment can be chosen from the following list:

- Eyes and ears
- Systematic classroom and school observations
- Official records

TABLE 20.2 *Choosing an Interpersonal Approach*

Interpersonal Behaviors	Decision
Nondirective: listening reflecting clarifying encouraging	High teacher/low supervisor
Collaborative: presenting problem solving negotiating	Equal teacher/supervisor
Directive informational: presenting problem solving directing alternatives	Low teacher/high supervisor

Characteristics of Teachers
levels of development   expertise   commitment

- Review of teacher and student work products
- Third-party review
- Written open-ended survey
- Check and ranking lists
- Delphi technique
- Nominal group
- Cause and effect diagrams
- Flowcharts
- Pareto charts

Explanations of each assessment technique can be found in Chapter 13.

Second, the team brainstorms activities that will cut across supervision tasks. The team can respond to these four questions corresponding to supervisory tasks:

1. What type and frequency of direct assistance must be provided to teachers to reach our instructional goals?
2. What meetings and discussions need to be arranged as part of group development for faculty to share and reach our instructional goals?
3. What professional development opportunities, such as lectures, workshops, demonstrations, courses, and visits, need to be provided for faculty to reach our instructional goals?

4. What is the necessary curriculum development, in terms of course content, curriculum guides, lesson plans, and instructional materials, to reach our instructional goals.

These tasks of supervision are explained in Chapters 16, 17, 18, and 19.

Third, the team makes a plan relating activities to goals. Techniques for writing plans are as follows:

- Affinity diagrams
- Impact analysis chart
- Gantt chart
- Force field analysis
- PDSA cycle
- Strategic planning

A description of each planning device can be found in Chapter 13.

Fourth, the team determines ways to observe the progress of the action plan as it is implemented in classrooms. Observations can be made with the use of the following instruments:

- Categorical frequency
- Performance indicator
- Visual diagramming
- Space utilization
- Verbatim
- Detached open-ended narrative
- Participant open-ended observation
- Focused questionnaire
- Tailored observation systems

Use of these instruments is explained in Chapter 14.

Fifth, the team chooses an evaluation design that will enable them to analyze data, determine whether objectives have been met, and decide what further actions need to be taken. The design can be quantitative, qualitative, or a combination of both. Questions to be asked in the evaluation include the following:

- What is the purpose of the evaluation?
- Who will evaluate?
- What questions need to be answered?
- What and how will data be gathered?
- How will the data be analyzed?
- How will the evaluation be reported?

To understand the components of a comprehensive evaluation, refer to Chapter 15.

Action Research: Vehicle for a Cause beyond Oneself

Previously, each task of supervision (direct assistance, group development, professional development, and curriculum development) was discussed separately. In reality, any effort to improve instruction must relate each task to the others. It is time to soften the boundaries between the tasks and show how action research can be the vehicle for their integration.

Action research is focused on the need to improve instruction, as perceived by the faculty. As instructional improvements are identified, faculty and supervisor plan related activities to be implemented in each of the tasks of supervision (see Figure 20.2).

Think of action research as a huge meteor falling into the middle of the supervision ocean. As it hits, it causes a rippling of water that activates the four seas of direct assistance, professional development, curriculum development, and group development. The rippling of water continues to increase in force until a giant wave gathers and crashes onto all instructional shores, sweeping away the old sand of past instructional failures and replacing it with the new sand of instructional improvement. Stepping away from the beach, let's look at some examples of action research related to supervisory activities.

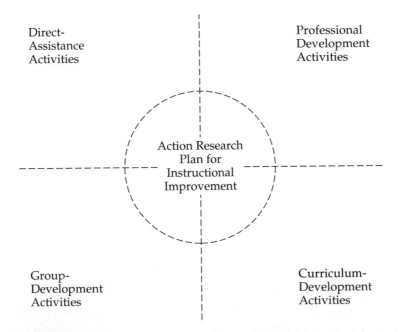

FIGURE 20.2 *Action Research as the Core of Related Supervisory Activities*

Example of Action Research

Matthews Elementary School is located in the heart of Austin, Texas. Matthews serves students from 32 different cultures. The student population includes children from the local Salvation Army shelter and city children's center. Matthews also serves the children of an international community of professors and graduate students from a nearby university. Approximately 50 percent of Matthews' students are classified as at-risk. The goal of action research at Matthews was to improve the school's balanced reading program. Needs assessment data gathered included student results on two reading tests, indicating that a large number of students were reading below grade level. Data on teacher perceptions of the reading program was gathered through surveys and interviews. Based on the needs assessment, the action plan called for acquisition of additional resources for the reading program, professional development for teachers, and more effective monitoring of the program.

In the first component of the action plan, teachers participated in discussion groups to identify needed resources. In response to these meetings, new nonfiction and fiction books, books on tape, and a variety of new instructional materials were added to the program. The professional development component included monthly meetings of support groups in which teachers learned new strategies, discussed concerns, and shared ideas. Balanced reading also was discussed at general faculty and vertical team meetings. A supervisor served as a mentor for new teachers, providing them assistance as they implemented balanced reading. Two literacy specialists served as support persons to all teachers, leading support groups, teaching demonstration lessons, and visiting classrooms. Teachers visited other schools to observe balanced reading lessons, participated in district workshops on balanced reading, and attended national reading conferences. The last component of the action plan was improved monitoring of the reading program. This included supervisors and reading specialists observing classrooms to determine if balanced reading was being implemented effectively and also to make sure that teachers were receiving the resources and support they needed. Teachers played a major role in monitoring. They assessed student progress daily by analyzing student work samples, keeping anecdotal records, and listening to students' oral reading. Additionally, teachers used a standardized reading assessment to measure students' reading levels in September, January, and May.

Year-end evaluation of the action research included teacher surveys and interviews as well as pre-post comparisons of student reading levels. Teachers reported a high commitment to balanced reading, understanding of the reading program, and confidence in their ability to implement the program. The teachers stated that they now had adequate materials to implement balanced reading and that strategies they learned through professional development enabled them to understand strengths and needs of students and to individualize student learning. Analysis of student achievement data supported teacher perceptions. Over the school years there were increases in the percentage of students—including the percentage of economically disadvantaged students—reading on or above grade level. By the end of the school year 85 percent of all students were reading on or above grade level.

Expanding Boundaries: Alternative Approaches to Action Research

The approach to action research emphasized in this book, as well as in most schools that use action research, is a problem-solving approach. A problem is identified, needs assessment data are gathered to find out more about the problem, an action plan is designed to solve the problem, the plan is implemented, and evaluation data are gathered to determine what progress has been made and what revisions in the action plan might be needed. There are alternative approaches to action research that schools may wish to consider, including interpretive and critical action research.

Interpretive Action Research

Teachers doing interpretive research are attempting to understand phenomena in schools and the meaning participants make of those phenomena. Examples that might be studied include a school's culture, classroom implementation of a new curriculum, and interactions between teachers and students during classroom discussions of controversial issues. For a more detailed example, let us say a group of teachers decided to carry out an interpretive study on the use of a new inquiry-based science program. Research questions might include the following:

1. What does the teacher experience during inquiry learning?
2. What does the student experience during inquiry learning?
3. How does the teacher describe learning that results from inquiry learning?
4. How does the student describe learning that results from inquiry learning?

To gather data on these questions, interpretive researchers might observe inquiry lessons and take extensive field notes on class activities, interactions between teachers and students and among students, and so on. Additionally, the teacher-researchers might conduct interviews with teachers and students on their experiences with inquiry learning and their interpretation of learning resulting from inquiry lessons. The researchers probably would find that different participants experience the same learning activities differently and construct different interpretations of inquiry learning. Through dialogue on alternative perspectives and interpretations identified in the action research, teachers can gain a more holistic understanding of the phenomena being studied. The dialogue, and increased understanding that results, can be the foundation for improved practice. For instance, based on the results of their interpretive research, teachers in our inquiry-learning example might modify the way they present science problems to students.

Critical Action Research

Critical research examines and challenges established, taken-for-granted practices that help maintain certain inequities, with an eye toward changing practice to increase equity. In particular, critical research examines power relationships that lead to inequity. External social, economic, and political forces that cause inequity also are examined, and ways to overcome those forces' negative effects are considered. An important process used by critical researchers is *praxis,* which denotes an interactive cycle of practice and theory building. In critical action research, praxis takes the form of an ongoing cycle of action and reflection aimed at emancipating groups and individuals from inequitable treatment.

Teachers engaged in critical action research on a high school's tracking system could begin the research by formulating a set of critical questions like the following:

- Whose interests are served by the existence of the tracking system?
- What cultural values are reinforced by the tracking system? What cultural values are delegitimized?
- What power relationships are present in the current tracking system?
- How does the tracking system reflect socioeconomic realities in the community that the school serves?
- How does the tracking system reflect ethnic and racial issues present in society?
- Who decides which students are placed in the various tracks?
- Who is placed at an advantage by the tracking system? Who is placed at a disadvantage?

Teachers engaging in critical action research find answers to these questions through repeated cycles of data gathering and dialogue on the meaning of the data. Eventually, the researchers begin to focus on a series of questions about changing the system to increase equity.

- How can we include parents and students in decisions about how to best meet student learning needs?
- How can the diverse learning needs of students be met in an emancipatory way?
- What methods of grouping students will benefit the least-advantaged students?
- How can student grouping promote democracy and social justice?
- How can the growth and development of all students be placed in the center of the decision-making process at this school?

Again, teachers would go about finding answers to these questions through repeated cycles of data gathering and dialogue. In time, teachers and other members of the school community would use research results as the basis for changes in decision making, student grouping, curriculum, and instruction. The test for the effectiveness of critical action research is whether equity has been increased in a meaningful way.

Shared Governance for Action Research

A shortcoming of earlier studies of school improvement and action research was the lack of descriptions of how individual schools or districts went about the process of change (Fullan, 1985, p. 398). Achieving "a cause beyond oneself" in pursuing collaborative and collective instructional goals for students sounds admirable, but how does a supervisor initiate and sustain such efforts? What follows is one explanation, using case studies from the public schools that are part of the League of Professional Schools (Glickman, 1992). The model of shared governance and schoolwide instructional change has been adapted and used in elementary, middle, and secondary schools in Georgia, South Carolina, Vermont, Michigan, and the United States Department of Defense Dependent Schools in Europe.

Premises

Three declarative premises underlie shared governance.

1. Every professional in the school who so desires can be involved in making decisions about schoolwide instructional improvements.
2. Any professional in the school who does not desire to is not obligated to be involved in making decisions about schoolwide instructional improvements.
3. Once a decision is made about schoolwide instructional improvements, all staff must implement the decision.

Thus, an individual can choose to be or not to be part of the decision-making process. However, once decisions are made, all individuals must implement the agreed-on actions. Operationalizing these premises allows a school to move forward with people who are interested in participating, without forcing any individual who is not interested into a corner. Afterward, an individual who did not wish to participate in making decisions has no grounds for complaint about decisions on schoolwide instructional actions. Perhaps when the next issue, concern, or topic is brought up for schoolwide action, nonparticipants who have been disgruntled with previous decisions will have a renewed interest in participating.

Principles in Operating Shared Governance for Instructional Improvement

1. *One person, one vote.* Each representative has the same rights, responsibilities, and equal vote as any other representative. Each teacher who sits on the representative schoolwide council has the same vote as the school principal or any

other administrator or formal supervisor. This means, in practical terms, that an individual administrator or supervisor cannot get his or her own way on decisions about instructional improvement, just as a single teacher representative cannot get his or her own way. Decisions are made by the group, so expertise, influence, and credibility are more important than power and authority.

2. *Limit decisions to schoolwide instruction within the control and sphere of responsibility of the school.* Action research and shared governance involves the core of a school's existence: curriculum and instruction, or teaching and learning. Areas for decision making should be schoolwide and instructional. Issues of day-to-day administration, contracts, school board policies, other schools, and personnel are not the concerns of shared governance for schoolwide action research. The scope of concerns for deliberations, decisions, and actions is always grounded in the question: What should *we* be doing *here* with *our* school to improve learning for *our* students?

This is not to dismiss the influence on student learning of external policies and operations, nor is it to suggest that changes to improve conditions for students should not be pursued at levels beyond the school. It is simply to suggest that unless a school has a clear, streamlined mechanism for keeping the focus on creating a dialogue about instruction within the school, shared governance will often dissipate into a depository of complaints about noninstructional concerns. Time and energy spent on complaining or proposing what other schools, parents, the central office, and school board should do (which the individual school has no legal or direct control over) take time and energy away from instructional changes that *can* be made. (Talking about others can be an excuse for not talking about ourselves.)

3. *Authentic feedback necessitates small groups.* To call a faculty meeting with a large staff for the intended purpose of an open, freewheeling discussion of ideas, opinions, and positions is at best misguided, if not outright manipulative. Large meetings result in input from the most confident, the loudest, and the most powerful persons—who are not necessarily the wisest, most insightful, or most interested persons. A true forum for intellectual discourse is a small group (ideally, 7 to 11 members); therefore, shared governance in large schools must operate in small groups.

Operational Model

The work of Schmuck, Runkel, Arends, and Arends (1977) has provided the basis for an operational model for shared governance, action research, and school improvement that uses the premises of individual choice of involvement and implementation by all and the principles of one-person, one-vote; focus on teaching; and small groups. The model discussed here is a compilation of various models used by schools in the League of Professional Schools (see Glickman, 1992; Allen and Glickman, 1992). Many schools use comparable models of operation and have their own specific versions. The goal is not to advocate a particular model of shared governance, but rather to achieve the premises and principles of shared governance and action research, leading to a purposeful, collective, and thoughtful school—a school that is the center of inquiry.

The Formal Groups.   Shared governance in this model involves three groups (see Figure 20.3). *The executive council* is a 7- to 11-member body, consisting of a majority of teachers with administrators. Parent and student representatives can serve as well. (For more details about representation of other groups, see Glickman, 1993.) Teachers could be democratically chosen from liaison groups (described in the following paragraph) or from among grade-level heads, team leaders, department heads, and union representatives. They could be elected at large from the faculty, or some combination of election and appointment could be used. They hold a term of at least three years and move off the council at staggered times. Teachers serve as chairperson and co-chairperson of the executive council. The principal is a member of the committee with the same rights and responsibilities as any other member. The executive council's responsibility is solely for acting on and monitoring schoolwide instructional improvement recommendations. *The council does not make recommendations;* it is an approving board. Recommendations must come from task force groups within the school. The executive council does not involve itself in administrative matters, school board policies, personnel matters, or issues that are departmental in nature. It acts on instructional improvement recommendations that the faculty has the legal power to carry out. This differentiation between instructional and administrative responsibilities helps avoid problems that can arise from delving into matters beyond the school's own control.

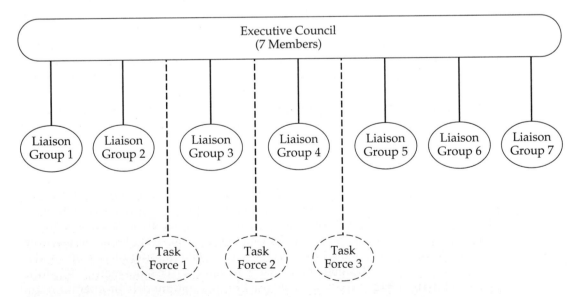

FIGURE 20.3 *Action Research as the Core of Related Supervisory Activities*

Liaison groups are formal groups set up as communication links between the faculty and executive council concerning needs, reactions, opinions, and ideas about schoolwide instruction. Liaison groups are an important unit for considering the faculty's ideas and opinions about assessing instructional goals and responding to proposed recommendations. For example, in the case of a school with 50 teachers, there could be seven liaison groups consisting of approximately 7 faculty members each. An alphabetized list of all faculty names is gathered and each person is assigned a number from 1 to 7. All 1s go to liaison group 1, all 2s go to liaison group 2, and so forth. This assignment procedure ensures that members in each liaison group come from various departments and grade levels. Each liaison group is a microcosm of the entire school. Each group elects a representative to the council. The executive council member can (a) call the liaison group together from time to time for a brief meeting to review a specific recommendation under executive council consideration, (b) gather written opinions about a particular proposal, or (c) simply drop by and talk to the various liaison group members.

Task forces are the last groups shown in Figure 20.3. These ad hoc task groups of volunteers are formed after the executive council has solicited feedback from all the liaison groups about perceived schoolwide instructional needs and reviewed any existing data on schoolwide instruction. The executive council then targets priority instructional areas for the next one to three years. Schoolwide priorities might be such matters as increasing instructional time, coordinating curriculum, improving student attitudes, teaching higher-order thinking, increasing student success rates, improving school discipline, improving school and classroom climate, improving the quality of feedback to students, or improving test scores.

Once the needs for improvement have been selected by the executive council, ad hoc task force groups are formed by recruiting volunteers who have an interest in and a commitment to the particular topic. At least one executive council member serves on each task force, but this person normally does not serve as chair of the task force. The task force volunteers meet, review their task, select their own chairperson, schedule meetings, and set a timeline for making a final recommendation for schoolwide action to the executive council. Depending on the topic, one task force might meet three times over three weeks to make a recommendation, whereas another task force might meet every other week for five months before making a recommendation.

Decision-Making Procedures.   When the task force is ready to make a recommendation, it makes its report in three parts: (1) goals and objectives, (2) action plan (what will be done, by whom, and when), and (3) evaluation (how the success of actions will be known). The executive council discusses the recommendations and either makes an immediate decision to approve (most councils use a consensus vote to approve a first-time recommendation) or, without the required vote, tables the recommendation until the next meeting. During the interim, the executive council members can discuss the recommendation and check with their respective liaison groups to gather input from the entire faculty. At the next meeting, a second vote can be taken. (Most councils use a two-thirds vote to approve a tabled recommendation.) By the second vote, the council will have a good sense of total faculty receptivity and the chances of successful implementation. Some issues are deemed so important by the council that the final decision is made by going back to the entire faculty, parents, and students.

Implementation. After a decision has been made, the executive council (with the task force) announces the approved plan to the school. The task force then disbands, and the executive council implements the plan. It becomes the responsibility of the executive council (including the principal) to enforce the schoolwide decisions and to oversee action research that monitors and evaluates the results.

Suggestions for Assisting Action Research

Beyond the governance structure described above, our work with schools using action research leads to additional suggestions for increasing the quality of teacher research. First, it is important that teachers receive basic preparation in gathering and analyzing data. Here we are not talking about making every teacher an expert in research design and statistical analysis. Rather, teachers should be introduced to a variety of simple data-gathering methods, both quantitative and qualitative. Also, teachers need to learn simple methods for reviewing and summarizing data and drawing data-based conclusions. Second, to ensure that no teachers or students are placed at academic, social, or emotional risk, the school governance body should establish a set of ethical guidelines for action research, along with a process for reviewing research proposals to make sure they comply with the guidelines. Third, resources need to be provided for action research teams. The most important resource needed by teacher-researchers is *time* to plan action research, gather and analyze data, and implement action plans. Finally, teachers should be provided opportunities to share action research with the school community, and even with teachers from other schools. Sharing action research gives recognition to the teacher-researchers, serves as a basis for reflective dialogue among teachers, and provides other teachers ideas for improving instruction in their own classrooms and schools.

Conclusion: Focus, Structure, and Time for Development

Supervision provides a focus, structure, and time for teachers to be engaged in dialogue, debate, research, decisions, and actions about instruction. Without focus, teachers will not discuss teaching, because it has not been an accepted norm for discussion in most schools. Without structure, there are no clear apparatus, procedures, and rules for how decisions are made and implemented. Without time, there is no functional or symbolic expression that teachers have the capacity to make collective and wise instructional decisions on behalf of students.

REFERENCES AND RECOMMENDED READINGS

Allen, L., and Glickman, C. D. 1992. School improvement: The elusive faces of shared governance. *NASSP Bulletin, 76(542),* 80–87.

Calhoun, E. F. 1992. *A status report on action research in the League of Professional Schools.* Paper presented at the annual meeting of the American Educational Research Association, San Francisco, April.

Calhoun, E. F. 2002. Action research for school improvement. *Educational Leadership, 59(6),* 18–24.

Corey, S. M. 1953. *Action research to improve school practices.* New York: Teachers College, Columbia University.

Fullan, M. 1985. Change processes and strategies at the local level. *Elementary School Journal, 85(3),* 391–421.

Glickman, C. D. 1989. *Shared governance at Ogelthorpe County High School.* Athens, GA: Monographs in Education.

Glickman, C. D. 1992. The essence of school renewal: The prose has begun. *Educational Leadership, 50(1),* 24–27.

Glickman, C. D. 1993. *Renewing America's schools. A guide for school-based action.* San Francisco: Jossey-Bass.

Glickman, C. D., and Wright, L. V. 1986. Decision making in schools. In P. R. Burden (Ed.), *Establishing career ladders in teaching: A guide for policy makers* (pp. 111–129). Springfield, IL: Charles C. Thomas.

Gottfredson, C. 1985. *Effective school battery: User's manual.* Odessa, FL: Psychological Assessment Resources.

Houser, N. O. 1990. Teacher-researcher: The synthesis of roles for teacher empowerment. *Action in Teacher Education, 12(2),* 55–60.

Hubbard, R. S., and Power, B. M. 1993. *The art of classroom inquiry: A handbook for teacher-researchers.* Portsmouth, NH: Heinemann.

Lewin, K. 1948. *Resolving social conflicts.* New York: Harper and Brothers.

McBee, M. T. 2004. The classroom as laboratory: An exploration of teacher research. *Roeper Review, 27(1),* 52–58.

Sagor, R. 1993. *How to conduct collaborative action research.* Alexandria, VA: Association for Supervision and Curriculum Development.

Schaefer, R. 1967. *The school as the center of inquiry.* New York: Harper and Row.

Schmuck, R. A., Runkel, P., Arends, J. H., and Arends, R. I. 1977. *The second handbook of organizational development in schools.* Palo Alto, CA: Mayfield.

Function of SuperVision

The chapters in Part VI address aspects of supervision that transcend traditional knowledge, skills, and tasks of supervision. Chapter 21 focuses on the change process, viewing it from both the supervisor's and the teacher's perspectives. Chaos theory is discussed in relation to change, and applied to schools and classrooms. Cultures of change are described, and we argue for changing the conditions of teaching. Chapter 22 discusses democratic and moral purpose. Ten moral principles of the "good school" are presented. The moral dilemma brought about by the No Child Left Behind Act is examined, and short-term as well as long-term strategies for addressing No Child Left Behind are proposed.

SuperVision, Change, and School Success

- ▶ **Assumptions about Change**
- ▶ **Change from the Teacher's View**
- ▶ **Chaos Theory and Change**
- ▶ **Chaos Theory Applied to School Change**
- ▶ **Implications of Chaos Theory at the Classroom Level**
- ▶ **Creating a Culture for Change**
- ▶ **Changing the Conditions of Teaching**
- ▶ **What Is School Success?**

Although not all change represents progress, progress—by definition—is not possible without change. Facilitating change necessary for instructional improvement is a supervisory function that cuts across all five tasks of supervision. Initiating a clinical supervision program (direct assistance), assisting teachers in deciding on schoolwide instructional improvement goals (group development), delivering a skill-development program in which teachers learn new models of teaching (professional development), moving from a discipline-based to an interdisciplinary curriculum (curriculum development), and assisting teachers as they conduct research on a new classroom management system (action research) are all examples of facilitating change. In this chapter, we will look at assumptions about change, change from the teacher's view, a developmental view of change strategies, creating a culture for change, changing the conditions of teaching, the role of supervision and supervisors in school improvement, and school success.

Assumptions about Change

After many years of research and reflection on change in schools, Michael Fullan (1991) proposed 10 assumptions about change. Our own experience with change efforts in schools leads us to agree with Fullan's assumptions:

1. Do not assume that your version of what the change should be is the one that should or could be implemented. On the contrary, assume that one of

the main purposes of the process of implementation is to exchange your reality of what should be through interaction with implementers and others concerned. Stated another way, assume that successful implementation consists of some transformation or continual development of initial ideas. . . .

2. Assume that any significant innovation, if it is to result in change, requires individual implementers to work out their own meaning. Significant change involves a certain amount of ambiguity, ambivalence, and uncertainty for the individual about the meaning of change. Thus, effective implementation is a process of clarification. . . .

3. Assume that conflict and disagreement are not only inevitable but fundamental to successful change. . . .

4. Assume that people need pressure to change (even in directions that they desire), but it will be effective only under conditions that allow them to react, to form their own position, to interact with other implementers, to obtain technical assistance, etc. . . .

5. Assume that effective change takes time. Unrealistic or undefined time lines fail to recognize that implementation occurs developmentally. Significant change in the form of implementing specific innovations can be expected to take a minimum of two to three years; bringing about institutional reforms can take five or more years. Persistence is a critical attribute of successful change.

6. Do not assume that the reason for lack of implementation is outright rejection of the values embodied in the change, or hard-core resistance to all change. Assume that there are a number of possible reasons: value rejection, inadequate resources to support implementation, insufficient time elapsed.

7. Do not expect all or even most people or groups to change. The complexity of change is such that it is impossible to bring about widespread reform in any large social system. Progress occurs when we take steps (e.g., by following the assumptions listed here) that increase the number of people affected. . . .

8. Assume that you will need a plan that is based on the above assumptions and that addresses the factors known to affect implementation. . . . Evolutionary planning and problem-coping models based on knowledge of the change process are essential. . . .

9. Assume that no amount of knowledge will ever make it totally clear what action should be taken. Action decisions are a combination of valid on-the-spot decisions, and intuition. . . .

10. Assume that changing the culture of institutions is the real agenda, not implementing single innovations. Put another way, when implementing particular innovations, we should always pay attention to whether the institution is developing or not. (pp. 105–107)*

Guskey's (1994, pp. 9–20) six guidelines for promoting professional development and change are consistent with Fullan's assumptions:

- Guideline 1: Recognize that change is both an individual and an organizational process
- Guideline 2: In planning and implementation, think BIG, but start SMALL (emphasis in original)
- Guideline 3: Work in teams to maintain support
- Guideline 4: Include procedures for feedback on results
- Guideline 5: Provide continued follow-up, support, and pressure
- Guideline 6: Integrate programs (integrate innovations into existing frameworks)

Change from the Teacher's View

Gene Hall and Shirley Hord (1987) have extended the work of Frances Fuller (1969) on teacher concerns (discussed in Chapter 4) and described seven stages of concern about school innovations (numbered from stages 0 through 6). Figure 21.1 describes each of these stages. Note that awareness as well as informational and personal concerns about the innovation relate to Fuller's self-concerns; management concerns about the innovation relate to Fuller's task concerns; and consequence, collaboration, and refocusing concerns about the innovation relate to Fuller's impact concerns. Teachers are not likely to move to higher stages of concern until their lower-stage concerns have been addressed.

To help us better understand stages of concern, Hord and associates (Hord, Rutherford, Huling-Austin, and Hall, 1987) have provided "expressions of concern" made by individuals at each stage of concern. Table 21.1 lists stages and expressions of concerns. The supervisor's role is to facilitate teachers' movement through stages of concern—*and* implementation of the innovation—by (1) assessing individual and group stages of concern and (2) meeting the needs of teachers and groups at various stages. The supervisor can assess teachers' stages of concern through conferencing, open-ended concerns statements, and questionnaires (see Hall and Hord, 1987).

Chaos Theory and Change

Chaos theory cuts across a wide number of disciplines, including biology, chemistry, mathematics, meteorology, and physics. The "new science" of chaos has two foci. The first is the exploration of the hidden order that exists within chaotic systems. The second is the study of how self-organization emerges from chaos (Hayles, 1990). Chaos theory involves a number of related concepts, not all of which are relevant to change in schools and classrooms. Several aspects

Impact   6   REFOCUSING: The focus is on exploration of more universal benefits from the innovation, including the possibility of major changes or replacement with a more powerful alternative. Individual has definite ideas about alternatives to the proposed or existing form of the innovation.

5   COLLABORATION: The focus is on coordination and cooperation with others regarding use of the innovation.

4   CONSEQUENCE: Attention focuses on impact of the innovation on student in his or her immediate sphere of influence. The focus is on relevance of the innovation for students, evaluation of student outcomes, including performance and competencies, and changes needed to increase student outcomes.

Task   3   MANAGEMENT: Attention is focused on the processes and tasks of using the innovation and the best use of information and resources. Issues related to efficiency, organizing, managing, scheduling, and time demands are utmost.

Self   2   PERSONAL: Individual is uncertain about the demands of the innovation, his or her inadequacy to meet those demands, and his or her role with the innovation. This includes analysis of his or her role in relation to the reward structure of the organization, decision making, and consideration of potential conflicts with existing structures or personal commitment. Financial or status implications of the program for self and colleagues may also be reflected.

1   INFORMATIONAL: A general awareness of the innovation and interest in learning more detail about it is indicated. The person seems to be unworried about himself or herself in relation to the innovation. She or he is interested in substantive aspects of the innovation in a selfless manner such as general characteristics, effects, and requirements for use.

0   AWARENESS: Little concern about or involvement with the innovation is indicated.

FIGURE 21.1   *Stages of Concern about the Innovation*

Source: Reprinted by permission from *Change in Schools: Facilitating the Process,* edited by Gene Hall and Shirley Hord, the State University of New York Press. © 1987 State University of New York. All rights reserved.

of chaos theory that have significance for educational change are reviewed here.

Nonlinearity

In a linear system simple cause-and-effect relationships exist; A causes B which causes C, and so on. A linear system is analogous to tipping over the first in a line of dominoes. The falling first domino knocks down the second, the second knocks down the third, and so on. A chaotic system is nonlinear. A nonlinear system is analogous to throwing a bowling ball toward a set of pins. Myriad variables come

TABLE 21.1 *Stages and Expressions of Concern*

Stages of Concern			Expressions of Concern
I M P A C T	6	Refocusing	I have some ideas about something that would work even better.
	5	Collaboration	I am concerned about relating what I am doing with what other instructors are doing.
	4	Consequence	How is my use affecting kids?
T A S K	3	Management	I seem to be spending all my time getting material ready.
S E L F	2	Personal	How will using it affect me?
	1	Informational	I would like to know more about it.
	0	Awareness	I am not concerned about it (the innovation).

Source: Taking Charge of Change by S. M. Hord, W. L. Rutherford, L. Huling-Austin, and G. E. Hall. Copyright 1987 by the Association for Supervision and Curriculum Development in the format Textbook via Copyright Clearance Center.

into play and interact with each other. The slightest variation in how the bowling ball is released may result in a strike in one frame, and a split or a gutter ball in the next.

Complexity

Chaotic systems take complex forms, making their precise measurement difficult if not impossible. Chapter 5's discussion on measuring the coast of Britain is an example of the problem with measuring complex forms; the method of measurement affects the measure. If one uses 200-mile-long rulers, the coast of Britain is 1600 miles long. If the rulers are 25 miles long, the length increases to 2,550 miles (Smith, 1995). As the length of the rulers becomes shorter, the length of the coast of Britain increases, on to infinity (Briggs and Peat, 1989).

Butterfly Effect

This phenomenon is technically known as *sensitive dependence on initial conditions*. This means that a small and seemingly unrelated event in one part of a system can have enormous effects on other parts of the system. Theoretical meteorologist Edward Lorenz made the term *butterfly effect* famous when he argued that a butterfly stirring its wings in Beijing today could unleash powerful storms in New York City next month. One implication of sensitive dependence on initial conditions is the impossibility of predicting not only next year's weather, but the long-term future of any chaotic system.

Fractals

A fractal is a geometric shape that is similar to itself at different scales. Mid-sized branches of a tree are remarkably similar in shape to the larger branches from which they come. Smaller branches, in turn, are the same shape as the mid-sized branches from which they come, and so on. Other examples of fractals include coastlines, mountains, clouds, rivers, weather patterns, and the human vascular system. Complex social systems can also reveal self-similarity on different scales: at each level of the system, specific patterns of organization and culture reappear.

Feedback Mechanisms

Chaotic systems contain feedback loops enabling outputs to feed back into the system as input. Feedback can bring stability or turbulence to a system. For example, a thermostat is a feedback mechanism that causes temperature stability. Conversely, when the sound from a loudspeaker feeds back through a microphone, it is rapidly magnified to create a disruptive shriek (Gleick, 1987). Feedback can also cause a system to move toward greater levels of complexity. Physicist Joseph Ford, for example, has referred to evolution as "chaos with feedback."

Turbulence

Turbulence can be caused from disturbances inside or outside of a system. Consider a river, flowing smoothly until it runs through a bed of rocks. The water is perturbed and becomes unstable. Turbulence can also be caused by a heavy rain that greatly increases the volume of water flowing through the river bed. The more complex a system is, the more subject it is to instability due to turbulence. If instability becomes great enough, a point of phase transition is reached; sudden, radical change takes place, resulting in either reorganization or disintegration.

Strange Attractors

Chaotic systems are not truly random. Rather, they possess patterns that are extremely complex and unpredictable, but that stay within certain parameters. Strange attractors are "deeply encoded structures" within chaotic systems (Hayles, 1990).

> The discovery that chaos possesses deep structures of order is all the more remarkable because of the wide range of systems that demonstrate this behavior. They range from lynx fur returns to outbreaks of measles epidemics, from the rise and fall of the Nile River to eye movements in schizophrenics. (Hayles, 1990, p. 10)

To summarize, chaos theory informs us that order and chaos are not opposites. Rather, in the words of Margaret Wheatley (1992) they are "mirror images, one containing the other" (p. 11).

Chaos Theory Applied to School Change

School improvement efforts traditionally have treated the change process as linear, with each step in the change effort affecting the next step in a simple cause-and-effect relationship. But despite linear organization charts and improvement plans, schools are not linear systems; they are *nonlinear,* chaotic systems. An implication for this reality is that, rather than viewing a change effort as a blueprint to be drawn and followed, it should be viewed as an organic process:

> Here the metaphor for change is the growth and development of a complex organism (for example a human being) rather than the operation of a simple machine. A complex organism begins life at a relatively small stage. Its development is not completely predictable. Its health requires interdependence, consistency, and balance among its various subsystems. Finally, organisms that flourish tend to be adaptable to changing environments. In fact, they are themselves in a constant state of change or "becoming." (Gordon, 1992, p. 73)

The fact that schools are nonlinear systems means that change cannot be controlled from above. It can only be nurtured by promoting a culture for change. The supervisor attempting to nurture such a culture needs to remember Fullan's admonition not to believe that the change the supervisor envisions is the one that should or even could be implemented. Rather it is the interaction of the supervisor's ideas about change with ideas from other members of the school community—and the interaction of the change process with many other variables within the school culture—that will determine the direction of change.

The *complexity* of schools means that neither external research on effective schools, nor legislated standards, nor the results of standardized achievement tests can, by themselves, precisely measure improvement needs or the level of success of improvement efforts. Keedy and Achilles (1997) argue that local educators must ask:

1. Why they want to change
2. What they want to achieve
3. How to go about the change process (p. 116)

We would argue that local educators need to ask a fourth question as well: *how to measure success.* Keedy and Achilles recommend that supervisors and teachers reach consensus on these questions through collaborative, critical inquiry informed by awareness of the change process.

The *butterfly effect* applies to school change: it is impossible to predict the long-term effects of school improvement efforts. This does not mean that formal planning for school change should not take place. It does mean that a different type of planning is needed. Planning in a chaotic system like a school should be medium range (one to two years) rather than long range (five to ten years). It should emphasize general goals, broad guidelines, and built-in flexibility (Gordon, 1992). Formal planning in an unpredictable system needs to focus on process rather than product, with the goal of producing "a stream of wise decisions designed to achieve the mission of the organization" (Patterson, Purkey, and Parker, 1986).

Like *fractals* in nature, schools reveal self-similarity in different scales. For example, a schoolwide staff development day, a department meeting, a classroom lesson, and a hallway interaction between a teacher and student might all reveal the same cultural characteristic. Thus reflective inquiry at the school, team, classroom, and individual level can help educators better understand their school culture, needed change, and pathways to improvement.

Once school improvement efforts are under way, feedback becomes essential for monitoring and assessing change. *Feedback mechanisms* need to be created and maintained. Feedback can take the form of student performance data, survey results, quality circles, third party reviews, and so forth. The important thing is that meaningful data on the results of change efforts be made available to teachers, and that they be given opportunities to reflect on the data and redirect their change efforts accordingly.

All complex systems experience *turbulence,* but efforts at change tend to increase its frequency and intensity. Turbulence is not always negative. Without some perturbance, the system would remain in a steady state and improvement would not be possible. However, too much turbulence (from outside or inside the school) can cause school improvement efforts to disintegrate. Keedy and Achilles (1997, p. 115) maintain that supervisors and teachers should construct a normative consensus—"a collective, critically examined, and contextually-based agreement" of essential school norms that they can hold fast to during times of turbulence. He maintains that it is this normative consensus (referred to earlier in this text as a "cause beyond oneself") that can hold a school together during the change process.

Finally, *strange attractors,* those deeply encoded structures within chaotic systems, have implications for school change. Is it possible for supervisors and teachers to create strange attractors within schools that will—albeit in unpredictable ways—create permanent patterns leading to school improvement? Policy makers have attempted to do just that, mandating such structures as site-based management, shared decision making, and parent choice (Keedy, 1995). However, these structures have all failed to lead to patterns of improvement. Keedy (1995) maintains that the design that should be embedded throughout the social fabric of schools—for our purpose a "strange attractor"—is *student-centered learning.* He also believes that embedding this design within traditional schools is an extremely difficult task, and that the best chance for making student-centered learning a school's underlying pattern is the design of new schools around that concept.

Implications of Chaos Theory at the Classroom Level

Chaos theory has implications beyond the school level. Classrooms and even individual students can be considered chaotic systems (the reader smiles and nods in agreement)! All joking aside, chaos theory is consistent with recent research that the brain learns in *nonlinear* ways. This calls into question a host of traditional classroom practices, including grouping students by age, separate subjects, a sequential curriculum, and discrete behavioral objectives (Rockler, 1990–1991; Tygestad, 1997; Bloch, 2005). Nonlinearity supports constructivist teaching and learning as discussed in Chapter 5.

Complexity implies that student learning can take many different forms and can be expressed in different ways. This means that teachers should place less emphasis on any single indicator of student aptitude or achievement. It especially calls into question use of the standardized achievement test as the sole measure of student growth (Rockler, 1990–91; Stiggins, 2002; Coladarci, 2002; Clark and Clark, 2000; Newell, 2002; Behuniak, 2002). Complexity suggests the use of multiple measures of student learning, matching different assessment measures to different learning goals. It also supports the use of authentic assessment methods. Finally, complexity gives credence to the idea of allowing students to participate in planning assessment and in making self-evaluation part of the assessment process.

The *butterfly effect* means that a wide variety of factors seemingly unrelated to a lesson plan (whether a student argued with a parent the night before, ate breakfast, or made a new friend on the school bus that morning) can lead to significant differences in what takes place in the classroom when the lesson is taught and how the lesson affects an individual student's learning. The butterfly effect ensures that no lesson will ever go completely as planned, or have the same effect on any two students. It indicates the need for teacher flexibility in teaching, as well as the need for individual attention to students, each of whom is experiencing a given lesson within his or her own personal context.

If the butterfly effect accounts for differences in classroom interactions and student outcomes, *fractals* are a metaphor for patterns that can be observed on different scales within the classroom. Systematic classroom observation can record behaviors and effects that cut across whole-class, small-group, and individual levels. Additionally, patterned behaviors and interactions can be observed from lesson to lesson. Reflective inquiry into classroom practice, whether in the form of clinical supervision, peer coaching, or action research, can help the teacher to identify patterns that foster and hinder student learning, and to alter the learning environment accordingly.

Feedback mechanisms can have positive or negative effects on classroom teaching and learning. For example, high-stakes testing (much to the chagrin of those who design the tests) can become a negative mechanism. In many cases, feedback on student performance on high-stakes tests has led teachers to ignore curriculum not measured by the test and teach to the test through "drill and kill" methods focused on practice test items. With all of the the unpredictability present in classrooms, beneficial feedback is critical for both teachers and students. For teachers, student performance data, direct student feedback, and classroom observation data can all assist teachers to improve classroom instruction. Skill at what Donald Schon calls "reflection in action" enables teachers to receive and analyze feedback and respond to that feedback while in the act of teaching. For students, feedback on their cognitive and affective performance—from teachers, parents, and peers—is an essential part of the learning process. The fact that in chaotic systems like classrooms output becomes input means that the artificial distinctions we often draw between learning and assessment need to be removed; in reality, learning and assessment cannot be separated.

Turbulence, like nonlinearity, supports constructivist teaching and learning. Trygestad (1997) points out that new knowledge, like turbulence, causes instability ("disequilibrium") before it is assimilated into a new conceptual scheme. The teacher's task is to first present perturbations that cause instability and activate conceptual change (Luffiego, Bastida, Ramos, and Soto, 1994), and then to support student reconstruction (Doll, 1986).

Finally, the improvement of teaching—like whole-school improvement—is dependent on the ultimate *strange attractor,* student-centered learning. Additional patterns within the fabric of classroom practice can foster student-centered learning, including reflective inquiry, instructional dialogue, and collegial support. It is not possible to predict precisely how these embedded patterns will change classroom instruction in the long run. Rather, they are designed to facilitate a process of continuous improvement.

And so ends our brief journey into the world of chaos, a world that elicits different reactions from those who enter it.

> Those who feel comfortable with order and reason, with symmetry, equilibrium, and stasis, will find life in the world of dynamic complexity quite challenging. On the other hand, those who are comfortable with being in the process, the flow of the system, those who can see the larger patterns beyond the endless change and dynamisms, those who can tolerate ambiguity and unpredictability, those people will find being in a complex system at the edge of chaos to be stimulating and rewarding. (McAndrew, 1997, p. 40)

Does not all that is said in the above quote about chaotic systems apply as well to modern schools and classrooms?

Creating a Culture for Change

The traditional literature on organizational culture treats culture and change as polar opposites, with one purpose of the culture being to *resist* change. Such resistance indeed seems to be part of the typical school culture. However, some school cultures actually foster positive change. What characteristics do these school cultures have that are not present in most schools? Those who have studied "cultures for change" have described very similar characteristics. Little (1982), Rosenholtz

(1989), Fullan, Bennett, and Rolheiser-Bennett (1990), Fullan (2001, 2002), and Harris (2002) all cite shared purpose, collegiality, and a spirit of continuous improvement. Simpson (1990), Fullan (2001, 2002), and Harris (2002) described sharing and collegiality, teacher empowerment, and participative/collaborative leadership. Leithwood (1992) described "transformational leadership" that fosters school reform through maintaining collaborative cultures, fostering teacher development, and improving group problem solving.

Saphier and King (1985) describe 12 cultural norms that foster school improvement:

1. Collegiality
2. Experimentation
3. High expectations
4. Trust and confidence
5. Tangible support
6. Reaching out to the knowledge bases
7. Appreciation and recognition
8. Caring, celebration, and humor
9. Involvement in decision making
10. Protection of what's important
11. Traditions
12. Honest, open communication (p. 67)

Rather than viewing school culture as a wall impeding change, a better way to define it is as a set of commonly held beliefs, values, norms, and assumptions that can result in change being resisted *or* embraced. Empowered individuals and groups are more likely to develop beliefs, values, norms, and assumptions that are congruent with risk taking, experimentation, and continuous improvement rather than with the status quo. Given the many problems facing our schools today, creating a culture for change has become a critical imperative for supervision and supervisors.

Changing the Conditions of Teaching

Any discussion on change in education would be incomplete if it did not address the conditions of teaching across the nation over the last several years. To say the least, these conditions have not been optimal. All of the research on change now available will be of little value if changing the conditions of teaching is not a central goal of both external and internal school improvement efforts.

- Change is needed, *away from* treating teachers as technicians expected to transmit curriculum developed by bureaucrats, using canned methods published by commercial interests, and measuring student learning through one-size-fits-all tests mandated by policy makers; *toward* treating teachers as professionals invited to make professional decisions about curriculum, instruction, and student assessment.

- Change is needed, *away from* overloading teachers to the extent that they are unable to develop the teacher–student relationships, engage in the reflective planning, and perform the critical self-assessment required for effective teaching; *toward* the manageable class and student load that are prerequisites for quality teaching.
- Change is needed, *away from* the physical and psychological isolation caused by outmoded school structures and norms of individualism; *toward* structures and norms that provide opportunities for professional dialogue and collaborative work.
- Change is needed, *away from* bureaucratic organizations in which teachers are overwhelmed by regulations and paperwork, or—worse yet—mistreated by authoritarian organizations more representative of old-style dictatorships than modern democracies; *toward* democratic school communities in which supervisors promote shared decision making, collegiality, and teacher leadership.
- Change is needed, *away from* policies that treat teachers as part of the problem and consider education a low priority in the allocation of resources; *toward* polices that value teachers as part of the solution and provide the human and material resources teachers need to improve schools and provide all students with a quality education.
- Change is needed, *away from* teaching as an unstaged career with minimal extrinsic rewards; *toward* teaching as a career in which teachers are properly inducted into the profession and are provided new responsibilities, appropriate support, increased recognition, and significantly increased salary at each career stage.
- Change is needed, *away from* diversity as a combination of colors and symbols; *toward* a vision of practice that values and honors respect and dignity as well as shared power and decision making.

Early in the twenty-first century, although many teachers face negative conditions, there also are efforts to improve the conditions of teaching. Many members of the business community, concerned citizens' groups, and policy makers are working to improve external conditions, and many supervisors have worked from the "inside" to make schools centers of democracy, inquiry, and dialogue. The door for improving external and internal conditions will never close; it is simply a matter of whether or not we care to step in and make a difference.

What Is School Success?

Ironically, the definition of school success has been left to near the end of this book. This has been done for a reason, however. The rationale for a school faculty making its own collective definition of school success should be apparent. In referring to studies of successful schools to support many of the propositions of this book, we mentioned schools that were achieving what they had set out

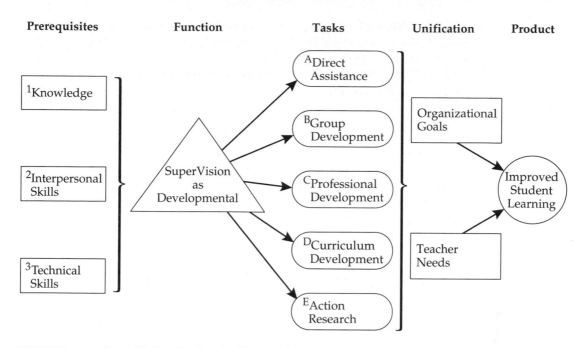

FIGURE 21.2 *SuperVision for Successful Schools*

to do, regardless of what those goals were. Some schools prioritize academic learning and achievement as their criteria for success. Some prioritize creativity and self-directed learning. Other schools prioritize problem solving, community involvement, and social cooperation as their criteria for success. Many schools want it all: they want to be successful in academics, creativity, self-directed learning, problem solving, community involvement, and social cooperation (Goodlad, 1984, pp. 33–60). Schools should strive to educate all students well, in ways consistent with education in a democratic society (Barber, 1993). Although we personally prefer schools that strive to have it all, that decision should be a local school matter. It is in the clarity of common purpose that action to improve instruction takes place.

With an understanding of what is meant by improved instruction and school success, we can fill in the remaining circle on the diagram of supervision for successful schools that has served as the map of this book (see Figure 21.2).

REFERENCES AND RECOMMENDED READINGS

Barber, R. R. 1993. America skips school. *Harpers, 287*(1722), 39–46.

Behuniak, P. 2002. Consumer-referenced testing. *Phi Delta Kappan, 84*(3), 199–207.

Bloch, D. P. 2005. Complexity, chaos, and nonlinear dynamics: A new perspective on career development theory. *The Career Development Quarterly, 53*(3), 194–207.

Briggs, J., and Peat, F. D. 1989. *Turbulent mirror: An illustrated guide to chaos theory and the science of wholeness.* New York: Harper and Row.

Clark, D. C., and Clark, S. N. 2000. Appropriate assessment strategies for young adolescents in an era of standards-based reform. *The Clearing House, 73*(4), 201–204.

Coladarci, R. 2002. Is it a house or a pile of bricks? Important features of a local assessment system. *Phi Delta Kappan, 83*(10), 772–774.

Doll, W. E. 1986. Prigogine: A new sense of order, a new curriculum. *Theory into practice, 25*(1), 10–16.

Fullan, M. 2001. *Leading in a culture of change.* San Francisco: Jossey-Bass.

Fullan, M. 2002. The change leader. *Educational Leadership, 59*(8), 16–20.

Fullan, M. G. 1991. *The new meaning of educational change.* New York: Teachers College Press.

Fullan, M. G., Bennett, B., and Rolheiser-Bennett, C. 1990. Linking classroom and school improvement. *Educational Leadership, 47*(8), 13–19.

Fuller, F. F. 1969. Concerns of teachers: A developmental conceptualization. *American Educational Research Journal, 6*(2), 207–266.

Gleick, J. 1987. *Chaos: Making a new science.* New York: Penguin Books.

Goodlad, J. I. 1984. *A place called school: Prospects for the future.* New York: McGraw-Hill.

Gordon, S. P. 1992. Paradigms, transitions, and the new supervision. *Journal of Curriculum and Supervision, 8*(1), 62–76.

Guskey, T. R. 1994. *Professional development in education: In search of the optimal mix.* Paper presented at the annual meeting of the American Educational Research Association, New Orleans, April.

Hall, G. E., and Hord, S. M. 1987. *Change in schools: Facilitating the process.* Albany: State University of New York Press.

Harris, A. 2002. *School improvement: What's in it for schools?* New York: Routledge Falmer.

Hayles, N. K. 1990. *Chaos bound: Orderly disorder in contemporary literature and society.* Ithaca, NY: Cornell University Press.

Hord, S. M., Rutherford, W. L., Huling-Austin, L., and Hall, G. E. 1987. *Taking charge of change.* Alexandria, VA: Association for Supervision and Curriculum Development.

Keedy, J. L. 1995. Teacher practical knowledge in restructured high schools. *Journal of Educational Research, 89*(2), 76–89.

Keedy, J. L., and Achilles, C. M. 1997. The need for school-constructed theories in practice in US school restructuring. *Journal of Educational Administration, 35*(2), 102–121.

Leithwood, K. A. 1992. The move toward transformational leadership. *Educational Leadership, 49*(58), 8–12.

Liberman, A. 1992. *The changing concerns of teaching.* Chicago: University of Chicago Press.

Little, J. W. 1982. Norms of collegiality and experimentation: Workplace conditions of school success. *American Educational Research Journal, 19*(3), 325–340.

Luffiego, M., Bastida, M. F., Ramos, F., and Soto, J. 1994. Systemic model of conceptual evolution. *International Journal of Science, 16*(3), 305–313.

McAndrew, D. A. 1997. Chaos, complexity, and fuzziness: Science looks at teaching English. *English Journal, 86*(7), 37–43.

Newell, R. J. 2002. A different look at accountability: The EdVisions approach. *Phi Delta Kappan, 84*(3), 208–211.

Patterson, J. L., Purkey, S. C., and Parker, J. V. 1986. *Productive school systems for a nonrational world.* Alexandria, VA: Association for Supervision and Curriculum Development.

Rockler, M. J. 1990–1991. Thinking about chaos: Non-quantitative approaches to teacher education. *Action in Teacher Education, 12*(4), 56–62.

Rosenholtz, S. 1989. *Teachers' workplace: The social organization of schools.* New York: Longman.

Saphier, J., and King, M. 1985. Good seeds grow in strong cultures. *Educational Leadership, 42*(6), 67–74.

Simpson, G. W. 1990. Keeping it alive: Elements of school culture that sustain innovation. *Educational Leadership, 47*(8), 34–37.

Smith, R. D. 1995. The inapplicability principle: What chaos means for social science. *Behavioral Science, 40*(1), 22–40.

Stiggins, R. J. 2002. Assessment crisis: The absence of assessment for learning. *Phi Delta Kappan, 83*(10), 758–765.

Tygestad, J. 1997. *Chaos in the classroom: An application of chaos theory.* Paper presented at the Annual Meeting of the American Educational Research Association, Chicago, March.

Wheatley, M. J. 1992. *Leadership and the new science: Learning about organization from an orderly universe.* San Francisco: Berrett-Koehler.

22

Supervision for What? Democracy and the Good School*

We first must reaffirm our commitment to education's public purpose and weave it into the fabric of our schools.

—National Commission on Service Learning, 2002

All children have the right to experience the joy of learning. We believe it is time for a new commitment to education reform in our country with the goal of giving every child the opportunity to be a part of a learning community that engages and inspires them to reach their full potential.

—Civil Society Institute, 2003

These two quotes taken from two broad-based nonpartisan national commissions strike a timely chord. Currently in state after state across the United States, the measure of school success or failure is how students perform on high-stakes achievement tests. These tests, usually consisting of multiple-choice items measuring cognitive learning at the lower level of Bloom's taxonomy, have become state legislatures' primary tools for bringing about school reform. The vision of many

*Portions of the introduction and the entire section "The Good School and Moral Principles" originally were published in S. P. Gordon (2001), "The Good School," *Florida Educational Leadership, 1*(2), 13–15. Reprinted with permission.

educational leaders is a higher percentage of students passing the test. Curricula are aligned with the test, teachers are teaching to the test, and increasingly, students' promotion or graduation depends on their test performance.

In this age of legislated learning enforced by legislated testing, there seems to be little room for a broader vision of school success. Yet in times like this, it is more critical than ever to make a clarion call for what many would consider a different and better vision of a successful school. This vision is not new, just currently unpopular. It is a vision of a school that is focused not solely on externally imposed standards and tests scores, but on the overall well-being, growth, and development of all students, indeed of all members of the school community. The vision is based on the premise that each individual possesses intrinsic worth as a human being and should, therefore, be afforded the educational opportunities prerequisite to a meaningful and fulfilling life (Baez, 2005).

Reform around Purpose

Listen to the voices of teachers talking about the same group of regular students they have during the school day:

Mr. A: The kids here are where the problem is today. These kids are just unteachable. There's nothing wrong with the curriculum. If I could just get the right students, I could teach and everything would be wonderful.

Ms. B: These students are just not real smart, and they don't want to learn. They're just putting in time.

Mr. C: There are kids here who really want to do a good job, but they have seen so much and heard so much that they often are distracted. Their perspective is gone. But they are basically really good kids.

Ms. D: My guys. They're very, very clever and brave kids. It's amazing how they are always figuring out what is going on around them. It is a job to keep up with their energy and channel it into learning experiences.

Without arguing over perception versus reality as reflected in those attitudes towards students, let us ask which of the views expressed are consistent with the founding principles of American society.

All men [and women] are created equal, that they are endowed by their Creator with certain inalienable Rights; that among these are Life, Liberty, and the pursuit of Happiness; that to secure these rights, Governments are instituted among men, deriving their just powers from the consent of the governed, that whenever any form of government becomes destructive of these ends, it is the Right of the People to alter or abolish it. (Declaration of Independence, 1776)

Take these words and make a few alterations and you have the central purpose of public education.

> All students are created equal; that they are endowed by their Creator with certain inalienable Rights; that among these are an education that will accord them Life, Liberty, and the pursuit of Happiness; that whenever any public school becomes destructive of preparing students for these ends, it is the Right of the People to alter or abolish it.

In essence, the reason we have public education is to enculturate students into the values of our democracy! To summarize Thomas Jefferson, public education has two corollary purposes: (1) to provide for an educated citizenry to participate in decisions about promoting the future good of our democratic society, and (2) to allow for leadership in a democratic society to develop from the merits, abilities, and talents of the individual. Leadership in a democratic society should not be accorded based on family privilege, economic wealth, religion, race, or group privilege (Lee, 1961).

The central question for all who educate is:

> What should we be doing in our schools, our curriculum, our placement and our scheduling of students, our allocations of resources, and our teaching to give every child his or her inalienable rights to life, liberty, and the pursuit of happiness? What is just, what is fair, what is democratic?

American schools are indeed better than they have ever been in reaching all students. But the challenge of American schools is not primarily that of achieving economic superiority in the world or of focusing on subject area achievement. The challenge is to rise to the far more demanding and crucially important standard of educating all students to be knowledgeable, proactive, resourceful, and responsible members of our democratic society.

Public schools must ensure a democratic threshold of learning experiences that give all students the knowledge, skills, compassion, and understanding to participate in human affairs. It is these requisites for democratic living that we should be returning to in determining decisions about standards, assessments, curriculum, professional development, placement, and grouping of students, as well as the ways that adults themselves function with each other. The supreme irony of public schools is that the only institution in the United States with the explicit purpose of preparing students for a democracy often operates in ways that demonstrate the lack of belief in such collective participation. Most schools do not include faculty, students, and parents in democratic decision making. Indeed, in many cases, where formal leaders wish for such involvement, many faculty, students, or parents would rather not be involved. Schools in the United States all too often operate in accord with dependency and hierarchical relations, not democratic ones. How can we as a country continue to sacrifice the lives of young men and women to protect and extend democracy as the best way of determining the common good while we stand unwilling to use the same beliefs in how we make decisions and set standards about the learning of our youth?

The Good School and Moral Principles

Few will argue with the central purpose of education described above, but if we begin to reflect seriously on it, then it leads to a set of moral principles that present a distinct challenge to conventional practice. These principles are in direct conflict with the essentialist philosophy, narrow curriculum, and restricted learning that accompany the standards and high-stakes emphasis of today. Let us, therefore, consider 10 moral principles that, taken together and taken seriously, foster development of a school much more likely to prepare students to use their education well in contributing to a better society.

Compassion

Truly effective leaders and teachers are fired by a spirit of compassion for all other members of the school community. Compassion should not be interpreted as maudlin sympathy, but rather as genuine empathy combined with a concern for the overall well-being of colleagues and students. In a "school of compassion," there is a great deal of interpersonal communication intended to understand the personality, needs, concerns, and interests of others, as well as commitment of time and energy to assist individuals to realize their human potential. Leaders are more concerned about the growth and development of individual teachers and students than just the latest composite test report. Teachers first teach students, not test objectives.

Wholeness

Authentic compassion for students leads to the realization that one cannot separate different aspects of student growth. The good school is concerned with all levels represented in Bloom's taxonomy, not just comprehension and application as typically measured by high-stakes tests, and certainly not just the narrow test objectives such instruments usually encompass. In addition to concern for cognitive growth, the good school is committed to students' physical, emotional, creative, social, and moral development. Not only is growth in all of these areas necessary for the development of the whole person, the different domains of learning are interactive and interdependent; growth in one domain is enhanced by growth in the others. The principle of wholeness applies to adult members of the school community as well. For example, the school needs to concern itself with teachers' pedagogical growth but also with their physical and emotional well-being, and with their creative, social, and moral development.

Connectedness

Schools have an obligation to break down artificial barriers to natural relationships in students' lives and learning. For example, the education provided to students must be relevant to both their present and their future, not focused on one at the expense of the other. Connections between different content areas must be made. And the world of the classroom needs to be connected to life outside the school, including the local, national, and world communities (National Commission on Service Learning, 2002). The principle of connectedness also means that members of the school community should not be restricted to a single role. Administrators, teachers, and students should all engage in leadership, teaching, and learning, albeit at different levels and with different emphases.

Inclusion

Inclusion, as a moral principle, combines the beliefs in equality and equity. It begins with equality; all students are of equal worth as human beings and as members of the school community. A belief in equality leads to a commitment to equity. Those who have physical, cognitive, emotional, or social disabilities need special assistance, including extraordinary measures if necessary, to enable then to remain members of the community and to lead fulfilling lives as students and later as adults. Additionally, the good school *reaches out* to all categories of students, for example, from low socioeconomic backgrounds, minorities, migrants, international students, non-English-speaking students, gay and lesbian students, and even students with serious behavioral problems.

Justice

Teaching about social justice certainly has its place in the school curriculum, but here we mean *providing justice* as a means of facilitating teaching and learning. Justice includes holding teachers accountable for effective instruction and holding students accountable for learning, but in an *educational* context accountability ought to mean the provision of feedback on one's performance and assistance for improving future performance, not the issuing of rewards and punishments.

At its core, justice means treating members of the school community in a fair and consistent manner. By being just with students, educators to some extent can counter the injustice that students may have been dealt by society. By modeling justice, educators can teach students to treat others justly. Such justice, repeated daily, can facilitate student learning in all areas and eventually lead to a more just society. Justice must also be provided to all adults in the school community. Adults who are treated justly learn better how to treat students justly. A school will very likely provide its students no more justice than it provides its staff.

Peace

Student misbehavior is one of the major school problems reported by supervisors and teachers. Especially troublesome is misbehavior that interferes with the right of other students to learn. Worse yet, in recent years there has been a frightening increase in student violence. Perhaps one way to approach this problem is to change from a school characterized by "effective student discipline" to a "school of peace." Moving toward this vision will require that supervisors, teachers, and students develop or enhance communication, collaboration, and conflict management skills. But it also will require that administrators, teachers, and students develop new self concepts; that they begin to view themselves not just as leaders or teachers or students but as *healers* and *peacemakers*. For those who argue that we cannot afford to spend school time learning about healing and peacemaking, our response should be that considering the growing incivility in our communities and schools, we can no longer afford *not* to engage in such learning.

Freedom

Learning and freedom—freedom to dream, to explore, to take risks, and to learn from failures—go hand in hand. Educators need freedom to grow professionally, and likewise, students need freedom to develop to their full potential. Granted, students and adults function at varying stages of development and thus possess varying capacities for responding to freedom. For some, freedom may need to be introduced gradually, initially presented as restricted choice. But it is the *directionality* of the school's efforts that is the important thing; all members of the school community should be moving toward increased freedom of choice in what they learn, how they learn, and how they demonstrate learning. This is a particularly difficult principle to accept for those who equate school reform with external control, an ironic phenomenon in a democratic society.

Trust

Consistent efforts on behalf of compassion, wholeness, connectedness, inclusion, justice, peace, and freedom can lead to trusting relationships among members of the school community. Trust is both a product of adhering to the other principles and a requirement for those principles to flourish over the long run. Authentic learning is based not only on the transmission of knowledge and skills but also on personal relationships, and trust is the ground on which those relationships are built. For all its importance, however, personal trust is not the only type of trust present in the good school. There also is trust in the moral principles to which the school is committed—trust that these principles, if adhered to, will result in a better education and more fulfilling lives for students and a better future for society.

Empowerment

As a moral principle, empowerment certainly includes involving members of the school community in decisions about matters that affect them. But it goes beyond this standard definition. It also means changing assumptions, norms, roles, and relationships that act as barriers to educators' and students' growth toward self-reliance and self-actualization. It includes not only an invitation to become involved in decisions concerning leadership, teaching, and learning, but also to acquire the information and skills necessary to engage in effective decision making in each of these areas. Finally, empowerment means instilling in educators and students a commitment to facilitate the empowerment of *other* members of the school community.

Community

We've referred to the "school community" throughout this book. The good school is a community of leaders, teachers, and learners, with individual members assuming all three roles. *Community* itself can be a moral principle if we understand the term as a group committed to the overall well-being, growth, and development of each member. An authentic community will develop values, norms, relationships, and practices consistent with this common purpose. Community members will engage in collective and individual actions for the well-being of both the community and its individual members. Collegiality and collaboration become a way of life. An additional aspect of community is *celebration*. The community celebrates its progress toward its vision, but also engages in anticipatory celebration of what it wants to be—it celebrates the future!

Priorities

Following the moral principles outlined above does not mean that a school ignores legislated standards of learning, externally mandated teacher evaluation systems, or high-stakes tests. What it does mean is that educators realize that schools need to go well beyond these well-intentioned, largely ineffective, and often counterproductive efforts to ensure that all students experience the growth and development necessary to become contributing members of society and to lead fulfilling lives. Educators in the good school realize that leadership, teaching, and learning based on moral principles offers the best chance for students to reach their human potential. What we are talking about then is a question of priorities. Educators committed to moral principles believe that if we base school reform on those principles, we will optimize meaningful student learning. They also realize that in some situations, the most efficient or immediate means of meeting external, simplistic measures of student learning may contradict moral principles. In such situations, they are prepared to choose the long-term good over expedient compliance.

Applying Moral Principles to a Moral Dilemma:
No Child Left Behind

The No Child Left Behind Act (NCLB) was enacted for the purpose of holding schools accountable for their students' academic progress and eliminating achievement gaps among student subgroups. NCLB mandates annual testing in reading and math for grades 3–8 and at least once in grades 10–12, with annual tests in science given once for grades 3–5, 6–9, and 10–12. States must set adequate yearly progress goals for districts, schools, and student subgroups, and use the state tests to determine whether schools are making adequate yearly progress toward 100 percent proficiency for all students by 2013–2014. NCLB requires state assessment results to be disaggregated by economic status, race, ethnicity, and limited English proficiency. The act mandates that all teachers be fully certified and licensed for the subjects they teach and that paraprofessionals have at least two years of college or pass a "rigorous" exam.

Districts and schools that meet or exceed adequate yearly progress goals or close achievement gaps are eligible for "State Academic Achievement Awards." Districts and schools that fail to reach their adequate yearly progress goals are subject to "improvement, corrective action, and restructuring" measures. Failing schools must allow students to transfer to a "better" school within the district and the district must pay for the students' transportation to the new school. Districts with schools that fail to meet standards for three out of four years must use a portion of their Title I funds to purchase supplemental educational services for eligible students. Eventually, failing schools may have their staff replaced or be taken over by the state.

At the surface level, NCLB seems to be a positive approach to problems facing public education today. After all, everyone can agree that all students deserve a quality education, achievement gaps among groups of students should be eliminated, and districts and schools should be held accountable for student learning. On closer examination, however, several aspects of NCLB are problematic. First, NCLB is severely underfunded in general, and the additional funds provided to poor districts are far from adequate for assisting poor schools to meet NCLB mandates. Second, the long-term requirements of NCLB may be impossible for most schools (including many effective schools) to reach. Some experts predict that as many as 75 percent of all schools eventually will be placed in the "needs improvement" category (Olson, 2002). Third, the strategies that NCLB uses to measure student progress are seriously flawed. NCLB does not provide for measuring yearly progress of the same group or subgroup of students. Neither the size of the achievement gaps among groups nor the size of gains by underachieving groups are relevant when determining adequate yearly progress. Finally, the primary tool for measuring student progress under NCLB, the high-stakes test, has produced a number of negative effects that have called into question its use as the sole measure of progress.

Most teachers do not believe that high-stakes testing is an accurate measure of student learning or school effectiveness (Reese, Gordon, and Price, 2004), yet they are under intense pressure to meet state testing goals (Brighton, 2002). Due to this pressure, many teachers spend more time than they wish teaching minimal skills and test-taking strategies (Jones et al., 1999; Reese, Gordon, and Price, 2004). The teaching of higher-order thinking and problem solving tends to be de-emphasized (Jones et al., 1999). As a result of the pressure to improve test scores, teachers become stressed and anxious, even when their students do well on the test (Jones et al., 1999). They feel frustrated and disappointed when students do poorly (Reese, Gordon, and Price, 2004). The negative effects of testing on their teaching and their students make many teachers feel powerless (Costigan, 2002). One study concluded that standards and high-stakes testing now is the number one reason experienced teachers leave the profession (Tye and Obrien, 2002).

Teachers are not the only educators negatively affected by high-stakes testing. Well-respected principals have been dismissed without warning solely due to low scores on a single set of tests (McGhee and Nelson, 2005). School counselors, who often coordinate the administration of state tests, report that testing has negative affects on their role as counselors. Many believe their role in testing inhibits their ability to provide counseling services and damages their relationships with teachers and students (Brown, Galassi, and Akos, 2004).

The most important effects of high-stakes testing, of course, are the effects on students. There is a growing body of evidence that improved scores on state tests do not mean increased student learning (Amrein and Berliner, 2002), and a narrowing of gaps on state test scores between Whites and minority students may actually mask increasing gaps between Whites and minorities on other measures of student learning (Klein, Hamilton, McCaffrey, and Stetcher, 2000). High-stakes testing does not increase students' motivation to learn (Reese, Gordon, and Price, 2004). Rather, the test causes stress, anxiety, and fear among many students (Brown, Galassi, and Akos, 2004), and the constant emphasis on test preparation can cause student burnout on testing (Reese, Gordon, and Price, 2004). The effects of testing on low-income minority students has been especially negative. Test prep materials and drill have replaced the normal curriculum in many schools serving primarily low-income minority students (McNeil, 2000). The oral drill, worksheets, practice tests, and frequent review that characterize test preparation for many minority students is reminiscent of the "pedagogy of poverty" written about by Haberman (1991) more than a decade prior to NCLB. This type of instruction leads to students' passive resentment and poor performance. It is not surprising, then, that graduation rates of African American and Hispanic students have decreased considerably during the era of high-stakes testing (Haney, 1999; Horn, 2003; Madaus and Clark, 2001).

It is not difficult to identify serious conflicts between the moral principles of the good school described above and NCLB. *The principle of compassion* calls for us to be more concerned about the growth and development of individual teachers and students than the latest set of test scores. *The principle of wholeness* requires us to teach the whole student, not just teach the narrow proficiencies typically measured by high-stakes tests. *The principle of connectedness* calls for connecting content from different subject areas and connecting students to the real world, not for the narrow curriculum and the artificial world of test preparation that

NCLB has led us to. *The principal of inclusion* is inconsistent with the pedagogy of poverty that forces low-income minority students to spend their school days in repetitive drill on minimal skills. *The principal of justice* cries out against the triage strategy used in many schools in which teachers focus intensive efforts on "bubble students" while spending less time and effort on students either likely to pass the test or perceived to have little chance of passing. We could go on. NCLB as currently written, despite the good intentions of those who made it the law of the land, contradicts all 10 of the moral principles described above.

The problems with NCLB that we have described place supervisors and teachers across the nation in one of the great moral dilemmas of our time. They cannot simply declare NCLB immoral and refuse to help students prepare for their state's high-stakes test. This course of action would put their students at a disadvantage, help to bring down sanctions on their school, and eventually result in their dismissal, after which they would no longer be of any value to their students. On the other hand, large numbers of supervisors and teachers believe that NCLB is doing many of our children more harm than good. Is it not wrong to simply comply with a system that has such negative effects? How should educators who believe that NCLB is harmful to students respond? Brighton (2002) notes that many teachers respond to this dilemma by attempting to "straddle the fence" between what they believe to be sound instructional practices and test preparation strategies. This approach attempts to create a balance between best practice and test practice. Although we believe there is some merit in this approach, we also believe that supervisors and teachers have a moral (and extremely difficult) obligation to directly confront the harmful effects of NCLB and work for changes in its provisions. Therefore, we propose both short-term and long-term strategies for educators to address NCLB, with both types of strategies carried out simultaneously.

Short-Term Strategies

These short-term strategies are intended to help schools meet the requirements of NCLB in ways that are consistent with the moral principles discussed earlier. The first set of short-term strategies is suggested for all schools:

- *Develop Curriculum:* Embed state standards and test objectives into a comprehensive curriculum that includes more holistic and meaningful learning opportunities. Brighton (2002) notes that standards can be integrated within meaningful units of study and used as scaffolding for larger concepts. Once the curriculum is developed, the larger curriculum goals rather than the discrete standards and test objectives must remain the focus of teaching and learning.

- *Do Not Eliminate Nontested Subjects:* Subjects like social studies, art, health, and physical education are important aspects of students' education, and thus schools have a moral obligation to include those subjects in their curriculum. Moreover, schools that maintain a rich curriculum tend to do better on high-stakes tests than schools that narrow the curriculum to tested content (Reese, Gordon, and Price, 2004).

• *Strive for Authentic Instruction:* Authentic instruction, including "higher-order thinking, deep knowledge and substantive conversation" as well as "connection to the world beyond the classroom" (Wehlage, Newman, and Secada, 1996, p. 32) results in increased student learning as measured by both standardized tests and authentic assessment (Marks, Newmann, and Gamoran, 1996). Authentic instruction can lead to significant improvement in academic performance for lower-performing as well as higher-performing students. Many of the "best practices" discussed in the literature are consistent with authentic instruction. These include "concept-based instruction, interdisciplinary connections, student-generated topics of study, authentic assessment, flexible grouping, and differentiated instruction" (Brighton, 2002, p. 31).

• *Make Extensive Use of Formative Assessment:* In effective schools, teaching is planned and modified based on ongoing and extensive gathering of informal data on students' daily progress. Teachers observe students' classroom performance, review student work products, engage in diagnostic discussion with students, and revise instruction accordingly.

• *Differentiate Instruction:* The one-size-fits-all drill and kill that many schools resort to in order to prepare students for the high-stakes test is neither good teaching practice nor an effective way to raise test scores. Teachers need to use a variety of instructional strategies to meet different student needs, including multiple strategies within the same lesson.

• *Limit Test-Taking Practice:* Students who are not taught test-taking strategies are placed at a disadvantage to students who are, so some preparation for taking a high-stakes multiple-choice test is necessary. The preparation needed, however, is a far cry from the common practice of using the test format day after day in lessons and assignments. Schools need to set limits on the amount of time and materials used to teach test-taking skills.

• *Provide Professional Development:* School-focused professional development possessing the characteristics described in Chapter 18 is essential to the improvement of teaching and learning. All professional development programs should include a teacher induction program as well as ongoing professional development assisting teachers with curriculum development, authentic instruction, informal assessment, differentiated instruction, and so on. Professional development also should deal directly with how to address the conflicts between NCLB and best practice.

The strategies discussed so far apply to all schools. Let us now consider additional short-term strategies that are especially relevant for low-income districts and schools.

• *Recruit and Retain Quality Teachers:* Provide incentives, resources, and rewards to attract and keep high-quality teachers in schools serving low-income students.

- *Develop Partnerships:* Collaborative partnerships are important to all districts and schools; however, schools serving low-income students must make special efforts to develop collaborative relationships with parents and other community members. This includes parent and community participation in school leadership and school improvement. Partnerships with higher education and business are other key ingredients for school improvement.
- *Focus on Analysis and Improvement:* Rather than pressuring, threatening, transferring, and dismissing principals and teachers in low-income schools with poor test scores, district leaders should collaborate with school personnel to complete a thorough data-based analysis of why scores are low, and work with the school to plan and implement a long-term, data-driven school improvement plan. A variety of data (not just state test results) should be used to plan for school improvement, and continued data gathering and analysis should guide ongoing school improvement efforts.

Long-Term Strategies

We believe that the short-term strategies outlined above will do much to ameliorate the harmful aspects of NCLB, improve test scores on high-stakes tests, and most importantly, improve student learning. However, when attempting to follow moral principles that lead to better schools, amelioration of harmful policies is not enough. We believe that the stakes for public education and public school students are so high that K–12 supervisors and teachers need to become directly involved in efforts to change public policy. They will not be able to do it alone, but will need to become part of a coalition of K–12 educators, parents, university educators, and enlightened businesspersons and policy makers who recognize the critical need for change. Members of this coalition will need to educate the general public, the corporate world, and politicians on the need for change, and push directly for new legislation at the state and federal level. Specific changes that should be on the reform agenda include the following:

- The development at national and state levels of more realistic long-term school improvement goals, with the involvement of various educational groups in the establishment of these goals
- A shift from reliance on the high-stakes achievement test as the sole measure of school effectiveness to the use of multiple measures, with the examination of the local school context a critical part of the assessment process
- Higher-level learning as a measure of student progress (for example, assessing students on their ability to solve real-world problems)
- Measurement of academic progress of the same groups and subgroups of students over time, with gains by the same group and subgroups used as indicators of school improvement

- Requirements to separate research-based teaching methods and school improvement strategies from ideology-based methods and strategies; to fund research on teaching/learning using a variety of research methods; and to promote teaching methods that are supported by multiple types of evidence gathered over time
- The provision of adequate resources for smaller school units, smaller classes, and professional development programs to foster high-quality teaching
- The provision of additional resources to low-income schools, allowing those schools to bridge the gaps with wealthier schools in quality of professional staff, physical facilities, and instructional materials
- The provision of additional resources, including adequate time, for underachieving schools to gather and analyze data on the causes of underachievement, and to plan and implement long-term school improvement programs focused on specific improvement targets

The use of moral principles to guide us toward "good schools" across the nation, as illustrated by the recommendations above, does not consist of embracing romantic abstractions. Rather, the road to the "good school" includes concrete actions to do what we can to improve schools within present limitations while we work together with others to remove these limitations and empower schools to be all that they can be. We will close this discussion of NCLB with two questions for readers to ponder, both individually and in dialogue with one another:

1. What can I do in the short term, either by myself or in collaboration with others, to protect students from external factors that are interfering with student learning?
2. What can I do in the long term, either by myself or in collaboration with others, to change external factors that are interfering with student learning?

SUMMARY

SuperVision and instructional leadership are foremost about the ideas of goodness, purpose, and the hope for all of our students. We have provided knowledge, technical and interpersonal skills, and domains, structures, and applications for achieving a purposeful school dedicated to the continuing improvement of teaching and learning. Please remember that competence without clear purpose results in directionless change, and purpose without competence provides inefficiency and frustration. We hope that you, the reader, in whatever role of instructional leadership, will add coherence and congruence to the education of all students in your own schools and districts. After all, this is the primary reason for why we chose to be educators—to practice what we believe.

REFERENCES AND RECOMMENDED READINGS

Amrein, A. L., and Berliner, D. C. 2002, March 28. High-stakes testing, uncertainty, and student learning. *Education Policy Analysis Archives, 10*(18). Retrieved October 29, 2005, from http://epaa.asu.edu/epaa/v10n18.

Baez, B. 2005. Schools and the public good: Privatization, democracy, freedom, and "government." *JCT, 21*(2), 63–82.

Brighton, C. M. 2002. Straddling the fence: Implementing best practices in the age of accountability. *Gifted Child Today, 25*(3), 30–33.

Brown, D., Galassi, J. P., and Akos, P. 2004. School counselors' perceptions of the impact of high-stakes testing. *Professional School Counseling, 8*(1), 31–39.

Civil Society Institute (2003). Draft statement for a national conversation about school reform and public education. Newton Centre, MA (Draft available at www.civilsocietyinstitute.org)

Costigan, A. T. 2002. Teaching the culture of high stakes testing: Listening to new teachers. *Action in Teacher Education, 23*(4), 35–42.

Gordon, S. P. 2001. The good school. *Florida Educational Leadership, 1*(2), 13–15.

Habermann, M. 1991. The pedagogy of poverty versus good teaching. *Phi Delta Kappan, 73,* 290–294.

Haney, W. 1999. *Study of Texas Education Agency statistics on cohorts of Texas high school students.* Boston: Center for the Study of Testing, Evaluation, and Educational Policy.

Horn, C. 2003. High stakes testing and students: Stopping or perpetuating a cycle of failure? *Theory into Practice, 42*(1), 30–41.

Jones, M. G., Jones, B. D., Hardin, B., Chapman, L., Yarbrough, T., and Davis, M. 1999. The impact of high stakes testing on teachers and students in North Carolina. *Phi Delta Kappan, 81,* 199–203.

Klein, S., Hamilton, L., McCaffrey, D., and Stretcher, B. 2000. *What do test scores in Texas tell us?* Santa Monica, CA: RAND Corp.

Lee, G. C. 1961. The precious blessings of liberty. In G. Lee (Ed.), *Crusade against ignorance:* *Thomas Jefferson on education* (pp. 27–28). New York: Columbia University.

Madaus, G., and Clarke, M. 2001. The impact of high-stakes testing on minority students. In M. Kornhaber and G. Orfield (Eds.), *Raising standards or raising barriers: Inequality and high stakes testing in public education* (pp. 85–106). New York: Century Foundation.

Marks, H. M., Newmann, F. M., and Gamoran, A. 1996. Does authentic pedagogy increase student achievement? In F. M. Newmann & Associates (Eds.), *Authentic achievement: Restructuring schools for intellectual quality* (pp. 49–73). San Fransisco: Jossey-Bass.

McGhee, M. M., and Nelson, S. 2005. Sacrificing leaders, villainizing leadership: How educational accountability policies impair school leadership. *Phi Delta Kappan, 86*(5), 361–372.

McNeil, L. M. 2000. Creating new inequalities: Contradictions of reform. *Phi Delta Kappan, 81,* 728–734.

National Commission on Service-Learning 2002. *Learning in deed.* Battle Creek, MI: W. K. Kellogg Foundation and the John Glenn Institute for Public Service. (Available from the W. K. Kellogg Foundation, (800) 819-9997, wkkford@iserv.net)

Olson, L. 2002. 'Inadequate' yearly gains are predicted. *Education Week, 21*(29), 1, 24–26.

Reese, M., Gordon, S. P., and Price, L. R. 2004. Teachers' perceptions of high-stakes testing. *Journal of School Leadership, 14,* 464–496.

Tye, B. B., and O'Brien, L. 2002. Why are experienced teachers leaving the profession? *Phi Delta Kappan, 84,* 24–32.

Wehlage, G. G., Newmann, F. W., and Secada, W. G. 1996. Standards for authentic achievement and pedagogy. In F. M. Newmann & Associates (Eds.), *Authentic achievement: Restructuring schools for intellectual quality* (pp. 23–48). San Francisco: Jossey-Bass.

Name Index

Subject Index

as directive control behavior, 115, 116, 250
as directive informational behavior, 124, 126, 250
as nondirective behavior, 142, 144, 251
as supervisory behavior, 94, 95
Priorities, of good schools, 343
Private self, in Johari Window, 97
Problem solving
as collaborative behavior, 133, 135
in direct assistance programs, 237
as directive control behavior, 116–117, 250
as directive informational behavior, 125, 127, 250
as nondirective behavior, 143, 144, 250–251
as supervisory behavior, 94, 95
Procedural technician role, 244
Professional development
adults as learners, 42–65
alternative formats for, 266–267
for beginning teachers, 266, 268–270
causes of ineffective, 167
characteristics of successful programs, 264–265
conditions necessary to promote, 155–156
curriculum development and, 297–299
defined, 10
ebb and flow of, 64–65
examples of effective programs, 267–272
extending concept of, 275–276
individualized, 109–110, 265–266, 267, 271–272
integrating levels of, 265–266
key considerations for programs, 274–275
life cycle development in, 57–58, 64
nature of, 225
need for, 263–264
No Child Left Behind Act of 2001 and, 347

peer-coaching programs, 109–110, 148, 156, 233–236
review of adult/teacher development models, 63–64
role development in, 60–61, 64
sociocultural context of, 61–63, 64
stages of, 273–274
stage theories of, 48–57
teachers as adult learners, 47–48, 150–151
teachers as objects or agents in, 276–278
transition events in, 58–60, 64
Program design, 206, 210
Program evaluation
decisions in, 207–209
implementation and, 207, 208
overall process for, 210–216
specific instructional programs, 206–207
for teacher empowerment, 216
Psychological isolation of teachers, 18
Public self, in Johari Window, 97

Qualitative observation, 84–86, 191–195
detached open-ended narrative, 192–193, 197
focused questionnaire observation, 84–86, 194–195, 198
participant open-ended observation, 194
verbatim/selected verbatim, 192, 193, 197
Qualitative research and evaluation, 201–205
characteristics of, 201–203
quantitative methods compared with, 201–203
using with quantitative methods, 203–205
Quality control, 176, 202–203
Quality teachers, 347–348
Quantitative observation, 183–191
categorical-frequency instruments, 184, 197
classroom culture and, 238

performance-indicator instruments, 184–186, 187, 197
visual diagramming, 186–191
Quantitative research and evaluation, 201–205
characteristics of, 201–203
qualitative methods compared with, 201–203
using with qualitative methods, 203–205

Race and ethnicity
in adult development, 62–63
discrimination based on, 27
Racism, 27
Rand Corporation, 165
Readiness, evaluating, 206–207, 210
Reality, in quantitative versus qualitative approaches, 201, 204
Reality shock, for beginning teachers, 21
Recognition-seeker role, 246
Reconstructionism, 82
Recorder role, 244
Reflecting
as collaborative behavior, 132, 134, 135–136, 250
on collaborative supervision, 138
as directive control behavior, 116
on directive control supervision, 121
as directive informational behavior, 126
on directive informational supervision, 130
as nondirective behavior, 141, 142–144, 145, 250–251
on nondirective supervision, 148–149
as supervisory behavior, 94, 95
Reflection in action (Schön), 332
Reinforcing
as collaborative behavior, 135
as directive control behavior, 117, 118, 250